Issues in Aging
(Vol. 2)

HOUSING AND THE AGING POPULATION

GARLAND REFERENCE LIBRARY
OF SOCIAL SCIENCE
(VOL. 803)

ISSUES IN AGING

GENERAL EDITOR: DIANA K. HARRIS

THE REMAINDER OF THEIR DAYS
Domestic Policy and Older Families in the United States and Canada
edited by Jon Hendricks and Carolyn J. Rosenthal

HOUSING AND THE AGING POPULATION
Options for the New Century
edited by W. Edward Folts and Dale E. Yeatts

HOUSING AND THE AGING POPULATION

Options for the New Century

Edited by
W. Edward Folts
Dale E. Yeatts

GARLAND PUBLISHING, Inc.
New York & London / 1994

Library of Congress Cataloging-in-Publication Data

Housing and the aging population: options for the new century /
edited by W. Edward Folts, Dale E. Yeatts.
p. cm. — (Garland reference library of social science ; v. 803.
Issues in aging ; v. 2)
Includes bibliographical references and indexes.
ISBN 0-8153-0610-5
1. Aged—Housing—United States.
I. Folts, W. Edward (William Edward) II. Yeatts, Dale E., 1952– .
III. Series: Garland reference library of social science ; v. 803.
IV. Series: Garland reference library of social science.
Issues in aging ; v. 2.
HD7287.92.U54H67 1994
363.5'946'0973—dc20   93-37739

Printed on acid-free, 250-year-life paper
Manufactured in the United States of America

For our wives and children. They have always been there when we needed them most.

Sandra Wright Folts
Steven Edward Folts

Linda Elgert Yeatts
Paul Elgert Yeatts
Peter Elgert Yeatts

Contents

Part III: The Private Sector

Part IV: Housing Issues for the Twenty-first Century

Series Foreword

This series attempts to address the topic of aging from a wide variety of perspectives and to make available some of the best gerontological thought and writings to researchers, professional practitioners, and students in the field as well as in other related areas. All the volumes in the series are written and/or edited by outstanding scholars and leading specialists on current issues of interest.

A major underlying theme of this present volume is to provide a basis for the discussion of housing issues concerning the elderly in the coming century. Written from a multi-disciplinary perspective, this book reviews the variety of housing alternatives presently available to older persons as well as discussing the changing demographic composition of the older population and how these changes will affect their housing needs in the future. Although written for those readers with a limited knowledge of housing options and issues, this volume also should be of interest to specialists in the housing field because of the wide range of material that it encompasses and the excellent coverage of the topics that it contains.

Diana K. Harris
University of Tennessee

Acknowledgments

A project such as this involves many people. Unfortunately, only a small number ever receive the recognition they so richly deserve. We would like to thank all those, in whatever capacity, who have contributed their time and energy so willingly to the completion of this project.

Obviously, we owe a great debt of gratitude to the individuals who wrote the chapters. Many of these individuals have sacrificed their time, and that of their families, to complete the assigned tasks, and we offer them our heartfelt thanks. We would also like to thank the series editor, Diana Harris, for her patience, cooperation, and unwavering support.

Both of us would like to thank our valued friend and colleague, Cora Martin of the University of North Texas. Her experience, tact, and ability to see the whole picture have provided us with valuable lessons for our professional and personal lives.

Two graduate assistants at Appalachian State University also deserve special recognition. Elliott Hermann and Alisa Wright were given the somewhat daunting task of compiling both the name and subject index for this project. Despite their numerous other responsibilities, they approached the task with an enthusiasm and dedication envied by all who dared to interrupt them.

Also deserving of special recognition is Joyce Rhymer who, as departmental secretary at Appalachian State University, helped us create and maintain the illusion of full attention to our other duties while successfully cloaking our preoccupation with this project. For her covert efforts on our behalf, we thank her.

Both of us would also like to thank Carol Ann Turner, Thomas M. Murphy, Bob Cole, Jeff Dwyer, Kenny Lee, and Rodney LeFant for their special help. Their persistence and insightful suggestions have been extremely helpful.

Finally, we would like to thank our families to whom this project is dedicated. Without their support, cooperation, and understanding we would never have been in a position to attempt, much less complete, this volume.

W.E.F.
D.E.Y.

Preface

A very wise person once told me: "You cannot understand housing problems without understanding the problems that are important to the people who live in those houses." That wise person was my mentor, friend, and colleague Dr. Gordon Streib of the University of Florida. His admonition was made in response to my rather naive suggestion that the "housing problems" of older people could be "solved" if only they were willing to give up their large houses and move into a variety of seemingly attractive but nontraditional housing arrangements. The realization that the impersonal "housing" issues I was interested in exploring involved the highly personal matter of "homes" not only made my intellectual life temporarily more difficult, but it changed forever the way I would consider the issue of housing.

Specialized housing for older adults, like so many of the important topics in our ever-changing world, is a complex issue involving not only the physical and social environments with which we humans surround ourselves, but also the highly personalized and emotionally charged issues of our underlying need for independence, our quality of life, and our overall attitudes about old age. Add to these the vague and sometimes arbitrary manner in which we attempt to measure housing adequacy, and the issue of housing for older adults becomes all the more important—if no less complex.

Housing means different things to different people. To some of us, housing is no more than a convenient way to shelter ourselves from the elements. To others, houses are an essential component of our preferred lifestyles and not only reflect who we are but provide reaffirmation of our sense of self. Still others among us, probably the majority, fit somewhere between these extremes. For this latter group, the persistence of a particular lifestyle can be important, but change and adaptation are possible and often even welcomed. One of the more obvious consequences of this is that there now exists a wide variety of housing types available to potential residents of all ages. However, cost and a basic belief in the single-family-detached dwelling unit as the only "normal" way to live have combined to make this wide array of choices practically unavailable to all but the wealthiest and the more adventurous of older adults.

The vast majority of older people do not live in the types of housing discussed in this or any other book on specialized housing. In fact, what makes these housing arrangements "special" is that they are largely ignored by the bulk of the populations for whom they have been designed. The obvious question becomes: why expend so much effort in attempting to understand nontraditional housing alternatives that are neither preferred nor desired by the majority of those for whom the alternatives are designed? The answer, we believe, lies in the fact that in a very few years the need for low-cost housing and the need for *coordination* and *integration* among those who provide housing and those who provide services will overtake both our resources and our resolve to address the issue. By focusing our attention on these issues now, we can be better prepared to meet the demographic imperative of the beginning decades of the twenty-first century.

Life will, of necessity, change. Whether it is for the better is largely an issue of personal perspective and political orientation, but that it will change is a fact. If we are to address the housing needs of the twenty-first century, we must first take a long hard look at the housing alternatives available today. Our vision for this book was to bring together authors from a variety of disciplines and perspectives who could introduce readers with little prior knowledge about the topic to the array of housing alternatives currently available to older adults. We also wanted to explore some of the more abstract issues that surround the topic of housing for the elderly. Finally, we wanted to provide a foundation for discussions about how the housing needs of the elderly will be dealt with in the coming decades.

We are just now emerging from a rather long period when the issue of housing was not a major national agenda item. Some would argue that it has never been a national priority. However, population projections and declines in the number of people who can afford home-ownership have combined to make housing a compelling national issue. The single-family-detached house that has represented the "American dream" to so many for so long is not likely to lose its attractiveness, but it might very well cease to be the "normal" housing arrangement for America's older adults.

Given the historically low priority that housing has received, it is not at all unreasonable to suggest that our previous approaches to the many issues related to housing will remain grossly inadequate. The inability of the "old" approaches to meet the housing needs of special populations are, we would argue, related to two issues: our system of publicly supported housing alternatives is overwhelmed with what is, for all practical purposes, an infinite need. Similarly, some especially promising private sector "solutions" have evolved into expensive "country clubs" for the wealthiest and healthiest of our older adult population. This obvious oversimplification is intended to draw our attention to the immediate need for a "new" approach: one that combines an increasing need for supportive services with the underlying need for affordable housing while, at the same time, taking into account the almost spiritual perspective from which Americans typically view their "homes." These will be among the important issues of the twenty-first century; it is to the discussion of these issues that we hope this volume contributes.

W.E.F.

Part I: Introduction

CHAPTER 1

Specialized Housing for Older People: Demographic, Socioeconomic, and Health Issues

David Boyd
W. Edward Folts
Dale E. Yeatts
Charles F. Longino

Specialized housing refers to various living environments that accommodate the particular needs of the population for which it is intended. There are many complex factors that will have an impact on the need for specialized housing for older Americans in the next century. Among the more important ones are demographic factors, socioeconomic factors, and factors related to the health and well-being of the older population. Golant (1992) has argued that because of these factors, the need for specialized housing for older Americans can be expected to increase dramatically as we enter the twenty-first century.

Demographically, more people than ever before are now at least sixty-five years old. The trend toward a larger older population, both in proportion and in absolute numbers, is projected to continue well into the twenty-first century until, sometime around 2050, the older population will be about 22 percent of the entire population. Further, while the older population is getting larger, another dramatic change is taking place—the older population is, itself, aging. Each of these changes in the age profile will have an impact on the need for specialized housing.

One of the primary socioeconomic factors affecting specialized housing is the income level of older persons. The utility of specialized housing is severely limited by the financial resources of those for whom it is designed. Obviously, even the most well-designed housing facility is of little value if those who would benefit from it are not able to afford it. One encouraging note is that the proportion of older Americans living below the poverty line has declined over the last three decades. At the same time, however, there have been increases in the number of older "near poor" (those with incomes below about 125 percent of the poverty level) and the "economically vulnerable" (those with incomes below about 150 percent–200 percent of the poverty level). The elderly population has become more diverse by growing proportionately at the other end of the economic spectrum as well (Crown, et al., forthcoming). These trends are likely to have a major impact on the suitability of future housing options.

Similarly, the health and well-being of America's older population suggests that specialized housing alternatives will be an increasingly important issue in the years to come, primarily because of the balance humans seek to maintain between their functional ability and the challenge of their living environments. Medical interventions continue to have their major beneficial impact on *acute* health problems. Unfortunately, the progress in treating *chronic* illness has not been as impressive. And, it is these chronic conditions from which older people are more likely to suffer. In fact, the true "medical miracle" of the twentieth century is not the much-sought-after conquest of the debilitating diseases of old age. Rather, it is that extreme frailty, illness, and even death are being pushed into older and older ages where few survived before. The result, so far at least, has been that we have added more healthy years to life for the "young-old," but, at the same time, we have added more unhealthy years of life for the "old-old." This irony, which has been noted by the U.S. Senate Special Committee on Aging (1991) on several occasions, has the most profound of policy implications in the area of housing.

The housing options available to older persons today represent a fragmented and widely diverse set of alternatives that lacks both coordination and comprehensiveness. In general, today's housing alternatives present the prospective older resident with a choice between independence and the availability of assistance. For reasons that will be explored in later chapters of this book, policies have been largely unable to incorporate both independence and assistance in a single setting. In fact, the current policy approach seems to view these concepts as antithetical in that one can be provided only at the expense of the other. The essential issue of how to make independence and assistance complementary is one that is likely to consume much of the housing debate in the years ahead.

For today's older persons, only a few housing options exist. That is also true of the entire population. The vast majority of persons in today's older population live in traditional single-family homes that they own. However, this should not in any way diminish the importance of exploring additional options, even if those options are "nontraditional" and innovative ones. Historical preferences in housing type notwithstanding, we are entering a period where adaptability and the willingness to innovate are going to be important components in our ability to meet the housing needs of the American public—regardless of their age, income, or health status.

Demographic Change and the Older Population

The United States is growing older, both in terms of the entire population and within the population of older (sixty-five plus) persons. From 1900 to 1990, the older population of the U.S. increased ten-fold from 3 million persons to 31.5 million persons (Table 1). Simultaneously, the proportion of older people in the population increased three-fold, from 4 percent to 12.6 percent (U.S. Senate Special Committee on Aging, 1991).

Table 1

Actual and Projected Growth of the Older Population: 1900–2050
(numbers in thousands)

Year	Total pop. all ages	55–64 No.	55–64 %	65–74 No.	65–74 %	75–84 No.	75–84 %	85+ No.	85+ %	65+ No.	65+ %
1900	76,303	4,009	5.3	2,189	2.9	772	1.0	123	0.2	3,084	4.0
1910	91,972	5,054	5.5	2,793	3.0	989	1.1	167	0.2	3,950	4.3
1920	105,711	6,532	6.2	3,464	3.3	1,259	1.2	210	0.2	4,933	4.7
1930	122,775	8,397	6.8	4,721	3.8	1,641	1.3	272	0.2	6,634	5.4
1940	131,669	10,572	8.0	6,375	4.8	2,278	1.7	365	0.3	9,019	6.8
1950	150,967	13,295	8.8	8,415	5.6	3,278	2.2	577	0.4	12,270	8.1
1960	179,323	15,572	8.7	10,997	6.1	4,633	2.6	929	0.5	16,560	9.2
1970	203,302	18,608	9.2	12,447	6.1	6,124	3.0	1,409	0.7	19,980	9.8
1980	226,546	21,703	9.6	15,580	6.9	7,729	3.4	2,240	1.0	25,549	11.3
1990	250,410	21,364	8.5	18,373	7.3	9,933	4.0	3,254	1.3	31,559	12.6
2000	268,266	24,158	9.0	18,243	6.8	12,017	4.5	4,622	1.7	34,882	13.0
2010	282,575	35,430	12.5	21,039	7.4	12,208	4.3	6,115	2.2	39,362	13.9
2020	294,364	41,087	14.0	30,973	10.5	14,443	4.9	6,651	2.3	52,067	17.7
2030	300,629	34,947	11.6	35,988	12.0	21,487	7.1	8,129	2.7	65,604	21.8
2040	301,807	35,537	11.8	30,808	10.2	25,050	8.3	12,251	4.1	68,109	22.6
2050	299,849	37,004	12.3	31,590	10.5	21,655	7.2	15,287	5.1	68,532	22.9

Sources: 1900 to 1980 data are tabulated from the Decennial Censuses of the Population and exclude Armed Forces overseas. Projections, which are middle series projections and include Armed Forces overseas, are from U.S. Bureau of the Census. "Projections of the Population of the United States, by Age, Sex, and Race: 1988 to 2060." by Gregory Spencer. *Current Population Reports* Series P-25, No. 1018 (January 1989). Obtained from U.S. Senate Special Committee on Aging, 1991.

In the future, from 1990 to 2050, the number of persons sixty-five and older is expected to more than double again, growing from 31.5 million to an estimated 68.5 million persons (Table 1). This number of older persons is projected to be about 22.9 percent of the total population. To put this into perspective, in 2020 nearly one in every four Americans will be at least sixty-five years old. Further, the U.S. Senate Special Committee on Aging (1991) has called attention to the fact that this increase in the older population will be quite unique:

> If current fertility and immigration levels remain stable, the older population will be the only age group to experience significant growth in the next century. (p. 4)

One way to examine the aging of the older population is to focus attention on the "oldest old"—those who are eighty-five years old and older. From 1900 to 1990, the "old-old" population grew from 123,000 to 3.3 million. During the same time period, its proportion of the total population grew from 0.2 percent to 1.3 percent (U.S. Senate Special Committee on Aging, 1991). Furthermore, the eighty-five plus population, which was only about 5 percent of the older population in 1900, had grown to nearly 10 percent of the older population by 1990.

This phenomenal growth in the oldest of age categories, often referred to in the popular press as the "graying" of America, can be further illustrated by the projected change in America's median age. From 1950 to 1990, the median age in the United States increased from thirty to thirty-three years—an increase of three years in forty years. For the period 1990 to 2050, the median age is projected to increase to forty-three years of age (U.S. Senate Special Committee on Aging, 1991). That is an impressive increase of ten years in only sixty years.

An equally impressive way to illustrate changes in the age distribution of the population in the U.S. is by comparing the projected proportions of older persons and youth. In 1900, young people (those less than eighteen years of age) comprised about 40 percent of the total population. Those who were sixty-five and older in 1900 made up only 4 percent of the population. By 1980, the age distribution of the U.S. had changed so that young people comprised only 28 percent and those at least sixty-five, 11 percent. It is projected that, by 2030, those sixty-five and older will have surpassed young people in proportion of the population 22 percent to 21 percent, respectively (U.S. Senate Special Committee on Aging, 1991). The baby boom of 1946–1964 (Atchley, 1991) and increased longevity through technological advancement have combined to produce most of this growth.

The changing age structure of the population is, therefore, a result of declining mortality rates across the entire life span and fluctuations in fertility rates for specific age cohorts (Harrington, Newcomer, and Estes, 1985).

Demographic Consequences for Specialized Housing

The projected demographic trends suggest that the need for specialized housing for older adults will increase substantially in the future. If all of the factors affecting housing need, other than demographic factors, remain constant in the future, the conclusions to be drawn would be relatively simple. If the sixty-five and older population is expected to increase by more than 34 million persons (100+ percent) between 1990 and 2030, the need for specialized housing can also be expected to increase. Perhaps even more important are the projected increases in the eighty-five and older population. This population is most likely to have significant deficits in its functional abilities (Atchley, 1991), and, therefore, most likely to need specialized housing of some kind. From 1990 to 2030 the projected increase in this population is 250 percent (from 3.3 million to 8.1 million). And the size of the population of persons eighty-five plus in the year 2050 is expected to be 15.3 million, an increase of 470 percent from 1990.

Socioeconomic Changes

In the past 30 years, the percentage of older Americans living in poverty has declined dramatically. In 1959, 35 percent of persons sixty-five and older were "officially" poor compared with 12 percent in 1990 (U.S. GAO, 1992). This dramatic change is one of the great success stories of our time, but while the elderly are about as likely as the nonelderly to live in "official" poverty, a much greater proportion of older Americans live near poverty than do those under the age of sixty-five (U.S. GAO,

1992). In 1989, for example, 27.2 percent of all persons age sixty-five and older were living below 150 percent of the established poverty level ($7,501 annually for an elderly couple), compared to 21.2 percent of persons under the age of sixty-five (U.S. Senate Special Committee on Aging, 1991). In successively older age categories, the proportion of persons living in or near poverty also increases (Longino, 1988). For example, in 1989, of all persons age eighty-five and over, 18.8 percent were living in poverty and 28.9 percent were living below 125 percent of the established poverty level (U.S. Senate Special Committee on Aging, 1991).

For women, staying married is associated with higher levels of income in current and past cohorts of the elderly. For poor widows, poverty is most often caused by loss of income upon the death of her spouse. For poor couples, however, poverty most often occurs within two years of retirement and is a direct result of the loss of income by the primary wage-earner (U.S. GAO, 1992). The vast majority of widows and of retired people, of course, are not poor.

A cursory examination of the relationship between elderly poverty and housing might suggest that elderly poverty has little bearing on housing since over three-fourths of older Americans own their own homes, and most own them "free and clear" (U.S. Senate Special Committee on Aging, 1991). Nonetheless, expenses related to homeownership such as taxes, utilities, insurance, repairs, maintenance, and remodeling to accommodate various age-related deficits, often represent a substantial expense among low-income older homeowners. Older persons with incomes at or near the poverty level may be unable to meet these expenses at all. Furthermore, for those not owning their own homes, housing expenses themselves can be equally demanding. In fact, according to the General Accounting Office (1992), in 1989 poor elderly renters (including those in subsidized housing) spent an average of about 46 percent of their total income on housing.

Ethnicity

In our society, socioeconomic status is demographically associated with ethnicity. Changes in the ethnicity of the older population, therefore, are also worthy of consideration in the context of socioeconomic status. As of 1989, the nonwhite and Hispanic populations in the U.S. contained much smaller proportions of older persons than the white population (U.S Senate Special Committee on Aging, 1991). Eight percent of African Americans, 5 percent of the Hispanic population and 7 percent of other races (Native Americans and Asian/Pacific Islanders) were over age sixty-five compared to about 13 percent of the white population. Projections for the future suggest that by the year 2030, 24 percent of the white population, 17 percent of the African-American population, and 13 percent of the Hispanic population will be at least sixty-five years old. Further, in 1990, white elderly people made up 86 percent of the older population. By the year 2050, this percentage is projected to drop to 68 percent (U.S. Senate Special Committee on Aging, 1991).

Table 2

Percent of Poor and Near-Poor Elderly Persons, by Age, Sex, and Race/Ethnicity, 1990

Sex and age	White		Black		Hispanic		Total	
	Poor	Near Poor	Poor	Near Poor	Poor	Near Poor	Poor	Near Poor
Both sexes								
65 +	10.1%	6.3%	33.8%	11.3%	22.5%	11.0%	12.2%	6.8%
65–74	7.6	4.9	29.6	11.0	20.6	10.4	9.7	5.4
75 +	13.8	8.6	40.6	11.9	26.2	12.4	16.0	8.9
Male								
65+	5.6	4.6	27.8	10.7	18.6	8.4	7.6	5.2
65–74	4.5	4.0	24.6	10.1	18.0	8.0	6.4	4.7
75 +	7.8	5.4	34.4	12.0	20.1	9.1	9.9	6.0
Female								
65 +	13.2	7.7	37.9	11.7	25.3	12.9	15.4	8.0
65–74	10.2	5.6	33.6	11.7	22.7	12.3	12.3	6.1
75 +	17.3	10.5	43.9	11.9	30.1	14.4	19.5	10.7

Source: U.S. GAO, 1992.

Table 2 presents information on those who experience what has been called "triple jeopardy" (Harris, 1990). These individuals are typically old, poor, and of minority status. As the data in Table 2 suggest, there is a clear disparity between groups of older people. In 1990, for example, only 16.4 percent of older whites were poor or near poor (125 percent of the poverty level), but 45.1 percent of older African Americans and 33.5 percent of older Hispanics were poor or near poor (U.S. GAO, 1992).

Gender

Gender is also implicated with socioeconomic status and race among the elderly. Women outnumber men in the sixty-five plus age group by a margin of three to two (U.S. Senate Special Committee on Aging, 1991). And, as was mentioned earlier, life expectancies for elderly women are projected to remain about seven years longer than those for men. This results in an over-representation of females in the sixty-five plus age group and is a major factor in the need for specialized housing for the elderly. For one thing, it means that housing for the very old is actually housing for very old women. And these very old women are typically alone, with limited financial resources and with a variety of chronic conditions that either directly cause functional deficits or that substantially increase the risk of such deficits.

The combined impact of poverty, ethnicity, and gender is illustrated by the fact that, in 1990, 7.6 percent of all males age sixty-five and older had incomes below the poverty line compared to 15.4 percent of females (Table 2). White males fared better than all males age sixty-five and older (5.6 percent versus 7.6 percent) and white females fared better than all females sixty-five and older (13.2 percent versus 15.4 percent) (U.S. GAO, 1992). With increasing age, poverty rates increase for both genders. In 1990, 7.8 percent of white males age seventy-five and older were living in poverty while for white females age seventy-five and older, 17.3 percent were in poverty (U.S. GAO, 1992).

The same general trends are found for other ethnic groups. For example, in 1990, 18.6 percent of Hispanic males were living below the poverty threshold while 25.3 percent of Hispanic females were living in poverty. Older Hispanics (seventy-five plus) also had higher rates of poverty than their younger elderly counterparts. Among the seventy-five plus Hispanic population, 20.1 percent of males and 30.1 percent of females had incomes below the official poverty threshold (U.S. GAO, 1992).

For older African Americans, the incidence of poverty was even more pronounced. For male elderly African Americans, 27.8 percent were poor while 37.9 percent of female elderly African Americans were living in poverty. As could be expected, poverty is even more prevalent among African Americans over the age of seventy-four. In 1990, 34.4 percent of males and 43.9 percent of the females in this age group were officially poor. Furthermore, the General Accounting Office reports that fully 53.8 percent—over half—of all African-American women over seventy-four years old had incomes within 125 percent of the official poverty level in 1990 (U.S. GAO, 1992).

Living Alone

The final demographic characteristic associated with socioeconomic status that we will examine separately is living arrangements, and in particular, living alone. Living alone is associated with poverty, ethnicity, and gender. As poverty has declined among the elderly, the proportion of older people living alone in their own homes has grown over the past several decades. The two factors, economic independence and residential independence, are linked. Widowhood is the primary event leading to living alone. Yet many widows who at one time would have joined the households of children now prefer to live in their own homes (Golant, 1992).

Because there is generally a drop in income associated with widowhood, there is a concomitant drop in income associated with living alone. In 1989, 22 percent of older persons living in poverty were also living alone (Table 3). Further, older persons in poverty were four times more likely to be living alone than living with a spouse (U.S. Senate Special Committee in Aging, 1991). This is in part an artifact of the measurement because poverty is based on household income; hence, the fewer persons in the household, the more likely it is to fall below the poverty threshold.

Ethnic differences also exist. The percentage of white older Americans in poverty who were also living alone was 18.8 percent in 1989. For the Hispanic elderly poor, 39.5 percent were living alone and 57.3 percent of elderly poor African Americans were living alone.

Table 3

Number and Percent of Elderly Below Poverty, by Race, Hispanic Origin, Sex and Living Arrangement, 1989

	Living arrangement of people below poverty level							
	Number (thousands)				Percent			
Race and Hispanic origin	Total	Alone	With spouse	With others	Total	Alone	With Spouce	With Others
All races								
Men	965	339	525	101	7.8	17.4	5.6	10.4
Women	2,404	1,705	390	310	14.0	23.3	5.2	12.7
Total	3,369	2,044	915	411	11.4	22.0	5.4	12.0
White								
Men	723	240	431	52	6.6	13.9	5.0	7.2
Women	1,819	1,339	318	162	11.8	20.0	4.6	8.5
Total	2,542	1,579	748	214	9.6	18.8	4.8	8.1
Black								
Men	221	96	80	46	22.1	48.2	13.7	21.0
Women	554	350	57	138	36.7	60.6	13.0	29.6
Total	766	445	137	183	30.8	57.3	13.4	26.6
Hispanic*								
Men	87	26	53	8	18.6	34.7	15.1	19.5
Women	124	62	33	29	22.4	41.9	12.4	20.4
Total	211	88	86	37	20.6	39.5	13.9	20.2

Source: Unpublished data from the March 1990 *Current Population Survey*. Obtained from U.S. Senate Special Committee on Aging, 1991.
Note: Details may not add to total due to rounding.
* Hispanic people may be of any race.

Among the older population, women are almost twice as likely to be poor than are men (14 percent and 7.8 percent respectively). Among all older women in poverty, 23.3 percent lived alone. Furthermore, the percentage of older poor women living alone was less for whites (20 percent) than for either Hispanics (41.9) or African Americans (60.6 percent) (U.S. Senate Special Committee on Aging, 1991).

Assets, Income, and Expenses

In 1988, assets produced 25 percent of the total income of older households (U.S. Senate Special Committee on Aging, 1991). However, as a source of income, the relative importance of assets was unevenly distributed among the elderly population, with 32 percent reporting no asset income and another 25 percent reporting asset income of less than $500 per year (U.S. Senate Special Committee on Aging, 1991).

Despite this, it is interesting to note that the elderly, as a group, owned more assets than the nonelderly. According to the U.S. Bureau of the Census, in 1988, the median net worth of elderly households was $73,471 compared to a median net worth of $35,752 for all households (Table 4). This difference is often explained in terms of "normal" life-cycle processes that result in an accumulation of assets over a lifetime. These would include savings, home equity, and personal property (U.S. Senate Special Committee on Aging, 1991).

However, when comparing the net worth of elderly households in 1988 based on the gender, living arrangement, and ethnicity of the residents, two facts stand out: (1) single males and single females each had less than half the net worth of married couples; and, (2) white elderly households had twice the net worth of Hispanic elderly households and four times the net worth of African-American elderly households (U.S. Senate Special Committee on Aging, 1991).

Table 4
Median Net Worth and Monthly Household Income,
by Age of Householder, 1988
(excludes group quarters)

| | | | Median net worth | |
Age	Number of households (thousands)	Median monthly household income	Total	Excluding home equity
Total	91,554	$1,983	$35,752	$9,840
Less than 35	25,379	2,000	6,078	3,258
35–44	19,916	2,500	33,183	8,993
45–54	13,613	2,604	57,466	15,542
55–64	13,090	2,071	80,032	26,396
65+	19,556	1,211	73,471	23,856
65–69	6,331	1,497	83,478	27,482
70–74	5,184	1,330	82,111	28,172
75+	8,041	977	61,491	18,819

Source: U.S. Bureau of the Census. "Household Wealth and Asset Ownership: 1988" *Current Population Reports* Series P-70, No. 22 (December 1990). Obtained from U.S. Senate Special Committee on Aging, 1991.

The single largest source of income for all elderly people in 1990 was Social Security (38 percent) (Harris, 1990). Pensions accounted for 18 percent, earnings accounted for 17 percent, and 3 percent was obtained from other sources. For the elderly poor, however, 71 percent of their income was derived from Social Security in 1990. Income assistance in the form of food, housing, and cash comprised another 20 percent of their income (U.S. GAO, 1992). The large majority of the financial resources of the older population was spent on housing, utilities, transportation, food, and health care. For persons age sixty-five–seventy-four, these expenses accounted for 74.1 percent of their total expenditures. For persons age seventy-five and older, 78 percent of their financial resources was spent for these necessities (U.S. Senate Special Committee on Aging, 1991). As a comparison, younger people spent 68 percent of their financial resources to cover these essential needs in 1990.

Obviously, the socioeconomic status of all Americans has much to do with the housing options that are available to them. The majority of older persons live in their own homes and have enough income and savings to retrofit their homes when their functional health decreases with advanced old age. They are the lucky ones who can control their environments enough to keep their living arrangements in balance with their level of physical functioning.

Others are not so lucky. For example, the appreciable minority of elderly persons who live at or near the official poverty level have few resources available to adapt their existing housing to match their increasing frailty. The inability to make existing housing arrangements more supportive can often encourage a move to a living environment that is more suitable to the individual's needs, if one can be found. The current lack of affordable housing designed with the very old in mind, except for those at the upper range of the economic spectrum, means that, apart from remaining in one's present housing arrangement or being institutionalized, few other real options exist.

Health and Well-Being

As a general trend, with increased longevity comes an increased probability of limitations in activity brought on by declining functional health. For that reason, those interested in housing for older Americans need to consider such issues as the current state of health of the older population, the impact of technological advances, and current health initiatives directed at meeting the needs of the older population. All of these issues will have a profound impact on the housing alternatives of the 21st century.

In a 1989 survey of the noninstitutionalized population of persons sixty-five and older, the vast majority (71 percent) rated their health as either excellent, very good, or good (U.S. Senate Special Committee on Aging, 1991). In that same survey, self-assessed poor health was associated with low income. Over 40 percent of those with family incomes under $10,000 rated their health as fair or poor compared to only 16.8 percent of those with family incomes over $35,000.

The built environment can either enhance or substantially hinder the functional abilities of older people, thereby profoundly affecting their independence. An examination of specific chronic health conditions experienced by those sixty-five and older suggests that as many as four out of five persons suffered from at least one chronic or disabling condition in 1989 (U.S. Senate Committee on Aging, 1991). Arthritis, hypertension, hearing impairments, and heart disease were the four most prevalent forms of chronic conditions occurring in the sixty-five and older population.

Table 5

Top Ten Chronic Conditions for People 65+, by Age and Race, 1989
(number per 1,000 people)

| Condition | Age | | | | Race (65+) | | |
	65+	45–64	65–74	75+	White	Black	Black as & of white
Arthritis	483.0	253.8	437.3	554.5	483.2	522.6	106
Hypertension	380.6	229.1	383.8	375.6	367.4	517.7	141
Hearing impairment	286.5	127.7	239.4	360.3	297.4	174.5	59
Heart disease	278.9	118.9	231.6	353.0	286.5	220.5	77
Cataracts	156.8	16.1	107.4	234.3	160.7	139.8	87
Deformity or orthopedic impairment	155.2	155.5	141.4	177.0	156.2	150.8	97
Chronic sinusitis	153.4	173.5	151.8	155.8	157.1	125.2	80
Diabetes	88.2	58.2	89.7	85.7	80.2	165.9	207
Visual impairment	81.9	45.1	69.3	101.7	81.1	77.0	95
Varicose veins	78.1	57.8	72.6	86.6	80.3	64.0	80

Source: National Center for Health Statistics. "Current Estimates from the National Health Interview Survey, 1989." *Vital and Health Statistics* Series 10, No. 176 (October 1990). Obtained from U.S. Senate Special Committee on Aging, 1991.

The types of health problems experienced by the older population are important because the most prevalent conditions are all chronic, not acute. The older population suffers from fewer acute conditions than do younger people. Acute conditions are characterized by rapid onset, short duration, pronounced symptoms, and a generally positive response to therapeutic efforts (Harris, 1990). In contrast, chronic conditions typically have a gradual onset, persist over a long period of time, and usually have no known cure. Since chronic conditions typically become progressively worse, persons with chronic conditions usually experience progressively greater activity restrictions.

Research involving persons seventy and older has consistently found that they are at substantially increased risk of experiencing difficulty when attempting to perform activities of daily living such as dressing, bathing, and walking (Kasper, 1988). In fact, it has been estimated that four out of ten persons age eighty-five and older actually could use assistance in carrying out at least one of the six everyday activities found in the most common measure of functional health (AARP, 1986). Activity restrictions have also been found to be more severe with increasing age, and are most severe among the elderly poor who are living alone.

One particularly disabling chronic health problem that becomes more prevalent with age is Alzheimer's disease. The incidence of "probable" Alzheimer's disease (the disease can only be accurately diagnosed at autopsy) was found to increase from 3 percent among those in the age group sixty-five–seventy-four, to 47 percent among those in the age group eighty-five plus (U.S. Senate Special Committee on Aging, 1991). The progression of this particular disease has profound implications for the need for specialized housing because, as an older person becomes progressively incapable of performing normal activities of daily living, he or she must become increasingly dependent on the environment for assistance.

The Impact of Modern Medicine

Public and occupational health as well as medical advances over the past century have been responsible for the prevention and control of many formerly fatal infectious diseases. These successes, along with a rising standard of living, have made it possible for an increasing number of persons to reach older and older ages. One consequence of the aging of the population has been a shift in the diseases from which people die. No longer do accidents and infectious diseases lead the list as the leading causes of death. Now chronic diseases, such as heart disease, cancer, and stroke lead the list, and other disabling diseases follow, such as arthritis, diabetes, and dementing illnesses (Rice, 1989). The easy victories that followed the introduction of germ theory in the last century are over. While there have been some advances in the treatment of such chronic conditions as heart disease, the focus has largely shifted from curing disease to maintaining and retarding its advance, a bitter pill for heroic medicine. Specialized housing designed to meet the needs of the elderly, especially for those in their seventh and eighth decades of life, simply must take into account the customary co-morbidity of the residents and this may mean a closer alliance between the public health community on the one hand and housing designers and policy advocates on the other (Estes and Rundall, 1992).

The two major publicly financed health-care programs, available to the elderly since 1965, are Medicare and Medicaid. Unfortunately, Medicare tends to emphasize acute care and it fails to fund health promotion and disease prevention as well as neglecting such chronic health needs as long-term care, in-home services, dental care, eyeglasses, and hearing aids. While Medicaid does finance long-term care, it has strict financial guidelines that limit eligibility to the poor. Further, only 36 percent of the eligible elderly take advantage of Medicaid (U.S. Senate Special Committee on Aging, 1991). In the latest health policy review that is underway in Washington, housing for the disadvantaged elderly may be seen as a potential opportunity to make health care more accessible to one segment of the older population, namely, those in the greatest need.

Conclusion

Several factors will affect the amount and types of specialized housing needed for older Americans. One of these factors is the changing size of the older population. Another is the formation of health policies that will affect health care research and services. A third is U.S. social policy affecting the socioeconomic conditions of older persons. Among the oldest old are concentrations of women, people in poor health, and those with inadequate incomes. Although this population may be in the greatest need for specialized housing, such persons are least likely to be able to afford such housing. As this more vulnerable part of the older population grows in size, along with the older population generally, there is likely to be increasing pressure for social policies aimed at addressing this issue. The electorate will age as well, and it is likely to be more sensitive to these issues than an electorate with a younger population profile.

One would hope that the numbers of people involved will compel them to reformulate our prevailing responses to the need for specialized housing for the elderly. The numbers, which often appear in the popular press in a variety of forms, suggest that we are not going to be prepared to meet the need for housing at any meaningful level. But consider this. It is a fact that nearly a quarter of the eighty-five plus population is currently institutionalized, most frequently in nursing homes. Based on the 1990 census data, that proportion translates into about 759,000 people. Using census projections for the size of the eighty-five plus population in the year 2050, and assuming that other factors, such as the health conditions of the very old remain generally as they are today, 23 percent translates into about 3,519,000 people. The ultimate question for housing specialists, then, is a deceptively simple one: How are we to accommodate these additional 2,760,000 individuals? As yet, neither the housing industry nor those involved in social policy have stepped forward with an adequate response. Perhaps as a major long-term care crisis moves from projected to actual reality, the response will be a multi-faceted one that includes better designed and more accessible specialized public housing for the vulnerable elderly who can continue, for a while at least, to remain residentially independent.

REFERENCES

American Association of Retired Persons (1992). *Your home, your choice.* Washington, D.C.: AARP.

—— (1990). *Understanding senior housing for the 1990s.* Washington, D.C.: AARP.

—— (1986). *Assessing elderly housing.* Washington, D.C.: AARP.

—— (1984). *Housing options for older Americans.* Washington, D.C.: AARP.

Atchley, R. (1991). *Social forces and aging* (365–378) and (chapter 19, 395–398). Belmont, CA: Wadsworth Publishing.

Crown, W., Longino, C.F., Jr. & Cutler, N. (forthcoming). *Journal of Aging and Social Policy.*

Crystal, S. & Beck, P. (1992). A room of one's own: The SRO and the single elderly. *The Gerontologist, 32*(5), 684–692.

Danigelis, N.L. & Fengler, A.P. (1990). Homesharing: How social exchange helps elders live at home. *The Gerontologist, 30*(2), 162–170.

Dunkelman, D. (1989). Housing at the crossroads. *The Southwestern, 5*(2), 19–30.

Estes, C. & Rundall, T. (1992). Social characteristics, social structure, and health in an aging population. In M. Ory, R. Abeles, & P. Lipman (Eds.) *Aging, health and behavior* (299–326). Newbury Park, CA: Sage.

Fairchild, T.J. & Folts, W.E. (1989). Elder housing policy in the 1990s: Problem or opportunity. *The Southwestern, 5*(2), 10–18.

Fairchild, T.J., Higgins, D. & Folts, W.E. (1991). An offer they could not refuse: Housing for the elderly. *Journal of Housing for the Elderly, 9*(1–2), 157–166.

Gerber, J., Wolff, J., Klores, W. & Brown, G. (1989). *Lifetrends: The future of baby boomers and other aging Americans.* New York: Stonesong Press.

Golant, S.M. (1992). *Housing America's elderly: Many possibilities/few choices.* Newbury Park, CA: Sage.

———— (1991). Matching congregate housing settings with a diverse elderly population: Research and theoretical perspectives. *Journal of Housing for the Elderly*, 9(1–2), 12–38.

Grigsby, J.S. (1991). Paths for future population aging. *The Gerontologist*, 31(2), 195–203.

Hare, P.H. (1991). The echo housing/granny flat experience in the U.S. In N.M. Lazarowich (Ed.) *Granny flats as housing for the elderly: International perspectives.* New York: Haworth Press.

Harrington, C., Newcomer, R.J. & Estes, C.L. (1985). *Long term care of the elderly: Public policy issues.* Beverly Hills: Sage.

Harris, D.K. (1990). *Sociology of Aging.* New York: Harper & Row.

Hipskind, M. (1991). *Elderly housing: Beyond shelter.* Unpublished paper: University of North Texas. Denton, TX.

Husaini, B.A., Moore, S.T. & Castor, R.S. (1991). Social and psychological well-being of black elderly living in high-rises for the elderly. *Journal of Gerontological Social Work*, 16(3–4), 57–78.

Kasper, J. (1990). Implications of an aging population for long-term care. In D. Harris (Ed.) *Sociology of Aging* 366–371. New York: Harper & Row.

———— (1988). *Aging alone: Profiles and projections.* A Report of the Commonwealth Fund Commission on Elderly People Living Alone: Baltimore, MD. 16–31.

Kaye, L.W. & Monk, A. (1991). Introduction. *Journal of Housing for the Elderly*, 9(1–2), 1–3.

Keigher, S.M. & Pratt, F. (1991). Growing housing hardship among the elderly. In S. Keigher (Ed.) *Housing risks and homelessness among the urban elderly.* New York: Haworth Press.

Keigher, S.M., Berman, R.H. & Greenblatt, S.T. (1991). Overview of the Chicago study of elderly persons at housing risk. In S. Keigher (Ed.) *Housing risks and homelessness among the urban elderly.* New York: Haworth Press.

Kingsley, G.T. & Struyk, R.J. (1991). Housing policy in the United States: Trends, future needs, and implications for congregate housing. *Journal of Housing for the Elderly*, 9(1–2), 39–57.

Lazarowich, N. M. (1990). A review of the Victoria, Australia Granny Flat Program. *The Gerontologist*, 30(2), 171–177.

Longino, C.F., Jr. (1988). Who are the oldest Americans? *The Gerontologist, 28*(3), 515–523.

Rice, D.P. (1989). The characteristics and health of the elderly. In C. Eisedorfer, D. Kessler & A. Spector (Eds.) *Caring for the elderly: Reshaping health policy* 3–26. Baltimore: Johns Hopkins.

Schroots, J.J.F., Birren, J.E. & Svanborg, A. (Eds). (1988). *Health and aging: Perspectives and prospects.* New York: Springer Publishing.

Serow, W.J., Sly, D.F. & Wrigley, J.M. (1990). *Population and aging in the United States.* New York: Greenwood Press.

U.S. Conference of Mayors (1986). *Assessing elderly housing.* Washington, D.C.: U.S. Conference of Mayors.

U.S. General Accounting Office (1992). *Elderly Americans: Health, housing and nutrition gaps between the poor and nonpoor.* Washington, D.C.: U.S. General Accounting Office.

U.S. Senate Special Committee on Aging (1991). *Developments in aging: 1990 Vol. 1.* Washington, D.C.: U.S. Government Printing Office.

CHAPTER 2

Planned Housing for the Elderly Since 1950: History, Policies, and Practices

Wiley P. Mangum

The focus of this chapter is the changes that have occurred in policies and practices since 1950 in the field of what has been termed retirement housing, senior housing, special housing for the elderly, purpose-built housing for the elderly, and planned housing for the elderly. Although distinctions could, perhaps, be drawn among these terms, they all refer to various types of noninstitutional housing and/or facilities and services that have been specially developed for older residents. The latter term is being used here partly because it seems the most general but mainly because it clearly denotes the deliberateness with which such housing has been developed for an older population.

The year 1950 was chosen as a starting point for this brief history of planned housing for the elderly for several reasons. First, it is chronologically distant enough from the present to enable us to discern and document significant changes in policies and practices and, yet, not so distant that the origins and roots of the changes have receded, perhaps irretrievably, into the mists of unrecorded history. Second, it is close to one of the world's great historical watersheds, the end of World War II. The ending of the war initiated numerous social and cultural changes in American society and allowed a resumption of concern with issues of aging, including housing, that had been interrupted by wartime mobilization. Third, it is close in time to the founding of such organizations as the Gerontological Society of America (1945), the National Council on the Aging (1950), and the American

Association of Retired Persons which was founded originally as the National Retired Teachers Association (1958). The actions of these and other organizations contributed to a sustained post-war "attack" on problems associated with growing older. Finally, serious concern with elderly housing issues may be said to have originated in 1950 when the first National Conference on Aging recommended greater federal emphasis on the housing needs of older persons (U.S. Senate Special Committee on Aging, 1991).

It is impossible to discuss changes in planned housing policies and practices without considering related changes that have taken place. At a minimum, these include changes in the characteristics of actual and potential inhabitants of planned housing for the elderly, changes in professional and lay attitudes toward such housing—centering on the issue of age segregation versus age integration—and changes in images of aging in American society. While it is clearly impossible to do justice to each of these changes in a single chapter, some consideration of them will be woven into the overall discussion of planned housing.

Even though the vast majority of older persons live in and will continue to live in conventional housing such as detached houses, apartments, and nonpark manufactured housing (formerly mobile-homes and, before that, house trailers), this chapter's focus on noninstitutional housing that has been specially designed and/or built for the exclusive use of older persons seems appropriate. While planned housing for the elderly may contain a relatively small and highly self-selected segment of the older population, it represents an important attempt to meet special housing and other needs of those older persons for whom conventional housing may be unsuitable or undesirable. Moreover, although planned housing—particularly retirement villages—was quite controversial in the early years of its development, it now appears to be well accepted as an alternative for the estimated 2 to 3 percent of older Americans who live in non-federally assisted housing (Golant, 1992). When those older persons living in federally assisted planned housing are included, the overall percentage of persons sixty years of age and over living in planned housing is approximately 5 percent (Mangum, 1982).

It should be noted that the preceding estimates are not based on all current nonconventional housing alternatives for older persons but, rather, those facilities that have been explicitly planned to house appreciable numbers of older persons, usually one hundred or more. Not included in the estimates are older persons living in shared housing, accessory apartments, cooperatives, ECHO housing, or nonpark manufactured housing. Based on calculations from estimates provided by Duensing (1988, p. 145), it appears that an additional 8 percent of the older population lives in such housing (mainly nonpark manufactured housing). Although these are important housing alternatives for older persons, with the exception of share-a-home type housing that will be discussed later, they are not planned housing in the sense that the term is being used here. Thus, they will not be included in the following discussion.

Planned housing has been developed over the years as a result of initiatives in both the public and private sectors of the United States, each of which has contributed distinctly different types of housing to the overall mix. We shall begin our historical survey of policies and practices in the public sector.

Public Sector Programs of Planned Housing for the Elderly

American society has always made a sharp distinction between activities thought to be appropriate to the private sector and those appropriate to the public sector. The provision of housing generally has been regarded as a private-sector activity, the main concern of which has been to satisfy the shelter needs and wants of individuals who can afford to pay market prices. The public sector, as a matter of public policy, has tended to concern itself with families and individuals who cannot afford market prices. For older persons, the private-public dichotomy has resulted in a variety of planned housing ranging from some rather architecturally splendid and amenity-rich retirement villages and continuing care retirement communities in the private sector to public housing, characterized by "economy of construction," in the public sector.

The social historian David Hackett Fischer (1977) has written that old age in the United States began to be viewed as a social problem around the year 1910. It was not until the Great Depression of the 1930s, however, that the general socio-economic plight and vulnerability of older persons really began to be revealed on a large scale. Besides providing a sociopolitical context within which the Social Security Act of 1935 could be passed, the Depression precipitated some concern for the housing of older persons and initiated its redefinition from an individual to a social and, hence, to a public problem. Organized public concern, principally at the federal level, is strictly a post-war development, however, and federal housing policy for older persons dates back only to 1956 (Gozonsky, 1965; Robbins, 1971). According to Robbins (1971, p. 44):

> Special Federal programs for elderly housing started with the Housing Act of 1956. Previously, the only specialized housing for the elderly had been such facilities as the county homes, church-supported homes, Federal and State homes for veterans, and privately endowed institutions. The Federal programs recognized that government resources should be made available if the housing needs of the elderly were to be met.

In 1956, the U.S. Government explicitly sought to improve the housing of poor older persons by amending the Housing Act of 1937 to make older individuals (i.e., sixty-two and over) eligible for low-rent public housing. Before 1956, only older persons who were members of families were allowed to occupy public housing. This legislation recognized some major demographic facts of particular gerontological import: most older persons are women (approximately 18.7 million as compared to 12.9 million men in 1990); most older women are widows (and many live alone); and older women are heavily over-represented among the aged poor (Atchley, 1991).

Federally Assisted Housing Programs
for the Elderly

In the United States, public sector programs of housing for the elderly exist for two major reasons: The market is unable or unwilling to provide sufficient affordable housing for older persons (or many younger persons) of limited means, and, for older persons with housing problems, economic and cultural changes over the years have reduced their options for and interest in living with relatives. From the 1950s to the late 1970s, the federal government seemed increasingly willing to act on these considerations by stimulating the construction of new housing for older persons. Beginning in 1981, during the Reagan administration, however, federal funding authorizations for new construction were drastically reduced. This represented a policy shift and was based on the Administration's position that new construction was unnecessary since sufficient housing stock already existed from which older persons could obtain housing. Moreover, the policy shift was related to increasing concern over the federal budget deficit and the negative effect that funding new housing construction had on the deficit.

The 1990 passage of the Cranston-Gonzalez National Affordable Housing Act (NAHA 1990) appears, however, to have returned the federal government to its former role in planned housing for the elderly:

> The Act authorized $27.5 billion in fiscal year 1991 and $29.9 billion in fiscal year 1992 to continue existing programs such as public housing, special housing programs for the elderly and handicapped, and rent subsidies, as well as the creation of several new programs. . . . Over a 2-year period, as many as 360,000 additional units could be added to the federally assisted housing stock. (U.S. Senate Special Committee on Aging, 1991, p. 295)

With the recent change in federal administration there is reason to believe that NAHA 1990 may be largely implemented. At the same time, however, the fact that governmental as well as general public concern over the federal budget deficit probably never has been greater may serve to dampen federal spending in many areas, including that of housing for the elderly.

Over a period of years, the federal government, acting principally through the U.S. Department of Housing and Urban Development, has developed a number of special housing programs for older persons of limited means. Most of these have been programs aimed at providing rental housing for older persons and the most important, judged by numbers of dwelling units provided, have been: public housing, Section 202 housing, and Section 231 housing.

Public Housing

Public housing, or the Low-Rent Public Housing Program, is the oldest and largest federally assisted housing program for low-income individuals and families, including older persons. Currently, residents pay rent in the amount of 30 percent of their net income to local housing authorities (LHAs) which construct and manage the housing. Differences between income from this source and operating expenses of the LHAs are reimbursed by the federal government.

Approximately 45 percent of the country's 1.4 million public housing units are occupied by older Americans (U.S. Senate Special Committee on Aging, 1991). However, the degree of age concentration of older persons in public housing varies. In a study conducted in 1986, it was found that in a sample of large public housing projects about 48 percent of older residents lived in units built for the elderly and handicapped, 15 percent lived in units built for the elderly but in mixed family/elderly developments, and 37 percent lived in unmodified family units in family developments (U.S. Senate Special Committee in Aging, 1991). For the last decade, most new public housing projects have been designed only for the elderly, primarily because there tend to be fewer management problems with, and less local opposition to, the construction of such projects (U.S. General Accounting Office, 1992).

Although public housing has provided shelter for many older Americans, it has not been without problems. Perhaps the most serious has been a lack of supportive services for older tenants who have aged in place. Technically, older tenants are supposed to be able to live independently in housekeeping units (with kitchen facilities) and to move, ideally to a more appropriate and formally supportive setting, when they can no longer do so. Evidently, however, managers of public housing have been reluctant to force older tenants to move, even when their physical health declines to the point where they should no longer live independently. Indeed, managers tend to consider terminating residency only when an older tenant manifests behavioral or psychiatric problems that may be disruptive or troublesome to other residents (Barker, Mitteness, & Wood, 1988; Bernstein, 1982; Sheehan, 1986). This apparently routine retention of increasingly frail older tenants, allowing them to age in place, has exerted additional pressure on public housing to provide supportive services.

In recent years, federal policy has permitted, but has never required, public housing projects to provide services for older residents and, consequently, those services that exist in individual projects have tended to develop in an idiosyncratic and uncertain manner. This uneven development of services for older persons in public housing generally can be attributed to shifting conceptions, and attendant policies, of what the federal government should be doing in the area of housing for the elderly. When federally assisted housing programs for older persons originated in the 1950s, the principal—some would say the only—concern of enabling legislation and official policy was in providing shelter. Tenants were expected to be in good health upon admission to a particular public housing project, to be able to live independently, and to move when and if they could no longer do so. Services were viewed as irrelevant to the housing mission of federal agencies and were discouraged if not officially prohibited.

Such conservatism was mainly a reflection of the incrementalism that characterizes the development of public policy; governmental agencies rarely, if ever, leap into bold new ventures, such as providing both housing and services de novo. Rather, they build slowly and piecemeal on existing policies and programs that, in the early days of federal participation in housing for the elderly, did not involve the concept of housing-related services. Indeed, the mere provision of special shelter exclusively for older persons probably was seen as a bold step in the context of the times. The policy conservatism also was rooted in the fact that the average age of early older tenants of public housing was considerably lower than it is now and, thus, the need for supportive services was not so evident. Moreover, the concepts of "the old old" (Neugarten, 1974) or "the oldest old" (Bould, Sanborn, & Reif, 1989; Rosenwaike & Logue, 1985), which served to underscore the need for services among the oldest segment of the population, had not yet entered the vocabularies or planning orientations of gerontologists and others concerned with housing for the elderly.

One service-relevant concept that has been around for a number of years, however, and that has been applied to some public and other types of planned housing is "congregate housing." The etymology of this term is uncertain but it may have originated in 1951 in a paper on "Difference of Adjustment: Segregated Old Age Communities vs. Unsegregated Communities" by Robert W. Kleemeier (1951). Later, Kleemeier (1961) elaborated on the term in a chapter on "The Use and Meaning of Time in Special Settings: Retirement Communities, Homes for the Aged, Hospitals, and Other Group Settings." In that context, "congregate," which generally pertains to the group aspects of housing settings for older persons, referred:

> ...not only to the size of the group, but also to the closeness of [the] individuals to each other and to the degree of privacy it is possible to obtain in the setting. (Kleemeier, 1961, p. 282)

Subsequently, however, the term has generally come to mean group housing for older persons in which certain kinds of supportive services are an essential element.

The federal use of the term "congregate" dates from the Housing and Urban Development Act of 1970 that attempted to stimulate the development of congregate housing on a national scale (Streib, 1990). As Streib points out, however, although such housing makes a great deal of sense for older persons, especially those at some risk of institutionalization, and despite program evaluations that have generally found congregate housing to be effective, there has yet to emerge a strong federal commitment to further development. In fairness to the federal government, however, it should be acknowledged that policy formulation and implementation of any kind are subject to the ineluctable political process in which incrementalism—or vacillation—appears to be inherent.

A final concept that has acquired housing and service relevance in recent years is that of "aging in place." When first coined in the early 1980s, the term merely referred to the fact of older persons remaining in their current housing. Now, however, aging in place, whether in one's own home or in a planned housing facility, is coming to be recognized as desirable for most older persons. Although it has not yet become a basis for policy, it is likely to be in the future (Pynoos, 1990). These considerations apply not only to public housing for the elderly but also to Section 202 housing, to which we now turn.

Section 202 Housing

Although public housing has provided the largest number of federally assisted dwelling units for older persons over the years, Section 202 rental housing for the elderly (and handicapped) has been regarded as the Department of Housing and Urban Development's primary program for providing housing specifically for the elderly. It was initiated almost thirty-five years ago as part of the Federal Housing Act of 1959. Since that time, it has undergone various transformations, including being temporarily phased out from 1969 until its reinstitution in connection with Section 8 rental assistance in 1974. During the Reagan and early Bush administrations, it was essentially dormant as far as authorizations for new construction were concerned but, as noted earlier, with the passage of the National Affordable Housing Act of 1990, it now appears to have new life. As of fiscal year 1992, however, the means of financing Section 202 housing has been changed from a direct loan program with Section 8 rental subsidies to nonprofit sponsors to a direct grant program with operating assistance (U.S. Senate Special Committee on Aging, 1991).

Section 202 was originally a program in which long-term (50 year), low interest rate (3 percent) loans were made by the federal government directly to private, nonprofit corporations to finance the construction or substantial rehabilitation of residential projects and related facilities to serve the needs of the elderly (i.e., persons sixty-two years of age or older) and the physically or mentally handicapped. Although it was viewed as being highly successful in this regard, it incurred the criticism that, as a public program, it was competing unfairly (through below market interest rates and a longer than usual amortization period) with the private sector in providing housing for the elderly. In addition, unlike public housing, which has always been targeted at low-income households, including the elderly, Section 202 housing was aimed originally at lower-middle income older persons, with minimum as well as maximum income limits as part of the admissions process. For several years and before gerontologists and policymakers began differentiating among subgroups of the elderly, this seemed appropriate; planned housing was being supplied to at least some of the older persons (sixty-two and over) who wanted or needed it, even if they were not at or below the poverty level. Similarly, the Older Americans Act of 1965 originally provided Title III supportive services to older persons (60 and over) who wanted or needed them, without regard to income. Increasingly, however, federal assistance to older persons has become targeted at those in greatest social and economic need, especially low-income minority individuals. Thus, changes in perceptions of whom should be served by Section 202 housing contributed to its temporary demise.

According to Lawton (1975), the program was terminated in 1969 primarily to reduce the appearance in the federal budget of large outlays of money to sustain the original program. Nevertheless, from 1959 to 1969, 45,000 housing units were constructed and the program was considered successful in that only one project was foreclosed during the original ten-year period (U.S. Senate Special Committee on Aging, 1991).

From 1969 to 1974, the Section 202 housing program was temporarily replaced by the Section 236 program of the Housing Act of 1968 (Lawton, 1975). Unlike Section 202, which was a direct loan program for nonprofit sponsors to provide housing for the elderly (mainly) and handicapped, Section 236 provided mortgage interest reduction payments to either profit or nonprofit sponsors to provide housing for limited-income tenants of all ages. With the reinstitution of Section 202 in 1974, in connection with Section 8 rental assistance, the Section 236 program was discontinued. During its five-year lifetime, however, about 192,000 units for the elderly were produced (Lawton & Hoover, 1981).

As of 1989, there were over 3,200 Section 202 projects nationwide, with over 230,000 occupied housing units (U.S. Senate Special Committee on Aging, 1990). Even so, there is still a great need for such housing, as reflected in lengthy waiting lists at 202 projects in most regions of the country.

Section 231 Housing

The Section 231 mortgage insurance program for elderly housing originated at the same time as Section 202; that is, with the Federal Housing Act of 1959. This program enabled both profit and nonprofit corporations to borrow money at market rates, with the mortgages insured by the federal government, to build housing with relatively few restrictions on tenant characteristics or type of environment provided (Lawton, 1975). Many nonprofit organizations, primarily church groups, took advantage of Section 231 to build "retirement centers" or life-care facilities that catered to relatively well-to-do older persons. At the same time, a number of profit-oriented corporations also used Section 231 to build rental apartments that were considerably more luxurious and aimed at more affluent older persons than was allowed under Section 202.

The experiences of the two types of sponsors were quite different, however. According to Lawton (1975), at one point only 6 percent of the church-sponsored projects, which focused on care as well as housing, had failed and had to be repossessed by the Federal Housing Administration whereas 45 percent of those sponsored by profit-oriented corporations, which focused mainly on housing, met this fate. The latter outcome was probably a classic instance of developers having misjudged the older housing market. As Kleemeier (1961) once suggested, regardless of their other reasons for doing so, older persons always enter planned housing with the thought that they may eventually require some degree of care. This seemed to be confirmed for me many years ago, while visiting a number of quite impressive but also quite unoccupied Section 231 projects in Southern California in the early 1960s. Several frustrated rental agents told me that the older persons who could afford such housing were not interested in the housing, per se, but they wanted certain supportive services that the projects did not provide.

According to Lawton (1975), after the large number of failures of Section 231 projects, especially in the private, profit-oriented sector, the Section 231 program was virtually abandoned by the federal government. Lawton (1975) also describes a variety of other federal programs such as the Section 221 (d-3) and the Section 515 Rural Housing programs that provided rental, purchase, rehabilitation of existing housing stock, or relocation payments for some older persons. As these programs were targeted at all age groups, they are not considered planned housing for the elderly and are, therefore, not included in this discussion.

State Housing Initiatives for the Elderly

Although most public-sector housing for the elderly has resulted from federal policies and programs, there have been some state initiatives. Some of these seem designed to supplement the federal effort in housing for the elderly whereas others may have been intended to take up some of the slack created during the 1980s when federal activity was sharply curtailed. It is beyond the scope of this chapter to provide a detailed history of state policies and programs in housing for the elderly, but some mention of activity in Florida, which has the highest percentage of older persons of any state in the nation, may be useful.

In Florida, the State Apartment Incentive Loan Program (SAIL) makes low interest rate loans to developers who agree to rent a portion of the units to low income tenants. During the first six months of loan availability each year, 45 percent of the loans must be reserved for elderly housing. Another component of the program provides loans for the repair of federally assisted housing for low income elderly. Another program, called Florida Fix, makes limited funding available to local agencies that provide home repair and weatherization to those with low incomes.

Programs such as these would be regarded by most people as reflecting a state interest in improving the housing of older persons. At the same time, however, there is an apparent lack of firm and ongoing state commitment to housing for the elderly. In 1986, the Florida Legislature established the Committee on Housing for the Elderly. This Committee was charged with developing an improved understanding of the housing needs of the elderly and promoting the development of living arrangements to meet these needs. Unfortunately, the Committee on Housing for the Elderly functioned only one year and was replaced in 1990 by the Affordable Housing Study Commission, which has a subcommittee on the elderly. This commission is not currently funded.

Private Sector Programs of Housing for the Elderly

In discussing private sector programs of housing for the elderly, it is necessary to distinguish immediately between profit-oriented and not-for-profit organizations that provide housing. It would be reasonable to suppose that profit-oriented housing is invariably more expensive than not-for-profit housing but this is not always the case. First, it is necessary to consider the meaning of "housing" in the two approaches. Profit-oriented housing facilities tend to focus on providing housing only, with any services as optional add-on expenses. Not-for-profit organizations, by contrast, have tended to focus more on providing care, with housing being simply one component of the total care package. By spreading expenses over the available client base, this can make some not-for-profit facilities quite expensive. Second, whereas profit-oriented housing facilities cater to customers who can afford to pay market prices, not-for-profit facilities may cater to low or moderate income older persons who are members of the sponsoring organization or they may cater to more affluent older persons who want comprehensive care, including housing.

Not-for-Profit Housing for the Elderly

Although some needy older persons have been cared for in monasteries and other charitable institutions in Western societies for centuries, the concept of nonprofit housing for the elderly is mainly a twentieth-century phenomenon. Even the general term "nonprofit" did not enter spoken English until 1900 to 1905 (Flexner & Hauck, 1987). Before the term originated, however, there was at least one instance of this type of housing in the United States. According to Gimmy and Boehm (1988), the first housing project for older persons was developed in the late 1800s by a religious organization to provide for retired clergy. Subsequently, not-for-profit housing has continued to develop, largely through the efforts of churches, fraternal associations, and other benevolent organizations to provide affordable housing and, possibly, some degree of care for their less affluent older members or for lower income older persons. By today's architectural and amenity standards, most of the facilities developed during the early period were quite modest. At the same time, however, general expectations for all kinds of material things, including early congregate housing, also were far more modest.

There are a number of types of noninstitutional not-for-profit housing. Three of the most important types are: shared housing; homes for the aged; and life-care facilities.

Shared Housing

Most of the types of planned housing discussed in this chapter represent rather marked departures from conventional housing occupied by families or single individuals. Whether profit oriented or not-for profit, they usually contain fairly large aggregations of older persons living in a purpose-built setting that may be located in a semi-residential, semi-commercial, or geographically remote area. Despite the general success of such housing in meeting the housing needs of various types of older persons, at one time it struck some professionals as being a rather artificial and possibly even socially pernicious way of doing so (Jacobs, 1974; Mumford, 1956; Vivrett, 1960). One type of planned housing that seems exempt from this concern has been "shared housing."

Shared housing may be thought of as a type of residential facility that lies somewhere between conventional housing and planned, purpose-built housing for the elderly. Physically, it usually takes the form of large, older, former single-family homes in ordinary residential areas housing several unrelated older persons under the supervision of a resident manager. As noted in the work on shared housing by Streib et al. (1984), it is aimed at older persons who may have some degree of frailty that makes living alone difficult but who do not need or want to be institutionalized. It also provides a quasi-familial setting for older persons, particularly older women, whose own families may no longer exist.

Unlike most other types of planned housing, the origin and history of shared housing in the United States is quite obscure. Apparently, however, it developed later than did the other types. Streib et al. (1984) discuss the history of "Share-A-Homes" in Orlando, Florida, with the original Share-A-Home having been founded by James Gillies in 1969. Similar shared housing facilities were developed in other states such as Illinois, Massachusetts, and Ohio in the 1970s (Daily, 1987; Herman et al., 1983).

According to Herman et al. (1983), shared housing is developing rapidly and, as of 1982, it was estimated that 300,000 older individuals occupied shared housing (Duensing, 1988). It is likely, however, that some of these were simply living, by invitation or agency arrangement, in the homes of older homeowners—house sharing—rather than living in the type of shared housing described by Streib et al. (1984) and other authors. Moreover, there is a rather substantial barrier, in the form of zoning ordinances and community resistance, to the development of any kind of group housing in single-family residential areas, whether it is for younger or older persons (Herman et al., 1983; Mangum, 1985; 1988).

Homes for the Aged

At one time in the United States it would not have been difficult to find housing and care facilities unselfconsciously called "homes for the aged" by their operators, their residents, and others. These facilities offered non-nursing personal care to from a few to a hundred or more older residents. In some of the less visible parts of the country and in some state bureaucratic classification schemes, it might still be possible to unearth a few. In the more euphemistic, image-manipulating, marketing-savvy, and relativistic times in which we now live, however, the term "home for the aged" is becoming unacceptable—a victim of its negative paternalistic connotation and a reproach to the more positive spin that gerontologists and others wish to place on aging. In the modern or, perhaps, the post-modern era, the combination of the words "home" and "aged" signifies a facility to which older people are consigned, however benevolently, when they are no longer capable of functioning on their own.

Today's society appears to be more comfortable with terms such as "assisted living," as well as others, that refer to facilities with commercially attractive names and that offer what is typically described as "limited" support to ordinarily active and healthy seniors when, and if, they need it. Despite this, homes for the aged still exist in considerable numbers, even if their names have been changed. However, as they have not exactly been grist for the mills of historians or statisticians, it is difficult to say when they began or how many there are. Most or all states have them and they are usually licensed by state departments of social welfare or some other state licensing agency for the purpose of providing nonmedical care and supervision for a specified number of older persons. Based on my own experience over the years, I would say that they have generally improved. This is partly due to licensing and regulation but, for the larger ones, it is also due to increasing competition and the efforts of community watchdog groups. Undoubtedly, as the number of very old persons increases in the United States, the number of such facilities will also increase.

Life-Care Facilities

As early as the late nineteenth century but mainly after about 1950, planned not-for-profit housing for the elderly, originally known as "life-care" facilities, began appearing (Somers & Spears, 1992). In today's much more marketing-oriented and sophisticated senior housing environment, such facilities are now known as "continuing care retirement communities" or CCRCs, and they are still operated mainly by nonprofit organizations. In fact, Somers and Spears (1992) reported that as of 1988, 95 percent–98 percent of all CCRCs were owned and managed by nonprofit organizations. Increasingly, however, profit-oriented corporations such as Marriott and Hyatt, as well as smaller companies, are developing and marketing quite sumptuous and amenity-rich CCRCs in many parts of the United States.

The basic function of CCRCs—to provide quite comprehensive and relatively luxurious housing and personal and nursing care for older persons who can afford it—has not changed much over the years. The mode of financing them has changed considerably, however. When life-care or life-lease (which did not involve a nursing care component) facilities first began, operational costs were to be covered either by having residents make a lump sum payment of a certain amount or assign all their assets, assuming they were sufficient, to the facility in return for lifetime care. Calculations of the cost of care were based primarily on age at admission, gender, and remaining life expectancy calculated from standard actuarial tables. For example, it might be determined that the approximate cost of lifetime care for a sixty-five-year-old female in good health (always a condition of admission) would be $125,000. If the applicant had assets of at least that amount and was otherwise acceptable, she would probably be admitted. In early life-care facilities, monthly fees for services provided, over and above the assets assigned, were either not charged or, if charged, could not be changed, due to the terms of an individual's life care contract with the facility.

Apparently, for the first several years of operation of various life-care facilities, this financial arrangement did not present a problem. As time went on, however, it became increasingly clear that the life-care fees collected were often insufficient to cover operating costs. This was partly a function of the contractual inability of facilities to increase residents' monthly fees but it was also because many residents tended to outlive their predicted remaining life expectancy. Why the longevity of life-care residents tends to be greater than that of older persons in general can only be a matter of speculation. It is reasonable to suppose, however, that contributing factors include such characteristics as life-long concern for health, higher income and education levels, and perhaps even genetic factors.

In contrast to other types of planned housing, the number of CCRCs appears to have been growing in recent years. Mangum (1982) estimated that there were 212 such facilities in all parts of the United States in 1975. By 1988, Somers and Spears (1992), citing the American Association of Homes for the Aging and Ernst and Young (1989), estimated that there were 527. This may be an underestimate, however, as Golant (1992), citing Chellis and Grayson (1990), reported that at the end of the 1980s there were close to 1,000 CCRCs in the United States serving 250,000 to 300,000 older persons. Indeed, this appears to be a rapidly expanding form of planned housing.

Profit-oriented Planned Housing

As noted earlier, profit-oriented planned housing for older persons did not begin developing until the older market was discovered and, in some ways, invented by housing entrepreneurs in the mid- to late 1950s. How an older market for planned housing may have come to exist cannot be fully addressed here but it undoubtedly resulted from a combination of factors. Among these were increasing affluence among a small segment of the older population who had proceeds from sales of homes as well as pensions and savings, along with social security, that could be used to purchase and live in planned housing; attitudes supportive of a move to such housing; and the allure of a "new and active retiree lifestyle" promoted by housing developers through advertising.

As an early example of the latter factor, about thirty years ago I saw a series of large, professionally produced billboards on a pleasantly meandering road leading toward Hemet, California, a naturally occurring retirement community. Each billboard proclaimed the wonders of retirement living in "Sierra Dawn Estates," a very posh adult mobile-home subdivision where the individually owned mobile-homes had to be state-of-the-art and where the spacious and well-landscaped mobile-home lots were owned instead of rented, as in the much more common "Mom-and-Pop" trailer parks of the day. From each billboard, the wise and benign countenance of Art Linkletter beamed down and it seemed to become even wiser, more benign, and *older* looking as the billboards got closer to Hemet. Mr. Linkletter, who was an extremely popular television personality of the 1950s and 60s, was shown on each billboard as a member of the Board of Directors of Sierra Dawn Estates. Not too surprisingly, he thought very highly of the place, as indicated by the sanguine and promotive words issuing from his billboard-borne lips. Judging from the bustling activity at the facility in its opening months, he was a very effective early practitioner of the art of celebrity endorsement.

It is possible to identify several types of profit-oriented planned housing that have developed largely over the last forty years. Among these are adult mobile-home parks, retirement villages, retirement hotels, and continuing care retirement communities of the profit-oriented variety. These vary along a number of dimensions, including sponsorship, design, cost, location, services, characteristics of the residents, and what I have termed "supportiveness." Supportiveness refers to the degree to which the housing environment provides for the routine and special needs of the resident, as well as the extent to which the resident is freed of the responsibility for maintaining the housing environment (Mangum, 1979). If the noninstitutional housing, both conventional and planned, of older persons is thought of as being arrayed along a continuum of supportiveness, then single-family houses would be considered the least supportive and continuing care retirement communities would be considered the most supportive. Supportiveness will be used as a concept for ordering the discussion of profit-oriented planned housing, beginning with adult mobile-home parks.

Adult Mobile-Home Parks

Mobile-homes, or manufactured housing or homes as they now tend to be called, are a fairly recent development, having been introduced to the U.S. housing market in 1930 (Haley, 1986). Adult mobile-home parks, as distinct from family parks (i.e., those that allow children), probably did not exist before around 1950. Unlike standard mobile-home parks, which tend to contain a mixture of lower income and relatively transient families and individuals of all ages, adult mobile-home parks cater almost exclusively to retired persons. From the park owner's perspective, older persons are generally more desirable residents than younger persons. They do not move as frequently as younger persons, they usually pay their rent on time, they are quieter, and, in general, they present fewer management problems.

Mobile-home parks are usually more supportive than conventional housing because of mutual aid among park residents, such as light-duty nursing during an illness. However, they are the least supportive type of planned housing because residents are expected to live independently and, traditionally, park managements have provided few services other than those related to recreation. Recently, however, perhaps in keeping with the apparently increasing phenomenon of aging in place, some park managements have begun providing or arranging for certain services. This seems to be particularly true in areas that have large concentrations of older persons. Unlike other forms of planned housing, which often stipulate a minimum age for occupancy (e.g., 50, 62, or 65), mobile-home parks rarely do. It is usually clear, however, from their advertising; e.g., "shuffle-board, potlucks, no children under eighteen," that the parks welcome only older or retired persons.

According to Golant (1992), who provides the most comprehensive recent discussion of manufactured-housing or mobile-home living for older persons, about 6 percent of older households in the United States live in manufactured housing and, of these, more than one half (54 percent) were in manufactured-home parks. It is difficult to say, however, how many or what percentage of the parks cater to older persons, as opposed to persons of all ages. Mangum (1982) estimated that, around 1975, there were 721 adult mobile-home parks in the U.S. This estimate was based on a count of such parks in *Woodall's 1978 Retirement and Resort Communities, National Edition*, a then well-known mobile-home park directory. Unfortunately, however, it is no longer being published and no other directory of mobile-home parks seems to exist.

Although mobile-home parks for older adults have never been as controversial regarding age segregation as have "fixed" retirement villages, they and manufactured housing, in general, have been criticized on the grounds of vulnerability to storm damage, especially from high winds. Thus, some persons have viewed them as being an undesirable housing alternative for older persons because they are unsafe. Nevertheless, through improved manufacturing procedures and materials and with greater concern for storm resistance, manufactured housing units may eventually become at least as safe as most conventionally built housing. Thus, despite the debate over safety, manufactured homes are and will continue to represent a suitable and attractive housing alternative for those self-selected older persons who choose them.

Retirement Villages

Except to their residents and staff, relatives of residents, service providers, and some others, most types of planned housing are probably invisible to the public. Few among us would even notice an architecturally unremarkable and unadvertised Section 202 highrise sitting unobtrusively on a side street in an undistinguished part of town. The retirement village is, on the other hand, usually quite visible and when people speak of retirement housing, probably the first type that comes to mind is a large retirement village typified by Sun City, Arizona or Leisure World in Laguna Hills, California. However, unlike the more modest federally assisted facilities whose history is well documented, the history of retirement villages is less clear.

Two terms usually have been applied to this type of planned housing: retirement village and retirement community. Both of these terms were used, at one time, more or less exclusively to refer to facilities catering to younger, more active and leisure-oriented older persons. These "communities" are fairly self-contained, with housing and a certain number of necessary services nearby. Now, however, with the exception of nursing homes, "retirement community" has been extended by some authors to almost every type of retirement housing: retirement villages, adult mobile-home parks, shared housing, retirement apartment complexes, retirement hotels, and continuing care retirement communities. One possible reason for this is that, quite apart from its sociological implications, the term "community" has a certain warmth and inclusiveness about it that appeals to everyone associated with the retirement housing industry. Older people are not merely admitted, decrepitly, to an old-age facility as they once may have been; they now go to live, as actively as possible, in a very special *community* of age peers. The following definition of retirement communities seems to capture the newer thinking:

> . . . retirement communities are aggregations of housing units planned for healthy, older people (at least fifty years of age), most of whom are retired. This housing aggregation should incorporate at least one commonly shared, nonresidential facility or service, and should be described by its developers, managers, and residents through marketing and other publicized material as a place for retirees to live. For [our] purposes, retirement communities are confined to those communities housing at least 100 healthy older adults. Moreover, if the community contains a health care facility, that facility may accommodate no more than half of the community population. Nursing or convalescent homes which call themselves retirement communities are therefore excluded. . . . (Marans et al., 1983, p. 87)

In this comprehensive conception of retirement communities, Marans et al. (1983) distinguished among three types of facilities that are being discussed here as retirement villages: *retirement new towns, retirement villages,* and *retirement subdivisions.* The distinctions are based mainly on the size of the resident population and the availability of on-site facilities and services. *Retirement new towns* have 5,000 or more residents and a multitude of facilities and services; they are essentially self-contained communities. *Retirement villages* house between 1,000 and 5,000 residents. Not only are they smaller than retirement new towns, but they are considered to be less self-contained. *Retirement subdivisions* vary in size but typically house around 500 residents and have a very limited number of services and facilities.

How retirement villages are viewed in an overall classification of planned housing is partly a function of when the classification was developed. When Marans and his colleagues (1983) developed their classification, planned housing had come of age, so to speak, was increasingly visible, and was, therefore, more readily classifiable into an overarching, integrated scheme. Over twenty years earlier Webber and Osterbind (1961, p. 4) developed a similar definition and classification of "retirement villages." They defined a retirement village as:

> . . . a small community, relatively independent, segregated, and noninstitutional, whose residents are mainly older people separated more or less completely from their regular or career occupations in gainful or non-paid employment. It is non-institutional in the sense that the population is largely free of the regimen imposed by common food, common rules, common quarters, and common authority.

They also provided the following classification of retirement villages:

1. Real-estate developments
2. Supervised and planned communities
   A.   Dispersed-dwelling communities
   B.   Trailer villages
   C.   Retirement hotels
3. Full-care homes and communities

Like the classification of Marans et al. (1983), which subsumes most types of noninstitutional planned housing under the single label "retirement community," Webber and Osterbind's (1961) classification does essentially the same thing using the label "retirement village." For general taxonomic purposes, this may be appropriate. However, the use of either "retirement community" or "retirement village" to encompass practically all types of noninstitutional planned housing obscures some very major differences among the types. Although it is true that "retirement villages," as the term is used here, and, say, retirement hotels, both cater to older persons, they are otherwise entirely different types of facilities. Moreover, retirement villages have changed substantially since Webber and Osterbind (1961) classified them. Consider, for example, the stated characteristics of the type of retirement village they (1961, p. 5) termed real-estate developments:

1. development and construction on a for-profit basis
2. single-family, detached dwellings
3. no provision for serving food or for medical or nursing care
4. ownership of living units in fee simple by residents

5. no restrictions on eligibility for residence except financial ability
6. small (if any) operating staff

At the time they were writing, these criteria would have fit existing retirement villages quite well, although even then there were exceptions. Some early villages, for example, did have lower age limits for residency and some had or intended to have on-site management. (See Streib, Folts, & LaGreca [1985] for an informative and interesting discussion of management issues in retirement villages or communities and LaGreca, Streib, & Folts [1985] for a discussion of the life stages of retirement communities). Even now, characteristics 1, 2, and 4 would still apply to most retirement villages, the larger of which have evolved to include, or have had developed nearby, medical and nursing care facilities for residents who wish to age in place.

One issue that may never be resolved is just where, geographically, retirement villages originated. In 1973, I suggested that they seem to have started in Florida, although I did not specify when (Mangum, 1973). At that time, I may have been thinking of facilities such as Moosehaven (which was not a real-estate development and might not even be considered a retirement village by some), which was founded in 1922 (Arnett, 1961). Other authors, however, have claimed that retirement villages originated in other parts of the United States. For example, Vivrett (1960) stated that only two retirement villages—Youngtown, Arizona and Ryderwood, Washington—had been developed as of 1960. More recently, Gimmy and Boehm (1988) have noted that the first planned "retirement community" was built in Arizona in 1954 by Elmer Johns and Ben Schleifer. Although Gimmy and Boehm (1988) did not name it, this retirement village may have been Youngtown and it was said to have inspired Del Webb to develop the first large "retirement community," Sun City, Arizona, in 1960.

Regardless of when or where they originated, retirement villages quickly became controversial. In a classic article titled, "For Older People, Not Segregation But Integration," Lewis Mumford (1956), a leading social critic of the day, argued that such large-scale organized living quarters for older persons are socially unnatural and should be avoided. Older people, he believed, should live amid all age groups in conventional neighborhoods. Obviously, his use of the terms "segregation" and "integration" was prompted by the 1954 U.S. Supreme Court decision (in Brown v. Board of Education) which mandated that racial segregation in schools be eliminated with "all deliberate speed." Nevertheless, it caught the mood of the times and may have stimulated other public figures such as the noted anthropologist, Margaret Mead, and the founder of the Gray Panthers, Maggie Kuhn, to condemn retirement villages. Mead referred to them as "golden ghettos" while Kuhn labelled them "playpens for the elderly." Both terms were apparently meant to suggest that not only had an uncaring society chosen to wall off older persons from other age groups but also to consign them to a life of complete, if pampered, social uselessness. As colorful and compelling as these ways of characterizing retirement villages may be, however, they do not accord well with the essentially positive empirical evidence of the impact of retirement villages on their residents and the surrounding community that has been developed by gerontologists over the last thirty or so years. For a review of early studies of retirement villages, see Mangum (1973; 1982) and for the most recent account of them see Golant (1992).

Not only are retirement villages interesting in more ways than can be indicated here, they also house a disproportionately large number of older persons in relation to the number of such facilities. If retirement villages are thought of as having 1,000 or more residents, then Marans et al. (1983) estimated that, around 1980, there were 85 such facilities containing 343,474, or 37 percent, of the 924,070 older persons living in 2,363 retirement communities in the United States.

Retirement Hotels

After retirement villages, retirement hotels occupy the next level of supportiveness in planned housing largely because their residents are freed of housekeeping responsibilities. Retirement hotels, in contrast to single room occupancy (SRO) accommodations of the hotel variety (Ehrlich, 1986), are considered to be planned housing for the elderly because they cater explicitly to older persons through the provision of meals in a central dining room, weekly maid service, and light recreation. Often they are listed in the yellow pages of telephone directories as retirement residences and they generally have highly visible signs indicating they are retirement hotels. Physically, some retirement hotels can be quite impressive but, typically, they are older hotel "properties" that are no longer commercially competitive.

Retirement hotels seem to have originated shortly after World War II, although their history has not been adequately investigated. Unlike most other forms of planned housing, which have been designed and built as retirement housing, retirement hotels represent an attempt to convert an existing structure from one use to another: from transient hotels to hotels with permanent guests. As I have suggested elsewhere (Mangum, 1973), the number of retirement hotels is likely to remain constant or decline since there is probably a fixed or dwindling supply of hotels suitable for conversion to retirement hotels.

Continuing Care Retirement Communities

Although CCRCs were discussed earlier under the heading of not-for-profit planned housing, it bears mentioning here that the private, profit-oriented sector is becoming increasingly interested in them. Evidently, this is due to the continuing growth of the older population, particularly the oldest segment who is most in need of the kinds of care services that CCRCs can provide. Also, even though new CCRCs tend to be expensive, there seems to be a substantial and increasing number of older persons who can afford them. Although the average age of persons who move into CCRCs is over seventy-nine (Golant, 1992) and, conceptually, they seem designed for the old old, they may become increasingly appealing to other types of persons, such as young old, single women who can afford them and who seem to appreciate the current and future supportiveness and security CCRCs provide.

Conclusion

This chapter has dealt with the history, including changes in policies and practices, of planned housing for the elderly since 1950. While its organization into public and private sector housing programs, and by types of planned housing within those sectors, may have facilitated discussion, it has also tended to foster the coverage of fairly narrow and specific issues and changes. In this concluding section, an attempt will be made to recast some of these issues and changes in a broader context as well as to bring in some additional considerations that may have implications for planned housing in the future.

During the approximately four decades that this chapter spans, numerous changes in the circumstances and perceptions of both older persons and housing have occurred in American society. In 1950, older persons were far less numerous and far less visible—demographically, politically, and as an ongoing aspect of societal consciousness and concern—than they are now. They were also just beginning to be viewed formally as a special age category with multiple problems such as lack of income, declining health and inadequate health care, negative attitudes and reactions toward retirement and use of leisure time, and inadequate or inappropriate housing. The image of aging and older persons that the rather grim statistics and professional pronouncements of the day fostered was decidedly negative but, at the same time, it paved the way for an unequivocally compassionate and fiscally supportive public response to their perceived plight. Planned housing for the elderly was part of this response although, as noted previously, it was viewed with some skepticism in the early years of its development.

Over time, the objective conditions of aging generally have changed for the better. Such factors as income, education, attitudes toward retirement, and the portrayal of aging and older persons by the mass media can easily be shown to have improved. Consequently, the image of aging in American society has generally become more positive. As Nelson (1982, pp. 136–137) has put it:

> From the 1950s through the 1960s the growth of aging
> programs and aging advocacy reflected public acceptance
> of an image of older people as persons in need....
> Beginning in the early 1970s, a growing number of
> "young-old" leaders in the aging movement began to turn
> their attention somewhat away from the question of
> "needs" and more to the issue of "opportunities."

Nelson (1982) goes on to note, to paraphrase the title of an
old song, that in the course of accentuating the positive about
aging, aging advocates did not attempt to eliminate the negative.
This, he believed, tended to sow policy confusion by:

> ... reinforc[ing] a set of images that variously characterize
> "older Americans" as dependent or independent; as
> appropriately retired or inappropriately excluded from
> work; as isolated or socially integrated; as frail or
> vigorous; as impoverished or affluent; as deserving of
> special status or subject to arbitrary discrimination; as well
> or ill; and so on. (Nelson, 1982, p.139)

In recent years, aging advocates have, to some extent,
overcome the policy dilemmas implied by these contradictory
images of aging by attempting to uncouple the "young-old"
from the "old-old." In the current approach to aging affairs, the
former are increasingly viewed as independently functioning
adults whereas the latter, with their demonstrably greater needs,
are to be the primary recipients of public policies and programs.
At the same time, however, aging is no longer as large a policy
issue as it was in the past. This is partly because the improved
conditions of older persons and the more favorable image of
aging have led to the supposition that older persons are now less
in need of sustained public benevolence. Mainly, however, it is
because no segment of American society can remain at the
forefront of public policy indefinitely. Thus, aging now shares
the policy stage with children's issues, among others, and must
compete with them for public resources. In view of such
considerations, it is impossible to predict the future of various
types of planned housing for the elderly with great accuracy.
Nevertheless, several things seem reasonably clear.

Planned housing for the elderly is now an accepted and
permanent part of the American housing landscape. The

question is not whether such housing should be provided but, rather, how best to provide it. For public sector programs, the rate of growth of the old-old segment of the population along with an increasing emphasis on the desirability of aging in place should lead to a growth of supportive services in public housing designed or designated for the elderly as well as in Section 202 and 236 projects. However, to accommodate rising expectations among older renters, new projects may need to be built to higher amenity standards and existing projects may need to be continuously upgraded. In any event, such housing should continue to have strong federal support, although ongoing concerns with the budget deficit may retard its production from time to time.

The destiny of planned housing for the elderly in the private sector is more difficult to forecast but it should also continue to grow, although perhaps at a slower rate than in the past. When retirement villages, for example, began developing in the 1950s, one of the main motivations for older persons' moving to them was ease of upkeep compared to then existing single-family homes. Now, however, there are many condominium complexes for adults of all ages in which external maintenance is provided and which are more centrally located than most retirement villages. There are also lawn services and many other home services, as well as recreational opportunities, that tended not to exist in the past but that are now readily available to older residents (with sufficient means) of ordinary housing. In other words, some of the reasons for moving to retirement villages may not be as compelling as they once were.

As noted earlier, continuing care retirement communities have been a rapidly growing form of housing/care for older persons and they will probably continue to grow at a faster rate than most other forms of planned housing. Traditionally, they have catered to older persons with considerable financial resources but they may become more accessible to those of more modest means. One of the reasons for this is that as more and more new facilities are developed, older and, presumably, less competitive facilities may need to be marketed to a less affluent segment of the older population.

Whatever the remainder of the twentieth century may hold for planned housing for the elderly, it is likely to become an even more vital part of our society in the twenty-first.

REFERENCES

American Association of Homes for the Aging and Ernst and Young (1989). *Continuing care retirement communities: An industry inaction: Analysis and developing trends 1989*. Washington, DC: Author.

Arnett, W.T. (1961). Designs of Florida retirement villages. In E.W. Burgess (Ed.), *Retirement villages* (pp. 43–52). Ann Arbor: Division of Gerontology, University of Michigan.

Atchley, R.C. (1991). *Social forces and aging* (6th ed.). Belmont, CA: Wadsworth.

Barker, J.C., Mitteness, L.S., & Wood, S.J. (1988). Gatekeeping: Residential managers and elderly tenants. *The Gerontologist, 28*(5), 610–619.

Bernstein, J. (1982). Who leaves, who stays: Resident policy in housing for the elderly. *The Gerontologist, 22*(3), 305–313.

Bould, S., Sanborn, B., & Reif, L. (1989). *Eighty-five plus: The oldest old*, Belmont, CA: Wadsworth.

Chellis, R.D., & Grayson, P.J. (1990). Summary and trends in life care. In R.D. Chellis & P.J. Grayson (Eds.), *Life care: A Long-term solution?* Lexington, MA: Lexington.

Daily, L. (1987). Housing options for the elderly. In J.A. Hancock (Ed.), *Housing the elderly* (pp. 227–244). New Brunswick, NJ: Center for Urban Policy Research, Rutgers University.

Duensing, E.E. (Ed.). (1988). *America's elderly: A sourcebook.* New Brunswick, NJ: Center for Urban Policy Research, Rutgers University.

Ehrlich, P. (1986). Hotels, rooming houses, shared housing, and other housing options for the marginal elderly. In R.J. Newcomer, M.P. Lawton, & T.O. Byerts (Eds.), *Housing an aging society: Issues, alternatives, & policy* (pp. 189–209). New York: Van Nostrand Reinhold.

Fischer, D.H. (1977). *Growing old in America*. New York: Oxford University Press.

Flexner, S.B., & Hauck, L.C. (Eds.). (1987). *The Random House dictionary of the English language* (2nd ed., unabridged). New York: Random House.

Gimmy, A.E., & Boehm, M.G. (1988). *Elderly housing: A guide to appraisal, market analysis, development, and financing*. Chicago: American Institute of Real Estate Appraisers.

Golant, S.M. (1992). *Housing America's Elderly: Many possibilities/few choices*. Newbury Park, CA: Sage.

Gozonsky, M.J. (1965). Preface. In F.M. Carp & W.M. Burnett (Eds.), *Patterns of living and housing of middle-aged and older people*. Washington, DC: U.S. Government Printing Office.

Haley, B.A. (1986). Are mobile-homes a solution to problems of low-income elders? In R.J. Newcomer, M.P. Lawton, & T.O. Byerts (Eds.), *Housing an aging society: Issues, alternatives, & policy* (pp. 217–228). New York: Van Nostrand Reinhold.

Herman, J., Anetzberger, G., & Beheim, N. (1983). Use of existing large homes for shared living. In Urban Land Institute, *Housing for a maturing population* (pp. 164–175). Washington, DC: Urban Land Institute.

Jacobs, J. (1974). *Fun city: An ethnographic study of a retirement community*. New York: Holt, Rinehart & Winston.

Kleemeier, R.W. (1951). *Difference of adjustment: Segregated old age communities vs. unsegregated communities*. Paper presented at the Northwestern University Centennial Conference on Problems of an Aging Population. Evanston, IL.

———— (1961). The use and meaning of time in special settings: Retirement communities, homes for the aged, hospitals, and other group settings. In R. W. Kleemeier (Ed.), *Aging and leisure: A research perspective into the meaningful use of time* (pp. 273–308). New York: Oxford University Press.

LaGreca, A.J., Streib, G.F., & Folts, W.E. (1985). Retirement communities and their life stages. *Journal of Gerontology, 40*(2), 211–218.

Lawton, M.P. (1975). *Planning and managing housing for the elderly*. New York: John Wiley.

Lawton, M.P., & Hoover, S.L. (1981). Housing for 22 million older Americans. In M.P. Lawton & S.L. Hoover (Eds.), *Community housing choices for older Americans* (pp. 11–27). New York: Springer.

Mangum, W.P. (1971). Retirement hotels and mobile-home parks as alternative living arrangements for older persons. In T.O. Byerts (Ed.), *Housing and environment for the elderly: Proceedings from a conference on behavioral research utilization and environmental policy,* December, San Juan, Puerto Rico (pp. 61–73). Washington, DC: The Gerontological Society.

———— (1973). Retirement villages. In R.R. Boyd & C.G. Oakes (Eds.), *Foundations of practical gerontology* (2nd ed.). Columbia: University of South Carolina Press.

———— (1979). Retirement villages: Past, present and future issues. In P.A. Wagner & J.M. McRae (Eds.), *Back to basics: Food and shelter for the elderly* (pp. 88–97). Gainesville, Florida: Center for Gerontological Studies and Programs, University of Florida.

———— (1982). Housing for the elderly in the United States. In A.M. Warnes (Ed.), *Geographical perspectives on the elderly* (pp. 191–221). London and New York: John Wiley.

———— (1985). But not in my neighborhood: Community resistance to housing for the elderly. *Journal of Housing for the Elderly, 3*(2), 101–119.

———— (1988). Community resistance to planned housing for the elderly: Ageism or general antipathy to group housing? *The Gerontologist, 28*(3), 325–329.

Marans, R.W., Feldt, A. G., Pastalan, L.A., Hunt, M.E., & Vakalo, K.L. (1983). Retirement communities: Present and future. In Urban Land Institute, *Housing for a maturing population* (pp. 86–111). Washington, DC: Urban Land Institute.

Mumford, L. (1956). For older people: Not segregation but integration. *Architectural Record, 119,* 191–194.

Nelson, D.W. (1982). Alternative images of old age as the bases for policy. In B. L. Neugarten (Ed.), *Age or need? Public policies for older people* (pp. 131–169). Beverly Hills, CA: Sage.

Neugarten, B. (1974). Age groups in American society and the rise of the young-old. *Annals of the American Academy of Political and Social Science, 415,* 189–198.

Pynoos, J. (1990). Public policy and aging in place: Identifying the problems and potential solutions. In D. Tilson (Ed.), *Aging in place: Supporting the frail elderly in residential environments.* (pp. 167–208). Glenview, IL: Scott, Foresman.

Robbins, I.S. (1971). *Housing the elderly: Background issues.* Washington, DC: White House Conference on Aging.

Rosenwaike, I., & Logue, B. (1985). *The extreme aged in America.* Westport, CT: Greenwood Press.

Sheehan, N.W. (1986). Aging of tenants: Termination policy in public senior housing. *The Gerontologist, 26*(5), 505–509.

Somers, A.R., & Spears, N.L. (1992). *The continuing care retirement community: A significant option for long-term care?* New York: Springer.

Streib, G.F. (1990). Congregate housing: People, places, policies. In D. Tilson (Ed.), *Aging in place: Supporting the frail elderly in residential environments* (pp. 75–100). Glenview, IL: Scott, Foresman.

Streib, G.F., Folts, W.E., & Hilker, M.A. (1984). *Old homes—new families: Shared living for the elderly.* New York: Columbia University Press.

Streib, G.F., Folts, W.E., & LaGreca, A.J. (1985). Autonomy, power, and decision-making in thirty-six retirement communities. *The Gerontologist, 25*(4), 403–409.

U.S. General Accounting Office. (1992). *Elderly Americans: Health, housing, and nutrition gaps between the poor and nonpoor.* (Report No. GAO/PEMD-92-29). Washington, DC: Author.

U.S. Senate Special Committee on Aging. (1990). *Developments in aging: 1989* (Vol. 1). (Report No. 101–249). Washington, DC: U.S. Government Printing Office.

―――― (1991). *Developments in aging: 1990* (Vol. 1). (Report No. 102–28). Washington, DC: U.S. Government Printing Office.

Vivrett, W.K. (1960). Housing and community settings for older people. In C. Tibbitts (Ed.), *Handbook of social gerontology* (pp. 549–623). Chicago: University of Chicago Press.

Webber, I.L., & Osterbind, C.C. (1961). Types of retirement villages. In Burgess, E.W. (Ed.), *Retirement villages* (pp. 3–10). Ann Arbor: Division of Gerontology, University of Michigan.

Part II: The Public Sector

CHAPTER 3

Public Housing: A Pioneer in Housing Low-Income Older Adults

Mary K. Nenno

Introduction

In 1989, about 1.4 million households headed by a person age 65 or over lived in federally subsidized housing. Of these households, about 517,000 resided in public housing, representing 38 percent of national public housing occupancy (U.S. Department of Housing and Urban Development, 1992).

The public housing program in the United States dates back to the Housing Act of 1937. As with many other public programs, the evolution of public housing was greatly influenced by the efforts of a single individual. Ms. Marie McGuire Thompson is largely responsible for transforming what started as a modest program designed to address some of the housing needs of low-income families into what is now a major component in meeting the housing needs of low-income older adults. In the course of a career extending well into retirement, Ms. Thompson served as a public housing manager from 1942–1948; executive director of an urban housing authority from 1949–1960; commissioner of the National Public Housing Administration from 1961–1968; advisor to the Secretary of the U.S. Department of Housing and Urban Development from 1969–1973; and (after her "retirement"), housing specialist for the

International Center for Social Gerontology. Ms. Thompson's contribution to public housing cannot be overstated and her impact on housing for frail and elderly people will continue to be felt for many years to come.

There have also been four pieces of legislation that have dramatically changed the direction of public housing. These statutes, combined with the efforts of Ms. Thompson and other state and local initiatives, have had the combined impact of clearly establishing low-income older people as a legitimate target for housing assistance.

The Housing Act of 1956

Although Public Housing, as a federal program, dates back to the 1930s, the Housing Act amendments of 1956 are generally identified as the first recognition of older adults as a distinct population in need of public housing assistance. It was not until the 1956 amendments were enacted that single elderly persons were made eligible for admission. Prior to that time, only an elderly person who was a residual member of a previously larger household was allowed to remain as a resident in public housing, and then, only for a period of thirty days. A more important contribution of the 1956 amendments was that they also authorized the Federal Public Housing Administration to assist in the construction of new housing or the remodeling of existing public housing in order to provide accommodations designed specifically for elderly households.

The decade of the 1960s was a period marked by rapid expansion of public housing for older persons. Table 1 reports the yearly proportions of public housing units occupied by older adults. In 1952, only about 6 percent of public housing residents were elderly and by 1957 that number had increased to only 11 percent. In 1970, however, the proportion of older residents had increased to 38 percent and by 1977 it had peaked at about 45 percent (for persons 62 years of age or older). Data for 1989, not reported in Table 1, indicate that occupancy of public housing by persons 65 years of age or older is currently around 38 percent of the total units. Although a part of this decline is due to the different age base (i.e., 65), it also reflects increased public housing occupancy by families (U.S. Department of Housing and Urban Development, 1992).

Table 1
Trends in the Percentage of Public Housing Occupied by Elderly Households, 1952–1977[*]

1952	6 %
1957	11 %
1968	32 %
1970	38 %
1972	41 %
1976	44 %
1977	45 %

[*] Households with heads of household sixty-two years of age or older.

Source: Robert Kolodny. 1984. *Exploring New Strategies for Improving Public Housing Management*. Washington, D.C.: Office of Policy Development and Research, U.S. Department of Housing and Urban Development, p. 30.

The opening of public housing facilities to occupancy by older adults stimulated public housing development in states where no previous activity had taken place. By 1978, six of these states: Iowa, Kansas, Minnesota, Nebraska, North Dakota, and Wisconsin, reported occupancy rates by older adults of over 66 percent (U.S. Department of Housing and Urban Development, 1980).

The Housing Act of 1970

While authorization for public housing agencies to construct or rehabilitate congregate housing facilities was not enacted until 1970, the seeds for the development of this housing type came in 1963. Backed by a statement of support by President Kennedy, a Memorandum of Understanding was signed by the Commissioner of Public Housing and the Commissioner of Welfare in the U.S. Department of Health,

Education and Welfare (HEW) on October 24, 1963 (Journal of Housing No. 10, 1963). The agreement called for a "pilot" congregate housing program specifically designed for older residents under which the Public Housing Administration would provide assistance for the same categories of space, equipment, and furnishings for which assistance is made available in self-contained dwellings. Further, these new facilities could include: (1) space for common eating arrangements, (2) kitchen equipment, and (3) space, furniture, and furnishings for lounges including a snack kitchen. The Department of HEW agreed that these facilities would be staffed and operated with local or state welfare funds that were reimbursable, in part, by the federal government. At the time the memorandum was signed, in 1963, one public housing congregate facility was under construction and there were applications pending for four others.

Local public housing agencies were cautious in developing congregate housing following the 1963 pilot program. There were two main reasons for this. First, a commitment was required in the form of a financial guarantee, made by a public source, insuring the continued operation of the dining facility. Second, many public agencies were reluctant to take on the additional responsibilities of support services for frail elderly persons when they did not have a secure source of funding and no staff who were trained to coordinate the services. Despite these deterrents, a few local agencies proceeded with plans to develop specially designed congregate public housing for older adults (Deetz, 1979).

The early history of congregate housing for the elderly can best be described as slow. However, the concept continued to receive public attention and support. This attention culminated in the provisions of the Housing and Urban Development Act of 1970 which authorized the use of up to 10 percent of all public housing development contract authority for the development of congregate housing for the elderly, the displaced, or the handicapped.

The Congregate Housing Services Program of 1978

Even as late as 1978 there remained serious constraints to program expansion, particularly in the area of providing support services. As a result, significant new incentives were made available under the congregate housing services section (Section 401) of the Housing and Community Development Amendments of 1978. This legislation authorized a comprehensive approach to funding the support services of congregate facilities located in public housing and in HUD Section 202 housing. This legislation resulted in a demonstration program involving thirty-three public housing agencies and thirty HUD Section 202 nonprofit housing sponsors (Housing and Community Development Amendments Act of 1978, Public Law 95–557).

The National Affordable Housing Act of 1990

Section 802 of the National Affordable Housing Act of 1990 restructured the Congregate Housing Services Program and expanded its coverage. Federal funding was made available for public housing and for housing provided under HUD Section 202, HUD Section 8, HUD Section 221–d–3, and HUD Section 229. Further, the new law included assisted housing provided under Sections 514 and 515 of the Farmers Home Administration (FmHA). Unlike the previous congregate housing services program, which provided for a 75 percent federal contribution, the 1990 law divides the costs among the federal government (40 percent), the local housing authority (50 percent), and the residents (10 percent) (Cranston-Gonzalez National Affordable Housing Act of 1990, Public Law 101–625). Under provisions of the new law, funds may be used for retrofitting individual units and common spaces. Further, meals are a required congregate service that must meet at least one-third of the daily nutritional requirements of the residents. Funds may also be used to pay for a service coordinator.

Although the 1990 law authorized $25 million in FY 1991 and $26 million in FY 1992, the Appropriations Committees of

Congress made available only \$18 million for FY 1991. This amount is sufficient to fund the sixty existing CHSP projects and an estimated sixty additional facilities. These additional programs would increase the number of older people served to only about 4,000.

Design and Development

When Victoria Plaza, the first public housing development specifically designed for the elderly, was opened in San Antonio, Texas on September 1, 1960 its design and management features rapidly became a model for other public housing developments. The extensive research phase preceding the construction of Victoria Plaza identified new and innovative concepts of how elderly housing should be designed and operated.

A progress report on elderly public housing, published in 1962, illustrates early efforts to meet the needs of older people (National Association of Management Redevelopment Officials, 1962). The following excerpts clearly illustrate the major unique elements of these efforts and call attention to the positive environment that was created.

In San Antonio, Texas

Victoria Plaza, considered to be one of the most dramatic examples of low-income public housing for the elderly built in the United States, is said to have become a mecca for those interested in seeing, first-hand, a new concept in public housing design and in seeing the incorporation of special features adapted to aged tenants into a public housing structure. Victoria Plaza is a nine-story, 185 unit building where the use of color and of imaginative materials—glass, tile, pre-cast exposed-aggregate panels—softens the otherwise austere slab concrete building. Maximum beauty and spaciousness was sought with the use of art works contributed by San Antonio artists in the public areas, both indoor and out, and by the use of open galleries that serve as corridors. Inside, divider closets in the individual units separate the living and sleeping areas and give the units maximum light and air. The first floor of the building contains a health, recreation, and counselling center that is open to all the elderly persons in the city. It has a Senior Center financed by private grants and gifts. Says one housing official: "The only way to translate the impact of Victoria Plaza is to go and see it." (p.460)

In Miami, Florida

Local support and community acceptance for the housing authority's Giant-Stride program to meet the housing needs of the city's low-income elderly have been strong factors in the success of the program. The housing authority now has four projects for elderly occupancy under management and one in planning. It also has done its share to provide the "extras" that bring Miami into the national limelight as a city with an elderly housing program that's full of imagination, innovations, ideas, and good sense. A community Senior Day Center program operates in cooperation with public housing projects. Presently operating elderly projects include: Abe Aronovitz Villas, with 55 units; Donn Gardens, with 64 units; the authority's newly acquired project that came "ready built and completely furnished," a purchase that provided "instant housing" for elderly families. The project provides 288 units in 36 buildings at six different locations. In planning for Miami's elderly: a 13-story high-rise, to be located near a medical complex and to feature a large Senior Day Center. (p. 461)

In Providence, Rhode Island

The first completed building in Providence's city center renewal area was Dexter Manor, an 11-story 200–unit public housing project designed especially for elderly occupancy. By using public housing as a residential re-use in the downtown renewal area, Providence proceeded on the recommendations of a human relations task force that advocated location of housing for senior citizens near the heart of the city. Dexter Manor puts the elderly a short walk away from stores, restaurants, and movie houses and across the street from a bus stop where they can catch transportation to Roger Williams Park and the Mall. (p. 461)

A year later, in 1963, the editors of the *Journal of Housing* summarized the state of public housing in the following words:

> Public housing for the elderly is assuming an important role in public housing programs in communities large and small across the country. Local authorities, with generally enthusiastic public support, have been able to devise and encourage particularly imaginative and creative plans for senior citizen housing—not only for the buildings themselves, but for special facilities and services to accommodate the particular needs of the elderly. Architects have been stimulated to incorporate new design ideas and innovations into plans for housing the elderly—with results often beautiful and distinctive. By encouraging the participation of various city departments and private community service agencies in the fields of recreation, welfare, [and] education, local authorities have found themselves in a position to cooperate in the provision of an extensive range of special services for elderly tenants. And, with the assurance of community support behind them, authorities have, in some cases, struck out in new directions to provide health maintenance programs in open recognition of the fact that health problems of the elderly are extensive and special and that any public program for senior citizens must take them into full account. (77)

As the elderly public housing program matured, a variety of structural types emerged, including manufactured housing. Vantage Glen, a mobile-home park for 164 low-income elderly couples and individuals, was opened in 1986 in the State of Washington. The development is a self-contained "Senior Village" located on a mass transportation route, close to medical facilities and a regional shopping center (Davis, 1986).

Beginning in the late 1970s, and continuing into the 1980s, the proportion of public housing occupied by elderly households leveled off at about 45 percent (Table 1). One reason for this was the increasing number of elderly units being constructed under other HUD-assisted housing programs. These included the HUD Section 202 Loan Program and HUD Section 8 Assisted Developments. As reported in Table 2, in fiscal year 1977, nearly two-thirds of all new commitments for HUD Section 8 Assisted Projects were for elderly occupancy.

Table 2

HUD-assisted Housing for the Elderly
(Units in Management)*

	1974	1979	1981
Public Housing	402,000	524,000	514,000
Section 8 New Construction (including Section 202)	——	110,000	266,000
Section 8 existing & Mod Rehab	——	134,000	207,000
Section 236	95,000	212,000	210,000
Section 8 substantial rehabilitation	——	11,000	28,000

*Between 1959 and 1968 the 202 program developed 45,000 units. After 1974, Section 202 was supported by Section 8 Assistance and is included under Section 8 new construction.

Source: Paul Burke. 1984. *Trends in Subsidized Housing, 1974–1981*. Washington, D.C.: Office of Policy Development and Research, U.S. Department of Housing and Urban Development, pp. 28–35.

Further, because of the rapid expansion of elderly housing under the newer HUD programs, there were some local housing markets where the immediate demand for new units had been met. To address this situation, after September 30, 1987, congress required a priority in public housing for the development of what it called "Family Housing" (United States Housing Act of 1937, Section 5 (j)(1)(d)). Finally, deep funding cuts in the construction program in the 1980s severely reduced the total number of new assisted housing units that could be built.

Training for Elderly Housing Management

Expansion of the mission of public housing to include units for the elderly meant that there was an increased need for persons trained in special management techniques. As a response to the increasing number of public housing facilities for the elderly, the National Association of Housing and Redevelopment Officials (NAHRO) undertook the development of a management training program.

For several years NAHRO studied existing facilities and identified the special concerns involved in managing elderly housing. The results of this effort were published in 1965 in two volumes. The first volume was a series of background papers written by experts in the fields of gerontology, elderly housing design, low-income economics, and community services for the elderly. The second volume dealt with management issues and contained training materials outlining specific management models, financing formulae, and administrative recommendations based on four demonstration training institutes (Bell, 1965, p. 90).

The NAHRO project confirmed that elderly housing management requires special knowledge and skills. As a result, the training materials include ten principles to assist in the training of managers for public housing (Bell, 1965, p. 91). These ten principles, listed below, are designed to call attention to the special needs of low-income elderly people and are a good indicator of the types of issues with which administrators of public housing must regularly deal.

1. The elderly represent a special group within the population and special management skills and knowledge must be used in administering public housing for the elderly.
2. Health is a primary concern of the elderly tenant. Therefore, the management function must include methods for identifying health problems and finding ways of dealing with them up to the point where independent living is no longer possible. The primary

responsibility for meeting health needs must rest with the medical and health resources of the community.

3. The long-term prospects of improved incomes for the elderly are not encouraging via employment; some improvement can be expected to come through federal Survivors, Old-Age, and Disability Insurance, pension plans, and improved social services.

4. The opportunity to develop their capacities and potentials through social participation and useful contributions to their community is of prime importance to the elderly. The responsibility for the provision of the recreational, educational, and leisure-time services that will help realize these potentials rests with the community.

5. Good public housing management for the elderly must create an atmosphere that prolongs useful living and retards, to the extent possible, the inevitably diminishing capacities of older people. It must also provide a sense of security for older people, a knowledge that help in time of crisis is always at hand.

6. Management policy must recognize that each tenant is an individual, whose adaptation to age is a result of his own life experience, education, and personality traits.

7. Housing for the elderly should be either so located or developed that normal needs of living (shopping, churches, medical assistance, and opportunities for association with all age groups) are readily accessible. In addition, such housing should be designed to recognize the reduced capacity of older persons to do things easily and quickly; to help create a feeling of emotional security; and to meet their changing ability to care for themselves. The public housing manager should have some knowledge of the principles behind the design of the housing units and community facilities of the project he manages—and should be trained to observe the experience of older persons living within it, so that he can transmit his observations for use in future designs.

8. There are a range of choices that can be applied to housing design (including size of development, building

types, and the degrees to which the aging desire proximity to other age groups). The approach depends on the site and the elderly to be served.

9. Excellence in design should be vigorously and insistently sought. Being "economical" has been mistaken to mean using what costs least. Economy should be seen in terms of value received. Beauty and aesthetic values have equal validity with the other goals.

10. For the protection of the elderly tenant, who is more prone to suffer crisis situations than tenants in other age categories, local housing authorities must adopt separate sets of formal and informal policies and practices in the areas of tenant selection, tenant relations, and community services.

Maintaining Independent Living

It was clear from early management experiences that, because of frailty, the risk of institutionalization for some public housing residents was dramatically increased. Many of these residents showed capacity to remain in independent housing if only supportive services were available. As early as 1963, efforts were made by the Public Housing Administration and the Department of Health, Education and Welfare to test a model congregate housing program for residents of public housing who required some support services in order to remain independent. It was not until 1970, however, that federal legislation authorizing public housing assistance for the construction of congregate housing was enacted. Still, the lack of access to support services for the congregate developments themselves continued to be a major deterrent to their establishment.

A significant breakthrough came in 1978 when legislation was enacted creating the Congregate Housing Services Program (CHSP). As noted above, in the period from 1980 through 1990, thirty-three public housing agencies and thirty HUD Section 202 sponsors provided support services to some 2,000 frail elderly and handicapped households. Nineteen of these projects were categorized as small projects (under 75 units); twenty were medium-sized (75–100 units); and twenty-four were larger projects (over 150 units). A total of fifty projects was specifically designed for the elderly, while thirteen were designed to meet the needs of younger impaired persons (U.S. Department of Housing and Urban Development, 1989).

The process used to select participants under the CHSP program involves identification of the needs of vulnerable persons by a volunteer professional assessment committee. This assessment technique involves determining a person's skill level in carrying out independent daily living, including typical tasks. The range of services relating to these needs includes meals, personal care, housekeeping, transportation, errands, chores, shopping, checking, and informal referral assistance. A package of appropriate services is developed for each person identified as requiring services.

At the direction of Congress, HUD was required to carry out a CHSP evaluation. The Department designed a four-year evaluation involving three components: (1) a process evaluation analyzing program start-up and initial operation, as well as comparisons of support services that grantees and similar projects were receiving prior to the initiation of the program; (2) a performance evaluation focused on the targeting of support services to those at risk and the tailoring of services to meet the identified needs; and (3) an impact evaluation examining the effects of CHSP on mortality rates and institutionalization rates and including assessments of functional health and the resident's quality of life. The HUD evaluation was begun in 1980 and was completed in 1985 (Sherwood, et al., 1985).

When the final evaluation was released to the public in 1986, it immediately sparked disagreement. The report indicated that the CHSP program experienced mixed success and stressed the lack of verifiable positive effects during the first fourteen months. These conclusions were strongly rejected both by local administrators and by those in academe (U.S. House of Representatives, Select Committee on Aging, 1987). Because of the HUD report, the Sub-Committee on Housing and Consumer Interests of the House Select Committee on Aging conducted its own analysis and released its own, more favorable, findings

(U.S. House of Representatives, Select Committee on Aging, 1987).

Included in the House of Representatives report (p. 11–13) were the following findings:

1. The CHSP and similar programs providing in-home services have been effective in preventing unnecessary institutionalization.
2. On orders from the Office of Management and Budget (OMB), HUD altered the tone and substance of the report of the independent evaluation for the expressed purpose of making the report consistent with the Administration's policy of eliminating the program.
3. The CHSP is a cost-effective alternative to institutional care.
4. The CHSP was effectively administered.
5. There is no evidence that CHSP services substituted for existing family or community services.
6. Recent changes in the HUD requirement for the provision of two meals per day have corrected an undue program emphasis on meals.
7. The CHSP had substantial positive benefits on the life satisfaction and general sense of well-being of its participants.

Despite these more favorable findings, the U.S. Department of Housing and Urban Development has called for the elimination of the CHSP program. In its budget proposal for fiscal year 1992–1993, the department of HUD provides no funding for CHSP, and proposes rescinding the funds appropriated for fiscal year 1991–1992.

One promising development in providing support services in government-assisted low-income housing is the increasing number of states that are initiating service program models. With assistance from the Robert Wood Johnson Foundation, ten states have carried out demonstrations providing integrated service programs for the elderly in over 200 developments. The goal of the program is to demonstrate that states, working with development owners and managers and the services network can provide and finance services in response to the needs and preferences of older residents (Policy Center on Aging, Brandeis University, 1991).

More directly applicable to public housing are nine state demonstrations funded by the U.S. Administration on Aging (AOA). These states are testing comprehensive state-wide efforts to link a consortium of relevant public and private sector agencies and organizations to increase supportive services to the elderly residents of federally-assisted housing. The two-year demonstrations concluded in 1992 and preliminary indications are encouraging (U.S. Administration on Aging, 1991).

Handicapped and Disabled Persons in Elderly Public Housing

Access to occupancy in elderly public housing by mentally disabled persons became an increasingly difficult management issue for public housing agencies in the late 1980s. Since 1959 the regulatory statutes governing residence in public housing have specifically included persons with disabilities. However, between 1959 and 1988, only small numbers of persons with disabilities, primarily those with physical limitations, actually applied for residence in public housing. The recent increase in the use of public housing by disabled persons can be directly traced to two legislative efforts designed to end discrimination directed at those with physical or mental impairments. Section 504 of the Rehabilitation Act of 1973 and Title VIII of the Fair Housing Act Amendments of 1988 both specifically prohibit discrimination based on handicapping condition (including mental disability) in all programs receiving financial assistance from the federal government (Gozonsky, 1991). These statutes further prohibit discrimination in the sale, rental or financing of public and private dwellings.

Beyond these statutory provisions, the continuing effort related to "deinstitutionalization" in state mental institutions increased the flow of persons, with a wide variety of mental impairments, back into the community. One indicator of the impact of this effort is an estimate by the National Institute of

Mental Health that the number of people residing in state mental institutions has declined by as much as 75 percent since the late 1960s (Lyons, 1991). The fact that this percentage represents a substantial number of people, combined with the fact that in almost all localities there exists a limited supply of private low-rent housing, means that the number of public housing applications by those with mental impairments has most certainly increased.

Faced with an influx of persons with mental impairments into elderly housing developments, public housing agencies grappled with policies to address occupancy concerns. Chief among these concerns was the issue of maintaining housing projects for elderly residents without disabilities while, at the same time, meeting the housing needs of mentally impaired persons. The issue is far from resolved. In fact, a recent study by the Government Accounting Office has documented that, when they became residents of elderly public housing facilities, about 31 percent of the mentally disabled households caused moderate or serious problems. The main problems are associated with specific behaviors such as substance abuse, excessive noise, and the presence of disruptive visitors. Further, almost half of large public housing agencies reported an increase in problems that directly involved mentally impaired tenants (U.S. Government Accounting Office, 1992).

A range of solutions have been proposed including: (1) providing separate public housing facilities for the elderly and the nonelderly mentally disabled; (2) providing alternative housing choices for the nonelderly mentally disabled, such as private-market rental housing assistance; (3) improving the delivery of community services; and (4) improving applicant screening guidance to public housing agencies.

It is clear that meeting the housing needs of nonelderly mentally impaired persons in local communities could have a lasting impact on elderly public housing, substantially altering the character of the program. At the policy level, decisions must be made concerning the efficacy of housing mentally impaired persons in facilities designed to meet the special needs of older adults.

Issues for the Next Century

At the beginning of the last decade of the twentieth century, public housing for the elderly is facing new challenges related both to the existing program as well as to emerging directions for the future. To meet this challenge, the popular and successful elderly public housing developments, pioneered in the 1960s and 1970s, require immediate attention in four areas if they are to remain a viable housing option.

First, most of the existing elderly public housing developments are now twenty-five to thirty years old. Many either currently require, or soon will require, physical modernization and refurbishment. An important part of this process will be to incorporate recent advances in standards for elderly housing, including design features, to accommodate elderly households which are aging in place.

Second, many of the earlier elderly developments did not incorporate community space adequate for all types of services including support services, meal services, and community activities. A plan to identify and retrofit selected public housing developments for congregate housing will need to be undertaken.

Third, many of the resources for bringing support services to elderly residents are available only on an ad-hoc basis. Long-term and integrated resources must be made available to meet the needs of this special population.

Fourth, because of the continuing issue of public housing occupancy by nonelderly mentally impaired individuals, a new policy to resolve the current confusion and uncertainty is needed. Additional separate affordable housing for these nonelderly individuals is the most widely discussed possible solution.

Public housing for the elderly is one important component in meeting the housing needs of low-income elderly persons. It is also an important part of the larger, more comprehensive approach that is emerging to meet the needs of the increasing numbers of older adults in the American population. The central role that public housing continues to play in housing older people requires constant attention at the policy level. Thus, there are several additional policy issues that will need to be addressed in the very near future.

While the availability of low-income elderly housing varies, at least locally, there remains an urgent need to assure that public housing is an option in all areas of the country. Unfortunately, despite this rather obvious need, recent federal policies have resulted in a dramatically reduced number of new federally-assisted low-income housing projects. Initiatives should be undertaken at the federal level, as well as state and local levels, to add to the existing supply of elderly housing through new construction and through housing rehabilitation.

Another issue vital to the future of public housing is the issue of developing an integrated system of support services. The piecemeal, ad-hoc approach to support services that currently exists should be replaced by a comprehensive and, more importantly, an integrated service delivery system. To this end a number of pilot programs are now in operation that should provide much needed information in this area. Further, at the national level, policies are being discussed which, if implemented, would integrate the resources of various federal programs around mutual concerns, particularly in the area of family self-sufficiency (National Commission on Children, 1991; National Association of Housing and Redevelopment Officials and American Public Welfare Association, 1991).

Also important is the need for adequate information about the housing supply in all areas of the country. The essential base for identifying housing and support service needs, and for addressing them, is at the local level. The 1990 National Affordable Housing Act requires each state or locality receiving federal housing assistance funds to develop a Comprehensive Housing Affordability Strategy (CHAS). The elderly, as a group, are among the special populations with housing needs that are required to be addressed.

One notable weakness in the CHAS program, however, is the lack of a requirement that the state or local agencies develop a strategy for an integrated support service delivery system that is related to housing. Despite this weakness, some localities are, in fact, attempting to develop and implement such a system (National League of Cities, 1991).

Finally, federal policy on housing and service needs of the elderly has followed two distinct courses of development. Housing policy has traditionally focused on programs created to provide housing to low-income but fully independent people. This focus is rapidly changing, both to serve frail elderly low-income persons and dependent, nontraditional families who require support services. A parallel, but distinctly separate, federal policy approach has been health-care assistance for low-income persons, largely through Medicaid, which has evolved into a major form of assistance for the elderly. However, the mounting costs of institutional care have forced national policy planners to experiment with service programs specifically designed to prevent unnecessary institutionalization. The Omnibus Budget Reconciliation Act of 1987 (OBRA) established need standards for living in institutions. However, the policies on long-term care and the policies on housing and social services continue to be treated as if they are two entirely separate issues.

This problem has not been entirely ignored as indicated by this cogent plea by Donald Redfoot, noted authority on the housing and service needs of older adults. In a report for the U.S. House Select Committee on Aging in 1987, Redfoot noted:

> This separation of housing and health services is no longer tenable as we address the growing need for long-term care. Housing programs have concentrated on the "bricks and mortar" issues of constructing and maintaining physical structures without addressing the service needs of residents. Health service programs have stemmed from the treatment of acute diseases and have, therefore, emphasized institutional-based care. Community-based social service programs developed with little regard to the housing needs of the elderly. The result is a patchwork of services with large gaps between fully independent living and the near total dependence that often characterizes nursing home care. (p. 2)

Among the many concerns important to public housing, the convergence of long-term care policies and policies related to affordable housing has become the most important issue facing efforts to meet the needs—both the housing needs and the service needs—of this nation's growing number of older adults.

REFERENCES

Bell, L. 1965. "Management Training Institutes for Public Housing for Elderly Advance New Job Concept." *Journal of Housing* 22:90–91.

Burke, P. 1984. *Trends in Subsidized Housing, 1974–1981.* Office of Policy Development and Research, U.S. Department of Housing and Urban Development. Washington, D.C.: U.S. Department of Housing and Urban Development.

Davis, B. 1986. "Focus on Vantage Glen." *Journal of Housing* 43:139–141.

Deetz, V. L. 1979. "Congregate Housing: A Growing Need." *HUD Challenge.* X-8; 18–19, U.S. Department of Housing and Urban Development. Washington, D.C.: U.S. Department of Housing and Urban Development.

Gozonsky, M. 1991. "A Look Backward at Linking Housing the Handicapped with the Elderly." *Seniors Housing Views*, nos. 4 and 6. Washington, D.C.: National Association of Home Builders.

Kolodny, R. 1990. *Exploring New Strategies: For Public Housing Management.* Washington, D.C.: U.S. Department of Housing and Urban Development.

Lyons, J. 1991. "With the Best of Motives." *Seniors Housing News: 5.* Washington, D.C.: National Association of Home Builders.

National Association of Housing and Redevelopment Officials. 1962. "Public Housing for the Elderly: Examples from Three Cities Show Variety, Originality." *Journal of Housing* (19): 8, 460–461.

———. 1963. "Localities Greet Elderly Housing Projects with Enthusiasm, Launch Them with Fanfare." *Journal of Housing* (20):10, 567.

———. 1963. "Public Housing for the Elderly: Expands in Numbers, Ideas; Enjoys Good Local Support." *Journal of Housing* (20): 2, 77–92.

National Association of Housing and Redevelopment Officials and the American Public Welfare Association. 1991. *Developing an Integrated Family Self-Sufficiency System: Road Blocks, Key Elements and Recommendations for Action.* Washington, D.C.: Author.

National Commission on Children. 1991. *Beyond Rhetoric: A New American Agenda for Children and Families.* Washington, D.C.: Author.

National League of Cities. 1991. *Children and Families in Cities.* Washington, D.C.: Author.

Policy Center on Aging, The Florence Heller Graduate School, Brandeis University. 1991. "Supportive Services in Senior Housing: Lessons from the Robert Wood Johnson Foundation Demonstration." Waltham, MA: Author.

Sherwood, S., J. Morris, C. Sherwood, S. Morris, E. Bernstein, & E. Gornstein. 1985. "Final Report of the Evaluation of the Congregate Housing Services Demonstration." Boston, MA: Author.

U.S. Administration on Aging. 1991. Conference of State Grantees on Supportive Services to Residents of Federally Assisted Housing for Older Persons. Washington, D.C.: Author.

U.S. Department of Housing and Urban Development. 1980. *1979 Statistical Yearbook.* HUD 338–8–UD.

———. 1984. *Fifth Annual Report to the Congress on the Congregate Housing Services Program,* July.

———. 1992. Washington, D.C. Office of Policy Development and Research. *Characteristics of Residents in HUD-Assisted Housing.*

U.S. General Accounting Office. 1992. *Public Housing and Issues in Housing the Mentally Disabled with the Elderly.* GAO–RCED–92–81. Washington, D.C.

U.S. Housing of Representatives, Select Committee on Aging, 1987. *Dignity, Independence and Cost-Effectiveness: The Success of the Congregate Housing Services Program.* Publication No. 100–650. Washington, D.C.

CHAPTER 4

The Housing Programs of the Department of Housing and Urban Development: Description and Issues

Jerold S. Nachison[1]

Introduction

When describing housing for the elderly, it is important to understand that housing is not only bricks and mortar. The physical structure is only a part of what housing means to the individual resident. This is partly because many frail older adults find their physical environment challenging and, thus, they are more "at risk" in the sense that small changes in their health status can make any particular living arrangement unsuitable. Since the 1950s, the special housing needs of older adults have been recognized by the federal government. As a result, a number of approaches and programs has attempted to meet the housing needs of the elderly through the provision of living space designed specifically for older people.

The United States Department of Housing and Urban Development (HUD) has been involved in providing housing to older adults since 1961 when the first project constructed with HUD Section 202 funds was occupied. At the time, there was much interest in building these projects both by nonprofit and for-profit owners. As a result, several hundred HUD projects were built under HUD Sections 202, 231 and 236, in the 1960s. Congregate housing was generally authorized across program lines as part of the Housing Act of 1970. In 1972, the Nixon administration placed a freeze on housing programs that lasted through 1975. Then, through HUD Section 202/8, HUD Section 8 new construction, HUD Section 221(d), and HUD Section 236 programs, there was a rapid increase in building resulting in over 300,000 units of housing for the elderly built during the 1970s.

In the late 1970s HUD Section 202/8 projects were funded at the rate of 20,000–30,000 units annually, which decreased to 16,000 in 1982. After 1982 Congressional approval of new units began a downward spiral. At about this same time period, construction of family housing essentially disappeared from the federal budget, with some replacement by voucher and certificate programs. By 1989, funding for HUD Section 202 projects had been decreased by Congress to approximately 6,000 units annually. Today, the only housing for the elderly being built with HUD assistance is under Section 202, which was approved for 9,400 units each year for 1991 and 1992.

Section 8 Rental Certificates

This program was authorized as low-income rental assistance under Section 8 of the U. S. Housing Act of 1974. Section 8 rental certificates currently pay the difference between 30 percent of an individual's adjusted income and the established fair market rent for the house or apartment being rented. HUD Section 8 is administered by a local housing authority, and individuals and families receiving the certificates may locate housing anywhere within the housing authority's jurisdiction. Further, recipients are free to negotiate a lease with the owner. The unit chosen must meet HUD's quality standards and the owner must be willing to accept the Section 8 certificate for the designated portion of the rent (HUD, 1989). Historically, Section 8 has been available in two forms:

1. Section 8 certificates are available as rental assistance to eligible individuals and families. There are approximately 1.2 million certificates currently in circulation, of which about 37 percent (434,000) are used by elderly persons.
2. Section 8 is also coupled with all Section 202 projects approved between 1976 and 1990. This subsidy is made directly to the project owner and not the individual. Approximately 200,000 people are currently housed in Section 202/8 projects.

A new version of Section 8 involves the use of what are called "rental vouchers." This program was established as a demonstration in 1983 and was converted into a permanent program in 1989. The voucher program is essentially the same as HUD Section 8 rental certificates except that the rent charged for a unit may exceed the fair market rent limit for a particular jurisdiction. In that event the voucher holder pays the additional cost. Another initial difference was that the voucher was "portable" in that it did not have to be utilized in the jurisdiction for which it was issued. Currently, both HUD Section 8 certificates and vouchers are portable. There are about 234,000 of the vouchers in circulation, of which about 21 percent (49,000) are to provide housing for older adults.

HUD Section 8 New Construction/ Substantial Rehabilitation

The HUD Section 8 New Construction and Substantial Rehabilitation program was authorized as low-income rental assistance under Section 8 of the U.S. Housing Act of 1974 and includes both standard multi-family projects and congregate housing. Projects were approved by action of the local HUD field office between 1976 and October 1983. Section 8 projects are owned either by nonprofit or limited-dividend owners. These projects are privately financed, and have a subsidy for a guaranteed number of units in order to assure rental assistance to tenants as well as sufficient income to cover mortgage payments. The contracts with HUD for this subsidy are for twenty years and are currently being renewed as they expire.

There are approximately 12,400 Section 8 projects with about 770,000 dwelling units of which nearly 71 percent (544,000 units) are utilized by the elderly. At the urging of the Reagan administration and due, in part, to the approval of what were perceived to be excessively expensive buildings in the late 1970s, this program was ended by Congress in 1983.

HUD Section 202

Although the Section 8 program is the largest of the HUD housing programs, the Section 202 program is probably the most visible and the best known. Section 202 was initially established by the Housing Act of 1959. Funds were first appropriated in October 1960 for a $20 million pilot program. Section 202 used low interest direct loans with a fifty-year payback period. Between 1959 and 1970 Section 202 was an "over-the-counter" program in which any interested sponsoring organization could go to a local HUD field office, present plans and get funding approval. The program was small but it produced excellent state-of-the-art housing utilizing the latest design ideas. Approximately 300 projects with 45,000 units were built with an average size of 133 units. About 25 percent of the projects had a mandatory meal plan included as a condition of occupancy (U.S. Senate, 1984). The program was suspended by the Nixon administration in 1970 and replaced with HUD Section 236. About 150 projects that had already been approved as well as a few completed projects were then converted to the Section 236 program.

HUD Section 202/8

With passage of the Housing and Community Development Act (HCD) of 1974, Congress combined Section 202 with Section 8 and authorized a new program designated as

Section 202/8. This revised program was implemented in 1976 with 30,000 units in 289 projects funded that year. Under the revised plan, the Section 202 program was converted to a national competition, with projects approved at the national level. The sponsoring organizations had to set up a single-purpose "borrower" corporation which received the funding award and thus owned and operated the project. Until 1990, borrowers could receive a direct loan from the federal government, at slightly below market rates, to finance construction. The loan was then repaid through a forty-year mortgage. Projects for the elderly approved through 1990 are coupled with 100 percent Section 8 rental assistance. The average size of projects approved between 1976 and 1980 was sixty-five units. HUD, under a directive from Congress, prohibited the implementation of mandatory meals programs in any project completed after April 1, 1987.

During the period 1981–1989, HUD imposed a severe "cost containment" policy on projects approved under Section 202/8. This policy was implemented to cut the cost of building the projects by utilizing cheaper materials and by eliminating two-bedroom units, downsizing one-bedroom and efficiency units, requiring a minimum of 25 percent efficiency units, cutting down or eliminating common space, meeting rooms and congregate facilities, eliminating elevators in two-story buildings or more than one elevator in multistory buildings, and prohibiting balconies or covered entrance ways.

Due to these restrictions, meals programs disappeared as many projects no longer had the necessary community or office space. Increasingly tighter regulations were imposed and with Fair Market Rents artificially suppressed by HUD policies (U.S. Senate, 1989) it became all but impossible to build projects in many parts of the nation without substantial sponsor contributions or supplemental financing from other sources. Tighter regulations at the field office level also increased the time it took to get a project through the approval stage. In fact, it became common for the process to take three years from initial selection to occupancy. These restrictions were loosened somewhat in 1989 and were subsequently all but removed by passage of the National Affordable Housing Act (NAHA) of

1990. Currently, there are approximately 3,000 Section 202/8 projects in the HUD inventory covering about 200,000 units. About 25,000 of these are in projects specifically for the nonelderly disabled.

The Section 202/8 program was highly modified by Section 801 of the National Affordable Housing Act of 1990. Among the major changes mandated by NAHA are:

1. Direct loans were abolished and replaced with a capital advance which does not have to be repaid if the project is utilized for its original purpose for at least forty years. This capital assistance effort operates essentially as a grant;
2. The cost of a project is based upon local cost standards rather than Fair Market Rents. Incentives are provided so that owners who build projects for less than the initial estimates may retain 50 percent of the savings for certain designated uses, and may retain 75 percent of the savings if they add certain energy efficient features;
3. Nonelderly disabled are no longer allowed to live in projects for the elderly financed under Section 202. New projects built under Section 202 from FY 1991 onward will only accept elderly persons for tenancy;
4. Project managers may now include staff who will coordinate supportive services in their budgets. Further, project rental assistance funds may be used to pay for a portion of certain necessary supportive services.

HUD Section 221(d)

HUD Section 221(d) consists of two types of mortgage insurance for privately-financed loans to build multi-family projects (which could include projects for the elderly). Initially authorized in the 1950s, Section 221(d) is an over-the-counter effort similar to the original Section 202 program, in which owners present plans and proposals to the HUD field office for approval (HUD, 1989). These projects may be owned by either a nonprofit or a limited dividend owner. Income limits for tenancy are not applicable for this program, but many of the projects do utilize Section 8 certificates. The major difference is that 100 percent of the mortgage may be insured by the government for nonprofit and cooperative mortgagors under Section 221(d)(3), but the government insures only 90 percent of the mortgage under 221(d)(4) irrespective of the type of mortgagor.

While this program has never been officially suspended, activity has been minimal since the mid-1980s. Currently, there are approximately 1,900 projects for the elderly insured under either Section 221(d)(3) or 221(d)(4), with about 140,000 dwelling units in the HUD inventory. About 15 percent (21,000) of the total number of units insured under Section 221(d) include a mandatory meals plan. However, a significant difference from the Section 202 program is that these projects are not specifically limited to the elderly and in many cases have large numbers of nonelderly disabled people living in them.

HUD Section 221(d)(3) Retirement Service Centers

This program, which was in operation from 1983 to 1989, consisted of federal mortgage insurance on privately financed projects. The program was specifically designed to develop congregate facilities for low- to moderate-income frail elderly who were expected to pay market rates for both rent and supportive services. Under this program 186 projects providing approximately 26,500 units were insured (HUD, Inspector General, 1990). Currently, 62 of the 186 projects (33 percent) are in default and are either in the foreclosure process or have already been foreclosed by HUD (Inspector General, 1990).

It appears that one problem with these facilities was that there were too few elderly in the narrowly defined income range targeted by the program to make it possible to support the numbers of projects being insured. This was especially true in a number of locations where these projects were concentrated— Cincinnati, Ohio, Phoenix, Arizona and Minneapolis-St. Paul, Minnesota (HUD, Inspector General, 1990). The reasons given for the program failure include poor loan underwriting, overly optimistic financial and marketing projections and inadequate reserves.

HUD Section 231

HUD Section 231 is federal mortgage insurance for privately-financed loans, initially authorized in 1959. It too is an over-the-counter effort in which owners present plans and proposals to the HUD field office for approval (HUD, 1989). These projects may be owned by either a nonprofit or a limited dividend owner. Currently, there are approximately 500 of these projects with about 67,000 dwelling units. Among that number, 340 projects and 41,000 dwelling units are specifically for the elderly.

HUD Section 236

HUD Section 236 was designed for rental and cooperative housing in which there was federal mortgage insurance on a private market-rate loan. It also provided interest reduction payments to reduce the effective interest rate to one percent. Section 236 was initially authorized under the Housing and Urban Development Act of 1968. Tenant eligibility was established with rental limits, and rental rates were either the basic rental charge based upon a one percent interest rate, or 25 percent of income, whichever was less. Some residents paid the fair market value for the apartments while others received rent supplement payments. Some of these projects have a mandatory meals program. Currently, nearly 80 percent of the 610 Section 236 projects (81,000 dwelling units) serve the elderly. Section 236 projects, generally, operate under similar occupancy rules as do those projects for the elderly under the Section 202/8 program. Section 236 was suspended in 1976.

HUD Section 232

HUD Section 232 started out as a program of federal mortgage insurance on privately-financed loans for nursing homes. However, more recently, board and care facilities and adult day care facilities may be included in connection with a nursing home. The authorizing legislation for this program was passed in 1968. There have been few projects approved in recent years, due to the limited availability of "certificates of need" for construction of nursing facilities issued by the individual states. However, under HUD regulations, these nursing homes may be owned either by a nonprofit or a limited dividend for-profit owner and there are approximately 1,600 nursing homes with 154,000 beds in the HUD inventory. These projects are financed by a private mortgage loan which is insured by HUD.

The Elderly in HUD Housing

The elderly assisted by HUD programs number approximately 1.3 million persons. These individuals are living in HUD-assisted housing, housing that is covered by HUD mortgage insurance, or they are receiving rental assistance for apartments in their communities. An additional 100,000 elderly in rural communities are served by what are essentially parallel programs of the Farmers Home Administration (FmHA).

In the 1960s, the "early" days of senior housing, it was not uncommon for elderly persons to move into projects when they were sixty-five or younger and in relatively good health. This has changed and the average age upon admission has risen steadily since the 1970s. Now, many residents are in their mid-seventies or even their early eighties when they first move into a HUD project. For the past twenty years or so, the trend has been for the average age of the elderly in HUD assisted or insured housing to increase approximately one year every two and a half years. Currently, the average age of elderly residents in HUD projects is about seventy-eight years. The elderly who are currently in HUD assisted housing are usually described as older and less affluent than their counterparts in the general community. They also tend to be women and minorities.

HUD defines frailty on the basis of performance of Activities of Daily Living (ADLs). A person who is deficient on at least one ADL is defined as "at risk" and a person deficient in three ADLs is defined as "frail." Currently, the frail elderly in HUD-assisted housing make up less than 10 percent of the total number of elderly residents but as many as 30 percent of the residents are "at risk" of becoming frail. These individuals represent the most important subgroup in terms of policy decisions and it is clear that this group will receive additional attention in the near future. Current estimates are that those elderly who are deficient in at least one ADL may include as many as 75,000–135,000 of those in HUD housing who are sixty-five and older (Struyk, 1989). Those who are "near frail" in that they need some assistance to carry out activities of daily living comprise an additional 365,000 elderly households among those in HUD projects.

Supportive Services and HUD Projects

The question of how to best provide supportive services for the elderly living in HUD-assisted and -insured housing is one which has been actively pursued since the 1960s. Unfortunately, little progress has been made in this area. Essentially, there is a housing system, represented by HUD, and a supportive services system, represented by the Department of Health and Human Services (HHS) and its predecessor agency the Department of Health, Education, and Welfare (HEW). Traditionally, each of these systems has operated independently of the other with little program or policy overlap. Locating the best mechanism for interdepartmental interaction between these two agencies has been a major, but as yet unresolved, political issue (Nachison, 1985).

The basic approach utilized by Congress to provide supportive services in housing for the elderly, until very recently, was to require coordination between HUD and HHS. Under this approach, HUD field staff would assist project sponsors in accessing the supportive services funded through HHS. It was attractive to have service funds targeted to these projects because the projects could offer office and community space from which services could be provided in a single location. Thus, ease of servicing and economies of scale were major attractions, at least theoretically, to service providers who needed to stretch dollars and keep costs as low as possible.

There is a substantial legislative history of congressional mandates for interagency coordination both for HUD and for HHS. The major congressional mandates include:

1. Section 203 of the Older Americans Act of 1965, as amended, required that the Commissioner "advise, consult and cooperate with the head of each federal agency or department proposing or administering programs or services substantially related to the purposes of the Act. . . ." (U.S. Senate, 1989, pp. 7–8).
2. Section 202(f) of the Housing Act of 1959 required that "housing and related facilities assisted therein will be in appropriate support of and supported by, applicable State and local plans . . . providing an assured range of necessary services for individuals occupying such housing." (U.S. House of Representatives, 1991, p. 300)
3. Section 209 of the Housing and Community Development Act of 1974 required that HUD "consult with the Secretary of HHS to insure that special projects for the elderly and handicapped . . . shall meet acceptable standards of design and shall provide quality services and management consistent with the needs of the occupants." (U.S. House of Representatives, 1991, p. 234)
4. Section 162(c) of the Housing and Community Development Act of 1987, since repealed, required "supportive services plans in all Section 202 housing describing the served populations, range of necessary services, manner in which services will be provided, and the extent of state and local fund availability for services provision." (U.S. Congress, 1988, p. 101)

There has been much controversy about the extent to which interagency coordination has been successful. Certainly, there is a long history of complaints from housing authorities and HUD projects about the difficulty of accessing services—both those from agencies supported by the programs of AoA and others within HHS. With only a very few exceptions, there has been little evidence of a true federal partnership in linking housing and services together (Nachison, 1985). There have also been direct suggestions that federal policy has actually discouraged effective and efficient linkages for housing and services (DeShane and Spring, 1989; and Pynoos, 1990).

One of the difficulties in getting services to residents in HUD facilities is that service providers may hesitate to go into the housing projects because of the perception that project locations are in dangerous neighborhoods. Another reason is the perception that since the housing projects are HUD-supported, services are already being provided.

There are two other factors which seem to have a negative impact on the provision of services:

1. HHS funds are allocated by Congress on an annual basis, and not usually in multi-year commitments. However, after a housing project is funded initially by HUD, there are several years of planning and construction before it is ready for occupancy. Thus, HHS agencies are extremely reluctant to promise future funding to projects approved by HUD. Further, nonprofit and other owners (and particularly local housing authorities) have been reluctant to build congregate housing for low-income elderly or market low-income housing to the frail elderly because of the apparent shortage of subsidized supportive services.

2. HHS funds are distributed to local jurisdictions on a formula basis. However, until the early 1980s, when Section 202 became formula-based, projects that were approved for HUD insurance and those directly funded by HUD were not funded on a formula basis. This produced a major mismatch, at the local level, between the number of HUD projects in a particular area and the availability of services in that area.

One example of successful interagency coordination between HUD and HHS occurred under the Title VII of the Older Americans Act (now Title IIIc). When AoA's nutrition program was implemented in the early 1970s, HUD and AoA signed a statement of understanding (HUD, 1975) which resulted in the location of over 1,000 meal sites serving over 30,000 elderly persons in HUD housing projects for the elderly.

It appears that Congress has reluctantly concluded that general interagency coordination, especially at a time of tight budgets and limited staff availability, is an inefficient way to provide services to the residents of HUD housing. However, it is not yet clear that an adequate approach to this problem exists. While the solution—a federal/state partnership—is difficult to achieve, there is mounting evidence that providing services to residents of HUD projects will improve their living environment as well as the quality of their lives. However, due to the competing jurisdictional interests, it has been especially difficult to get Congress to focus on the issue of linking housing and services. Only in recent years has there been an attempt to reach a consensus on how to bring the housing and supportive services communities together.

In 1990, Congress enacted the National Affordable Housing Act. This law contains a new version of interagency coordination for dealing with supportive services for the elderly and builds on a similar approach used under the Stewart B. McKinney Homeless Assistance Act of 1987. The new approach includes the use of what are called "incentive" dollars aimed at attracting resources from other agencies. Under this plan, HUD projects will have staff whose job is to work with HHS to insure that services are available for the residents and that HUD dollars will be available to pay for some portion of the cost of the services. The intent is to leave the major responsibility for funding supportive services with HHS agencies, or other third parties, but provide HUD with the staffing and the financial tools to substantially ease the problem of attracting the dollars from other sources.

Supportive Services for Frail Older Adults

It is generally accepted that HUD programs are outside the long-term care system. One reason is that housing for the elderly, historically at least, has been directed at those who were capable of independent living. Another reason is the fear that if owners begin to convert dwelling units or entire projects to medically based care programs, the projects would rapidly lose their character as "noninstitutional housing." Further, housing management does not currently look upon supportive services as health-care related but rather as services necessary to maintain an acceptable level of independent functioning.

At the federal level, however, the line between supportive services and health-care services in housing is becoming less distinct. For example, there currently exist HUD Section 202, 231 and 236 projects with board and care wings or nursing wings attached. There are also projects with entire floors converted for use as either board-and-care or medically oriented facilities. One Section 202 project, now being built in New York City, has "suites" of three or four one-bedroom apartments and a two-bedroom apartment. A personal care aide will reside in one of the bedrooms and provide support to the other residents of the suite. However, the policy focus is still on housing for the independent elderly.

The Congregate Housing Services Program (CHSP)

The Congregate Housing Services Program was funded initially by Title IV of the Housing and Community Development Amendments of 1978. This program provided HUD dollars and allowed projects to purchase supportive services directly. The program was available to both public housing and HUD Section 202 projects. Funds were awarded in either three- or five-year renewable grants and could be used for two meals a day, personal assistance, housekeeping, transportation, or other supportive services approved by HUD. Participants were required to pay a fee for services on a sliding scale established by the individual projects. Staff were also hired to perform resident assessment and case management. A "professional assessment committee" reviewed the degree of frailty of the residents of an approved project to determine eligibility.

The CHSP was modified after its early years. Initially, only one ADL deficiency was required for a resident to be eligible to receive meals and other supportive services. This resulted in the provision of services, particularly meals and housekeeping services, to a broadly focused group including some individuals who did not actually need the services (Sherwood, 1985). Thus, the ADL-deficiency requirement was increased to two in 1984 and to three in 1987. Also in 1987, the two meals-per-day requirement was changed to one meal per day with additional meals optional. The fee-scale requirement was also modified to require a minimum fee of 10 percent of adjusted income for all participants.

Initially, there were 63 projects funded under the CHSP. One of the grants was canceled and four grantees chose to discontinue federal assistance. As of 1991, 58 CHSP projects are still providing services to about 1,900 persons, of whom 1,300 are elderly, 400 are nonelderly disabled and the remainder are temporarily disabled individuals. HUD provides over 62 percent of the funds for the projects serving the elderly, and about 34 percent of the costs for the projects serving the nonelderly disabled.

The CHSP was revised under Section 802 of NAHA. The major differences from the original program include the following (U.S. House of Representatives, 1990):

1. There is a match requirement in which HUD will provide up to 40 percent of the total funds, the participants pay at least 10 percent of the cost of the services, and the grantee or other third parties pay at least 50 percent of the cost of the services;

2. The universe of eligible projects has been expanded to include programs of the Farmers Home Administration, HUD Section 8 new construction and substantial rehabilitation, and HUD Section 221(d) and Section 236 projects for the elderly. Further, eligible applicants have

been expanded to include states, Indian tribes and units of general local government;

3. Projects are required to accept food stamps as partial or full payment of the meal fee and to utilize surplus foods from the Department of Agriculture;

4. A service coordinator is specifically mandated to provide case management and services coordination support to the program participants; and,

5. Retrofitting and renovation of facilities are included as eligible expenses.

The degree to which applicants to the revised CHSP are able to put together sufficient matching funds and qualify for funding is the first real test of the incentive concept for projects serving the elderly. There is some concern that applications may be limited, due to possible difficulties in meeting the matching requirements, in a time of very tight state and local budgets. However, at least two states are apparently planning to enter the competition in the first year. Also, there is growing interest, at the project level, for the CHSP program.

Services and the National Affordable Housing Act of 1990

Section 801(g) of the National Affordable Housing Act of 1990 (NAHA) describes supportive services for the frail elderly which are eligible expenses and may be specifically integrated into the revised HUD Section 202 program. It also allows a project to hire personnel to coordinate the delivery of services to residents who need them. Similarly, NAHA Section 808 allows similar expenses in the existing HUD Section 202 and 202/8 programs for the elderly. The main components of the statute are twofold:

1. Approvable supportive services under either program may be meals, housekeeping, personal assistance, transportation, health-related services, and others. The services may also be provided to nonresidents of the

project if such provision will not adversely impact the cost-effectiveness or the operation of the program, or add to the need for program subsidy. HUD will pay 15 percent of the cost of approvable services.

2. A service coordinator may be hired to access and ensure the coordination of supportive services from the community to eligible residents.

These statutory changes are major. For the first time, the federal policy regarding eligible operating budget expenses for service coordinators and supportive services has been clarified nationally, at least in the Section 202 programs. Traditionally, payments for services were clearly prohibited. And, service coordinators were allowed in some facilities and disallowed in others until HUD issued standardized policies for service coordinators in May 1991. While funds for supportive services are still prohibited in the old Section 202 program due to a lack of appropriations, HUD is moving forward to implement service coordinators under both old and new Section 202 programs. These changes represent another test of the incentive approach for HUD projects. If a service coordinator has some HUD funds available in addition to community and office space, it should be easier to attract other resources into the project to meet the needs of the residents.

One of the impediments to effective interagency coordination has been the issue of "who pays" for supportive services (Nachison, 1985). This is an issue that is just now beginning to be addressed through statutory amendments. The issue, put simply, is which level of government should subsidize services and under what circumstances? Regardless of the final mechanism, the approach must be a partnership involving the federal, state, and local levels.

Currently, in this regard, there are at least three promising avenues for service subsidy. They include:

1. A modification of Medicaid and Medicare to allow a general entitlement for home-based community services for all low and some moderate income people whether they live in subsidized housing or not. This would involve some co-payment from the individual. One

approach along this line was a bill (HR 3426) which was defeated in 1988. If enacted, this bill would have expanded the home-based component of Medicaid and Medicare into universal coverage thus eliminating the current stigma attached to Medicaid. The basic concept could still be a possible ingredient of future efforts. Under a general entitlement, a project-based service coordinator would function primarily as a broker of services. However, the major responsibility, to link the individual to necessary services, would be a simpler task than exists in the current system in which services may not be affordable or even available.

2. A more experimental concept would be an expansion of the Social Health Maintenance Organizations (SHMO) now being tested in four cities (Struyk, 1989). A SHMO would be available to all elderly in a community. In a SHMO, a prepaid amount covers a special insurance and prepaid service package for the elderly. Thus, a SHMO has several advantages: (1) one organization is responsible for organizing acute and chronic care; (2) the SHMO would enroll a cross-section of the community; (3) payment is by prepaid fee, which may be from the individual, Medicaid or Medicare; and (4) because it is at risk, the SHMO has incentives to find the best way to deal with the cost of chronic and acute care (Pynoos, 1989). Proponents of the SHMO say that it is cheaper than Medicaid, and, with education, low-income people can learn that the cost of the investment in the prepaid plan is worthwhile and a benefit in terms of receiving care when needed. It should be noted, however, that the concept has had difficulty starting up in all the test sites and, thus, the number of services offered has been less than if there were greater community support (Struyk, 1989).

3. A much more limited option would deal only with the low-income residents of HUD-assisted and -insured housing. This may be a more realistic approach, at least in the short run. There would be a modification to the other existing HUD statutes in order to provide specific

supportive services to residents in Section 8, Section 221 (d), and Section 236 projects.

The Elderly and the Impaired

Another highly volatile issue has emerged regarding who can be served in housing for the elderly. The issue involves the appropriateness of housing nonelderly disabled (including the mentally ill) in the projects designed for elderly persons. At its base, this conflict is the result of the lack of available housing for nonelderly disabled in the community.

Under current regulations, nonelderly disabled (primarily the physically impaired) may live in no more than 10 percent of the dwelling units in any HUD Section 202 project, but nonelderly disabled may live in any of the other HUD insured or assisted projects for the elderly, generally without restriction.

Since the passage of the Fair Housing Act of 1988 there has been tremendous pressure on the owners of projects for the elderly (other than in HUD Section 202 and some Section 236 projects) to operate in a "nondiscriminatory" manner and allow nonelderly disabled to live in them. Because the definition of elderly in these programs includes nonelderly disabled, there has been little apparent legal basis for continuing the elderly preference in any of the HUD programs—other than HUD Section 202. Owners, who have set up their management structures to serve the elderly are now forced to take in many nonelderly, including the mentally impaired, for whom there is no basis for services in the existing regulatory agreement between the project and HUD. Similar pressure is also being put on the Section 202 projects. The result of these changes is that the nonelderly population may now be 30–40 percent of the tenants in some HUD projects that were designed for the elderly. As the composition of the projects changes, the remaining elderly become more and more fearful of their safety and many move out even if to a "less adequate" housing situation.

The end result has been a dramatic decrease in available HUD dwelling units for low-income elderly people. The evolving ad-hoc system is one in which neither the needs of the elderly nor the needs of the nonelderly disabled are adequately met. The advocates for the disabled say they have no choice but to press for further access to housing originally designed for the elderly. This is because, in most cases, there is an insufficient amount of appropriate housing for the nonelderly disabled, particularly the mentally ill, in the general community. Advocates for the elderly, on the other hand, want to narrow the regulatory definitions in order to halt the influx of the nonelderly into what they see as "elderly housing." While this latter approach would solve an immediate problem for the managers and sponsors of housing for the elderly, it does not address the need for additional housing for the nonelderly disabled. That issue must be addressed by Congress and the individual states.

NOTE

1. The author is an employee of the United States Government. The ideas and opinions expressed in this chapter are solely those of the author and may or may not reflect the official position of the federal government.

REFERENCES

Assistant Secretary for Housing and the Administrator of Social and Rehabilitation Services of the U.S. Department of Health, Education, and Welfare. (1975). "Memorandum of Agreement in Housing and Social Services Cooperation." Washington, DC: U.S. Department of Housing and Urban Development.

Assistant Secretary for Housing, U.S. Department of Housing and Urban Development and the Commissioner of the Administration on Aging. (1976). "Joint Working Agreement on

Housing and Social Services for the Elderly." Washington, DC: U.S. Department of Housing and Urban Development.

DeShane, M.R. & Spring, N.L. (1989). "Integrating Services Between Subsidized Housing Facilities and the Aging Services Network: Present Difficulties and Future Needs," *Oregon Journal of Gerontology*, 2–4.

Nachison, J. (1985). "Congregate Housing for the Low and Moderate Income Elderly: A Needed Federal-State Partnership," *Journal of Housing for the Elderly*, 3(4), 65–66.

——— (1985). "Who Pays? The Congregate Housing Question," *Generations*, Spring, 35–42.

Pynoos, J. (1990). "Public Policy and Aging in Place," in D. Tilsen (ed.), *Aging in Place*. Glenview, IL: Scott Foresman and Company, 169–197.

Senate Select Committee on Aging. (1989). "Compilation of the Older Americans' Act of 1965," Washington, DC: U.S. Senate.

——— (1984). "Section 202 Housing for the Elderly and Handicapped: A National Survey," Washington, DC: U.S. Senate.

Sherwood, S. (1985). "Evaluation of the Congregate Housing Services Program, Executive Summary," Roslindale, MA: Hebrew Rehabilitation Center for the Aged.

Struyk, R. (1989). "Providing Supportive Services to the Frail Elderly in Federally Assisted Housing," Washington, DC: The Urban Institute.

U.S. Congress. (1988). "Housing and Community Development Act of 1987." P.L. 100–242, U.S. Senate and U.S. House of Representatives, 1988, Washington, DC, Page 101 STAT 1859.

U.S. Department of Housing and Urban Development. (1979). *Housing for the Elderly and Handicapped*. Washington, DC: U.S. Department of Housing and Urban Development.

U.S. Department of Housing and Urban Development, Office of the Inspector General. (1990). "Multi-Region Audit of the Insured Retirement Service Centers Program." Washington, DC: U.S. Department of Housing and Urban Development.

———. (1975). "Participation in Nutrition Programs for the Elderly." Washington, DC: U.S. Department of Housing and Urban Development.

———. (1989). *Programs of HUD*. Washington, DC: U.S. Department of Housing and Urban Development.

———. (1990). *Retirement Service Center Program Evaluation*, Washington, DC: U.S. Department of Housing and Urban Development.

U.S. House of Representatives. (1991). "Basic Laws on Housing and Community Development." Washington, DC: U.S. House of Representatives.

———. (1990). *Cranston-Gonzales National Housing Act*, Washington, DC: U.S. House of Representatives.

U.S. Senate Select Committee on Aging. (1989). "The 1988 National Survey of Section 202 Housing for the Elderly and Handicapped, Report of the Select Committee on Housing and Consumer Interests of the Select Committee on Aging," Washington, DC: U.S. Senate.

Part III: The Private Sector

CHAPTER 5

Naturally Occurring Retirement Communities in Urban and Rural Settings

Michael E. Hunt
John L. Merrill
Carolyn M. Gilker

The most prevalent form of alternative housing for older people in the United States is often overlooked. This housing option has come to be known as a naturally occurring retirement community (NORC). NORCs are a nearly invisible housing option for several reasons. First, they are neither planned nor designed for older residents, but occur naturally. Second, NORCs tend to be age-integrated since there are no age restrictions on residency. Lastly, NORCs are not advertised as retirement communities nor are they considered as such by their residents, owners, or managers.

A NORC can take any one of several forms. It can be an apartment or condominium complex, a particular neighborhood, a vacation or resort area; it can be in a rural area, a small town, or a city. In short, the concept of a naturally occurring retirement community is most useful if it is considered a phenomenon, rather than a place—the phenomenon of a particular location attracting and retaining older residents, even though that location was not originally intended to do so.

NORCs are of interest for several reasons. The first is that we know very little about them even though they are so prevalent. In a survey of 1500 randomly selected adults age fifty-five and older, the AARP (1990) found that 27 percent of the sample lived in NORCs, neighborhoods or apartment buildings where 50 percent or more of the residents were age sixty or older. In contrast, only 5 percent lived in planned retirement communities. Of the 30 million Americans sixty-five years of age or older, as many as 8 million may be currently living in NORCs. The AARP survey also found that older people living in NORCs disliked fewer things about their housing than people living in purpose-built retirement housing. NORC residents tended to be the poorest and oldest segment of the older population, but they were also very satisfied with their lifestyle, which they felt was less stigmatized than retirement housing.

A second reason to investigate NORCs is to learn more about their attraction for older adults. And, NORCs may also provide lessons that can improve the quality of purpose-built housing for older people.

This chapter specifically discusses two types of NORCs: apartment complexes and rural areas. These types of NORCs differ in various ways. The first is in their respective settings. For example, apartment-complex NORCs are typically found in urban settings. The second difference is in physical description. An apartment complex is an easily defined place, while a rural NORC is often an amorphous area. The third difference is related to the characteristics of the residents and the features that initially attracted them.

Apartment Complex NORCs

Apartment complex NORCs are defined as apartment buildings that were not designed or planned for older people but in which over half of the residents are at least sixty years old. The question of how apartment complex NORCs develop has been addressed by Hunt and Gunter-Hunt (1985). They conducted case studies of three apartment complexes in Madison, Wisconsin that had attracted numerous older residents. In each case, neighborhood features turned out to be more critical to the development of the NORC than were features of the facility itself. The most important neighborhood features were safety and proximity to shopping and services.

Hunt (1988) has approached the question of why some apartment complexes become NORCs through structured interviews with seventy-two individuals aged sixty and older, who were residents of one of three apartment NORCs in Madison, Wisconsin. He reports that proximity to their previous homes was an important attractor, as was the presence of friends or family in the NORC. Respondents were also asked why they had moved from their previous residence. The most frequently mentioned reason was that their former living arrangement was too large and that upkeep was becoming a problem. Isolation was also mentioned as were failing health and loss of a spouse.

Surprisingly, cost was rarely mentioned as a factor that contributed to the decision to move to a NORC. This may be partially explained by the fact that the older people interviewed in this study had already chosen to move to the NORC. Therefore, these older adults had previously determined that the NORC was within their current economic means. However, the cost of living in a NORC could become a problem at a later date as a result of rent increases.

In most cases, participants in the study indicated that they had heard about the NORC by word-of-mouth from a friend or relative. The fact that two of the three NORCs did not advertise supports the importance of individual referrals as the dominant means of attracting residents.

In a subsequent study on the attraction of NORCs, Hunt and Ross (1990) provided descriptive measures of the relative importance of various apartment complex attributes in attracting older and younger people to apartments that have and have not become NORCs. The major differences found between the NORC and non-NORC older residents concerned the relative importance of social and physical characteristics of the housing. Older NORC residents placed more importance on social factors, such as proximity of friends and age peers, than did the older non-NORC residents. The latter group, instead, generally placed more importance on the distance of stores and leisure activities, the physical attributes of the housing, and the design of the living unit itself.

Although Hunt and Ross (1990) found some differences in the response patterns of younger and older NORC residents, the major finding of this comparison was the generally similar patterns regarding the importance of the attributes. Younger residents were seeking a safe place to live that was also convenient to leisure activities, public transportation, and work. While apartment features were more important to younger residents overall, the similarities between age groups were more impressive than the differences. Older residents were also seeking a safe place that was near friends or family and near a grocery store.

NORC Resident Characteristics

Hunt (1988) found that about 80 percent of a sample of NORC residents were widowed women living alone. Overall, about two-thirds of the older residents were between the ages of sixty and seventy-five, and the remaining one-third were older than seventy-five years. It was also found that these NORCs had evolved by residents "aging in place," as well as "in-moving" by retirement-age individuals. In fact, about half of the elderly residents had moved into the NORC between the ages of sixty and seventy-five, about one-fifth at seventy-five or older, and nearly one-third at under sixty years of age.

It was also found that older residents tended to move from nearby neighborhoods, with over 75 percent of the participants moving to the NORC from the same part of town as the NORC. These findings are consistent with 1980 Census data that show the older population is more likely to move locally or within the same state than between states. According to these data, only 3.6 percent of older people made interstate moves between 1975 and 1980.

NORC Resident Satisfaction

Most older NORC residents liked NORC living better than their previous living arrangement. Moving to a relatively small apartment that was not as spacious as their previous home was difficult for some. However, they were willing to trade off qualities of the living unit for the benefits offered by the location of the NORC (being near friends, relatives, and shopping), that reduced feelings of isolation and reduced maintenance responsibilities (Hunt and Ross, 1990).

Maintenance of the NORCs by management was very important to NORC older residents. The degree to which management was perceived to maintain the building and grounds appeared to be important to the evolution of the NORCs because word-of-mouth was the primary means by which other older people heard about the community. This suggests that if residents became disenchanted with management, word-of-mouth recruiting would cease and the evolution of the NORC would slow or even be reversed.

Reasons for Leaving

To address the issue of why older residents leave a NORC, Hunt and Ross (1990) asked participants if they planned on moving away. About 60 percent answered no, 30 percent answered maybe, and less than 10 percent reported plans to leave. Participants who answered maybe or yes to this question were asked why. The two most common answers were related to the need for additional health care and a need for less costly living arrangements. However, few people actually moved away for either of these reasons. Other reasons that people gave for planning to move related to the design of the NORC. For example, barriers such as stairs were mentioned as problems for some elderly residents.

The remaining participants were also asked if anything could have been done to help retain those people who had moved away. Unexpectedly, the most common response was that nothing *should* have been done. And, although the second most common response was to provide in-home care, most respondents felt that, if people needed health care, they should move to a place where it could be better provided. Taken together, these somewhat surprising answers illustrate that most of these older NORC residents were happy with the fit between their needs and desires and what the NORC offered.

NORC Evolution

There appear to be three main categories of factors involved in the evolution of apartment NORCs: (1) location, (2) management, and (3) design (Hunt, 1988). Location seems to be the chief initial attraction of a NORC. The two aspects of location that appear to be important are proximity to friends and family and proximity to familiar shopping and service facilities. Management was found to be a critical factor in maintaining a stream of referrals to the NORC. Since older residents tended to expect and sometimes even demanded that the NORC be well maintained and since most older residents were initially attracted by word-of-mouth, it is evident that management played a key role in fostering the evolution of the NORC. Finally, the design of a NORC does not seem to be an attraction, but rather a potential barrier to continued independent living.

Rural NORCs

NORCs do not appear to be exclusively urban phenomena. Older adults also move to rural areas not planned or marketed specifically as retirement areas, thus creating rural NORCs. The definition of a rural NORC, at this point at least, is fairly broad and not very precise. Rural NORCs can be areas adjacent to natural amenities, such as lakes or rivers, or they can be small towns. The common characteristic is that there is a relatively high concentration of persons who moved to the area when they were sixty years of age or older. Although there has been very little research specifically focusing on rural NORCs, there is a large body of literature related to older people who move to rural areas.

Part of the growing need to study rural NORCs is the impact that older persons and their financial resources have on rural economies. Because of their positive financial impact, rural communities are interested in identifying those factors that can attract this population. Many municipalities have noticed the potentially positive economic impact of increasing numbers of older people moving to rural towns. Hot Springs, Arkansas, for example, received national attention recently when a full-time staff person was hired to recruit older adults as residents. There have also been reports that rural communities whose economies are based on retirees have outpaced other communities in per-capita income growth (Richards, 1988). In many rural communities, transfer payments, dividends, interest, and rent income of older residents are a major contribution to a county's economic base. For example, in 1984 money from these sources accounted for between 42.8 percent and 60.7 percent of resident income in the ten Wisconsin counties with the highest concentrations of older persons. For the state as a whole the proportion was only 32.1 percent (U.S. Bureau of Economic Analysis, 1986).

Smith et al. (1986) contend that the incomes of a growing retirement population can be viewed as a new and emerging basic industry for some rural areas. Retirement-related transfer payments are somewhat immune to the cyclical trends of the national economy. Therefore, communities that attract retirees and incorporate their transfer incomes into the community's economic base implicitly exercise a strategy of local development and diversification that fosters greater stability as well as growth. Finally, increases in cash transfer income have been found to be positively associated with growth in retail sales—more so than other sources of income (Bain, 1982).

Migration Patterns of the Elderly

Litwak and Longino (1987) proposed that there are three types of elderly migrations associated with different periods of the life course. The first type of move tends to closely follow retirement. Movers are often married couples, in good health, with better than average financial resources, and appear to be motivated by a concern for making a change to a new lifestyle (Longino et al., 1991). Wiseman (1980) called this type of move "amenity" migration. Typical of these amenity migrants would be those moving to retirement communities in the Sunbelt region or nonmetropolitan small town settings.

The motivation for a second type of move arises when older people develop chronic disabilities making everyday household tasks difficult to perform (Litwak and Longino, (1987). Motivation for this type of move is usually compounded when deficits from widowhood and disability are combined. These moves tend to be to places offering a more convenient lifestyle near services, shopping, friends, and family. For this reason, this second type of move is called a "convenience" move. Convenience moves may include return migration from the Sunbelt back to Northern areas, as well as moves within one's own neighborhood. Persons making convenience moves tend to be older and more frail than those making post-retirement amenity moves.

The third type of move proposed by Litwak and Longino (1987) is motivated by limited kin resources and involves moving from a setting that involves almost exclusive care by kin to an institutional setting. These moves have been called "assistance" moves and tend to be short-distance local moves.

Migration patterns have also been studied for those who move to a nonmetropolitan area from a metropolitan area and for those who move between nonmetropolitan areas. Sofranko, Fliegel, and Glasgow (1983) and Glasgow and Beale (1984) found that urban origin migrants were younger, less likely to be living alone, and had higher incomes than the rural migrants. Differences in settlement patterns have also been documented. Sofranko, Fliegel, and Glasgow (1983) found that two-thirds of older urban origin migrants who moved to selected high net inmigration counties chose to live in the countryside while only 45 percent of the older rural origin migrants who had come into the same counties chose the countryside. Similarly, Voss and Fuguitt (1979) found that as a consequence of amenity seeking, the settlement pattern of the elderly migrants to nonmetropolitan areas is more dispersed than that of the existing local population.

Types of Rural NORCs

Based on this demographic research and their own continuing research on rural NORCs in Wisconsin, Hunt and Merrill (unpublished) have identified three types of NORCs in rural areas: (1) natural amenity NORCs, (2) convenience NORCs, and (3) amenity/convenience NORCs that exhibit characteristics of both categories. The categories of the typology are based on the degree to which a rural NORC has attracted migrants seeking either amenities or assistance and the attributes of the NORCs themselves.

The natural amenity NORC primarily attracts younger, healthier, and more affluent older persons who move to a rural area because of its natural environment or in order to escape an urban lifestyle. These people tend to come from farther away, move because of a pull toward this new area for its natural amenities, and tend to live on or near a lake or in the woods. Initially they are not typically concerned with living near the services in town. Older people moving to natural amenity NORCs are less likely to have familial ties to the area than are those who move to convenience NORCs. In fact, the natural amenity movers are often former seasonal migrants.

A convenience NORC primarily attracts local people who are moving a shorter distance from one nonmetropolitan location to another. These people tend to have less income and less education. They move to be closer to relatives, due to widowhood, or because of a need to be closer to the town and its services. This group would also include many persons who exited the farming industry during the 1980s (Bentley and Saupe, 1989). People are attracted to a convenience NORC due to a push out of their old homes that are too far from needed health and related services. Convenience NORCs are less likely than amenity NORCs to be located in tourist or resort areas. This is partly because movers to convenience NORCs are not attracted to natural amenities since they already live in nonmetropolitan areas, partly because housing in amenity NORCs may not be affordable and partly because they may not feel as strong a kinship with amenity migrants as with fellow convenience migrants. Thus, a convenience NORC allows older people to benefit from a socially supportive and convenient environment, while living independently in an age-integrated setting.

The third type of rural NORC, the amenity/convenience NORC, exhibits characteristics of both of the other types. It is perhaps the most interesting of the three types because these NORCs are attractive to both types of older adults identified by migration research—those seeking amenities and those seeking assistance. These NORCs must, therefore, contain a mix of services and attributes found attractive to both of the migrant groups. For rural areas actively attempting to attract older residents, becoming a NORC of the third type would seem desirable since it would increase inmigration while, at the same time, accommodate the changing needs of the older population as they age.

Based on the existing migration data and the Wisconsin study by Hunt and Merrill, it is possible to construct a reasonably clear description of what attributes are attractive to natural amenity versus convenience migrators. Proximity to water (lakes or rivers) seems to be one of the most attractive attributes of natural amenity NORCs. The climate of the region is also an influential factor. Areas that already have a high percentage of older residents also attract more elderly. Important predictors of the presence of amenity NORCs are the percentage of the labor force employed in retail and services such as hotels, motels, restaurants, and other entertainment. The presence of health-care services is not a major attraction of the amenity migrants and the size of the largest nearby city tends to be negatively related to their migration into an area. Migrants to convenience NORCs are concerned with reducing their cost of living and making their access to services more convenient. As in amenity NORCs, the presence of numerous older residents is an attraction.

Discussion

NORCs are clearly an attractive housing alternative for older people in both urban and rural settings. They are also deemed beneficial by their hosts. Apartment NORCs have been found to be desirable by their resident managers and management companies (Hunt and Ross, 1990). Resident managers reported that older residents were desirable tenants because they are long-term residents who pay their rent and cause minimal wear and tear on the apartment. As discussed above, rural NORCs are attractive to their host communities largely because of the economic benefits they provide. This mutual attraction produces a highly desirable living environment for older people.

One way to maximize our understanding of NORCs is to consolidate what is known about urban and rural NORCs. The literature on migration patterns provides a conceptual basis for this effort. In rural areas, two types of moves have been identified: amenity and convenience. In urban areas, the move to an apartment NORC has been identified as a move of convenience. Thus, the underlying motivation and attraction of apartment NORCs and rural convenience NORCs are likely to be similar, yet quite different from the circumstances surrounding a move to a rural natural amenity NORC. Older migrants to natural amenity NORCs are typically relatively young and affluent and move with their spouse to a recreation area where they have vacationed in the past. Older migrants to rural convenience NORCs are likely to be similar to those moving to apartment NORCs. These individuals are likely to be relatively older and less affluent, they are likely to be widowed, and they are likely to be seeking a more supportive social environment and a more convenient lifestyle.

A pressing question facing NORCs of all kinds is how, and whether, to accommodate the changing needs of older residents as they age-in-place. Those who manage and operate apartment complex NORCs must choose whether to expand or establish services as they become necessary. Of special concern is whether the provision of services will lessen the desirability of a particular location to younger residents. Ironically, if younger people shy away from a NORC, it may also become less desirable to many older people as well. A workable compromise for apartment complex NORCs wishing to retain an age mix of residents appears to be providing community-based services to those in need. Other NORCs may decide to allow themselves to evolve into "housing for the elderly." This seems to occur more often in condominium or cooperative housing than in rental housing since the former are under the control of the residents and not a management company as is more typical of rental housing.

Rural communities near amenity NORCs must also address the changing needs of residents. As these amenity migrants age and desire a more convenient lifestyle and social support, nearby rural communities may be expected to accommodate these changing needs. Rural communities wishing to do so could benefit from the lessons learned from apartment complex NORCs. The prevalence of this "second move" has been documented by Longino et al. (1991).

Another question concerning NORCs relates to their future. Amenity NORCs are more affected by the economy, since they are not need-driven. People move to amenity NORCs to achieve the "good life" and, in times of recession, such a move can be postponed. On the other hand, moves to apartment and convenience NORCs are more need-driven—the need for convenience and a sense of community to alleviate isolation. Therefore, it seems reasonable to expect that the demand for convenience and apartment NORCs will continue to increase as our population ages. The demand for amenity NORCs is not as easily predictable.

A final lesson to be learned from NORCs is that key features of alternative housing for older people are a sense of community, convenient shopping and health care—whether or not these were the initial attractions. How well these features are provided, along with appropriate amenities, seems to be an indication of the success a place has in not only attracting, but also retaining, older residents.

REFERENCES

AARP (1990). *Understanding Senior Housing in the 1990s: An AARP Survey of Consumer Preferences, Concerns and Needs.* Washington, D.C.: American Association of Retired Persons,

Bain, J.S. (1982). "Transfer payment impacts on rural markets: a regression analysis." Unpublished manuscript, University of Wisconsin, Department of Agricultural Economics, Madison.

Bentley, S. & W. Saupe. (1989). *Farm exit and migration in Southwestern Wisconsin* (Report No. 151). Madison: University of Wisconsin–Extension, Community Economics.

Glasgow, N. & C.L. Beale. (1984). Rural elderly in demographic perspective. *Rural Development Perspectives,* U.S. Department of Agriculture, v. 1–3, 22–26.

Hunt, M.E. (1988). The naturally occurring retirement community. In G.M. Gutman & N.K. Blackie (Eds.), *Housing the Very Old* (pp. 161–172). Burnaby, British Columbia: The Gerontology Research Centre.

Hunt, M.E. & G. Gunter-Hunt. (1985). Naturally occurring retirement communities. *Housing for the Elderly, 3,* 3–21.

Hunt, M.E. & J.L. Merrill. (unpublished). A Rural Housing Alternative for Older People: Naturally Occurring Retirement Communities. Unpublished research funded by the Agricultural Experiment Station of the University of Wisconsin, Madison.

Hunt, M.E. & L.E. Ross. (1990). Naturally occurring retirement communities: A multiattribute examination of desirability factors. *The Gerontologist, 30*(5), 667–674.

Litwak, E. & C.F. Longino. (1987). Migration patterns among the elderly: A developmental perspective. The *Gerontologist, 27* (3), 266–272.

Longino, C.F., Jr., D.J. Jackson, R.S. Zimmerman, & J.E. Bradsher. (1991). The second move: Health and geographic mobility. *Journal of Gerontology, 66*(4), S218–S224.

Richards, B. (1988, August 5). An influx of retirees pumps new vitality into distressed towns. *The Wall Street Journal*, pp. 1, 6.

Smith, G.W., D.B. Willis, & B.A. Weber. (1986). *Transfer payments, the aging population, and the changing structure of the Oregon and Washington economies* (Report No. 30). Corvallis, OR: Oregon State University, Western Rural Development Center.

Sofranko, A.J., F.C. Fliegel, & N. Glasgow. (1983). Older urban migrants in rural settings: Problems and prospects. *International Journal of Aging and Human Development, 16*(4), 297–309.

U.S. Bureau of Economic Analysis. (1986). *Local Area Personal Income 1979–1984,* Volume 1, Washington, D.C.: U.S. Government Printing Office.

Voss, D.R. & G.V. Fuguitt. (1979). *Turnaround Migration in the Upper Great Lakes Region.* Madison: Applied Population Laboratory, Department of Rural Sociology, University of Wisconsin, Population Series 70–12, August, 1979.

Wiseman, R.F. (1980). Why older people move: *Theoretical issues. Research on Aging, 2*(2), 141–154.

CHAPTER 6

Leisure-oriented Retirement Communities

W. Edward Folts
Gordon F. Streib

In recent decades, a small but important segment of American elderly have chosen to move to retirement communities. Among the more popular of the various types of retirement communities are what can be described as leisure-oriented retirement communities (LORCs). The development of this type of specialized housing is an important result of a general demographic trend common to most complex industrialized societies. This trend, which includes a more favorable mortality pattern, resulting in a larger proportion of older persons, coupled with the fact that many older persons are retiring at an earlier age while they are in good health, makes the retirement community an increasingly important housing alternative. Furthermore, there is a large segment of the elderly population which, through a combination of Social Security, private pension plans, and personal savings, is able to enjoy a standard of living that is similar to that which it enjoyed while working. The combination of these factors provides a context within which some older adults are able to choose from among several housing alternatives. One alternative, of course, is to remain in their single-family detached houses. However, an increasingly important alternative is the modern leisure-oriented retirement community. The growth of this type of community has been enhanced by a general trend toward greater acceptance of leisure roles in retirement and a decline in the importance of the work ethic in American society (Ekerdt, 1986).

Retirement communities have been regarded somewhat negatively by many gerontologists and by some of the general public. There are a variety of reasons for such disapproval, ranging from the assertion that the elderly are "banished" to ghettoes in order to remove them from contact with the "working world," to the contrasting view that they are escaping to a hedonistic lifestyle (Jacobs, 1974) and avoiding their responsibilities as participating members of society. A related objection specifically focuses on the fact that the communities are, by definition, age-segregated. This objection is based on a traditional and idealistic view that old and young should live in close proximity and share a common way of life. An additional reason for negative attitudes toward retirement communities may stem from the fact that most of them are commercial developments and there have been widely publicized instances of unscrupulous developers taking advantage of older residents. This phenomenon, however reprehensible, is not unique to retirement communities—it can and does occur in developments for all age groups.

Still, these and other generally negative attitudes remain despite a cumulative set of research findings (Barker, 1966; Bultena and Wood, 1969; Malozemoff, Anderson, & Rosenbaum, 1978; Messer, 1967; Osgood, 1982; Rosow, 1967; and Teaff, Lawton, Nahemow, & Carlson, 1978) establishing both a preference for the retirement community lifestyle among older people and positive outcomes associated with high density age-segregated environments. Furthermore, despite all of these reservations, the fact remains that many elderly people continue to view retirement communities as attractive and desirable alternatives to living in more traditional housing arrangements.

The modern retirement community, as an alternative living arrangement, must be placed in the broad context of a largely urbanized and industrialized society characterized by relatively high levels of mobility among all age groups (Streib, 1990). The preference for separation of the generations into age segregated communities is part of a complicated cultural drift which stimulates age-concentrated environments and is epitomized by the phrase, "intimacy at a distance." One essential element of this process is the establishment of Social Security and private pension programs which not only permit generational separation but which actually encourage the establishment of service and recreational programs aimed at distinct and separate age groups.

There is another consideration that may be involved in the choice of age-concentrated environments and that has been largely neglected by gerontologists, sociologists, and environmental psychologists—namely, that American society is increasingly characterized by individualism, competitiveness, and anomie. In the last period of life, when career considerations are generally not relevant, people may seek a different style of life embodying a more *Gemeinschaft* orientation (Toennies, 1957)—a shared community experience, characterized by a higher degree of reciprocity, mutual support, interdependence, and cooperation than is typically found in age-heterogeneous communities.

An additional element, often overlooked, is the need for personal security. For many older persons, retirement communities represent a more protected and safer living environment. Related to this feeling of security is the fact that some elderly do not want to be compared to younger working persons who are actively participating in the mainstream of competitive economic life. These elderly persons prefer the LORC environment where they are not "unique" for having withdrawn from gainful employment.

Still others choose retirement communities because they believe such communities are characterized by what Atchley (1975) has described as "rural ideals." He says:

> Rural areas are conceptualized as being small in scale and dominated by social patterns which emphasize personalized interaction, informality, simplicity, slow social change, and little social differentiation. (2)

This description certainly fits many existing retirement communities, even some of those which are located on the fringes of large metropolitan areas.

Taken together, the motivations just discussed represent a more plausible explanation for why older people move to retirement communities than either of the extreme explanations involving older people who are "pushed" away from society or who escape to a hedonistic lifestyle.

Since retirement communities are, first of all, housing arrangements, they must be considered as part of the housing market in the United States. As such they are also part of the private enterprise system. Although there have been a variety of governmental programs to provide housing for older (and younger) persons, some of which are described in other chapters of this book, most of the housing market in the United States is controlled by private enterprise. Currently, there are almost half a million housing units for the elderly with some form and level of federal subsidy or support (Golant, 1992). However, this number represents only a small proportion of the housing utilized by the elderly in the United States and is greatly exceeded by the number of dwelling units available in retirement communities.

In studying retirement communities, one must keep the market mechanism in the forefront of the analysis, for it is fundamental to how these communities are established and evolve. Retirement communities are business enterprises and they emerge from an interesting and unique market situation stemming from the gerontological, demographic, and sociological developments discussed earlier. The developers of retirement communities witnessed the changing social situation of older adults and, in response to what they perceived as a housing need, developed large age-segregated communities for healthy and active retired people.

These early developments were not merely profit-making enterprises based upon the short-term desire to maximize gain. Rather, at the very heart of the market mechanism that produced these living arrangements is an assumption of growth and an optimism about the future that is quite unique. Early developers were optimistic in their definition of the situation. Specifically, they believed their efforts would result in a desirable age-concentrated "lifestyle" that would provide housing and other amenities to older people while, at the same time, yielding an acceptable return on their investment. What makes this especially interesting is the fact that the context in which these developers operated had many features that were beyond their control and which often combined to make their enterprise generally more difficult to establish and, sometimes, resulted in the failure of a community. Despite these obstacles, the early developers started with an optimistic and confident definition of the situation—a necessary condition for the establishment of a modern retirement community.

Leisure-oriented Retirement Communities: Issues Relating to a Definition

Leisure-oriented Retirement Communities (LORCs) can be distinguished from both Continuing Care Retirement Communities (CCRCs) and more supportive forms of living by the simple absence of a formalized network of supportive services directed at the activities of daily living (ADLs). As the name implies, the emphasis of LORCs is on leisure activities and the provision of opportunities and facilities to pursue those activities. Thus, while a great deal of personal support is typically found in LORCs (Streib, Folts & LaGreca, 1985), supportive activities tend to be informal and the emphasis is clearly on leisure pursuits.

LORCs have been a subject of interest to gerontologists for several decades. As early as the 1920s retirement "villages," precursors to the modern retirement communities, were being developed to provide low-cost housing to retired individuals self-selected because of membership in a particular religious denomination or fraternal organization. Sometime around 1960, changing attitudes toward retirement and a dramatic increase in the number of healthy older individuals with adequate retirement incomes combined to produce a significant surge in both the number and the quality of LORCs. As entrepreneurial developers began to establish LORCs in the Sunbelt states, the rather simple and austere retirement village model that was established in the 1920s began to evolve into a luxurious "club-like" environment with physical facilities designed to encourage and enhance leisure pursuits. Thus, LORCs such as Leisure World and Sun City, as well as others, began to appear in Florida, California, Arizona, and the other so-called retirement or Sunbelt states.

The period since that initial surge has been marked by two distinct trends. First, the existence of a large population of healthy older adults with adequate incomes attracted the attention of entrepreneurial developers interested in establishing facilities based on a "leisure lifestyle." In order to attract and keep residents, these developers designed elaborate leisure and recreational programs as integral components of community life. In addition, although LORCs retained their relative economic advantage over the same lifestyle in age-integrated communities, emphasis was clearly shifted away from the retirement community as a low-cost housing alternative to the retirement community as a leisure-oriented lifestyle choice. The result has been the creation of two broad types of LORCs: those for affluent residents with a rich array of activities and services, and a more modest type of LORC for persons with lower incomes, providing low-cost housing and limited kinds of activities.

Although the establishment of age-concentrated communities as a viable alternative living arrangement can be traced to the efforts of religious and fraternal organizations attempting to meet the rather narrowly defined needs of their own members (Heintz, 1976; Haas, 1980; Winklevoss and Powell, 1984), entrepreneurial developers, sensitive to the potential market for such communities, have had a profound impact on the evolution of the modern LORC. In fact, the impetus to innovate is, in large part, due to the competition among early developers—most notably Del Webb, developer of the Sun City communities, and Ross Cortese, developer of the Leisure World communities (Streib, Folts, & LaGreca, 1986).

The second trend involved the provision of formalized health care services as one component of community residence. The emergence of "life-care retirement communities," and later "continuing care retirement communities," as distinct retirement community types has meant that a significant segment of both the nonprofit and for-profit retirement "industry" has begun to emphasize health-related services and caregiving. Despite this shift toward supportive services, discussed more fully in other chapters of this book, LORCs are likely to remain an important component in the housing options that are available to the active young-old population.

By the decade of the 1970s, all types of retirement communities had modified their somewhat unfavorable image as low-cost "elderly housing." To be sure, even today, some stereotypical "trailer parks" for older adults remain—especially in Florida, California, and Arizona. But, as more and more relatively affluent elderly people chose to live in the comparative luxury of the modern retirement community, the "trailer parks" began to be identified less with the elderly and more with low-income residents.

The recent gerontological literature dealing with retirement communities may be described as concerning itself with two main issues: resident satisfaction and age segregation. In one study, Jacobs (1974) presented a view of retirement communities that reflected a generally negative assessment. However, the cumulative research findings suggests that age-concentrated living environments are not only preferred by a substantial proportion of elderly individuals but those who actually live in retirement communities tend to be highly satisfied with the lifestyle (Barker, 1966; Bultena & Wood, 1969; Messer, 1967; Malozemoff, Anderson, & Rosenbaum, 1978; Osgood, 1982; Teaff, Lawton, Nahemow, & Carlson, 1978; and Streib, Folts, & LaGreca, 1986). Indeed, so convincing are these data that even among the most vocal critics of retirement communities the argument appears to have shifted away from issues related to life satisfaction and toward an almost exclusive concern with the issue of age segregation.

Implied in much of the retirement community literature is an attempt to come to terms with the question of whether elderly people have common needs that can be met more efficiently by the concentration of those needs (i.e., literally and physically concentrating the elderly in one area) or whether the whole retirement community enterprise is an attempt to "push" elderly people out of the mainstream of society. The question itself further implies that the older residents of these communities are either unable or unwilling to make conscious choices about their lifestyle preferences. This extreme line of thought involves the unfounded assumption that the needs of society are met by segregating older people into small geographic areas and providing just enough services to make the experience tolerable. Also implied by this line of reasoning is a particularly passive older population whose real needs are not addressed and who are unwilling to take an active role in the design and maintenance of their lifestyles.

Not only is this picture incorrect as it applies to the larger issue of leisure-oriented retirement communities, but it is an example of the type of stereotypical thinking surrounding the issue of housing for older adults. In thirty-six LORCs studied by a University of Florida research team in the mid 1980s, residents were not only able to make their preferences known, but they were typically not at all hesitant to take the necessary steps to shape their environment and meet their particular needs. Thus, the LORCs studied in this research were not so much housing designed *for* older people as they were expressions of the housing preferences *of* older people. In fact, so actively involved were the LORC residents in maintaining their chosen lifestyles that many residents in the surrounding communities actually felt threatened by what they perceived to be the extraordinary political, social, and economic influence of the LORC residents.

In attempting to understand the modern leisure-oriented retirement community it is important to carefully define what is being examined. This is not at all as easy as it might seem. The basic question is: what is a leisure-oriented retirement community? The answer, as it turns out, is not a very precise one. The essential elements of a retirement community were first delineated by Webber and Osterbind (1961, p. 4). They defined a retirement community as:

> a small community relatively independent, segregated, and non-institutional, whose residents are mainly older people separated more or less completely from their regular or career occupations in gainful or non-paid employment.

In a more recent effort, Golant (1992) has provided us with an elegantly simple yet adequately precise working definition for leisure-oriented retirement communities as: "planned age-segregated housing for active and independent retirees" (p. 67).

The definitional problems are not all that is confusing about LORCs. Some LORCs have included supportive services as an integral part of their lifestyles. Others have specifically chosen not to include any type of services. Still others exclude some services, such as health-related services, but include others, such as transportation, housekeeping and lawn care. Though problematic in a research and definitional sense, the flexibility and fluidity with which LORCs meet the changing needs of their resident population is not only one of their major attractions but it is precisely the reason LORCs will continue to be a viable housing option well into the next century.

One approach to this definitional problem is to focus on the supportive services themselves in the attempt to make a distinction between environments that are "leisure-oriented" and those which are focused on the supportive needs of the residents. Although this tactic is by no means a final solution, it is a conceptually helpful device. Specifically, Folts, (1987), has made the distinction between "convenience services" and "necessary services." While the types of services in these two categories may be precisely the same the difference is that "convenience services" make life easier and "necessary services" make life possible. Estes (1991) also helped to elaborate the distinction, although in an entirely different context, when she suggested that existing programs for older adults consisted primarily of "life-enhancing" services as opposed to the more important "life-supporting" services. As it relates to our discussion the "life-enhancing" and "convenience" services would be found in LORCs while the "life-supporting" and "necessary" services would be found in continuing care retirement communities and other such facilities focused on the health care needs of the individual residents.

The Importance of Activities in Leisure-oriented Retirement Communities[1]

A significant consideration in the decision process of those who have relocated to leisure-oriented retirement communities is the opportunity to occupy themselves in a variety of pleasant and rewarding leisure activities (Bultena and Wood, 1970). Many of these activities are those in which the persons have engaged earlier in life. Furthermore, an additional attraction is that by moving to a leisure-oriented retirement community, an older adult enhances his or her opportunities to explore new interests and hobbies.

In general, activities in LORCs are carried out in a neighborly and friendly setting that is close to where people live. It is typically not necessary for residents to cope with traffic, night driving, parking problems, or the fear of crime when participating in a wide range of activities. The location of a golf course, swimming pool, or tennis court only minutes away is a definite advantage to those who wish to use these recreational facilities. All of these factors, plus the physical and psychological security of an age-dense community and the support of new neighbors and friends, has resulted in strong positive evaluations of retirement communities by those who move there.

The focus on activities in LORCs is particularly important for attracting new residents. In fact, the provision of recreational activities, such as a golf course, may be a prime stimulus for people to consider relocation. Then too, for people who do not have work responsibilities, there may be a strong desire to fill time with enjoyable activities or to explore new interests. In a typical LORC, people do not have especially strong work-role identities. Put simply, retirement community residents are generally not interested in an individual's former occupation or income. More important is the individual's new identity that is partially defined by the activities he or she chooses, the skill with which he or she carries them out, and his or her overall sociability and personality. Thus, activities become extremely important in socializing individuals to their new environment and in facilitating their adaptation to the process of relocation.

In LORCs, activities are more than merely entertainment for they provide the setting for the development of new friendships and associations. Typically, people who have moved to LORCs greatly expand their range of activities and, while trying new things, also develop new competencies. Husbands and wives, who may have followed different patterns of activity in their earlier years, may choose to embark on joint projects and may cultivate new interests together. The importance of these "new" activities has been clearly stated by Kelly (1982, p. 228):

> One issue that remains to be investigated is whether leisure identities can replace those related to other roles in providing meaning and integration to life in the third age. Can leisure become, for some, a central set of role identities around which life can be reoriented?

The answer to this question is decidedly affirmative for many of the older people who choose to relocate to leisure-oriented retirement communities. The rich array of activities offered serves to provide a "new life" and typical residents are overwhelmingly positive about their "third age."

Another reason activities are important is that developers of LORCs emphasize them in their marketing effort to attract new residents. The emphasis on active, engaged, happy, older people is highlighted in brochures, videos, and other promotional materials, and is usually quite successful in dispelling any notion that a retirement community, especially a LORC, is a place for "old folks" to sit in a rocking chair and "mark time" before moving into a nursing home. Some newly retired people are especially attracted by a LORC environment in which everyone is busy pursuing individual preferences and interests. This is especially important when the LORC lifestyle is in direct contrast to a former lifestyle where the old person may have felt "left out" while their neighbors went off to work or to pursue other activities.

Activities Available in Leisure-oriented Retirement Communities

The variety of activities offered in a typical LORC is extensive. An abbreviated list of the types of activities scheduled in one middle-income LORC with about two thousand residents includes:

1. Social: Pot luck suppers, dances, movies, bridge, pinochle, travel club, group outings to nearby entertainment events, state clubs, singles club.
2. Sports: Golf, swimming, tennis, fishing, boating, shuffleboard and various tournaments and competitions.
3. Crafts and hobbies: Ceramics, lapidary, quilting, fabric painting, stamp collecting, gardening, coin collecting.
4. Arts, music and dramatics: Art classes, chamber music, choral groups, theater troupes, concerts.
5. Educational: Lectures, foreign language classes, study clubs, investment groups, book review, library committee.
6. Health and fitness: Exercise groups, hiking clubs, yoga, Weight Watchers.
7. Self-governance: Various committees and activities related to operating the day-to-day and long-term operation of the community.
8. Religious: Bible study, weekly religious services, hymn singing.
9. Service and philanthropic: Good neighbor groups, money-raising activities for various organizations, either within the community or for broader charitable needs outside the LORC.

The wide range of activities offered by this typical LORC facilitates both differential disengagement and differential engagement (Streib and Schneider, 1971). There are also attractive choices for a variety of age groups and different energy levels. Newly retired persons typically choose tennis lessons, line dancing, swimming, and the travel club. Older residents usually prefer such activities as card playing, movie night, and pot luck suppers. However, the availability of such a wide range of activities, and their close proximity to one's own home, means that it is easier to remain socially engaged in a LORC than in a "normal" age-integrated neighborhood.

It is significant that in the LORC just described, which was first studied by the Florida researchers ten years ago, the activities program has been modified to include an Alzheimer support group, Meals-on-Wheels, Good Neighbors Club Assistance, and Home Health Services. This is a clear illustration of the adaptation of a leisure-oriented retirement community to the phenomenon referred to as "aging-in-place."

Governance as an Activity in LORCs

The role of self-government as an activity is important since it is an activity more often occurring in retirement communities than in age-integrated neighborhoods. Self-governance occupies considerable time and effort in some retirement communities. In others, it consists primarily of organizing the recreational activities, sports competitions, hobby groups, and social functions. In some LORCs there is a recreation director who either organizes the events or serves to stimulate, coordinate, and assist the residents in these efforts. In still other LORCs, an elected board of directors is responsible for the day-to-day operation of the community. Typically the board hires a manager but they may monitor his or her performance closely and consult on all decisions.

In studying decisionmaking in thirty-six LORCs, Streib, Folts, & LaGreca (1985) reported that most LORC residents appear content to allow other residents, or in the case of the larger communities, a competent and above all a benign management, to make most of the day-to-day and month-to-month decisions. However it was also reported that, when a crisis does develop, a substantial number of the residents can be mobilized and they can act more quickly than the residents of nonretirement communities. While residents typically express a desire not to be constantly involved in self-government, they do want to be involved in decision-making if a situation arises that is threatening to their interests or their enjoyment of the LORC lifestyle. Most residents seek stability and many are threatened by change. However, for a small number of residents, power and decision-making represent a challenging continuation of earlier roles and involve the use of skills and competencies developed and used during their working years.

As a LORC ages and as its residents age-in-place, a shortage of persons able and willing to fill leadership positions emerges. Persons who have leadership skills and are willing to serve eventually feel they have taken "their turn." Thus, an inflow of new residents is usually needed for self-government to function effectively.

Another interesting finding from this research was that in all thirty-six communities studied, a few persons were perceived as instigators of discord. Some of the more active of these persons were able to create considerable mischief by outwardly opposing the existing power structure and by attempting to escalate trivial issues into "causes" that severely hampered efforts at self-government.

Social Stratification and Activities in LORCs

Leisure-oriented retirement communities provide a unique perspective on the class structure of the larger society. There is considerable variation in the economic levels of the residents, the value of dwelling units, and the facilities and amenities offered by LORCs. The communities may vary from small manufactured homes (the small trailer parks are an example), to luxury communities with homes valued at many hundreds of thousands of dollars. The affluence of the residents is also reflected in the kinds of recreational facilities that are available. A LORC designed for those with modest resources will typically have a small recreation hall for community meetings, dances, shared meals, and opportunities for playing cards and bingo. Holidays, birthdays, and other special occasions are held in the community hall which becomes the center of social life for the residents.

At the high-income end of the economic scale, there are extensive facilities which typically include a large club house, one or more golf courses, tennis courts, and one or more large swimming pools. The presence and size of a swimming pool is one indicator of the difference between modest LORCs and their more luxurious counterparts. As one ascends the economic scale, pools become larger and "fancier" with more elaborate support facilities such as extensive lounging space, a whirlpool bath, exercise machines, and changing facilities. It is interesting, however, that the proportion of LORC residents who actually swim tends to be quite small. There may be exercise groups, and water ballet swimmers, but they usually involve only a small number of persons. Residents like having a pool available, even if they don't use it often. In this sense then, a pool may be a mark of the social status of the community—an example of Veblen's conspicuous consumption (1953) as well as a recreational or exercise locale.

One activity that is stereotypically associated with retirement communities is shuffleboard. While it is true that some retirement communities have a great interest in shuffleboard activities, with leagues, competitions and elaborate play-off scheduling, other LORC residents view it as an "old peoples' activity." In several of these communities the residents have actually had the shuffleboard courts removed or modified for other purposes.

The class structure of residents of LORCs manifests itself in some interesting ways. In small and lower-income communities, the streets and yards are quite busy, particularly in the morning, as members meet, talk and exchange greetings, discuss the activities of the community and events in the larger world. As one ascends the community class hierarchy, the amount of visible street activity tends to decline. Part of the street-level social activity relates to the sheer size of a community, the size of the lots, and the distance between the dwelling units. In small communities the residents live closer together, and the opportunity for friendly, neighborly relations is enhanced in comparison to LORCs where residents live farther apart. In LORCs with high-income residents there is a greater amount of travel which reduces the amount of neighborly contact because the residents are often not at home.

While there may be a considerable range of incomes and affluence within higher-income LORCs, activities do not appear to be class-related. Generally speaking, as mentioned earlier, LORC residents are not primarily interested in previous occupational status or income level. Thus, the LORC environment tends to have a leveling effect on class structure. Previous position and status are not especially relevant in the realm of some activities, for when people play golf or bridge, the important factor is the person's ability as a golfer or a bridge player, or whatever the activity is at hand. If a person is a particularly accomplished golfer (or particularly bad at it), these traits become more significant than past accomplishments in the labor force.

Developmental Stages in Leisure-oriented Retirement Communities

While variety and flexibility are characteristic of LORCS, there are structural regularities that are common to most of them. The basis for the discussion that follows is a two-year research effort conducted in the mid 1980s by researchers at the University of Florida. The research involved thirty-six leisure-oriented retirement communities located in Arizona, California, Florida, and New Jersey (LaGreca, Streib and Folts, 1985).[2] Interviews with key informants, including developers, residents, and officials in the surrounding communities, were used to provide in-depth data on leisure-oriented retirement communities selected for their size and geographic location. Analysis of these data suggested that there were common "life-stages" through which these LORCs passed in their evolution from developer-owned sites to resident-owned living arrangements. An adaptation of that life-stage approach provides a useful tool for understanding the modern LORC.

Leisure-oriented retirement communities may include almost any type of housing. Some are a loosely organized collection of single-family detached homes located on large lots that are in close geographic proximity. Others consist of multi-unit buildings with small undivided lots. Still other LORC communities contain mobile homes or "manufactured housing." In some of the LORCs the residents own the dwelling units but rent the land. In others, both the land and the dwelling units are owned by the individual residents. Still other communities offer alternative ownership arrangements such as cooperatives and condominiums. Condominium arrangements involve individual ownership of dwelling units and common ownership of facilities and public buildings. LORCs organized as cooperatives are increasingly rare but some still exist. In a cooperative arrangement, residents typically own stock in a not-for-profit corporation that actually holds title to the property. In either condominium or cooperative arrangements, the physical facilities are jointly owned by the residents and decisions are typically made by a vote of the entire community. It is also common to find several different ownership arrangements present in a single LORC.

Because of the diversity of housing and ownership styles, it is difficult to categorize LORCs with any precision. However, the Florida research focused on a fundamental difference in LORC communities—land ownership. If residents do not own the land upon which their dwelling units are situated, there is a variety of controlling influences such as corporations, family partnerships, single owners, business partnerships, and others that have an impact on the stability of the community. On the other hand, if residents do own the land upon which their dwelling units are located, the ultimate responsibility for the long-term viability of the community is entirely in the hands of the residents themselves. Thus, LORCs may be separated into those where the residents own the land upon which their dwelling unit is situated, labeled a Type I LORC, and those where the residents do not own the land upon which their dwelling unit is situated, labeled a Type II LORC.

If one considers programs and activities as defining characteristics of LORCs, regardless of whether they are Type I or Type II, the aging of the residents and its association with changes in the community have important social psychological and social structural outcomes. In Table 1, the detailed ten stages of the life-stage research have been truncated into three broad stages: Establishment, Transitions, and Maturation. These stages are useful in understanding how the evolution of LORCs is related to the activities they offer. This is especially important since it is the activities that are central to the definition of a Leisure-oriented Retirement Community.

Table 1
Retirement Communities and Their Life Stages

Life Stages	Activities
STAGE 1 Establishment	
Marketing Initial sales Residents move in	Erection of club house and provision of facili- ties for recreational activities and sports social programs
STAGE 2 Transitions	
From developer to new owner to resident ownership and self-government	Activities added or dropped according to residents' wishes. Maintenance and preservation of facilities for marketing to new residents
STAGE 3 Maturation	
Maintain physical facilities, emergence of new issues and Discussion and decision about adding supportive care facilities. Replacement of "old timers" by newcomers	Aging-in-place of first residents. Effort problems. to secure new leadership for arrival of new cohorts: creation of "newcomer" clubs and "good neighbor" groups. Volunteer support groups.

As the residents age-in-place, there is a slow and quite pervasive shift in the leisure orientation of a LORC. For example, there is a growing need for health care, social supports, and personal caregiving. Furthermore, as these health-related activities increase in scope, some residents become spectators rather than active participants in programs requiring physical ability.

When a LORC reaches what we have called "Maturation," a kind of balance between the residents and the community structure occurs. Residents, community leaders, managers, and developers all hope (and often expect) that the equilibrium found in the maturation stage will tend to maintain itself over a long period of time. However, this may occur in some LORCs and not in others. One intervening factor that mitigates the aging of the community organization is that some of the older and sicker residents leave and younger, healthier residents take their places. In those LORCs in which this replacement process occurs with some regularity the leisure orientation is maintained. When the two aging processes involving residents and community organization follow a parallel trajectory of adaptability then there is a minimum amount of change in the defining character of a leisure-oriented retirement community. However, when substantial numbers of residents "age in place," fundamental changes in the LORC are made necessary by the changing needs of the resident population. These changes can substantially alter the leisure orientation of a particular community.

The "life-stages" approach is also useful in exploring the structural adaptations that are necessary for the long-term viability of LORCs. Recently established Type I communities are generally involved in a process of transition in the decision-making power and responsibility, from the developer to the residents themselves. This process typically involves a cooperative effort that results in a fairly substantial amount of "training" in the mechanisms and techniques involved in day-to-day decisionmaking.

Residents in Type II communities, on the other hand, are typically involved in matters unrelated to the long-term viability of the LORC. This difference in orientation, which might be subtle in the beginning, becomes more important as the residents' needs increase and as decisions are made about supportive services.

Ultimately the social ties that are structurally encouraged by the Type I ownership arrangement, which are absent in the Type II community, may create feelings of mutual responsibility among the residents (Gemeinshaft) and provide the flexibility needed for long-term viability in the face of changing resident needs. Furthermore, a Type II LORC may be at higher risk because the ownership arrangement may discourage the type of community feeling that accompanies a long-term commitment to the LORC lifestyle.

Conclusion

In this chapter, our primary purpose has been to provide an overview of the salient characteristics of what we have called leisure-oriented retirement communities. At least three important related issues remain unresolved. First, it is by no means certain that leisure-oriented retirement communities can retain their recreational orientation in the face of a demographic imperative that demands increasingly extensive and, probably more importantly, increasingly intensive support services. The long-term viability of LORCs will depend primarily on the existence of a sufficiently large population of healthy "young-old" individuals who are both willing and able to relocate to the nontraditional lifestyle and housing arrangements that the modern LORC embodies. It is not likely that developers will continue to establish large city-sized LORCs such as Sun City, Arizona and Leisure World, Laguna Hills, California. Rather, more modest and more "service-rich" environments are likely to dominate future efforts at retirement community construction. These "new wave" retirement communities may very well focus on the service component at the expense of leisure activities.

Another issue that remains is the continuing debate about the social desirability of age-segregated living arrangements. Although the urgency of this issue is somewhat diluted by demographic projections of the size and financial resources of the future older population, the argument still attracts attention.

In all likelihood, the issue will be neither finally resolved nor even addressed at the policy level in any meaningful way. What is more likely is that the debate will grow increasingly hostile between those who view age segregation as a primarily positive means to provide social support for individuals with similar interests and needs and those who view age segregation as yet another example of the "disposability" of the older generation. That is unfortunate, for it misses the point. Lost in the debate about social desirability are the preferences and needs of tomorrow's older population.

Finally, recent discussions of living arrangements, as they relate to the older population, have typically implied that older Americans are in need of special treatment simply because they are old. We should be aware that there is a distinction between discussions of housing arrangements *for* older people and discussions of the housing arrangements *of* older people. The two are not the same and the subtle difference between those two words is very much related to a cultural predisposition toward treating old age as something that happens to other people. The fact is *we* are tomorrow's older generation. And, it is the range of housing alternatives we explore today that will make up our options in the future. That sobering thought alone should compel us to divert our attention from the age-segregation issue and face squarely the issue of how to maximize our housing options while at the same time reducing our personal environmentally based limitations. It is our considered opinion that the modern leisure-oriented retirement community has a firm claim to being a part of that issue.

NOTES

1. This section of the chapter and the following have been adapted from Gordon F. Streib (forthcoming). Also, Table 1 was originally published in Streib (forthcoming).

2. The life stages research was conducted by researchers at the University of Florida supported by a research grant from the National Institute on Aging (NIH) of which Gordon F. Streib was the Principal Investigator. A more detailed account of the life stages research is found in the final report, "Retirement Communities: Their Structure and Process" (1984). The authors of the report were Gordon F. Streib, Anthony J. LaGreca, and W. Edward Folts.

REFERENCES

Atchley, R.C. 1975. *Rural Environments and Aging*. Washington, D.C.: The Gerontological Society.

Barker, M.B. 1966. *California Retirement Communities*. Berkeley: University of California Printing Department.

Bultena, G. and V. Wood. 1969. The American retirement community: Bane or blessing? *Journal of Gerontology* 24:209–218.

———. 1970. Leisure Orientation and Recreational Activities of Retirement Community Residents. *Journal of Leisure Research* 2:3–15.

Ekerdt, D.J. 1986. The Busy Ethic: Moral Continuity Between Work and Retirement. *The Gerontologist* 26: 239–244.

Estes, C. 1991. The New Political Economy of Aging: Introduction and Critique, pp. 19–36 in *Critical Perspectives on Aging: The Political and Moral Economy of Growing Old*. Edited by M. Minkler and C. Estes. Amityville, NY: Baywood.

Folts, W.E. 1987. *The Structural and Environmental Dimensions of Florida's Continuing Care Retirement Communities*. Unpublished doctoral dissertation. University of Florida, Gainesville.

Golant, S.M. 1992. *Housing America's Elderly: Many Possibilities/Few Choices*. Newbury Park, CA: Sage Publications.

Haas, W.W. III. 1980. *The Social Ties Between a Retirement Village and the Surrounding Community*. Unpublished doctoral dissertation. University of Florida, Gainesville.

Heintz, K. 1976. *Retirement Communities: For Adults Only*. New Brunswick, New Jersey: The Center for Urban Policy Research, Rutgers University.

Hunt, M.E., A.G. Feldt, R.W. Marans, L.A. Pastalan, and K.L. Vakalo. 1984. *Retirement Communities: An American Original*. New York: Haworth Press.

Jacobs, J. 1974. *Fun City: An Ethnographic Study of a Retirement Community*. New York: Holt, Rinehart, and Winston, Inc.

Kelly, J.R. 1982. Leisure in Later Life: Roles and Identities, pp. 268–292 in *Life After Work: Retirement, Leisure, Recreation, and the Elderly*. Edited by N.J. Osgood. New York: Praeger.

LaGreca, A.J., G.F. Streib, and W.E. Folts. 1985. Retirement Communities and Their Life Stages. *Journal of Gerontology* 40: 211–218.

Malozemoff, I., J. Anderson, & L. Rosenbaum. 1978. *Housing for the Elderly: Evaluation of the Effectiveness of Congregate Residences*. Boulder, CO: Westview Press.

Messer, M. 1967. The Possibility of an Age-Concentrated Environment Becoming a Normative System. *Gerontologist* 7:247–251.

Osgood, N. 1982. *Senior Settlers: Social Integration in Retirement Communities*. New York: Praeger.

Rosow, I. 1967. *Social Integration of the Aged*. New York: The Free Press.

Streib, G.F. 1990. Retirement Communities: Linkages to the Locality, State, and Nation. *Journal of Applied Gerontology* 9:405–419.

———. forthcoming. *The Life Course of Activities and Retirement Communities in Activity and Aging*. Edited by J.R. Kelly. Newbury Park, CA: Sage Publications.

Streib, G.F., and C.J. Schneider. 1971. *Retirement in American Society: Impact and Process*. Ithaca, N.Y.: Cornell University Press.

Streib, G.F., W.E. Folts, and A.J. LaGreca. 1984. Entry into retirement Communities: Process and Related Problems. *Research on Aging* 6:257–270.

———. 1985. Autonomy, Power, and Decision-making in Thirty-Six Retirement Communities. *The Gerontologist* 25:403–409.

———. 1986. Retirement Communities: People, Planning, Prospects, pp. 94–103 in *Housing an Aging Society: Issues, Alternatives, and Policy*. Edited by R.J. Newcomer, M.P. Lawton, and T.O. Byerts. New York: Van Nostrand Reinhold.

Teaff, J.D., M.P. Lawton, L. Nahemow, and D. Carlson. 1978. Impact of Age Integration on the Well-being of Elderly Tenants in Public Housing. *Journal of Gerontology* 33:126–133.

Toennies, F. 1957. *Gemeinschaft and Gesellschaft*. East Lansing: Michigan State University Press.

Veblen, T. 1953. *The Theory of the Leisure Class: An Economic Study of Institutions*. New York: Mentor Books.

Webber, I.L., and C. Osterbind. 1961. Types of Retirement Villages. In *Retirement Villages*. Edited by E.W. Burgess. Ann Arbor: University of Michigan.

Winklevoss, H.E., and A.V. Powell. 1984. *Continuing Care Retirement Communities: Financial and Legal Analysis*. Homewood, IL: Irwin.

CHAPTER 7

Continuing-Care Retirement Communities[1]

Susan B. Brecht

The origins of today's continuing care retirement communities (CCRCs) can be traced to residential communities developed by various church groups to meet the housing and service needs of their elderly clergy and parishioners. Before Social Security, and at a time when there were few private pension programs, churches of various denominations began responding to an increasing need by their retiring clergy for all types of supportive services. The early response primarily addressed the housing needs of these individuals. Soon after these first "retirement communities" were established, older parishioners became interested in what they viewed as a "care-for-life" concept. Many of these elderly parishioners had reached an age where they no longer worked and some were experiencing difficulties meeting the costs of retirement living. Partly because of this growing need, denominationally sponsored retirement homes, which were originally open only to retired clergy, began extending their care to members of the denomination. Frequently, such facilities offered housing and care for the life of the individual in exchange for a nominal fee or for an outright transfer of the individual's assets.

Lifecare and Continuing Care Facilities

Some of the early facilities, typically referred to as lifecare communities, were developed in the Pacific Southwest, the North Central, and the Middle Atlantic and Northwest regions of the United States and many are still in operation today. For example, Hollenbeck Home opened its doors in Los Angeles in 1895. In addition, several other communities currently in operation began in California in the early years of the twentieth century. These early facilities include: The Scripps Home opened in Altadena in 1913, Solheim Lutheran Homes in Los Angeles established in 1923 and The Heritage in San Francisco, which opened in 1925.

These early communities typically combined housing and supportive services such that residents could expect to live and receive care in the same facility for the remainder of their lives. Care was frequently provided in exchange for personal assets. Those who moved to the early communities enjoyed the security of knowing that they would not have to be concerned about arranging or paying for care as their needs increased.

The lifecare concept has undergone major changes since that time. These changes were the result of a rapidly increasing need for such services and the fact that the "nursing home" had emerged as the institutional source for health-related care for older people. In response to these changes, new retirement communities were developed with nursing home beds and some existing facilities added nursing services to their supportive service package. One good example of this trend is Hollenbeck Home which opened its skilled nursing facility in 1954, more than half a century after it originally opened as a retirement home.

The lifecare retirement community, and its more modern form the continuing care retirement community (CCRC), both grew out of these early denominational efforts to care for specific groups of individuals. For many years these facilities operated with little regulation, offering housing and services on a fee-for-service basis. Typically, residents paid a specified entrance fee and a monthly fee.[2] This concept embodied a self-insured health-care component that addressed the future need for nursing care among the residents. As the costs of providing increasing levels of health care accelerated, residents were assured that they would pay no more than a specified monthly fee that was tied to the cost of their independent living unit. For example, at Foulkeways, a lifecare community in the Philadelphia area, when a permanent move is required from an apartment to the nursing home, the resident pays only the basic monthly fee for the studio apartment, the smallest unit offered by Foulkeways. In 1989 the costs for a nursing home bed in the same area ranged from $80 to $110 per day, or $2,400 to $3,300 per month. At that time Foulkeways residents paid only $890 per month for similar levels of care.

The insurance element inherent in the traditional lifecare concept has been compared to a pension plan by Winklevoss and Powell (1984). The reason is, they assert:

> [Lifecare communities receive revenues] in advance of the cash payments required for meeting promised benefits . . . the payment of a CCRC entry fee plus recurring monthly fees is designed to advance-fund the cost of future health care for a CCRC resident. (p. 77)

Inherent in this concept is substantial economic risk. Essentially a lifecare community needed to create a fee structure that was based on an assessment of future health care utilization and future costs of the pool of individuals residing within it. Some of the lifecare community failures that were experienced in the early years, and again in the 1960s, were related to problems inherent in the financing scheme. Despite these failures, as Winklevoss and Powell have noted:

> [The] practice of basing fees on the unit size (real estate basis) rather than an entrant's age or physical condition (actuarial basis) persists despite industry-wide agreement that the product is the intangible, insurance-like concept of continuing care and not the living unit itself. (p. 34)

Other serious problems in the lifecare concept identified by Winklevoss and Powell include:

> the practice of using life expectancies to amortize entrance fees into the community's income stream and the lack of a clear distinction between mortality rates applicable to

> those living in apartments versus those residing in health care centers. (p. 292–293)

These factors, combined with a lack of stringent health and economic admissions criteria, have created major financial and operational problems for some communities and will very likely continue to do so for others in the future.

In response to the concern over accurately predicting future long-term health-care utilization and costs, some facilities, developed in the late 1970s and early 1980s, "unbundled" the health-care costs. This had the impact of eliminating the insurance component from the lifecare community. Such communities may still include housing and health care in their service continuum, but they usually do not include the future costs of health care in the entrance or monthly fees. Instead, when a resident has to make a permanent move (or in some cases, a temporary move) to the nursing home, the care provided in the nursing home is provided on a fee-for-service basis. While some communities offer various forms of discounting health-care coverage, such as a specified number of free days in the health center or a daily rate for permanent transfers that is below the normal daily rate being charged to those who entered the nursing home directly from the outside community, the practice of advance-funding future health care costs has diminished in the CCRC industry.

Endowment Fees and Monthly Fees

Once the practice of offering a "lifetime of care" in exchange for assets was abandoned, the typical payment mechanism that replaced it involved the combination of an entrance fee and a monthly fee. The entrance fee, variously referred to as an "upfront fee" or an "endowment fee," was designed to cover the development costs associated with each dwelling unit and to provide a reserve for future health-care costs. This entrance or endowment fee was typically considered to be nonrefundable. However, even in the early years of the industry, the issue of refundability was dealt with in different ways by different organizations. In some facilities, for example Rydal Park in Rydal, Pennsylvania, residents who withdraw from the community during the first 50 months receive a prorated refund of their entrance fees.

Monthly fees, on the other hand, are typically tied to the cost of operating the community and usually depend on the type and cost of dwelling unit selected and the number of people residing in the unit. In the early years of this industry, the monthly fees were calculated on the date of occupancy and were rarely increased. The current practice, prompted by the economic realities of operating such a facility, is to periodically increase monthly fees (usually no more than once a year) and to tie these increases directly to inflation and the increased costs of operating the community.

Currently, the payment of an entrance fee and monthly fee is typically required only when a resident enters an independent living unit of a community. For those communities providing nursing care, the circumstances under which one moves to the community determine the fee for such care. Direct entry into the nursing home component from outside the retirement community typically requires payment of a daily rate commensurate with the market rate for such accommodations in the general geographic area. Those who transfer to the nursing component from the residential portion of the retirement community usually pay either a specified monthly fee (as described earlier) or a daily rate similar to the local rates at nursing homes.

Refundable Entrance Fees

During the 1980s, facilities were developed that offered refundable entrance fees. The concept was pioneered by Life Care Services (LCS), a company that had worked with not-for-profit sponsors on traditional endowment fee projects. LCS created an approach that, in effect, capitalized the project through the entrance fees. Basically structured as an interest-free loan to the nonprofit sponsor, the program refunded 90 percent of the entrance fees when a resident died or withdrew from the community. The LCS program was developed in response to fluctuations in interest rates and to the need for additional capital, required at some communities, because of the depletion of endowment funds. Examples of the LCS program exist at several projects, including Beacon Hill in Lombard, Illinois, and Friendship Village of South Hills in Pittsburgh, Pennsylvania.

The LCS program is by no means the only response to refundability. Other communities, such as Williamsburg Landing, in Williamsburg, Virginia, provided residents (or their estates) a full refund of the entrance fee upon permanent transfer to the nursing center, death, or voluntary withdrawal from the community. The amount of an entrance fee that is refundable varies widely. For instance, The McAuley, in West Hartford, Connecticut, refunds two-thirds of the entrance fee at withdrawal and the remainder is nonrefundable at any time. At the Court at Palm Aire, in Pompano Beach, Florida, residents have a choice between two entrance fee programs, with different terms of refundability, or a straight monthly rental option.

Several major factors influenced the emergence of refundable entrance fees. Perhaps most important was the consumer. Many older adults were interested in the concept of continuing care, but found the financial arrangements to be unacceptable. Often, entrance fees amounted to a substantial proportion of an elderly household's assets. As elderly consumers and their adult children became more sophisticated, their demands regarding the financial arrangements of continuing care reflected this sophistication. Although refundable entrance fees were typically 50 percent higher than their nonrefundable counterparts, many people were willing to pay the additional cost in order to enhance the value of their estates.

Another factor that influenced the introduction of refundable entrance fees was the entrance of private for-profit developers into the retirement housing industry. For these developers, nonrefundable entrance fees produced a substantial amount of taxable income over a very short period of time. The refundable entrance fee, however, represented a loan and, because they were a form of debt, reduced the tax burden on the developer considerably.

Finally, the refundable entrance fee was frequently associated with the uninsured or fee-for-service form of continuing care. Because of this, those who believed that they would never need to move to the nursing home, a common belief among potential residents, refundable fees were an attractive arrangement because residents believed they would have to pay only for the health-care services they used while at the same time payment of such fees guaranteed the resident the right to remain in the community for life.

Monthly Rental

During the last two decades, numerous communities have been developed that avoid the entrance fee concept entirely. These communities operate on the basis of a monthly rental charge to residents. An example of this type of arrangement is The Lafayette, in Philadelphia, Pennsylvania. The Lafayette consists of 300 independent-living units and a full 120-bed nursing unit. Frequently, however, the rental communities embrace the congregate care model and do not include a nursing home component. Laventhol & Horwath's 1987 Retirement Housing Industry Survey indicated, for example, that of the sixty-three participating rental communities, thirty-one did not have nursing centers on the premises (p. 34). In contrast to offering a contract that, for the most part, promises lifetime residency, the rental communities may offer a yearly or even monthly lease. Rental communities cover the entire cost of debt financing and the operating expenses through their monthly fees. This results in monthly fees that are generally quite a bit higher than the monthly fees charged by typical lifecare or continuing care communities.

Equity Models

Another payment approach that has only recently emerged is the condominium or cooperative arrangement. There are a few early examples of such communities, particularly in the Minneapolis area, but most projects that offer residents an equity opportunity were developed during the latter half of the 1980s. Condominium and cooperative projects offer residents of independent living units an opportunity to share in the ownership of the community, either through shares in the corporation (cooperative) or by holding a fee-simple title to their dwelling unit (condominium). Condominium and cooperative projects offer an attractive option for those looking for the benefits of owning real estate. These benefits include the deduction of mortgage interest and the use of the one-time-only $125,000 capital gains roll-over for those over the age of 55. Another benefit is the potential for appreciation in the value of the dwelling unit. The condominium or cooperative payment approach has been applied to both continuing care communities and congregate care communities.

The Canterbury in West Hartford, Connecticut, does not have a nursing home component but offers residents shelter and services until they need to make a permanent move. In contrast, Beaumont at Bryn Mawr, Pennsylvania, offers its independent-living units through purchase of certificates of membership in a nonprofit cooperative. The certificate of membership, along with a proprietary lease agreement, entitles residents to occupy a dwelling unit in the community for the remainder of their lives. And, the residents are provided a full range of care services, including independent living, assisted living, and nursing care.

Not-for-Profit Organizations

The retirement housing industry has been dominated, for much of its history, by nonprofit religious and fraternal organizations. Throughout the United States, substantial numbers of facilities are still owned and operated by religious denominations, fraternal organizations, or private not-for-profit groups. In Philadelphia, for example, many of the original sponsoring organizations are still in operation today. In Philadelphia, perhaps the country's oldest such organizations, Kearsley Christ Church Hospital and Ralston House, are rivals for the distinction of being the first to provide care to the elderly. Both of these organizations trace their origins back to the beginning of the nineteenth century. In fact, in Philadelphia, no less than eight currently operating sponsoring organizations were operating facilities providing care to the elderly by 1910. Each of the eight has successfully changed to meet the changing needs of the elderly population and each now provides a continuum of care on their various campuses.

Philadelphia has become the center of the continuing care retirement industry with over forty continuing care retirement communities currently flourishing within its boundaries. Nearly all of these communities are owned by not-for-profit organizations. Perhaps best known outside of Philadelphia are the Quaker-sponsored lifecare communities. These facilities are known for their success in operating a traditional self-insured model which offers each resident the opportunity to move through the various levels of care without significant changes in the monthly fees they must pay.

Laventhol & Horwath's 1987 study of the retirement industry included data on 173 retirement communities. Among those reporting, 86 percent were owned by a nonprofit organization. By 1993, the American Association of Homes for the Aging, which is the national association representing not-for-profit organizations, had over 6,000 members throughout the United States. While many of the not-for-profit retirement communities were originally developed with multiple levels of care, others grew out of a nursing home base. As mentioned earlier, not-for-profit organizations pioneered the creation and evolution of what we know today as the continuing care retirement community. The history of the emergence of the CCRC model reflects, in many ways, the evolution of the not-for-profit organizations responsible for creating this industry.

There are a growing number of not-for-profit organizations which own and/or operate numerous continuing care retirement communities. As the industry has matured, there has been increasing value placed upon the management experience of these not-for-profit organizations. The lending community places tremendous value on this experience and the influence that fraternal and religious sponsors have on their constituents.

In an industry where the success of marketing and operations are critical, the strength of an experienced not-for-profit organization with a known constituency can make the difference in attempting to obtain financing.

This valuable experience can be utilized in other ways too. For example, some not-for-profit organizations, such as Parkside Senior Services near Chicago and Walker Methodist Homes in Minneapolis, have become consultants and offered their expertise in development, marketing, and management to others interested in establishing retirement communities.

For-Profit Organizations

In recent years, proprietary (for-profit) organizations have increased their involvement in all segments of the retirement housing industry. However, their initial involvement was in the form of providing contract services to the nonprofit organizations that owned facilities. One of the first proprietary organizations to provide a full range of services from development, to construction, to marketing and management, was Lifecare Services Corporation (LCS), a subsidiary of The Weitz Company headquartered in Des Moines, Iowa. Lifecare Services became involved in the industry in 1961. LCS has provided services to more retirement communities throughout the country than any other U.S. developer and has recently begun to retain ownership of the properties it is developing. Other proprietary companies that have offered similar contract services for more than a decade include American Retirement Corporation and Retirement Centers of America.

The proprietary organizations have not, however, limited their involvement to providing contract services. As the industry broadened in its approach to programming and payment structures, many proprietary organizations, including large publicly held companies such as Marriott and Hyatt, developed and owned properties. During the 1980s, numerous retirement communities were developed by much smaller proprietary organizations. Local and regional development companies began to enter the industry, many in response to declines in their traditional housing, commercial, and office markets. In an annual survey conducted by *Contemporary Long Term Care* (CLTC) in 1989, 56 percent of the organizations providing data were proprietary. The growth of for-profit involvement in the industry is highlighted by comparing these 1989 responses with those from CLTC's first industry survey in 1987, when only 37 percent of the respondents represented for-profit organizations.

It is difficult to know how many facilities were planned and developed by these smaller companies because the industry still lacks a uniform statistical database that tracks such information. For many such organizations, entrance into retirement housing brought surprises because of the unique nature of the business. Although retirement communities have a clear similarity to real estate development, particularly multifamily housing, many developers learned through difficult experience that they had, in fact, entered a unique type of service industry, one that combined the elements of real estate with those of hospitality and health care and one aimed at a demanding clientele whose needs changed and grew as time passed. For some organizations, this challenge was both unexpected and, in some cases, insurmountable. Many of the proprietary developers sought a way to get out of the industry through the sale of properties that were either still in the pre-opening stage or opened but not yet full.

Health-Care Providers

Another major category of entrants into the retirement housing industry is health-care providers. These include both those who focus primarily on long-term care and some whose traditional focus is acute care. In 1983, *Modern Health Care* (MHC), a news magazine covering all aspects of the health care industry, began to include data on lifecare in its annual multi-unit provider survey, reporting on both nursing home chains and multi-hospital systems that operated lifecare facilities. The data revealed that nine nursing home chains operated ten lifecare communities in 1981 and that fifteen multi-hospital systems operated thirty-seven such facilities. These data were embedded near the conclusion of an article entitled "Nursing Home Chains Scramble for More Private-Paying Patients," and received little editorial comment in the text. After 1983 the number of facilities represented by the multi-facility health-care providers grew rapidly, as did the number of players. By the 1986 survey, the retirement industry warranted its own article, and forty-four nursing home chains were operating 279 retirement communities and fifty-two hospital systems owned, leased, or managed 171 such communities.

The interest and subsequent involvement of health-care providers was generated by several factors. Responding to the overall attention that retirement housing received during the 1980s, many health-care providers recognized this housing as a natural extension of their existing levels of care. In some cases, providers owned land that was either vacant or underutilized, and the development of a retirement community enabled them to increase the value of a nonincome-producing asset. Another factor for hospitals was the desire to continue to capture the business of older consumers, who otherwise were discharged after relatively short in-patient stays due to the pressures of the prospective payment system for Medicare reimbursement. For many providers, the operation of a retirement facility furthered their existing mission to serve the elderly in a community while, at the same time, providing an opportunity to develop a revenue stream far less affected by changes in reimbursement formulae. However, the financial difficulties that many hospitals were experiencing by the late 1980s meant going back to basics for financial survival. Capital-intensive projects, such as retirement centers, were no longer possible for some health care providers.

Financing Approaches

The financing of CCRCs was, for many years, dominated by the use of tax-exempt bonds. This had substantial advantages, particularly for the nonprofit sponsors who dominated the industry. These bonds offered a long-term debt-financing source with favorable and fixed interest rates and allowed for the funding of the capitalized development expenses. On the other hand, tax-exempt bonds for retirement facilities typically involved substantial financing costs and high reserve requirements. For proprietary organizations, tax-exempt financing was more restrictive, adding to a project's capital costs.

As the industry, capital markets, and tax codes have changed, however, financing mechanisms have broadened as well. The passage of the 1986 Tax Reform Act had a significant impact on the means by which real estate could be financed. This change was also felt by the retirement housing industry. The general federal requirements associated with tax-exempt mortgage revenue bonds became more restrictive. An annual volume limitation was placed on each state of $75 per individual, or a maximum of $250 million per state. For proprietary developers, additional restrictions required that 20 percent or 40 percent of the residential units had to be occupied by tenants 50 percent or 60 percent below the area's median gross income. The impact of the 1986 Tax Reform Act was to virtually eliminate the use of tax-exempt bond financing for market-rate retirement housing communities owned by for-profit organizations.

The not-for-profit sponsor was still able to access the tax-exempt bond market after the passage of the 1986 Tax Reform Act. The true not-for-profit corporation, as defined by Section 501(c)(3) of the Internal Revenue Code, had no limit placed on its amount of indebtedness and was not subject to the state volume restrictions (Peregrine & McNulty, 1988). However, there were several limitations for a 501(c)(3) corporation using tax-exempt financing, including such things as a limitation of $150 million per exempt organization or related group of exempt organizations. This restriction had an impact only on large multi-facility owners or large health-care systems. Further, 95 percent of the net proceeds of the bonds were to be used to provide facilities that were owned by a governmental unit or by a code 501(c)(3) exempt organization. In addition, no more than 2 percent of the proceeds could be used for issuance costs with additional limitations on the debt service reserves, advanced refunding, and the interest that could be earned on the bond proceeds. Furthermore, unlike the early days of tax-exempt bond financing, today's markets require that a sponsor/owner bring significant equity to the capital structure of the deal. Depending on the strength of the project, it is not uncommon for 10 percent equity to be contributed.

Financing by commercial lenders, savings and loan associations, insurance companies, foreign companies and individual investors has broadened the base of capital available for retirement community development. However, for many of these potential sources of capital, interest in retirement housing has been modest at best. Conventional lenders, to the extent that they became involved at all, preferred short-term construction loans to long-term permanent financing. Where permanent loans were available, they typically were based on a 15- to 25-year amortization but then usually did not exceed a 10-year term and required a balloon payment.

The lending community has shown a general lack of familiarity with retirement communities. Thus, concerns regarding lending for single-use facilities and fears about the viability of retirement housing generated by publicity over failed facilities have greatly limited the amount of money available. Further, the tremendous downturn in conventional real estate markets, felt by many of the nation's savings and loan and commercial banking institutions in the late 1980s and into the 1990s, exacerbated by the highly restrictive posture of bank regulations, even further reduced the availability of conventional mortgages.

Generating equity for the development of CCRCs has been accomplished in several ways. For some nonprofit sponsors, a cash infusion has been made from a parent corporation, philanthropic fundraising, or land donation. For the proprietary organizations, equity has, to a limited extent, been generated through syndication. The changes brought about by the Tax Reform Act of 1986 have had a serious impact on syndication by imposing restrictions on the utilization of tax losses by investors. Some syndications based on economic value and generation of cash returns are still taking place; however, they involve relatively small projects.

Finally, financing is being facilitated for some projects through the use of resident entrance fees. However, the ability to use this approach has been limited by regulations imposed on continuing care communities in numerous states. Communities that are structured as condominiums or cooperatives are utilizing the residents' capital to finance facilities. Through residents' purchase of the condominiums or shares in the cooperative, project financing (restricted primarily to construction loans) can be facilitated.

Long-Term Care Insurance

During the 1980s, the emergence of long-term care insurance offered by commercial insurance companies had an impact on the retirement community industry. In 1983, approximately twenty commercial insurers offered policies with coverage including long-term care. By 1989, 118 companies had long-term care policies. However, fifteen companies dominated 75 percent of the market (O'Connor, 1990). By 1989–1990, the Health Insurance Association of America estimated that approximately 1.5 million people held long-term care policies.

Long-term care policies were originally sold on an individual basis. However, as some retirement housing providers began to re-evaluate the self-insurance inherent in the lifecare concept, the interest in incorporating commercial long-term care insurance increased. Several companies began to pioneer the use of group long-term care insurance in continuing care/lifecare communities. One of the first to experiment with this concept was Metropolitan Life at Williamsburg Landing, which opened in Williamsburg, Virginia, in 1985.

Several other companies, including Unum, Ætna, Travelers, and Cologne Reinsurance, have entered the group insurance business focusing on retirement communities. As of January 1990, these companies, along with Metropolitan, had sold 179 group-sponsored or quasi-group programs to CCRCs (Kunerth, 1990). The leading provider as of early 1990 was Unum Life Insurance Company. Its program has been endorsed by the American Association of Homes for the Aging, which has undoubtedly contributed to the number of programs that Unum has in place (estimated by Kunerth [1990] to be 118 group-sponsored programs as of January 1990). The CCRC-based insurance programs include both voluntary and mandatory participation provisions, depending on the insurer and the program. In some cases, the facility sets the eligibility criteria, whereas in others, the insurance company serves as the "gatekeeper."

Regulatory Change

The rapid growth in the CCRC industry, coupled with facility failures in the 1960s and 1970s, has resulted in increasing state regulatory legislation, nearly all of which is aimed at CCRCs that charge entrance fees. At the beginning of the 1980s, few states had statutes specifically regulating retirement communities. By 1990, however, thirty-four states had passed CCRC legislation (Table 1).

Table 1
States with CCRC Legislation

State	Responsible Agency
Arizona	Division of Insurance
Arkansas	Insurance Department
California	Department of Social Services
Colorado	Division of Insurance
Connecticut	Department of Aging
Delaware	Secretary of State
Florida	Department of Insurance
Idaho	Department of Finance
Illinois	Department of Public Health
Indiana	Department of Securities
Iowa	No agency designated
Kansas	Department of Insurance
Louisiana	Department of Commerce
Maine	Department of Human Services
Maryland	State Office on Aging
Massachusetts	No agency designated
Michigan	Insurance Bureau, Securities Division
Minnesota	No agency designated

Missouri	Division of Insurance, Dept. of Consumer Affairs
New Hampshire	Department of Insurance
New Jersey	Department of Community Affairs
New Mexico	State Agency on Aging
New York	Department of Health
North Carolina	Department of Insurance
Ohio	No agency designated
Oregon	Department of Aging
Pennsylvania	Department of Insurance
Rhode Island	No agency designated
South Carolina	Health and Environmental Control
Tennessee	Department of Insurance
Texas	Department of Insurance
Vermont	Department of Insurance
Virginia	Department of Insurance
Washington	Department of Health
Wisconsin	Department of Insurance

Source: American Association of Homes for the Aging

Existing statutes vary with regard to the specific aspects of the retirement community industry they regulate. However, as noted by Parrillo and Bertelsman (1987), the five major categories that are consistently included in regulatory statutes include:

1. Pre-opening requirements—The community may be required to have state certification and to disclose certain financial information to residents. Some states also impose a minimum presale requirement prior to granting a permit;
2. Contracts between the residents and community— Regulations may address the form and content of the resident contract, promotional materials, resident rights, resident councils, liens and terms of withdrawal from the community;
3. Health care requirements—The community may be required to obtain a Certificate of Need (CON) to provide home health care, assisted living or nursing home care and to meet life safety codes for medical

facilities. Other CON requirements may include required admission of a certain number of nonresident Medicaid patients, a restriction on external marketing of the nursing home or other state requirements for construction of a nursing home facility;

4. Financial requirements—Regulations may require escrow deposits before and after occupancy, reserve requirements, performance bonding, annual audits and govern fee adjustments and refunds;

5. Remedial procedures—The steps taken if fraud, deception or serious financial problems exist or if the community refuses to disclose required information.

Perhaps one of the most important events related to regulation has been the amending of New York State's insurance law in 1989 to allow development of CCRCs. Until that time, New York law prohibited the development or operation of CCRC or lifecare communities. Primarily due to nursing home scandals that surfaced in the 1960s, New York's legislature enacted laws that prohibited health-related facilities and nursing homes from requiring prepayment for basic residential health-care services exceeding three months. The wording of the law not only prevented any lifecare communities from being developed in New York, it also had the impact of slowing the development of other noninsured models of retirement housing. As a consequence, New York, with one of the nation's highest concentrations of older adults, was substantially undeveloped in relation to housing for the elderly.

Glossary of Terms

There has never been uniform agreement as to the precise meaning of the terminology used to describe the different types of retirement communities currently available. Organizations, such as the American Association of Homes for the Aging (AAHA) and the National Association of Senior Living Industries (NASLI), the two major trade associations serving this industry, have made efforts to clarify the definitions. However, uniformity in the definitions is made more difficult because of entrenched differences in the regulatory definitions developed by the various states.

One illustration of the difficulty in standardizing the definitions becomes clear when considering the different agencies charged by the states with regulating the industry. Although the issue is by no means a simple one, in general, states give regulatory power to those agencies responsible for specific elements of the housing industry believed to be in need of state regulation. As Table 1 indicates, many states give regulatory power to their Departments of Insurance while others select the Departments of Health as the appropriate regulatory agency. Other states have placed regulatory responsibility in the hands of their Departments of Social Services, Departments of Aging, Departments of Commerce, Departments of Human Services, Departments of Community Affairs, and, in one case, the Department of Health and Environmental Control.

Given the fragmented nature of the development of regulatory statutes governing the retirement housing industry, it is not likely that uniform definitions will be developed in the foreseeable future. However, there are some terms about which there is some agreement at the consumer and research level, even if not yet at the regulatory level. A glossary of these selected terms has been developed by both AAHA and NASLI and is included.

American Association of Homes for the Aging/ Ernst & Young Definitions[3]

Continuing Care Retirement Community

A continuing care retirement community (CCRC) is an organization that offers a full range of housing, residential services and health care in order to serve its older residents as their needs change over time. This continuum consists of housing where residents live independently and receive certain residential services such as meals, activities, housekeeping, and maintenance; support services for disabled residents who require assistance with activities of daily living; and health-care services for those who become temporarily ill or who require long-term care.

Based on the concept of self-insurance, every continuing care arrangement involves a contract between residents and the CCRC that, at a minimum, guarantees shelter and access to various health care services for the balance of the resident's lifetime. In return, the resident agrees to pay a lump-sum entrance fee (analogous to an insurance premium) upon moving to the community and monthly payments thereafter.

A wide variety of contracts are employed by continuing care retirement communities to specify the particular services and benefits afforded to residents in return for entrance and monthly fees. Indeed, for various reasons, it is relatively common for a CCRC to offer several different contract types or variations of one type of contract.

An Extensive Continuing Care Contract

Includes shelter, residential services, and amenities. It also offers unlimited long-term nursing care for little or no substantial increase in monthly payments, except normal operating cost and inflation adjustments.

A Modified Continuing Care Contract

Includes shelter, residential services, and amenities. However, a specified amount of long-term nursing home care is provided for little or no substantial increase in monthly payments, except normal operating cost and inflation adjustments. After the specified amount of nursing care is used, residents pay the full per diem rates for nursing care required, or, in some cases, a discounted per diem rate.

A Fee-for-Service Continuing Care Contract

Includes shelter, residential services, and amenities. Emergency and short-term nursing care are included in the contract, but access to long-term nursing care is guaranteed only at full per diem nursing care rate.

NASLI Definitions[4]

Continuing Care Retirement Community (CCRC)

A community established to provide a continuum of care to people of retirement age. This type of community offers housing, health care and various residential supportive services depending on a resident's level of independence.

CCRCs range from a single high-rise development to a large "village-like" campus of many different housing types. Admission is usually limited to seniors who are in good mental and physical health and of sound financial status. CCRCs offer a variety of recreational, health maintenance and social programs as well as conveniences such as barber/beauty services, banking services, a restaurant-quality dining facility, a library, a convenience store, 24-hour emergency call system, community transportation, pharmacy services, and meeting rooms.

At a minimum, CCRCs have independent living units and access to health-care facilities (they may be either assisted living units and/or nursing facilities); and offer a contract for more than one year that guarantees shelter and access to health-care services such as nursing home care.

CCRCs do not all provide a full or "lifetime" delivery of health care. The terms Continuing Care Retirement Community and Life Care Community were formerly used interchangeably but have become less synonymous in recent years because many CCRC operators have begun to limit their financial responsibilities for nursing care in their contract agreements.

Full service, modified, and fee-for-service are three types of CCRCs. The continuing care contract, or residency agreement, between the resident and the owner of the facility is the differentiating factor between the various types of CCRCs.

Full-Service CCRC or Lifecare Community

The contract provides for full or lifetime health care as needed at no substantial increase above the monthly payments made in the independent living unit. If the resident depletes his or her financial resources, the CCRC assumes the burden of payment. This type of agreement is generally considered a "lifecare" contract.

Modified-Service CCRC

The owner guarantees access to a nursing home bed and provides partial coverage of the cost of that care. The CCRC contract establishes a limited number of days of care covered fully in the monthly fees, after which time the resident pays either a reduced or full market per diem rate for nursing care.

Fee-for-Service CCRC

The contract provides for housing, residential services, and emergency and infirmary nursing care. This type of community is frequently built adjacent to or is affiliated with a local nursing facility. Access to long-term nursing care is guaranteed in the contract, but unlike other types of CCRCs, residents must pay full per diem rates.

Several states have instituted licensing laws for CCRCs. Generally the laws focus on Full-Service CCRCs or Modified-Service CCRCs and Exempt Fee-for-Service CCRCs from licensing if they do not guarantee access to a nursing bed.

Lifecare Community (LCC)

A Lifecare Community (LCC) or Life Care Retirement Community (LCRC) provides full lifetime health care as needed to residents at no substantial increase above the monthly payments they made living in an independent living unit in the LCC. If the resident depletes his or her financial resources, the LCC assumes the burden of payment. The type of agreement is generally considered a "lifecare" contract. Financial arrangements usually include a substantial entrance fee plus monthly charges. This health security is financed by either "risk pooling" where part of the front-end fees are "reserved against" the future liabilities assumed by the facility, or through a "periodic premium" which is simply an amount of money charged each month as part of the monthly fee to support the care which is to be delivered to each of the residents as needed. While "continuing care retirement community" has become in recent years the generic term used to define housing that provides a continuum of care, the phrase "life care community" predates it. In the 1930s when nonprofit organizations were providing care to their older members, they conceived the program of a continuum of care as a lifetime obligation.

NOTES

1. This chapter is the revised version of a chapter that appeared in: *Retirement Housing Markets: Project Planning and Feasibility Analysis*, edited by James F. Sherman, Copyright © 1991, John Wiley & Sons, Inc. Reprinted by permission of John Wiley & Sons, Inc.

2. Some older retirement communities such as Hollenbeck Home still incorporate an assignment of assets structure for their residents.

3. Used with permission from American Association of Homes for the Aging and Ernst & Young, Continuing Care Retirement Communities: An Industry in Action (Washington, DC: American Association of Homes for the Aging, 1989).

4. Used with permission from National Association of Senior Living Industries (NASLI), NASLI Dictionary of Terms of Senior Citizens and the Industries That Serve Them, Annapolis, MD.

REFERENCES

Kunerth, A.M. (1990). "Nationally Underwritten LTC Programs in CCRCs—How Good a Deal for Residents?" *Retirement Housing Report*, June.

Laventhol & Horwath. (1988). *Retirement Housing Industry, 1987*, Philadelphia: Author.

O'Connor, J. (1990). "LTC Insurance Booming, Despite Growing Pains," *McKnight's Long-Term Care News*, July.

Parrillo, J.W. and H.K. Bertelsman. (1987). "Regulations in the Retirement Housing Industry," in Laventhol & Horwath, *Retirement Housing Industry, 1987*, Philadelphia: Author.

Peregrine, M.W. and L.K. McNulty. (1988). "Tax Exempt Financing Faces an Uncertain Future," *Retirement Housing Report*, August.

Winklevoss, H. and A. Powell. (1984). *Continuing Care Retirement Communities: An Empirical, Financial and Legal Analysis*, Homewood, IL: Richard D. Irwin, Inc.

CHAPTER 8

Sub-institutional Facilities: Board-and-Care Homes[1]

Lorin A. Baumhover
R. Steven Daniels
John Gillum
Carolyn L. Clark-Daniels

The Elderly and Long-Term Care

The elderly population of the United States is growing rapidly. Between 1990 and 2035, the number of individuals over age sixty-five will increase from 12 percent to 20 percent of the total population, with the greatest growth among those age eighty-five and over. Each year 645,000 individuals reach age sixty-five (American Association of Retired Persons [AARP], 1991).

Most elderly individuals enjoy good health and are able to live independently. However, some require a degree of long-term personal and/or medical care due to chronic conditions or other physical or mental impairments. Long-term care refers to any continuing provision of housing, personal, and/or economic assistance to individuals with functional deficits. The need for long-term care increases with age. While only 2 percent of the elderly population between the ages of sixty-five and seventy-seven are in need of long-term care, approximately 24 percent of those over eighty-five need such care. Overall, about 5 percent of the elderly population resides in long-term care facilities at any given time. Three percent of these individuals live in nursing homes and 2 percent occupy other types of facilities (Atchley, 1991).

Residents of long-term care facilities are most likely to be in their mid- to late-eighties, widowed, and suffering from one or more physical limitations. Many of these individuals have no income other than Social Security (SS) or Supplemental Security Income (SSI) (Down & Schnurr, 1991). Although the greatest need for long-term care is among the elderly, other populations, including the developmentally disabled of all ages and those suffering with debilitating diseases, also require such care (Liebig & Lammers, 1990).

The types of living arrangements currently available may be thought of as falling along a continuum of support levels. Single-family houses provide the lowest level of support. Retirement villages, high-rise apartment buildings, and mobile-home parks for retirees afford moderate levels of support because the householder is freed from some maintenance responsibilities and neighbors are close at hand. Long-term care facilities represent the highest level of support (Streib, Folts, & Hilker, 1984).

Too often, long-term care facilities are narrowly defined as nursing homes. This limited view ignores an array of formal, informal, institutional, and noninstitutional care settings (Kemp, 1990) including shared living homes, board-and-care homes (BCHs), lifecare communities, and private residences in which family members care for a dependent relative. So too, providers of long-term care are not limited to health care professionals and paraprofessionals but include other practitioners and family members as well (Liebig & Lammers, 1990).

The responsibility for the care of many dependent elderly has slowly shifted from the family to public and private facilities. During the nineteenth and early twentieth centuries, dependent elderly individuals were usually cared for by their families (Brubaker, 1987). Today, many families lack the resources, time, or expertise required to provide adequate assistance to elderly relatives.

Furthermore, changes in social policies and government funding have served to further increase the demand for long-term care facilities. *Wyatt* v *Stickney* (1971a, 1971b, 1972a, 1972b) and its associated case law (*Wyatt* v *Aderholt*, 1974) imposed minimum standards of care on mental institutions. These standards, although improving conditions in care facilities, escalated the cost of institutionalization. Most states addressed the financial burden by releasing mental patients and developmentally impaired individuals into the community, often referring them to alternative types of long-term care facilities. State and federal government agencies, such as departments of human resources or the Veterans' Administration, also have referred or discharged individuals to long-term care facilities.

Nursing homes have been unable to keep up with the increased demand. Government restrictions regarding the addition of new Medicaid reimbursable nursing home beds have produced, in part, a general shortage of beds in nursing homes. As a result, a dramatic increase has occurred in the number of alternative types of long-term care facilities, including BCHs, such that the number of BCHs is increasing more rapidly than the number of nursing homes (U.S. Bureau of the Census, 1987; U.S. Bureau of the Census, 1991).

An Overview of Board and Care

The board-and-care home of today is an outgrowth of the old-style boarding home or rooming house where individuals rented spare rooms in their homes to supplement their incomes and/or gain companionship. These facilities typically provided food and lodging to tenants who included ". . . traveling salesmen, transient workers, and out of town guests" (Down & Schnurr, 1991, p. 21). Although modern BCHs provide more services than old-style boarding homes or rooming houses, they maintain the same "homey" atmosphere. Many people find BCHs ". . . more satisfying, more natural, and less costly" (Baggett, 1989, p. 9) than institutional care facilities.

Board-and-care homes may be described as places where residents receive lodging, meals, some help with the activities of daily living ([ADLs] such as bathing and grooming) and assistance with instrumental activities of daily living ([IADLs] such as transportation). BCH operators can also provide residents with social support and opportunities for community contact. Providing transportation to church or recreation centers gives elderly individuals with limited mobility a sense of continuing involvement and allows them to maintain friendships (Down & Schnurr, 1991). These homes offer housekeeping and personal help to those who are unable to live alone but who do not need, or cannot afford the level of care provided by nursing homes (Down & Schnurr, 1991).

Adult foster homes, group homes, homes for the aged, rest homes, personal care homes and domiciliaries are all classified as types of board-and-care homes (Down & Schnurr, 1991). Each of these names implies slightly different facility characteristics. For example, domiciliaries are usually larger and somewhat more institutional in nature than foster homes, which are typically small, family-type facilities (Baggett, 1989). Because of the range of services provided and the different ways in which the facilities can be classified, considerable confusion exists over the various types of these noninstitutional long-term care facilities for the elderly (Stone & Newcomer, 1985; see also Benjamin & Newcomer, 1986; Dobkin, 1989; Mor, Gutkin, & Sherwood, 1985).

Most BCHs are owned by individuals, primarily by older widows (Baggett, 1989), but churches and civic organizations sponsor some of the larger facilities (Down & Schnurr, 1991). All BCHs operate for profit; however, most of the smaller facilities experience only marginal financial success. One of the main problems facing the smaller homes is the lack of business training and relative inexperience of the operators; many experience difficulty with bookkeeping and government records. Larger homes tend to have trained administrators with business experience (Baggett, 1989).

Beyond reminding residents to take their medication, BCH staff are generally not permitted to provide medical care. However, because BCHs are often looked upon as low-cost alternatives to nursing homes, some level of medical care is often available for the residents. Existing research suggests that the residents often require a larger amount of such care than should typically be provided in a BCH. Unfortunately, many BCH operators lack training for administering even minimal medical assistance, resulting in potentially harmful situations.

Although state and federal agencies utilize BCH services by referring individuals to or placing them in these facilities, the various levels of government make no direct reimbursement to the homes. BCHs are not eligible to receive Medicare, Medicaid, or other forms of direct government compensation. However, because most residents rely on SS and SSI to meet their expenses, BCHs do receive indirect government support (Baggett, 1989).

Federal and State Regulation of Board-and-Care Homes

A few federal statutes and incentives address BCH regulation. The most directly relevant statute, the Keys Amendment to the Social Security Act (Section 1616[e]), provides that each state will establish or designate an agency to be responsible for the creation, maintenance, and enforcement of standards for any "institutions, foster homes, or group living arrangements" in which a "significant" number of SSI recipients reside (Solomon, 1989). These standards cover such areas as admission policies, safety, sanitation, and protection of civil liberties. Each year, states must certify that they are in compliance with the Act. Failure to comply is punishable by a reduction in benefits to the residents of housing units that fail state standards. Unfortunately, the amendment provides no mechanism for the identification of group living arrangements. States are required to certify the quality of care received in BCHs, but have no federal or state guidelines to aid in their location.

Lack of information at the state level about BCHs makes it difficult for organized social service networks to make decisions regarding placement of dependent individuals. Some states require licensing and inspection of BCHs meeting certain size or organizational criteria (e.g. over six residents, or operating as a domiciliary) and thereby have at least partial information about the number and location of facilities. Unfortunately, no other formal means of identifying or monitoring BCHs exists.

Some controversy continues over the desirability of additional legislation for BCHs. The lack of regulation allows some unlicensed facilities to operate in violation of health, fire, or building codes (Streib, Folts, & Hilker, 1984). However, government regulation may result in increased operating costs that would not allow small or medium size homes to operate profitably (Down & Schnurr, 1991).

Previous Research on Board-and-Care Facilities

Most of the research on noninstitutional long-term care is anecdotal and incomplete. Some nonsystematic investigations have been conducted; however, most of this research has focused on conditions in individual BCHs rather than more general applications (see, e.g., U.S. House Select Committee on Aging, 1989). Therefore, what is most needed by current policymakers is basic, descriptive information.

The General Accounting Office (GAO) conducted the first organized study aimed at identifying and monitoring BCHs (USGAO, 1979). Because the vast majority of BCH residents were old, blind, or disabled, GAO speculated that a significant proportion of these residents received SSI. Relying on State Data Exchange (SDX) tapes from the Social Security Administration, GAO was able to produce lists of addresses at which three or more unrelated SSI recipients resided. Eliminating apartment buildings, trailer parks, institutions, hotels, and residences housing recipients with the same surname, GAO found that approximately 50 percent of a random sample of addresses in Camden County, New Jersey, and Baltimore, Maryland, met the criteria for BCHs.

GAO interviewers found that the mentally ill and mentally retarded (MI/MR) constituted 90 percent of residents who received SSI disability and over 50 percent of all residents. Most were aware that their SSI checks came from the Social Security Administration, but over half could not recall the amount. Sixty-eight percent of the respondents endorsed their checks over to the owner of the BCH but a majority did not receive the required $30 per month spending money from the facility managers. Three-quarters of the residents were on prescribed medication and over half needed assistance in actually taking it.

The facilities themselves were generally in poor condition. Over half of the BCH operators had no background in health-related professions and only one-third had received some kind of specialized training. Nevertheless, virtually all operators provided twenty-four-hour supervision of residents and some form of medical management. In short, most of the facilities studied provided types of care for which the operators had received no training and for which the facilities were inadequate.

The U.S. Department of Health and Human Services, Office of the Inspector General conducted the second major review of the BCH industry (USDHHS-OIG, 1982). Unlike the GAO study, the USDHHS-OIG study focused on federal and state responses to developments in the industry. The OIG surveyed state agencies and examined ongoing federal research, focusing on policy recommendations meant to increase federal leverage in an area where federal incentives were few. Although several of the federal research projects produced results regarding conditions in licensed and unlicensed BCHs, few of the findings were reported in the USDHHS-OIG report.

Mor, Sherwood, and Gutkin (1986) examined data from an Administration on Aging-financed study of licensed residential care homes in Michigan, Illinois, Massachusetts, Georgia, and Florida. These facilities ranged in size from small foster homes to large institutions. Most of the residents of these homes were over 70, female, and widowed. Over half received SSI. Although most residents were not physically ill, a majority required help with personal care. Over a third exhibited some evidence of mental dysfunction. Despite these characteristics, over 70 percent were happy with their current living situation. External evaluations revealed that over 85 percent of the residents resided in homes that provided care at least marginally commensurate with their physical and mental status. As expected, the level of satisfaction varied with the quality of the match.

The Denver Research Institute (DRI) conducted the most extensive federal project (Dittmar, 1989) between 1979 and 1983 in seven states (California, Colorado, Florida, Massachusetts, Minnesota, Texas, and Washington). DRI drew a purposive sample of homes from major urban areas. Most of the homes were originally private residences of considerable age (forty-three years on the average) that had been used as BCHs for approximately fifteen years. A majority of the facilities were large and somewhat crowded. Most provided fire alarms and smoke detectors, but not sprinkler systems. Individuals or couples owned a majority of the homes. The typical owner was a white, married female with less than a college education who had worked for over twelve years in the residential care industry. The typical home charged $442 per client per month and the federal government subsidized approximately one-third of this amount, primarily through SSI and Social Security payments to residents. Only about 21 percent of the residents used the owner/operator as their SSI payee. The average client was a sixty-seven-year-old white female who had lived at the home for approximately forty months. Roughly 44 percent of the residents suffered some mental impairment. Most of the residents were in good health, although about one-third suffered physical impairments severe enough to restrict their social functioning.

The American Association of Retired Persons Consumer Affairs Program Department ([AARP-CAPD], Dobkin, 1989) conducted the most recent systematic survey of BCHs in Maryland. The AARP-CAPD study investigated the impact of the administrative structure of Maryland's boarding home regulations on BCH effectiveness. The CAPD staff interviewed small purposive samples of BCH operators, residents, and regulators. In general, BCH operators expressed uneasiness about over-regulation and low compensation. State regulators voiced frustration with the continuing referral of clients from social service agencies to unlicensed homes, the poor quality of many residences, the poor training of many operators, the lack of cooperation among responsible state agencies, and their own inability to identify unlicensed homes. The AARP-CAPD staff concluded that BCH programs needed to be centralized under a single state agency for greater visibility and accountability. Furthermore, AARP-CAPD found that the licensing and certification process needed simplification. They also noted that the amount of reimbursement for care should be increased and most operators needed better training.

The results of these surveys, and other research, suggest that the current system is in need of change; however, attempts to create new policies and directives are hampered by lack of information. Rapidly increasing costs, administrative and financial fragmentation, and lack of coordinated case management are only a few of the difficulties facing the BCH industry (Morris & Youket, 1981; see also, Brubaker, 1987; Callahan, 1981; Dilworth-Anderson, 1987; Montgomery & Hatch, 1987; Quadagno, Sims, Squier, & Walker, 1987; U.S. House Select Committee on Aging, 1989). To date, studies of the BCH industry have primarily used purposive samples of licensed facilities. With the exception of the GAO pilot study, none of the national or state surveys has attempted to randomly assess conditions in both licensed and unlicensed facilities.

Although BCHs represent an increasingly important component in the long-term care system, very little information is available on the number of facilities, the characteristics of operators and residents, services provided, or even the quality of such living arrangements. Still less in known about referral patterns, health status of residents, and the level of care provided by operators (Baggett, 1989; Down & Schnurr, 1991). One effort to address this need for information was a study conducted in the State of Alabama.

A Study of Board-and-Care in Alabama

The purpose of the study described here was to examine selected characteristics of BCHs in the state of Alabama. Included in this study were both licensed and unlicensed homes. The specific objectives of the research included: a determination of the characteristics of BCH residents; BCH operators; BCH facilities; and examination of the levels of health care provided by operating BCHs. Further, this research addressed the issue of identifying a referral network among BCHs.

The researchers selected three cities as representative of Alabama Metropolitan Statistical Areas (MSAs). The cities chosen were Huntsville (Madison County), Tuscaloosa (Tuscaloosa County), and Birmingham (Jefferson County). To identify both licensed and unlicensed BCHs in Madison and Tuscaloosa Counties, the study employed the procedure developed by the GAO (1979). The researchers compiled a list of addresses from computer listings for each city where three or more individuals received Supplemental Security Income (SSI) payments. Health and social service agency personnel supplemented the list. After eliminating known apartment buildings, trailer parks, hotels, mental institutions, domiciliaries, and residences housing individuals with the same surname, the staff verified the BCH status of the remaining homes. Identification of facilities in Jefferson County was considerably less complicated since Jefferson is the only county in Alabama that independently licenses and inspects BCHs.

The research team developed, pretested and employed three survey instruments in this study. The first instrument elicited information about characteristics and qualifications of BCH operators. The second instrument gathered information about facility residents. A third instrument assessed the physical structure of the BCHs.

A three- to four-person team visited each site with the permission of the operator. Visits occurred between 9:00 A.M. and 4:00 P.M. and lasted from one to two hours. The visits incorporated owner/operator interviews, environmental audits, and assessments of a sample of up to eight residents in each home. All interviews took place on site.

The interview with the owner/operator took approximately thirty minutes to one hour to complete. The fifty-item instrument gathered information about sociodemographic characteristics; qualifications of the operators; and additional information concerning facility policies and rules, services provided, licensure, and knowledge of a referral network. The DRI instruments provided most of the questions used in the current study (Dittmar, 1989).

The interview with residents employed a seventy-four-item questionnaire. The instrument included questions about sociodemographic characteristics; cognitive capacity; physical condition; social activity; and subjective and objective measures of health. The questions for this instrument originated in several sources including the *Statewide Survey of Alabama's Elderly* (ACOA & UABCA, 1988); *The Short, Portable Mental Status Questionnaire* ([SPMSQ] Pfeiffer, 1975); *Board and Care for Elderly and Mentally Disabled Populations* (Dittmar, 1989); and the *OARS Multidimensional Functional Assessment Questionnaire* ([OMFAQ], Duke University Center for the Study of Aging and Human Development, 1975). The SPMSQ assessed the cognitive functioning of the selected residents. Testing by Pfeiffer (1975) has calibrated error ranges for different ethnic backgrounds and educational levels. Respondents who scored in the "severe intellectual impairment" category received no further questions. If residents could not provide complete information about themselves, the facility operator furnished the remaining information.

The survey instrument also assessed the degree of social isolation by measuring the extent to which activities were restricted to the BCH. The physical ADL scale from the OMFAQ appraised the degree of physical functioning. This scale includes questions on eating, dressing, grooming, walking, transfer from bed, bathing, and continence. Research evaluations reported by Mangen and Peterson (1984) indicate a test-retest reliability of .92 for the physical ADL. In addition to the OMFAQ scale, the survey included questions from the Alabama survey (ACOA & UABCA, 1988) on the use of physical aids and on the quality of resident's vision, hearing, and dentition.

A checklist derived from the Jefferson County Boarding home inspection report assessed the quality of the home. The questionnaire covered the structural integrity of the dwelling; the presence of plumbing, a working kitchen with necessary equipment, and electricity; the existence of fire equipment including fire alarms, fire extinguishers, smoke detectors, and sprinkler systems; and the presence of facilities to ease the movement of elderly residents in, out of, and around the residence. These latter facilities included properly spaced stairs, railings, and well-lighted corridors. The survey also addressed the provision of necessities such as linen, bedding, toiletries, towels, and laundry facilities. One of the most significant factors for determining the quality of the facility was its level of cleanliness. The environmental audit required researchers to evaluate the overall cleanliness of the kitchens and bathrooms, the condition of bedding, and the smell of the facility.

Descriptive statistics, primarily frequency distributions, served to summarize the data. Results of these analyses appear in Tables 1 through 11.

Results

Residents

Individuals selected for inclusion in the study were at least sixty years of age. As shown in Table 1, subjects ranged in age from sixty to nintey-five with a mean age of seventy-two. Reflecting life expectancy and gender differentials, two-thirds (64 percent) of those surveyed were female and 43 percent were African American, a surprisingly large number because only about 21 percent of the state's sixty-five-plus population is African American. A slight majority (55 percent) had less than a high school education and the vast majority (92 percent) were unmarried. Half of these were widowed and one-fourth were either divorced or separated. Only one individual had a job outside of the home.

One of the questions under investigation in this study concerned the existence of a referral network between board-and-care operators and other social-service and health-care providers. Table 2 shows information about length of stay, prior residence, and referral source. Even though the majority of the residents was fairly recently arrived (over half reported living there less than two years), the mean length of residence was 4.3 years with 14 percent having lived in the same house for over ten years. Regarding prior residence, information from interviews revealed a common pattern for the 38 percent who moved from independent living arrangements to the BCH. Faced with increasingly more difficult health problems, many found that they needed additional help that was unavailable to them on a day-to-day basis. In addition to this group, another one-third previously lived in institutional settings such as group homes, mental hospitals, or acute care hospitals. Among this group, most resided in homes for the mentally impaired.

Table 1
Characteristics of Residents

Characteristics	Number	Percent
Age		
60–65	28	31.5
66–75	27	30.3
76–95	34	38.2
Sex		
Male	44	36.1
Female	78	63.9
Race		
White	68	56.7
African American	52	43.3
Education		
<12	57	54.8
12	34	32.6
>12	13	12.6
Marital Status		
Never Married	14	16.3
Married	7	8.1
Widowed	43	50.0
Sep./Divorced	22	25.6

Source: Lorin A. Baumhover et al. 1991. Subterranean Networks of Board and Care for the Elderly: A Survey of Boarding Home Operators and Residents.

Table 2
Length of Stay, Prior Residence,
Mobility, and Referral Source

Characteristic	Number	Percent
Length of Stay		
1 year or less	14	31.8
2–3 years	15	34.1
4–20 years	15	34.1
Prior Residence		
Own Home	33	37.5
Institution	42	32.8
With Relatives	14	15.9
Other	12	13.8
Distance Moved		
In Neighborhood	9	10.6
In Town	44	51.8
Out of Town	32	37.6
Referral Source		
Friend	5	6.1
Relative	30	36.6
BCH Operator	11	13.4
Hospital	12	14.6
Social Worker	9	11.0
Other	15	18.3

Source: Lorin A. Baumhover et al. 1991. Subterranean Networks of Board and Care for the Elderly: A Survey of Boarding Home Operators and Residents.

Almost two-thirds (62 percent) had previously lived in the same town, with the remaining one-third living in the same state but in another town. Only one person had lived out-of-state immediately prior to moving into the board-and-care home. While a relative was the single most important referral source (37 percent), health and social service professionals played major roles in referring these elderly residents to boarding homes. Forty percent of all referrals came from BCH operators, social workers and hospital workers. The number would have been even greater if additional information were available about the composition of the "other" referral category. Despite this, professionals accounted for one-fourth of direct referrals.

Table 3
Residents' Income and Expenses

Variable	Number	Percent
Income Sources		
SSI	50	45.0
SS	35	31.5
Family	6	5.5
Other	20	18.0
Income Amount (Monthly)		
SSI < 200	10	20.0
201–400	1	22.0
> 400	7	14.0
SS < 300	7	14.0
301–400	7	14.0
> 400	8	16.0
Monthly Charge		
< 300	12	30.0
300–370	13	32.5
371–930	15	37.5

Source: Lorin A. Baumhover et al. 1991. Subterranean Networks of Board and Care for the Elderly: A Survey of Boarding Home Operators and Residents.

In general, these residents had both modest incomes and modest expenses. Table 3 illustrates that almost half received SSI payments and about one-third received Social Security checks. Family members contributed little to the upkeep of these BCH residents. Some (8 percent) of the residents worked in the home doing domestic "chores" to supplement their incomes but none earned over $45 per month. Seventy percent received less than $400 monthly from either SSI or Social Security. The mean monthly SSI check for the residents was $318, while for Social Security, monthly checks ranged from $42 to $700 with a mean amount of $396. For the few (6 percent) receiving income from their families, the amount averaged about $51 monthly. Only 7 percent received any other kind of pension: three individuals reported VA benefits and four were unsure where their income came from. Clearly, the majority (77 percent) relied on federal dollars for their basic support.

The low incomes of these residents were matched by low rates for room and board. Many home operators reported that they accepted the residents' SS or SSI check as payment-in-full for all board-and-care charges. Some residents paid more than others because those residents had greater income. Monthly charges ranged from $100 to $930 with a mean cost of $371 per month.

Table 4
Physical and Instrumental ADLs
Completed by Residents and Others

Variable	Number	Percent
ADLs*		
Eating	77	96.2
Dressing	72	90.0
Grooming	70	87.5
Walking	71	88.8
Transferring	78	97.5
Bathing	62	77.5
Toileting	79	98.7
IADLs+		
BCH Operators	47	62.0
Relative	24	31.5
Others	5	6.5

* completed by self
+ primary helper

Source: Lorin A. Baumhover et al. 1991. Subterranean Networks of Board and Care for the Elderly: A Survey of Boarding Home Operators and Residents.

In looking at the daily activities of these residents, passive activities such as watching television (90 percent) or listening to the radio (64 percent) occupied much of their time. While almost two-thirds reported going for walks (64 percent) and talking on the telephone (61 percent), most spent their time involved in tasks that required little or no social interaction.

Table 4 includes information on both physical and instrumental ADLs. Local licensure requirements in some areas mandated that all BCH residents demonstrate their capability to extricate themselves from the facility in case of a fire. In addition, local requirements assume that these individuals are not sufficiently disabled or disoriented to warrant nursing home placement. Approximately 90 percent reported they were capable of carrying out necessary ADLs with the possible exception of bathing or showering.

A closer examination of IADLs revealed a different picture. In examining the residents' ability to handle personal affairs, such as managing money and making medical appointments, about three-fourths (74 percent) reported they needed help in handling these kinds of personal tasks. When asked who was their primary helper, or the single individual they would turn to first for assistance, BCH operators were identified most often. Residents reported that they relied on the BCH operators two to one over family members or other helpers. Whereas either personal attachment or proximity could explain this reliance on BCH operators and staff, an alternative explanation is the absence of living family members or other potential caregivers. A majority of BCH residents (53 percent) also ranked operators as the second choice of helper over family (33 percent) and others (14 percent).

Table 5 reports the residents' subjective evaluation of their personal health. A slight majority (51 percent) of residents reported their health as only fair or poor. When comparing their current health to last year, about one-third felt better, one-third felt the same, and one-third felt worse. Nevertheless, only 27 percent reported that their health interfered with their normal activities and an overwhelming majority (82 percent) considered their health better than or the same as others their age.

Table 5
Residents' Assessment of Personal Health

Personal Health	Number	Percent
Overall Health		
Excellent	6	7.5
Good	33	41.3
Fair	23	28.8
Poor	18	22.4
Compared to Last Year		
Better	29	35.8
Same	27	33.3
Worse	25	30.9
Interferes w/Normal Activities		
Yes	22	26.8
No	60	73.2
Compared to Others		
Better	35	47.9
Same	25	34.2
Worse	15	17.9

Source: Lorin A. Baumhover et al. 1991. Subterranean Networks of Board and Care for the Elderly: A Survey of Boarding Home Operators and Residents.

Most (82 percent) residents reported they were getting the health care they felt they needed. When asked where they usually went for health care, as Table 6 reports, about three-fourths (73 percent) of respondents chose a private physician or clinic over an emergency facility, hospital, or public health department. Residents reported a different pattern of reliance, however, when comparisons were made between how they usually got to health care and how they got to health care when they had a medical problem or emergency. Although the role of family members changed little, BCH operators assumed a much greater responsibility for transporting these residents in case of need. While subjects reported operators provided only about 10 percent of the usual transportation to health care, operators were the most likely (66 percent) to be called upon when a medical problem developed.

Table 6
How Residents Accessed Health-Care System

Variable	Number	Percent
Usual Health Care Provider		
Private Physician	41	37.6
Clinic	39	35.8
Emergency Facility/Hospital	23	21.1
Health Dept.	6	5.5
Usual Transport		
Relative	23	33.3
BCH Operator	7	10.1
Public Transportation	39	56.6
Emergency Transport		
Relative	21	27.6
BCH Operator	50	66.0
Public Transportation	5	6.4

Source: Lorin A. Baumhover et al. 1991. Subterranean Networks of Board and Care for the Elderly: A Survey of Boarding Home Operators and Residents.

Residents were asked a series of questions about their use, source, and knowledge of medications they used on a daily basis. These results appear in Table 7. Ninety percent took at least one prescription drug daily, 60 percent took two or more and about one-third (30 percent) took more than three medications per day. In addition, some 40 percent took at least one other nonprescription medicine on a daily basis. By combining prescription and nonprescription drugs, BCH residents consumed, on average, at least three separate medications daily.

Interviewers attempted to determine the extent of multiple drug-taking behavior by ascertaining if medications came from more than one physician or from more than one pharmacy. About 20 percent of the respondents didn't know if their medications came from multiple sources, one-fourth (28 percent) reported more than one physician prescribed drugs for them and one-third (36 percent) reported receiving drugs from more than one pharmacy.

Table 7
Number, Type, and Source of Medications
Used by Residents

Medication	Number	Percent
Daily Prescription Drugs		
None	5	9.8
1	16	31.4
2	14	27.5
3–4	8	15.7
5–6	8	15.7
Daily Nonprescription Drugs		
None	23	59.0
1	11	28.2
2–3	5	12.9
Purpose of Drug		
Understands	31	50.9
Some understanding	10	16.3
No understanding	20	32.8
Medication Schedule		
Completely understands	28	49.1
Somewhat understands	8	14.1
Cannot explain schedule	21	36.8

Source: Lorin A. Baumhover et al. 1991. Subterranean Networks of Board and Care for the Elderly: A Survey of Boarding Home Operators and Residents.

Possibly more serious, however, was the very limited understanding that these residents had concerning the purposes of their medications and of their specific medication schedules. Although over half the residents were able to explain the therapeutic justifications for all their medications, 16 percent had only limited understanding and about one-third were not at all able to explain why their medications had been prescribed.

Another very important issue involves the care and accuracy with which older BCH residents take their prescribed medications. When interviewers questioned residents about opening medicine containers, reading instructions, or getting their medicines, very few of the residents reported they had any problems in managing their medications. Observations by the research team, however, revealed that most BCH operators stored the medications, reminded residents to take specific drugs and, at times, administered the medications themselves. Thus, one reason why older residents reported no difficulties in managing their medications was that BCH operators provided these services for them.

BCH Operators

BCH operators interviewed in this study were predominantly African American, married, and female. The operators were typically fifty-five years of age with at least a high school education (see Table 8). Almost 95 percent rated their health as good or excellent. Although over half reported experiencing some degree of job-related stress, most also reported that they had relief staff (80 percent) and some time off (84 percent). About one-fifth of the operators reported their facility was not staffed twenty-four hours a day.

Unlike those in previous studies, 80 percent of the operators in this study reported having some specialized training in boarding home operation, although no evidence existed on the specific nature of such training. These operators had been in the business for a considerable time with an average of nine years experience in BCH management.

Table 8
Operator Characteristics

Characteristic	Number	Percent
Race		
White	16	41.0
African American	23	59.0
Gender		
Male	2	5.1
Female	37	90.2
Marital status		
Married	30	76.9
Divorced	6	15.4
Widowed	3	7.7
Education		
<12	8	21.0
12	14	36.8
>12	16	42.2
Health—self rating		
Excellent	13	33.3
Good	24	61.5
Poor	2	5.1
Terrible	0	0.0
Get time off	32	84.2
Have relief staff	31	79.5
Received specific training	30	81.1
Under considerable stress	20	51.3
Own multiple BCHs	14	36.8
Manage multiple BCHs	12	33.3

Source: Lorin A. Baumhover et al. 1991. Subterranean Networks of Board and Care for the Elderly: A Survey of Boarding Home Operators and Residents.

Operators enjoyed considerable autonomy in determining the types of residents accepted, rules of conduct, services provided, and degree of resident autonomy. Most homes had prohibitions against residents who were potentially dangerous to themselves or others and those with substance abuse problems (see Table 9). In addition, over 60 percent of the homes would not accept individuals with severe physical impairments. Because residents must be able to exit the building without assistance in the event of an emergency, operators were apparently reluctant to accept responsibility for residents who were unable to function independently.

Table 9
Types of Residents Accepted in the Facility

Characteristics	Number	Percent
Elderly	39	100.0
Prescription medication	39	100.0
Previously institutionalized	32	82.1
History of mental illness	31	79.0
Confused	28	73.0
Mentally impaired	27	69.2
Mentally ill	17	47.2
Severe physical disabilities	15	38.5
Combative	12	30.0
Hostile	11	28.2
Alcoholic	10	25.6
Drug abuser	7	17.9

Source: Lorin A. Baumhover et al. 1991. Subterranean Networks of Board and Care for the Elderly: A Survey of Boarding Home Operators and Residents.

Over 60 percent of the homes posted rules governing conduct. While most (75 percent) allowed residents to smoke and had designated smoking areas (81 percent), few (14 percent) allowed alcohol consumption on the premises. Residents could receive visitors in 71 percent of the homes, but regulations usually governed the visiting hours in those homes. Half of the homes also restricted the hours during which residents could leave the premises. This is not too surprising since most of the BCHs in the study were located in areas identified as high-crime areas.

Table 10
Services Provided to Residents

Service	Number	Percent
Make medical appointments	29	74.4
Remind to take medications	28	73.7
Keep prescription medicines	22	64.7
Keep OTC medicines	19	54.4
Manage money	19	52.8
Help take medicine	18	47.4
Help make phone calls	14	36.8
Help bathe	13	35.1
Help write letters	12	30.8
Help dress	9	24.3
Help with toileting	8	20.5
Help shave	7	20.0
Help eat	3	8.1
Help brush teeth	3	8.1

Source: Lorin A. Baumhover et al. 1991. Subterranean Networks of Board and Care for the Elderly: A Survey of Boarding Home Operators and Residents.

Services provided by BCHs were generally appropriate to noninstitutional care facilities (see Table 10). Most provided residents some assistance with ADLs. In-house recreational activities were available in most of the homes, and residents in over half of the facilities participated in outside activities. Most operators provided transportation for shopping, recreational activities, church, and medical or dental appointments.

Over half of the operators managed residents' money, and 51 percent were designated as the Social Security payee for at least one resident. The vast majority (85 percent) of those who managed residents' money kept records of expenditures.

Nearly all of the homes kept some type of resident records. These records generally consisted of the resident's name, the name of the resident's nearest relative, the name of the resident's physician and a list of the resident's current medications. In some cases the records contained the name of the resident's dentist and social worker.

In providing meals, 74 percent of the operators said they consulted a dietician and nearly two-thirds reported cooking for special diets. Although one-third of the homes reported having cooks on staff, the operator or a home employee other than a cook were usually responsible for meal preparation.

Nearly three-quarters of the operators assisted residents in scheduling medical appointments. Nearly 60 percent of the home operators reported that they kept residents' over-the-counter and prescription medicines in kitchen cabinets, indicating that residents did not control their own medications. While almost three-quarters of the operators reminded residents to take medicines, nearly half also administered medications. Since operators generally lacked medical training, such assistance is inappropriate. These findings support previous studies indicating that BCH operators sometimes provided services in excess of what is allowable in the regulatory statutes.

A surprisingly high degree of support existed among operators for BCH regulation (68 percent in favor) and licensure by the state (76 percent in favor). In view of the varying numbers and types of permits, certificates and inspections required to operate a BCH, support for regulation may indicate a preference for uniform standards and reporting procedures.

BCH Structures

A majority of the facilities operated in older buildings (the mean age of the homes was forty-five years) originally constructed as private residences and not as boarding homes. The structures were of moderate size with an average maximum occupancy of ten boarders. These facilities had been boarding homes for an average of ten years. Many of the buildings had not been modified for current usage and were therefore inappropriate or unsafe for the current inhabitants (see Table 11).

Although the majority of homes surveyed had only one level, 41 percent had two or more floors and several also had basements where residents lived. Basic safety features, such as handrails at staircases were absent in 20 percent of the multilevel structures. Access to the front door was difficult in 13 percent of the facilities either because of exterior steps without handrails or the absence of a ramp. Lack of these features could retard or prevent physically impaired individuals from exiting the building during an emergency.

Table 11
Safety Features in Homes

Feature	Number	Percent
Fire extinguishers	37	92.5
Smoke detectors	35	85.4
Outside stairs have rail	32	80.0
Windows unblocked	29	70.7
Outward opening exits	27	67.5
Exits clearly marked	27	67.5
Emergency plan posted	20	52.6
Inside stairs have rail	20	80.0
Exterior ramps	12	29.3
Fire sprinkler system	5	12.8

Source: Lorin A. Baumhover et al. 1991. Subterranean Networks of Board and Care for the Elderly: A Survey of Boarding Home Operators and Residents.

Fire safety equipment, including extinguishers, smoke detectors, and sprinklers, was not present in all facilities. Fire and safety hazards observed in the homes included rooms with blocked windows (30 percent), unmarked exits (32 percent), and inward opening doors at main exits (32 percent). In nearly half of the homes, the operators had not posted emergency plans. Four of the homes had unvented space heaters in residents' bedrooms and common rooms. These situations highlighted a failure to ensure the safety of the boarders.

Although nearly three-quarters of the buildings appeared to be in good condition, many of the homes had damaged plaster, holes in the walls, and "spongy" or weak floors. In some homes, mechanical or electrical items such as ventilation fans were not operable. Lack of maintenance and the resulting structural deterioration suggested that boarding home income was not sufficient to cover necessary repairs.

Privacy and personal space for residents, essential elements of a home environment, were lacking in many BCHs. Basic amenities, such as sufficient drawer space and individual closet storage space for each boarder, were not consistently provided. Furthermore, residents' rooms did not have telephones in 85 percent of the homes.

Discussion

The profiles of residents, operators, and homes were fairly consistent across the homes visited. The typical elderly resident was a previously-married, 72-year-old white female, with less than a high school education—although nearly half the residents were African American. The residents moved to the boarding home from a variety of dwellings ranging from their own homes to institutional settings. Approximately equal proportions of relatives and health-care professionals made referrals to the homes. Some homes had high turnover of residents while others catered to long-term residents. The dominant source of income for most residents, and thus for most BCH operators, was Social Security or SSI.

Most residents had somewhat limited physical and mental capacities. Although the vast majority of residents could perform the basic ADLs, most had difficulty with IADLs, which they relied on the BCH operator to provide. They reported their personal health as somewhat poorer than they hoped; yet most residents argued that their health did not interfere with their normal activities and they were better off than most. The relatively passive activities, such as watching television and listening to the radio, in which they engaged may explain the lack of interference from their health. A more serious shortcoming was the relative lack of knowledge they had about their medicines and medication schedules. Half of all residents did not have sufficient knowledge to administer their own medications. Yet most residents reported no problems with taking medication. Clearly, the BCH operators had acquired a central role in the health care of these residents.

The research reported here suggests other instances where the role of the BCH operator is central to the life of the BCH residents. The typical operator was African American, married, and female with at least a high school education. For most operators, Social Security or SSI checks were the sole source of payment for BCH charges. Over half the operators were the designated payee for at least some of their residents. However, the income received was barely sufficient for the BCH operation.

Although 80 percent of the boarding home operators surveyed reported special training, their training was generally not directly related to BCH operation. Training often consisted of past work experience in health care settings, especially as nurses and nurses' aides. Most operators had never operated BCHs before owning and operating the current facility.

Despite the lack of training specific to boarding homes, the operators exercised significant control over the type of resident admitted to the home, the rules of conduct in the home, the type of services provided, and the overall autonomy of the residents. A majority of BCH operators explicitly excluded residents with severe physical limitations, behavioral problems, or chemical dependencies. Most operators limited the types of behaviors allowed in the home, setting rules concerning smoking and consumption of alcohol. A majority of operators also provided services related to the independent functioning of the residents, including the scheduling of medical appointments, medication management, and financial management. Finally, the operators of most facilities limited the movements of their residents by setting curfews and visitation hours.

The homes themselves were generally in fair to poor condition. Most were older structures located in the sections of Birmingham, Tuscaloosa, and Huntsville (all in Alabama) characterized by generally low-income housing. Because the homes were designed primarily as single-family dwellings, few had been adapted to the needs of a partially dependent population. Many had significant obstacles to access, particularly a lack of ramps and handrails. Approximately one-third to one-half of the homes had significant safety problems including blocked windows, unmarked exits, and inward-opening doors.

The overall lack of maintenance suggests that revenues were not sufficient to cover the costs of needed repairs.

Overall, the Alabama surveys revealed a reasonably close match among residents, operators, and facilities, confirming much of the earlier research (Dittmar, 1989; Dobkin, 1989; Mor, Sherwood, & Gutkin, 1986; USDHHS-OIG, 1982; USGAO, 1979) A significant portion of the board-and-care industry consists of the poor taking care of the poor. BCHs in Alabama were not exceptions. Nevertheless, boarding homes in Alabama, even licensed facilities, may be providing services that exceed their legal appropriateness. It is clear that some residents currently living in BCHs would be more safely housed in facilities providing higher levels of care such as domiciliaries and nursing homes. Conversely, some nursing home residents do not require the level of care provided in those facilities and may better be served in facilities with lower levels of care.

Unfortunately, the development of long-term care facilities in the United States has been fragmented and incomplete. No systematic mechanisms for the development of private or public oversight have been developed. Considerable variation exists between states, and even between counties within the same state, regarding licensure and certification requirements. In addition, little is known about current facilities and little planning has been done concerning the demands that demographic, economic, social, and political changes may impose on the long-term care system. The availability of board-and-care beds is increasing, yet there is little evidence that appropriate planning is being carried out for these new homes. Such limited policy development does not bode well for the future.

Conclusion

Incremental policy decisions and private market forces have produced a subterranean referral network for non-institutional long-term care in the United States. This network, consisting primarily of health-care professionals who refer individuals to BCHs, does not operate as a coordinated system. Further, there is little coordinated governmental oversight of the

BCHs themselves. Many homes have no supervision at all while several agencies regulate others. For example, in Alabama the Department of Human Resources, the Department of Public Health, the Department of Mental Health, and the US Department of Veterans Affairs all have some regulatory responsibility over the board-and-care industry. In Jefferson County (Birmingham), the Jefferson County Department of Health also directly monitors the industry. Each of these agencies has its own mandates and regulations that frequently place contradictory demands on BCH operators and facilities.

The Alabama data suggest that the match between resident, operator, and facility is fairly good. Nevertheless, the potential for both intentional and unintentional mistreatment exists. The most serious problems would appear to arise from the level of medical care provided by most BCHs. Although some operators have experience in the health-care industry, the administration of medication and the provision of personal care by untrained or undertrained BCH employees poses a significant health risk to BCH residents. This is especially true because the typical Alabama BCH resident takes three medications daily and approximately half of the residents have little or no under-standing of either the medication or the schedule for administration.

Despite these shortcomings, board-and-care homes play an important subsidiary role in the provision of long-term care. The only source of income for many elderly and developmentally disabled individuals is Social Security or SSI. BCHs, by accepting these checks as full payment, provide food and shelter for individuals who might otherwise be homeless. For many of these individuals, family members are either unavailable or unwilling to be involved in their lives. In addition, many board-and-care operators were found to be compassionate, caring individuals who became operators, in part, because of their desire to help those worse off than themselves. The homes operated by these individuals, by and large, provide a safe haven for an often-exploited population.

Unfortunately, the aging of the American population and, in particular, the aging of the minority population, is likely to place increasing stress on such an ad-hoc system of care. The increasing demand for such facilities is likely to attract the unscrupulous as well as the caring operator. National and state governments need to do a better job of coordinating and supervising the growth of the industry now, before the demand becomes so great that such coordination and supervision are impossible to implement.

NOTE

1. The research reported in this chapter was supported by the University of Alabama's Research Grant Committee and a University of Alabama at Birmingham, Center for Aging, Small Research Grant. Neither university is responsible for the content or interpretation of this material.

REFERENCES

Alabama Commission on Aging & University of Alabama at Birmingham Center for Aging (ACOA & UABCA). (1988). *Statewide survey of Alabama's elderly*. Montgomery: Alabama Commission on Aging.

American Association of Retired Persons. (1991). *A profile of older Americans*. Washington, DC: Author.

Atchley, R.C. (1991). *Social forces and aging: An introduction to social gerontology* (6th ed.). Belmont, CA: Wadsworth.

Baggett, S.A. (1989). *Residential care for the elderly: Critical issues in public policy*. Westport, CT: Greenwood Press.

Baumhover, L.A., Daniels, R.S., Gillum, J., & Clark-Daniels, C. (1991). *Subterranean Networks of Board and Care for the Elderly: A Survey of Boarding Home Operators and Residents*. Center for the Study of

Aging, University of Alabama: Center Published Monograph, May.

Benjamin, A.E., & Newcomer, R.J. (1986). Board and care housing: An analysis of state differences. *Research on Aging*, 8, 388–406.

Brubaker, T.H. (1987). The long-term care triad: The elderly, their families, and bureaucracies. In T. H. Brubaker (Ed.), *Aging, health, and family: Long-term care* (pp. 12–22). Newbury Park, CA: Sage Publications.

Callahan, J.J., Jr. (1981). Delivery of services to persons with long-term-care needs. In J. Meltzer, F. Farrow, & H. Richman (Eds.), *Policy options in long-term care* (pp. 148–181). Chicago: University of Chicago Press.

Dilworth-Anderson, P. (1987). Supporting family caregiving through adult day-care services. In T. H. Brubaker (Ed.), *Aging, health, and family: Long-term care* (pp. 129–142). Newbury Park, CA: Sage Publications.

Dittmar, N. (1989). Facility and resident characteristics of board and care homes for the elderly. In M. Moon, G. Gaberlavage, & S.J. Newman (Eds.), *Preserving independence, supporting needs: The role of board and care homes* (pp. 1–26). Washington, DC: AARP Public Policy Institute.

Dobkin, L. (1989). *The board and care system: A regulatory jungle.* Washington, DC: American Association of Retired Persons, Consumer Affairs Program Department.

Down, I.M., & Schnurr, L. (1991). *Between home and nursing home: The board and care alternative.* Buffalo: Prometheus Books.

Duke University Center for the Study of Aging and Human Development. (1975). *Multidimensional functional assessment: The OARS methodology* (2nd ed.) Durham, N.C.: Duke University Center for the Study of Aging and Human Development.

Kemp, B.J. (1990). The relationship between rehabilitation and long-term care. In P.S. Liebig & W.W. Lammers (Eds.), *California policy choices for long term care* (pp. 195–214). Los Angeles: University of Southern California Ethel Percy Andrus Gerontology Center.

Liebig, P.S., & Lammers, W.W. (1990). Overview: California policy choices for long-term care. In P. S. Liebig & W. W. Lammers (Eds.), *California policy choices for long term care* (pp. 1–6). Los Angeles: University of Southern California Ethel Percy Andrus Gerontology Center.

Mangen, D.J., & Peterson, W.A. (Eds.) (1984). *Research instruments in social gerontology: Vol. 3 Health, program evaluation, and demography.* Minneapolis: University of Minnesota Press.

Montgomery, R.J.V., & Hatch, L.R. (1987). The feasibility of volunteers and families forming a partnership for caregiving. In T. H. Brubaker (Ed.), *Aging, health, and family: Long-term care* (pp. 143–161). Newbury Park, CA: Sage Publications.

Mor, V., Gutkin, C.E., & Sherwood, S. (1985). The cost of residential care homes serving elderly adults. *Journal of Gerontology, 40,* 164–171.

Mor, V., Sherwood, S., & Gutkin, C. (1986). A national study of residential care for the aged. *The Gerontologist, 26,* 405–417.

Morris, R., & Youket, P. (1981). The long-term care issues: Identifying the problems and potential solutions. In J.J. Callahan, Jr. & and S.S. Wallack (Eds.), *Reforming the long-term care system* (pp. 11–28). Lexington, MA: D.C. Heath and Co.

Pfeiffer, E. (1975). A short portable mental status questionnaire for the assessment of organic brain defect in elderly patients. *Journal of the American Geriatrics Society, 23,* 433–441.

Quadagno, J., Sims, C., Squier, D.A., & Walker, G. (1987). Long-term care community services and family caregiving. In T. H. Brubaker (Ed.), *Aging, health, and family: Long-term care* (pp. 116–128). Newbury Park, CA: Sage Publications.

Solomon, C.D. (June 28, 1989). *Board and care homes and the Keys Amendment.* Washington, DC: Library of Congress, Congressional Research Service.

Stone, R., & and Newcomer, R.J. (1985). The state role in board and care housing. In C. Harrington, R.J. Newcomer, C.L. Estes, et al., *Long-term care for the elderly: Public policy issues* (pp. 177–196). Newbury Park, CA: Sage Publications.

Streib, G. F., Folts, W.E., & Hilker, M.A. (1984). *Old homes—new families: Shared living for the elderly.* New York: Columbia University Press.

U.S. Bureau of the Census. (1987). *Statistical Abstract of the United States: 1987* (107th ed.). Washington, DC: U.S. Government Printing Office.

———. (1991). *Statistical Abstract of the United States: 1991* (111th ed.). Washington, DC: U.S. Government Printing Office.

U.S. Department of Health and Human Services, Office of the Inspector General. (April, 1982). *Board and care homes: A study of federal and state actions to safeguard the health and safety of board and care home residents*. Washington, DC: Department of Health and Human Services.

U.S. General Accounting Office. (Nov. 19, 1979). *Identifying boarding homes housing the needy aged, blind, and disabled: A major step toward resolving a national problem* (HRD–80–17).

U.S. House, Select Committee on Aging, Subcommittee on Health and Long-Term Care. (1989). *Board and care homes in America: A national tragedy* (Committee Print, Pub. no. 101–711). 101st Congress, 1st session. Washington, DC: U.S. Government Printing Office.

Wyatt v. Aderholt, 503 F. 2d. 1305 (5th Cir., 1974).

Wyatt v. Stickney, 325 F. Supp. 781 (M.D. Ala., 1971).

———, 334 F. Supp. 1341 (M.D. Ala., 1971).

———, 344 F. Supp. 373 (M.D. Ala., 1972).

———, 344 F. Supp. 387 (M.D. Ala., 1972).

CHAPTER 9

Temporary Housing: Adult Daycare and Respite Services

Jan W. Weaver

A number of demographic, socioeconomic, and health-related characteristics affect the housing preferences of older adults. Research has shown that the majority of today's older persons live in a community setting rather than in institutions (Soldo & Brothman, 1981; Walsh, 1981; Conrad & Guttman, 1991). Since approximately half of these individuals are impaired in some way (Soldo & Brothman, 1981), variations in living arrangements occur and are affected by a wide array of factors including functional ability, personal preference, health status, social factors, financial security, and other social and familial circumstances.

The diversity in living arrangements for older adults is also dependent upon the availability of noninstitutional health and social support systems that provide a variety of services for promoting independence and thus maintaining the older person in the community. This system, often referred to as a continuum of care, includes programs such as adult daycare, homecare, support services, and other forms of respite that bridge the gap between independent living and institutional care.

Adult Daycare

Adult daycare has experienced rapid growth and development in recent years and has been quite successful in meeting the needs of its constituents. Adult daycare programs began as a response to a growing need for noninstitutional but supportive environments. In the late 1960s, the U.S. Senate Special Committee on Aging began to investigate whether federal funds were being utilized to support substandard long-term care. Boykin and Lamy (1978) note that by 1971:

> It was generally recognized that nursing homes and other institutional settings were being over-utilized and that aged people were being warehoused. The cost of institutional care was enormous, and there were dubious benefits to the patient beyond serving sheer physical needs. (p. 683)

As a result of these and other findings, adult day health models began to emerge for experimental demonstration.

The adult daycare concept was adapted from geriatric day hospitals appearing as early as the 1940s in the former Soviet Union, the United Kingdom, and from psychiatric day treatment centers in the United States. A physician, Lionel Cosin, known by many as the "father of adult daycare," initiated the first British geriatric day hospital in 1950 and, in the late 1960s, transplanted his model to the Cherry State Hospital in Goldsboro, North Carolina (Kelly & Webb, 1989). By the early 1970s, experimental day programs began emerging as noninstitutional service systems operated as alternatives to nursing homes. At the time, the total annual cost of nursing home care was $3.2 billion, with 61 percent provided by public funds (Boykin & Lamy, 1978, p. 683).

As these numbers continued to increase at a rapid rate, Congress identified the need to plan alternatives to long-term care and it authorized the Department of Health, Education, and Welfare (HEW) to design and conduct demonstration projects that would provide the basis for future changes in Medicare and Medicaid policy (Boykin & Lamy, 1978). In 1973, amendments to Title XX of the Social Security Act and Title III of the Older

Americans Act resulted in funding for community and home-based care alternatives including adult daycare, case management, counseling, foster care, nutrition, homemakers, information and referral, recreation, and transportation (Kelly & Webb, 1989). HEW, predecessor of the Department of Health and Human Services (DHHS), agreed to make Medicaid funds available for adult daycare in 1974, thus encouraging alternatives to nursing home placement. Congress further facilitated Medicaid funding for expanded use of alternative long-term care by authorizing state waivers for community-based services in the Omnibus Budget Reconciliation Act of 1981 (Billings, 1982).

The number of adult daycare centers increased gradually at first from about a dozen in 1973 to approximately 1200 in 1986 (National Council on the Aging, 1987). Since 1986, adult daycare has become known as "one of the fastest-growing options in long-term care" (Conrad, Hughes, Campione, & Goldberg, 1987, p. 18) with nearly 3,000 centers currently located in all fifty states (National Institute on Adult Daycare, 1992).

Adult daycare is a generic term describing programs that provide daytime health care and social services for individuals in need of rehabilitation or health maintenance. Prior to 1984, practitioners attempted to separate and classify health and social models, but since that time, a number of centers have developed a much broader range of both types of services as dictated by the needs of the programs' participants. In response to this trend, the National Institute on Adult Daycare (NIAD) developed its standards as generic guidelines for quality care and good practice, regardless of focus, and revised earlier standards which advocated separate models based on whether health care services were provided (NCOA, 1990).

In the 1990 revision of the standards, NIAD "rejected the idea of discrete models perpetuated by a long-standing tradition of separation of social and health services in state licensing agencies and state/federal funding sources" (NCOA, 1990, p. xiv). NIAD's more recent position is based on the belief that specifically defined models limit a program's ability to adapt to the changing needs of its participants. Accordingly, NIAD developed the following definition of adult daycare:

> Adult day care is a community-based group program
> designed to meet the needs of adults with functional
> impairments through an individual plan of care. It is a
> structured, comprehensive program that provides a
> variety of health, social, and related support services in a
> protective setting during any part of a day but less than
> 24-hour care. Individuals who participate in adult day care
> attend on a planned basis during specified hours. Adult
> day care assists its participants to remain in the
> community, enabling families and other caregivers to
> continue caring at home for a family member with an
> impairment. (NCOA, 1990, p. iv)

Most of what is known about adult daycare nationally is
the result of three nationwide studies. The National Institute on
Adult Daycare (NIAD) sent out questionnaires to all 1,200 adult
daycare centers known to exist in 1985 and received responses
from 874 of them (Von Behren, 1988). The purpose of the NIAD
study was to examine differences in program and participant
characteristics and to investigate relationships between licensing
categories and funding sources. Another study, the Adult
Daycare Assessment Procedure (ADCAP) (Conrad, Hanrahan, &
Hughes, 1990), measured structural components, process issues,
and the population characteristics of 834 centers located
throughout the U.S. The third study, conducted by Weissert and
his colleagues (1990), involved sixty adult daycare centers in
different geographic locations in the U.S.

All of these studies presented data collected in 1985–1986.
Among the findings were that a large number of adult daycare
programs are housed in multipurpose centers such as senior
centers, nursing homes, hospitals, or churches. Other programs
are free-standing. Typical staffing for these centers included a
director, often trained as a nurse or social worker, and an
assistant plus some or all of the following: nurses, therapists,
social workers, case managers, recreation/activity aides, nursing
assistants, custodial workers, van drivers, administrative/
clerical personnel, and office staff (Weissert et al., 1990, p. 18).
Consultant agreements were often utilized for the services of
physicians, therapists, or dieticians and in-kind staffing was
sometimes available for fiscal managers or bookkeepers. Overall,
the conclusions of these studies supported the concept that adult

daycare is a program containing a range of both basic and professional services.

Specific services in adult daycare centers tend to vary in accordance with participant needs and facility resources. Indeed, it is precisely this flexibility that makes adult daycare a viable alternative. Most centers, however, offer recreational therapy, exercise, a midday meal, morning and afternoon snacks, assessment, and social services. In addition, many centers provide medical supervision, nursing care, personal care, counselling, education, rehabilitation, and transportation.

This range of services provided by adult daycare is representative of an underlying philosophy directed at improving each participant's quality of life. Key elements in the treatment program for each person include the therapeutic milieu and the individualized, interdisciplinary plan of care.

Each service plan is based on an assessment of the individual's physical, mental, and social status, which includes an evaluation of functional skills, support systems, and financial resources. The community, as well as the individual participant, benefits from this approach since service mobility within the adult daycare system allows each center to respond appropriately when individuals' needs change. Thus, the opportunity exists for exploration and implementation of services unique to the profile of a specific community (Kelly & Webb, 1989).

Potential users of adult daycare exhibit the same heterogeneous characteristics as the general population. As Soldo and Brothman (1981) point out, the elderly population differs not only by age and historical, cultural, and educational experience, but also in family-friendship networks, interests, financial status, and health characteristics. A diversity of living arrangements and housing accommodations are utilized, often based on the person's health, personal resources, and degree of dependency. In general, adult daycare participants are similar in that they typically have at least minimal functional limitations. According to NIAD's 1985 national survey, the average adult daycare participant is seventy-three years old, Caucasian, female, with a monthly income of $478, and living with relatives or friends (Webb, 1989, p. 4). Similarly, the Weissert study found that the average age of participants was almost seventy-eight years, with just under 20 percent being older than eighty-four years, and most were unmarried Caucasian females who did not live alone. Further, more than half the participants were functionally impaired and almost 40 percent suffered from a mental disorder (Weissert et al., 1990, p. 12).

The growing population of older individuals with various forms of dementia has resulted in the expansion of adult daycare services to accommodate the care of persons with Alzheimer's disease and related disorders. Many programs have taken measures to improve the quality of care for participants with dementia by providing additional specially trained staff and special programming aimed at the needs of participants with dementia. Staff education in these centers typically emphasizes the special needs of individuals with dementia along with management of behavioral difficulties. Additional adaptations by some programs have involved environmental design features such as barrier-free building designs that incorporate bright, glare-free lighting, diminution of background interference, and considered use of signs and color schemes (Conrad & Guttman, 1991, p. 101).

One of the primary attractions of adult daycare is the opportunity for older participants to remain in their community while, at the same time, they receive needed health, social, and support services. A variety of research studies supports the assertion that, as Billings (1982) put it: "the quality of life for elderly people who remain in the community and receive care is better than for those who enter long-term care facilities" (p. 2). The quality of life for frail older adults is related to what has been called a "trinity" of factors: housing, income, and good health (Billings, 1982, p. 4). Redfoot and Gaberlavage state that "housing is a key factor in the quality of life for older people: it provides a secure and meaningful old age or magnifies the disability and isolation that too often accompany advanced years" (1991, p. 35). Chronic health problems or disabilities are often exacerbated by substandard housing conditions and inadequate services combined with limited income (Billings, 1982, p. 4).

Adult daycare offers obvious advantages over some of the other long-term care options. These advantages include a possible reduction in feelings of isolation and the creation of a supportive yet flexible temporary living environment. Further, social interaction and support by peers are benefits that are not often experienced in other care alternatives such as home care. Adult daycare services may also be a significant advantage for family caregivers since it provides respite from their 24-hour care responsibilities and permits continued participation in the workforce while allowing close familial relationships to continue.

A 1986 study by Zimmerman identified the primary areas of family functioning that were helped by participation in adult daycare. Positive aspects of participation reported by caregivers included not only the obvious attention to the needs of the participant, but also attention to the caregiver. Among the more important of these latter needs was that participation allowed the caregiver the time to perform usual household chores, spend time with family, do shopping, visit with friends, engage in recreational activities outside the home, and attend to the needs of other family members (Zimmerman, 1986).

Satisfaction with the care received in adult daycare centers has been addressed by a few researchers. According to the Weissert (1990) national survey of adult daycare, for example, satisfaction with adult daycare was particularly high with 82.2 percent of the elderly participants and 92.3 percent of their caregivers reporting the highest level of satisfaction. Ninety-six percent of the elderly participants reported complete satisfaction with their transportation to and from the center, 91 percent reported satisfaction with the amount of attention they received from the staff, and 91 percent expressed contentment with the program hours (Weissert et al., 1990, p. 19).

Another recent study (Asbury & Smyth Henry, 1991) explored the reasons caregivers were reluctant to initiate use of adult daycare services. The survey identified barriers to program utilization including caregivers' internal reluctance associated with guilt, denial, or fear; logistical problems such as lack of transportation or unsuitable hours of operation; and financial concerns relating to disease duration and the eventuality of nursing home placement (Asbury & Smyth Henry, 1991).

The cost of adult daycare varies from state to state and even from program to program. The National Institute on Adult Daycare found that the average per diem cost was $31 with a median of $20 (Von Behren, 1986). Payment for adult daycare services comes from a variety of sources including participant fees, Medicaid, Title III-B of the Older Americans Act, and various local funding programs. In addition, state mental health funds and the Veterans' Administration will, in select locations, reimburse for adult daycare services received by eligible participants.

Not all participants pay the full fee. In the Weissert study, for example, only about 45 percent of all participants were identified as paying some part of the charges for their care "out of pocket" (1990, p. 35). Many programs offered a sliding-scale fee system that sets rates based on the participant's income and ability to pay. Programs offering this form of payment system reported that its purpose was to make it possible for the individual on a fixed income to receive necessary services while remaining in the community setting. Other programs reported offering scholarships funded through various community resources to assist needy recipients in payment of adult daycare charges. Most centers with a sliding-scale and those offering scholarship opportunities also had to rely on additional funding sources such as United Way, fundraising, corporations, foundations, churches, and other forms of local support.

Government contracts used most often by adult daycare programs include Medicaid, Title XX, and Title IIIB. Medicaid funding for adult daycare has increased significantly in recent years accounting for 41 percent of center revenues in 1989 (Burke, Hudson, & Eubanks, 1990, p. 34). In 1986, the Adult Daycare Assessment Procedure (ADCAP) (Conrad et al., 1990) found that 47 percent of center participants were eligible for Medicaid (p. 45). Participants' monthly income, according to ADCAP, averaged $557 (Conrad et al., 1990, p. 45).

Title XX of the Social Services Block Grant program, which allows states to provide home and community care services for eligible elderly or disabled individuals, is another major source of funding for adult daycare. Title XX requires cost-sharing in some states and has traditionally been oriented toward the social model program although it may also support health components under certain specified conditions.

Title IIIB monies are available in some areas for scholarship programs, or for administrative overhead, or for specific services. Generally, Title IIIB supports transportation and social, recreational, educational, and nutritional services. Other public support is sometimes available through city or county funding.

Medicare generally does not pay for adult daycare although it may reimburse for medical services provided in an adult daycare center that is certified as a comprehensive outpatient rehabilitation facility. However, according to the adult daycare study by Weissert et al. (1990), only 2.9 percent of the centers surveyed were certified for Medicare.

Protection for the public using adult daycare comes in two primary forms: licensing and certification. Licensure, as a condition of operation, is the strongest control (Von Behren, 1992) since it grants an organization permission to provide services which would otherwise be unlawful. Certification, on the other hand, sets forth conditions of participation for funding. Licensing is mandatory in thirteen of the forty-one states that responded to the 1991 NIAD survey of state agencies (Von Behren, 1992, p. 1). Certification affects only those centers that desire state or federal funding (except in states such as Alabama, North Carolina, and Rhode Island that mandate certification for all centers) (Von Behren, 1992, p. 2–3).

Licensing and certification requirements commonly vary from state to state due to the absence of federal guidelines. In general, however, the requirements specify types of services, staff composition, administrative policies and procedures, and facility characteristics (Weissert et al., 1991, p. 54). To obtain and maintain licensure or certification, providers must demonstrate a minimum level of competence in these areas. Standards are enforced by an inspection process in which sanctions are imposed for failure to comply with the regulations (Weissert et al., 1991, p. 54).

Respite Care

The importance of respite for family caregivers is becoming increasingly clear as social trends dictate greater involvement of family members in the long-term care of older relatives (Rathbone-McCuan, 1990; Moore, 1987; Archbold, 1982). Respite care, as a temporary housing option, is generally defined as any service that focuses on temporary relief for families who provide ongoing care. The timing of respite may be either planned in advance (e.g., vacations, business trips, visits to relatives) or required as a consequence of an emergency (e.g., the primary caregiver may be suddenly hospitalized or incapacitated) (Rathbone-McCuan, 1990, p. 551–52).

Respite has been identified as an important factor in maintaining psychological as well as physical well-being for the family caregiver and in preventing premature or inappropriate institutionalization for the patient. In many instances, respite is not a single mode of care but rather an array of different patterns that are broadly defined and diversely provided either in or out of the care recipient's home (Rathbone-McCuan, 1990, p. 548). Adult daycare, of course, provides respite to the family caregiver while meeting the physical and social needs of the participant. Other respite services are available in many locations in the form of in-home services, support groups, or short-term out-of-home care.

In-home respite care allows the elderly person to remain in familiar surroundings while giving the primary caregiver some temporary relief from the demands associated with providing care. In-home respite is arranged either informally (i.e., with friends, neighbors, churches, volunteer groups, or other family members) or through an agency, and varies with respect to duration, the caregiver's level of need, and the care recipient's level of functioning. Respite care arranged by agencies is based on the principle that needs are to be determined by the caregiver in a nonintrusive manner in order to assure family autonomy (Ehrlich & White, 1991, p. 687). A range of services is offered by many agencies including personal care, homemaker-chore services, or companion care that not only allow time off, but also relieve the caregiver from performing certain tasks.

Support Groups

Support group intervention is designed to provide caregivers with emotional support, information, and coping strategies relative to the caregiver's role and degree of burden. These groups are either professionally led or peer led with a strong emphasis on sharing feelings, experiences, and stress-reduction methods. The professionally led groups target emotional and/or informational intervention while the peer-led groups tend to be less formal with an emphasis on personal experiences. The information model groups provide a combination of cognitive material, self-enhancement and/or behavioral management skills (Biegel, 1991, p. 215).

Informal support groups generally offer the opportunity to share ideas for overcoming difficult and stress-producing caregiving responsibilities. For these support groups, research findings indicate only a minimal reduction in actual caregiver burden or physical symptomatology (Biegel, 1991, p. 220), but studies also indicate that support group participants report a variety of benefits from the group experience. Examples of these benefits, according to Biegel (1991), include:

> increased knowledge, the provision of practical information, reduced anxiety, improvements in family communications, and helpful interaction with group members in learning new problem solving skills. (p. 229)

These benefits are often important in helping family caregivers make informed and ethical decisions regarding their caregiving role and the various choices available in respite services.

Congregate Housing

Licensed boarding homes, foster family care homes, personal care residences, and continuing care retirement communities offer 24-hour residential care and services ranging from supervision to skilled nursing care. Some locations offer short-term care away from the home setting, thus providing respite for family members who care for an elderly or disabled relative. The customary approach to this form of respite is to utilize these settings for temporarily housing the older adult when the family caregiver is absent for any reason. The congregate setting, in the form of a foster home or a board and care facility, often provides meals and housekeeping services to several residents. Personal care facilities tend to be more institutional and, according to the National Center for Health Statistics definition, offer at least three personal care services (Sherman, 1990, p. 495). Continuing care retirement communities offer a range of services from independent living to skilled nursing care at one site.

These facilities are both nonprofit and proprietary and are generally licensed by state health and human service agencies. In addition, public or private institutions, including hospitals and nursing homes, sometimes offer temporary stays for elders whose families need respite. Although these out-of-home respite options are frequently more accessible than in-home care, it is often more costly and can have a "potentially negative effect on the aged person who must endure a series of disruptions associated with entry and discharge" (Rathbone-McCuan, 1990, p. 553).

Medical Home Health Care and Hospice

Medical home health care and hospice, although not targeted to provide respite for the family member, are important alternatives to institutionalization that generally benefit both the patient and the caregiver. Home health care provides rehabilitation and health promotion while focusing on the care of an individual during an episodic illness. Services are offered by a variety of community agencies and organizations including governmental health agencies, voluntary nonprofit agencies, private nonprofit agencies, proprietary agencies, and programs based in hospitals or extended care facilities (Hogstel, 1985, p. 9). Regardless of the type of organization, most home health agencies provide an array of interdisciplinary services. These services typically include skilled nursing care, social services, homemaker-home health aide assistance, medical equipment and supplies, physical therapy, occupational therapy, speech pathology, and nutrition counseling.

Hospice is a specialized service for the patient and his family that emphasizes supportive and palliative care during the last stages of a terminal disease. According to the hospice philosophy, dying is not seen as a medical problem, but rather as a natural event in the life cycle that involves the patient, the family, and the community.

A range of health services is provided in hospice by an organized interdisciplinary team in a variety of settings including free-standing hospice facilities, the patient's own home, a hospital, or a long-term care facility. The most suitable setting for hospice is determined based on the team's assessment of the individual's physical condition, home situation, attitude toward the illness, and interaction with family members (Zimmerman, 1981, p. 31).

The interdisciplinary nature of hospice care is one of its most important features. Physicians, nurses, social workers, therapists, chaplains, and volunteers coordinate functions in order to assure that the physical, psychological, and social needs of the patients and their families are being addressed. The special emphasis placed on the care of both the patient and the family helps to resolve not only problems relating to the patient's illness but also the emotional strain associated with an impending loss. In addition, hospice workers provide counseling and referral to assist clients with financial needs, living arrangements, and any additional health care and social services that are deemed necessary along with bereavement services for a period of time following the patient's death.

Hospice focuses primarily on symptom management rather than on control of the disease itself. Symptom control is accomplished with a minimum of diagnostic or invasive therapeutic procedures and directed at psychosocial as well as physical problems. As a result, "hospice patients receive relatively little technological, but a great deal of personal attention" (Zimmerman, 1981, p. 30). The patient is at the center of the decisionmaking process with the freedom to make choices in accordance with personal values and in collaboration with the hospice professionals.

Service Coordination

The large number of in-home and community-based programs that have emerged in recent years have made service coordination an important issue. As the availability of community services combined with the number of individuals in need of such care continues to grow, coordination efforts are essential. Hughes (1986) suggests a comprehensive approach to service coordination and points out that:

> . . . the effectiveness of public dollars for long-term care could be maximized if existing fragmented public funding streams were pooled to finance a coordinated array of long-term care services. (p. 221)

One of the original objectives of the Older Americans Act was "efficient community services which provide social assistance in a coordinated manner and which are readily available when needed" (Fortinsky, 1991, p. 39). Although coordination has not been achieved in most communities, Area Agencies on Aging as well as individual service agencies have made remarkable progress in "forging interorganizational alliances and pooling funds to offer a wide array of services within a fairly accountable framework" (Fortinsky, 1991, p. 39). As the aging network becomes increasingly complex, it is imperative that each organization know how to link individuals receiving their care with any other service deemed necessary.

Conclusion

Adult daycare and other respite services are important options in the continuum of care for chronically ill or otherwise impaired older individuals for at least two reasons: (1) they provide necessary health care and social support for individuals who prefer to remain in their homes, and (2) they are more cost-effective than traditional institutional care. These comprehensive programs match the participants' needs with appropriate levels of support in order to enhance their ability to live in a community setting. For those older adults who experience decreasing health and declining economic resources, modifications and adaptations in living arrangements are often required. The diversity of services that are incorporated into community care programs may mean the difference between institutionalization and what is at least an acceptable level of functioning within the community.

As the elderly population continues its rapid growth, current public policy becomes more concerned with future trends in chronic health-care services and levels of federal expenditures. By the year 2040, it is estimated that there will be 67.3 million United States citizens (22 percent of the total population) sixty-five years old or older (Manton & Saldo, 1985). Assuming that the rates of old-age mortality decline only gradually, 13.3 million of these individuals (4 percent of the total population) will be in the eighty-five and over age group (Manton & Soldo, 1985). The expanding numbers of this so-called "oldest-old" group produces higher rates of disability and poverty and will have a major impact on health and social service systems in the U.S. over the next few decades. Soldo and Manton point out that if current morbidity and service use rates remain constant, there will be a five-fold increase in the numbers of the very old functionally dependent in the community by 2040 (1985, p. 286).

Future patterns of community long-term care services will be shaped not only by increases in the number of individuals with functional disabilities, but also by the availability of informal care-providers and changes in federal and state reimbursement policies. While the elderly population is increasing, the size of the American family is decreasing (Koff, 1988) which means less family-based support and increasing reliance on outside services for elderly people.

In addition, paying for services will become increasingly problematic for elderly persons who are forced by public policy to spend themselves into poverty. Currently, middle-class citizens faced with immense bills for long-term care must "spend down" their assets to gain eligibility for Medicaid. At the same time, recent cost containment initiatives have restricted existing Medicaid coverage for home and community-based care, thus increasing reliance upon expensive hospital and nursing home care (Koff, 1988, p. 14). These trends must be addressed in order to assure that the future demand for adult daycare and respite services is adequately met.

REFERENCES

Archbold, P.G. (1982). All-consuming activity: The family as caregiver. *Generations*, 6(2), 12–13.

Asbury, C.H. & Smyth Henry, R. (1991). Day programs for dementia: Responding to the market. *Perspective on Aging*, July–October, 25–28.

Biegel, D.E. (1991). *Family Caregiving in Chronic Illness*. Newbury Park, CA: Sage.

Billings, G. (1982). Alternatives to nursing home care. *Aging*, March April, 2–11.

Boykin, S.P. & Lamy, P.P. (1978). Day treatment—A new care modality. *Hospital Formulary*, September, 683–686.

Burke, M., Hudson, T. & Eubanks, P. (1990). Number of adult daycare centers increasing, but payment is slow. *Hospitals*, November 5, 34–42.

Conrad, K.J. & Guttman, R. (1991). Characteristics of Alzheimer's versus non-Alzheimer's adult daycare centers. *Research on Aging*, March, 96–116.

Conrad, K.J., Hanrahan, P., & Hughes, S.L. (1990). Survey of adult daycare in the United States. *Research on Aging*, March, 36–56.

Conrad, K.J., Hughes, S.L., Campione, P.F., and Goldberg, R.S. (1987). Shedding new light on adult daycare. *Perspective on Aging*, Nov.–Dec., 18–21.

Ehrlich, P. & White, J. (1991). TOPS: A consumer approach to Alzheimer's respite programs. *The Gerontologist*, October, 686–91.

Fortinsky, R.H. (1991). Coordinated, comprehensive community care and the Older Americans Act. *Generations*, Summer/Fall, 39–42.

Hogstel, M.O. (1985). *Home Nursing Care for the Elderly*. Bowie, MD: Brady.

Hughes, S.L. (1986). *Long-Term Care Options in an Expanding Market*. Homewood, IL: Dow Jones-Irwin.

Kelly, W. & Webb, L.C. (1989). The development of adult daycare in America. In L. C. Webb (Ed.), *Planning and Managing Adult Daycare*. Owings Mills, MD: National Health.

Koff, T.H. (1988). *New Approaches to Health Care for an Aging Population*. San Francisco: Jossey-Bass.

Manton, K.G. & Soldo, B.J. (1985). Dynamics of health changes in the oldest old: New perspectives and evidence. *Milbank Memorial Fund Quarterly/Health and Society*, 63(2), 206–285.

Moore, S.T. (1987). The capacity to care: A family focused approach to social work practice with the disabled elderly. *Journal of Gerontological Social Work*, 10(1), 79–98.

National Council on the Aging. (1987). *Directory of Adult Daycare in America*. Washington, D.C.

———. (1990). *Standards and Guidelines for Adult Daycare* (2nd ed.). Washington, D.C.

National Institute on Adult Daycare. (1992). *Position paper: Public policy statement*. Washington, D.C.: National Council on the Aging.

Rathbone-McCuan, E. (1990). Respite and adult day services. In A. Monk (Ed.), *Handbook of Gerontological Services* (2nd ed.). New York: Columbia University Press.

Redfoot, D. & Gaberlavage, G. (1991). Housing for older Americans: Sustaining the dream. *Generations*, Summer/Fall, 35–38.

Sherman, S.R. (1990). Housing. In A. Monk (Ed.), *Handbook of Gerontological Services* (2nd ed.). New York: Columbia University Press.

Soldo, B.J. & Brothman, H.B. (1981). *Housing whom? Community Housing Choices for Older Americans*. New York: Springer.

Soldo, B.J. & Manton, K.G. (1985). Health status and service needs of the oldest old: Current patterns and future trends. *Milbank Memorial Fund Quarterly/Health and Society*, 63(2), 286–319.

Von Behren, R. (1988). *Adult Daycare: A Program of Services for the Functionally Impaired*. Washington, D.C.: National Council on the Aging.

———— (1986). *Adult Daycare in America: Summary of a National Survey.* Washington, D.C.: National Council on the Aging.

———— (1992). *A very preliminary summary of the NIAD 1991 survey of state agencies/contacts re: licensing, certification, and fiscal information.* Unpublished report to the National Council on the Aging.

Walsh, T.J. (1981). *Costs of home services compared to institutionalization.* Community Housing Choices for Older Americans. New York: Springer.

Webb, L.C. (1989). Where do we start? In L.C. Webb (Ed.), *Planning and Managing Adult Daycare.* Owing Mills, MD: National Health.

Weissert, W.G., Elston, J.M., Musliner, M.C., & Mutran, E. (1991). Adult daycare regulation: Déjà vu all over again? *Journal of Health Politics, Policy, and Law,* 16(2), 51–66.

Weissert, W.G., Elston, J.M., Bolda, E.J., Zelman, W.N., Mutran, E., & Mangum, A.B. (1990). *Adult Daycare: Findings from a National Survey.* Baltimore: Johns Hopkins University Press.

Zimmerman, J.M. (1981). *Hospice: Complete Care for the Terminally Ill.* Baltimore: Urban.

Zimmerman, S.L. (1986). Adult daycare: Correlates of its coping effects for families of an elderly disabled member. *Family Relations,* April, 305–311.

CHAPTER 10

Homesharing for the Elderly: An Option for Independent Living

Dale J. Jaffe
Patricia Pawasarat
Elizabeth Howe

Homesharing is a situation in which two or more unrelated persons live together in a single house or apartment. Residents share common areas such as the kitchen and living room, but each has private space such as a bedroom and, perhaps, a sitting room. Homesharing was a common practice during the nineteenth and early twentieth centuries when nonrelative boarders were taken in by homeowners to help pay the costs of maintaining a home. By the 1920s, however, the practice of taking in boarders had fallen from favor largely because privacy became highly valued and because of the availability of suitable alternative living arrangements (Hareven, 1989).

In the late 1970s the rapidly increasing number of elderly homeowners living alone, coupled with the continuously escalating costs of maintaining a home, fostered the re-emergence of boarding and lodging as a housing option for the elderly. Unlike earlier times when homeowners and boarders had to seek each other out independently, today's homesharers are often served by a growing number of social service programs whose purpose is to set up shared living "matches" that will meet the needs of both the homeowner and the potential boarder (Jaffe, 1989).

Types of Shared Housing Arrangements

Schreter (1986) has developed a typology of shared housing arrangements based on their relationship to social service networks. In order of increasing program involvement they are: (1) self-initiated; (2) agency-assisted; and (3) agency-sponsored shared housing.

According to Schreter, "self-initiated shared housing is a private arrangement negotiated by nonrelatives who choose to share a dwelling unit as 'housemates'" (1986: 123). There is no social service program involvement in this type of arrangement and housemates may find one another through referrals from acquaintances, advertisements, or prior relationships. This type of arrangement is common among young adults, but may be found among older adults and the elderly as well.

Arranging self-initiated homesharing may be difficult for elderly people, especially those who are frail. Sharing their homes with strangers makes them vulnerable to abuse, and a great deal of care and time may be spent by the homeowner, and his or her family, in screening potential boarders for compatibility and trustworthiness. Because homesharing arrangements are typically short-lived, the stress associated with locating and securing appropriate boarders may outweigh the potential benefits of homesharing. Further, impartial third-parties may not be available to help negotiate fair and complete contracts regarding requirements of and restrictions on each of the housemates. Despite the difficulties associated with self-initiated shared housing, it has been found that among elderly persons this is the most common of the three types of homesharing arrangements (Schreter, 1986).

Potential homesharers who are unable to initiate shared housing on their own may turn to an agency for assistance (Schreter, 1986). The levels of agency involvement vary among the many programs. At a minimum, matching services introduce homeproviders and homeseekers, but many also provide additional services such as pre-screening, contract negotiation, and counselling. The level of assistance is typically a function of a program's operating philosophy and the availability of staff which, in turn, are dependent on the mission and level of funding available to the agency.

Depending on the program, agency assistance may alleviate some of the stress involved in securing a housemate. Although the longevity of the homesharing match may not be increased through agency assistance, having a ready pool of potential homesharers may increase the likelihood of future matches. Many agencies provide reference checks on potential boarders obviating this task for elderly homeowners and increasing confidence in the potential success of the match. Where pre-screening is available, expectations of homeowners and homeseekers are matched which eliminates the necessity of interviewing obviously incompatible homeseekers. In addition, agencies may provide sample contracts or participate in negotiations between homeowners and homeseekers which may be of great benefit to inexperienced homesharers.

Agency-sponsored shared housing, sometimes called "group home" living, is an arrangement in which several elderly residents share a single dwelling. In this arrangement an agency typically locates, maintains, and manages the dwelling. Housekeeping services such as cooking and cleaning and personal care services may also be provided by the agency (Schreter, 1986).

Agency-sponsored shared housing provides several obvious benefits for elderly residents. Residents are not responsible for seeking or interviewing housemates, and vacancies in the house do not affect the residents' cost of living. Although the composition of the group may change, new contracts do not have to be negotiated each time one of the homesharers leaves. Also, residents are spared the worries of maintaining a home and they share in the cost of maintenance via their boarding fees.

There are disadvantages to this arrangement as well. Obviously, the elderly resident must leave his or her own home and take up residence in an unfamiliar place. Residents do not have much control over the composition of the household and, if the arrangement proves unsatisfactory, relocation may be difficult. Further, personal independence and autonomy may be more limited in group-home living than in traditional living arrangements. While an individual's level of independence is related to physical or mental limitations, all residents in these types of living arrangements must relinquish some decision-making power to the sponsoring agency. This may range from something as innocuous as adhering to predetermined meal times to more limiting restrictions regarding visitors or the freedom to come and go as they choose. In addition, the age segregation inherent in most agency-sponsored shared housing may create a less stimulating environment than an inter-generational homesharing match.

Agency-sponsored shared housing is generally less expensive than institutional care, but it may be more costly than remaining in one's own home. The group home is, however, an especially attractive living arrangement type for those who are physically or mentally frail and those who cannot safely remain in their own homes.

Agencies sponsoring group homes are most frequently nonprofit and may own or lease one or several homes. Anywhere from four to twenty residents may share a home with the typical number of residents being eight (Mantell & Gildea, 1989). The remainder of this chapter will focus on agency-assisted shared housing, primarily because the processes and problems associated with agency-sponsored shared housing differ substantially from arrangements in which elderly people remain in their own homes, and because little research has focused on self-initiated shared housing arrangements.

Major Research Studies and Client Characteristics

Most of the research upon which this chapter is based was conducted in the mid to late 1980s when social scientists and gerontologists became aware of a growing interest in homesharing among social service agencies. A brief overview of some of the studies of the agency-assisted model will serve to illustrate both the range of research topics pursued and the general characteristics of the individuals who become involved in homesharing matches.

In-depth case studies of particular programs, based on many interviews and written agency materials, have been conducted in both Madison, Wisconsin and Burlington, Vermont. In 1983, as part of a larger evaluation of Independent Living's Homeshare Program in Madison (See Howe, Robins, and Jaffe, 1984), Jaffe (1989) conducted qualitative open-ended interviews with nineteen homesharers and seventeen home-seekers who had participated in agency-assisted matches. From these interviews, information on thirty different matches was collected which provided a description of the participants' view of the entire homesharing experience from the decision to participate to the dissolution of the match.

Jaffe found that homesharers in Madison were predominantly white, single, female, and ranged in age from sixty-three to ninety-four. These individuals had lived in their homes an average of thirty-two years. The socioeconomic status of homesharers ranged from working class to upper-middle class. Typical homeseekers were white, female, mostly working-class, and ranged in age from nineteen to twenty-nine. All matches were intergenerational and based on a service exchange in which elderly homesharers provided lodging and young homeseekers provided assistance of various kinds.

Jaffe also found that both homesharers and homeseekers were experiencing transitions. For homesharers, increasing costs of living and/or declining physical health forced them to seek solutions to their increasing dependence. Homeseekers, on the other hand, were moving toward increasing independence, but were either financially or emotionally too insecure to live on their own. The transitory nature of both groups caused matches to be of limited duration. As homesharers became increasingly dependent homeseekers became increasingly independent which often resulted in the dissolution of the match.

Danigelis and Fengler (1991) provide an intensive case study of another homesharing program located in Burlington, Vermont. They studied Project HOME from the program planning stage, beginning in fall of 1981, through the first five years of its operation. Data were collected using applicant questionnaires, follow-up questionnaires, program logs, and interviews with matched participants, project directors, and staff.

They reported that client characteristics varied depending on whether the applicant was seeking a housing or service arrangement. They also found that homesharers were predominantly single, nonworking females, seventy or more years of age, with annual incomes over $7,000. Homesharers seeking service arrangements were somewhat older, less well educated, less likely to be working, and slightly more affluent than those seeking housing arrangements. Homeseekers were mostly single females under the age of 30 with annual incomes below that of homesharers. Homeseekers desiring service arrangements were more likely to be female, had less education, were less frequently employed, and had lower annual incomes than those seeking housing arrangements. In general, the findings suggest that matches were mostly intergenerational with homesharers having higher socioeconomic status than homeseekers.

A number of additional studies support the findings that homesharers are typically over the age of sixty, single, white, retired, and female. They are generally older than homeseekers, and, although not affluent, they have incomes that are generally greater than homeseekers (Maatta, Hornung, Hart, & Primm, 1989; Pynoos & June, 1989; Thuras, 1989; Jaffe & Wellin, 1989).

Homeseekers are somewhat more difficult to categorize. Although most are single, white, and female, they vary greatly in age and employment status. This finding, however, may be an artifact of the economic and social conditions that existed in the particular locations studied. In areas with large concentrations of young college students and tight housing markets, homeseekers are more likely to be students under the age of thirty (Jaffe, 1989). In areas with high housing costs, homeseekers may be older, unemployed, underemployed, or retired (Pynoos & June, 1989; Thuras, 1989). Further, as will be discussed later in this chapter, the characteristics of both homesharers and homeseekers may be influenced by the type of arrangement an agency chooses to promote.

Noticeably lacking is the participation of minorities in agency-assisted homesharing arrangements. Although researchers have documented that few racial or ethnic minorities become either homesharers or homeseekers, the reasons are not yet understood. In the case of agency-assisted homesharing, there may be several reasons why minorities do not participate. As Stack (1975) has shown, the extended family is much more of a reality among poor African-American families than it has ever been among whites. Several generations of families may share housing for economic reasons and this may preclude the necessity of living with nonrelatives. In addition, extended kinship networks of nonrelatives who have been socially "adopted" by families, may share housing and expenses.

In fact, and for a variety of reasons, many African-American families do engage in self-initiated shared housing. This may account both for Schreter's (1986) finding that among elderly participants this is the most prevalent form of home-sharing and the fact that minorities are noticeably under-represented in agency-assisted homesharing. Another reason may be that economically disadvantaged elderly minorities may not have homes or apartments large enough to accommodate a housemate or their dwellings may be located in areas in which homeseekers choose not to live.

Agency-assisted Homesharing Programs in the U.S.

The period from 1970 to the late 1980s was one of rapid growth in the number of agency-assisted shared housing programs. In 1970 there were approximately 25 such programs in the U.S. but by 1988 the number had increased to over two hundred (Mantell & Gildea, 1989). Initially, homesharing programs were located primarily on the East and West coasts. In recent years, however, the idea has spread throughout the U.S. so that by 1986, nearly half of all new programs were located in the Midwest and the Sunbelt states (Robins & Howe, 1989).

Homesharing programs are typically found to be one component of multi-function agencies providing a wide variety of services. In 1986, for example, agencies serving the elderly, such as Area Agencies on Aging and senior centers, sponsored 39 percent of all homesharing programs. Housing authorities and housing opportunity agencies sponsored 17 percent, and general social service agencies sponsored an additional 31 percent (Robins & Howe, 1989).

Although sponsoring agencies may be large and provide numerous services, homesharing programs generally are quite small. In 1984 Jaffe and Howe found that only 12 percent had three or more staff members, and 36 percent had one or fewer full-time equivalent staff members. Programs often supplemented paid staff with volunteers and some relied completely on volunteers. About 34 percent of funding was provided by Community Development Block Grants and 23 percent by the Older Americans Act, but some funds came from private donations or state and local government grants. In any case, funding for homesharing programs was characteristically limited in both magnitude and duration.

Robins and Howe (1989) found that community size and the proportion of elderly residents were the most reliable predictors of whether a community would have a homesharing program. In general, programs were not found in communities with fewer than 100,000 residents (Robins & Howe, 1989). However, several small rural communities with especially high concentrations of elderly people were found to have homesharing programs (Maatta, Hornung, Hart, & Primm, 1989). Areas in which housing costs are high, rental vacancies are few, and elderly home ownership rates are high may also be fertile ground for the development of homesharing programs (Jaffe, 1989).

Matchmaking

There are several things that must occur before agency-assisted matches can be established. The first step is making the public aware that a program exists. Agencies may use a variety of methods to increase public awareness. Among the more common methods are newspaper ads, the use of public bulletin boards, and speeches at public meetings.

After potential homesharers and homeseekers have become aware of the existence of this housing option, they must analyze their alternatives before making the decision to share. Homesharers must decide whether they are willing to give up some of their privacy in exchange for the opportunity to remain in their homes. Homeseekers must decide whether they are willing to devote time and work in exchange for relatively less expensive housing.

Once the decision to share has been made, homeseekers and homesharers contact the assisting agency. What happens next depends on agency goals and staff availability. If a full-service agency is contacted, the client will be asked to make an appointment to speak with a counselor. During this initial meeting clients are advised as to what they may reasonably expect from a homesharing arrangement. Called reality counselling, agents try to ensure that clients are willing to engage in equitable exchanges and are aware of the general characteristics of people available to share. At this stage many potential clients decide that their desires cannot be met and choose not to participate in the program.

If a client decides to participate, he or she is asked to fill out an application providing the agency with information on the available space, their needs, their personality characteristics, and their personal habits. In a full-service program an agent may visit the home of the sharer to determine its suitability for sharing, and reference checks may be made on homeseekers.

Using the pool of applications, agents try to match clients with complementary needs and personalities. Generally the homesharer is contacted and given information on several potential housemates. Meetings between clients are arranged and may be attended by agency representatives, but the decision to engage in a match is left up to the clients. Once clients agree to a match, the agency will help to prepare a written contract specifying the particulars of the exchange. Often a specified trial period is set up during which partners can evaluate their compatibility. If clients decide at the end of the trial period that they are not compatible, the arrangement can be terminated without either partner feeling they have failed.

Depending on the type of arrangement, program agents may provide follow-up phone calls and/or visits to the home to monitor the progress of the match and help with any problems. Jaffe and Howe (1989) found that agencies can be helpful in ensuring that contractual obligations are met, but have less success dealing with matters of personal compatibility. They stress that housemates must be left to decide what their affective relationship, if any, will be.

Many homesharing agencies began with the intention of serving only the elderly but found that few elderly people applied as homeseekers. As a result, most agencies now serve people of all ages, and most matches are, in fact, inter-generational. Similarly, many agencies began with the intention of providing only service matches or only housing matches and found that the needs of many clients could not be met. Consequently, many programs have expanded their operations to include both types of matches to serve a broader range of clients and produce more matches. Many also have expanded their services in an attempt to increase the "success" rate of matches.

Types of Agency-assisted Homesharing Programs

Based on program goals, Jaffe and Howe (1988) have identified three types of shared housing programs and the major characteristics of each. The type of program established may be determined by restrictions imposed by a funding agency or by community characteristics. The three types are: Housing Oriented; Service Oriented; and Mixed Orientation.

The primary goal of housing oriented programs is to provide homeseekers with affordable housing by making use of underutilized space in the homes of the elderly. Jaffe and Howe (1988) found that 73 percent of housing-oriented programs existed in communities where housing vacancies were low and rents were high. And, 71 percent required at least one elderly person in each match. The primary benefit to homesharers is the rental income received from the homeseekers. This is supported by the finding that 84 percent of homeseekers paid rent but provided no services to elderly homesharers.

Primarily because clients are not physically or mentally impaired, housing oriented programs typically provide less agency involvement in matches than do service and mixed programs. Some programs do no more than provide lists of prospective homesharers and homeseekers. Others may provide counselling prior to matching, assistance with contracts, and/or follow-up services, but only 29 percent were found to provide all these services (Jaffe & Howe, 1988).

Service-oriented homesharing programs exist primarily to provide low-cost in-home care to frail older adults, and most of these programs require at least one member of the match to be elderly. Jaffe and Howe found that in only 25 percent of these matches do homeseekers pay rent. Rather, services are generally exchanged for room and board and, in cases where the homesharer requires substantial assistance, the homeseeker may be paid a nominal wage as well. The primary benefit to homeseekers is low-cost or no-cost housing. For the elderly homesharer, who often cannot afford to hire professionals to perform routine home maintenance, repairs, or personal care, service programs strive to provide a low-cost alternative.

Jaffe and Howe (1988) found that 80 percent of service-oriented programs followed a counselling model providing a full range of services from reality counselling prior to matching through reference checks, contract negotiation, home visits, and follow-up on the progress of the match. Agencies with a mixed orientation attempted to fill the needs of both homeseekers, requiring low-cost housing, and homesharers, requiring services in exchange for room and board. They further report that only about 60 percent of these programs required an elderly person in each match, and about 42 percent of homeseekers paid rent indicating both housing and service orientations were served.

Mixed programs provide services based on the type of match. Housing matches generally receive less agency support than service matches, but many programs offer whatever assistance they have available to promote successful matches. About 50 percent of mixed programs were found to provide a full range of services similar to those offered by service programs (Jaffe & Howe, 1988).

The Problem of Program Evaluation

It is extraordinarily difficult to assess the success of agency-assisted shared housing programs. Robins and Howe (1989) found that between 1983 and 1986 the failure rate of programs was about 22 percent, but what this means is not clear since programs have not been in existence long enough to have established a normal attrition rate. So too, lack of stable funding, rather than unsuccessful programming, may be responsible for the failure of some programs. The fact that the absolute number of programs has risen dramatically in the past decade, despite the number of failed programs, suggests that a shift in sponsoring agencies may be responsible for some closings. Robins and Howe (1989) have found that agencies exclusively serving the elderly are losing ground to general social service agencies following a trend toward more service-oriented programs. Thus, the failure of one agency may be the result of the inception of a homesharing program in another agency.

Assessing a program's success in terms of the number of matches accomplished is also difficult. Jaffe and Howe (1988) found that about 38 percent of applicants were matched, with the average number of matches in a year being 54 (although the range of matches was 3 to 450). The small average number of matches is due, at least in part, to the reluctance of healthy elderly people to share their homes with available homeseekers. Many homeseekers are young and many homesharers would prefer a middle-aged housemate. Also, many prospective homesharers are in poor health, require substantial assistance, and may be reluctant to pay a housemate for services. It is often difficult, if not impossible, to match these clients.

The duration of matches, which intuitively might seem to be a predictor of program success, is also problematic. The nature of the clients and their reasons for homesharing make it unlikely that even compatible matches will be of long duration. Initially healthy elderly homesharers may become incapacitated and require services that the current housemate may be unable or unwilling to provide. Frail homesharers may become so physically impaired that home care is no longer feasible.

Homeseekers, too, are generally in transition. Many are students, some are unemployed, and some are displaced homemakers. For each of these categories, the individual's life situation is likely to change in ways that impact their desire or willingness to participate in homesharing. Few homesharing arrangements, even those that participants deem successful, last more than one year and many last less than three months (Jaffe & Howe, 1988). When homeseekers are students, matches may be designed to last no longer than a school semester or school year.

Barriers to Future Growth and Development

Four barriers to the development and growth of shared housing programs have been identified by Mantell and Gildea (1989). First is lack of financial support. Most programs serve clients who cannot afford to pay more than a nominal fee for matching services. Thus, programs must rely on outside funding for continued existence, and the few available staff members must use valuable time, which could otherwise be devoted to client services, to apply for funds. When funding is received, it is often unstable, making future planning difficult, especially as it relates to growth.

Second, program evaluation difficulties must be overcome to allow funding agencies to judge the effectiveness of programs. Most current evaluations focus on the number and duration of matches which are not very good indicators of program success. Agencies must formalize their goals and recordkeeping methods to indicate the full range of services provided to clients.

Third, zoning codes often place strict limitations on the location of shared housing arrangements. In most states, homes in areas that have been designated as "single-family" areas can be shared only by relatives. In areas designated "multi-family," restrictive codes may make homesharing financially unfeasible because it is likely that "multi-family" dwellings are required to be equipped with costly items such as external fire escapes, sprinklers, and fire doors. City planners must be educated in the many benefits of shared housing in an effort to change both zoning ordinances and the way in which shared housing is categorized.

Fourth, federal and state laws often penalize homesharers with a reduction in public benefits, such as SSI, when homes are shared. This may seriously reduce the financial benefits of homesharing and discourage its use by the elderly.

Using data from in-depth interviews, Jaffe (1989) has developed a typology of homesharers, homeseekers, and homesharing matches that is based on varying levels of dependence.

Homesharers

"Independent homesharers" were physically and socially active, healthy elderly persons who basically sought a housing arrangement in which lodging was exchanged for rent. They required someone to perform occasional heavy household chores for which they were willing to offer reduced rent, but they did not require routine household or personal services.

"Transitional homesharers" were subject to functional limitations due to chronic diseases such as arthritis or emphysema and were likely to experience declining health. They required a housemate willing to assist with routine housekeeping, cooking, and errands, but required few, if any, personal services. In exchange, these homesharers offered free room and board to homeseekers.

"Dependent homesharers" were physically frail and required personal and household services. Also in this group are mentally impaired individuals who required nearly constant supervision. They sought a service arrangement in which free room and board was supplemented with a monthly stipend.

Homeseekers

Jaffe found that "independent homeseekers" were generally older graduate students or permanently employed persons who were often involved in serious relationships typically leading to marriage. They did not require supplemental income nor free room and board but wanted a temporary, inexpensive place to live. Busy schedules precluded them from providing more than occasional services, and they sought housing arrangements.

"Transitional homeseekers" were typically advanced undergraduates, the newly graduated, or people who had recently left jobs and were making decisions about whether to return to school or seek other employment. Less financially stable than independent homeseekers, they were willing to provide routine household services in exchange for free room and board, but did not have time to provide substantial personal care to a homesharer.

"Dependent homeseekers" were generally younger people who had recently left their family homes, many to continue their schooling. With few social contacts and severely limited funds, these homeseekers were willing to provide a wide array of household and personal services to homesharers in exchange for free room and board and supplemental income.

Matches

"Independent matches" were characterized by a great deal of social distance between homesharers and homeseekers, each of whom had independent social lives. The independent homesharers involved in these matches clearly controlled the amount and type of social interaction by setting and enforcing house rules, and the relationship between housemates was generally formal and business-like. The lack of personal interaction reduced opportunities for conflict, and matches generally lasted for no longer than the initially negotiated contract period (e.g., one semester or one year).

"Transitional matches" were the most unstable of the three types of matches, largely due to the changing needs of both homesharers and homeseekers. Elderly homesharers in transition may experience increasing functional limitations which move them toward a more dependent status at the same time that homeseekers may be moving toward greater independence. As a result it was found that transitional matches frequently terminate prior to the end of the negotiated contract period.

The social lives of transitional housemates are more intertwined than in independent matches. Because homesharers are dependent on homeseekers for routine household services, they are less able to maintain social distance. Housemates converse frequently and informally, but do not usually discuss matters of a highly personal nature. They may regularly engage in recreational activities of mutual interest, and often consider themselves friends.

Dependent matches are, by their very nature, intimate relationships in which homeseekers generally have influence over very frail elderly homesharers. The intimate personal nature of services brings the housemates together in substantial physical interaction which often results in the disclosure of personal confidences and a sense of family. Because homeseekers must devote a great deal of time to caring for dependent homesharers, housemates may become primary sources of mutual social interaction as well. Emotional attachments between housemates and a sense of responsibility on the part of the homeseeker often lead to the renewal of these matches at the end of the contract period, and many matches end only because of the death or institutionalization of the homesharer.

Based on the survey of program administrators, Jaffe and Howe (1988) found that 55 percent of all matches may be classified as independent or housing arrangements, 40 percent as transitional limited-service arrangements, and only 5 percent as service-oriented dependent arrangements. Further, independent matches presented the fewest set-up difficulties and dependent matches the most, but transitional matches were the most difficult to maintain.

Benefits to Homesharers

Homesharers do not all receive the same benefits, although there are benefits to all. Perhaps the most important benefit is that homesharing permits aging in place. In the United States about 76 percent of the elderly own their homes (Robins & Howe, 1989) and have lived in these homes for much of their lives (Jaffe, 1989; Danigelis & Fengler, 1991). Although mortgages are generally paid, homes are aging, along with their occupants, and often require repairs and maintenance that place a severe financial strain on some elderly people. For healthy independent older adults, homesharing may provide the additional income needed for major repairs and taxes, and homeseekers may provide minor repair services as part of their rent. For the frail elderly, homeseekers may provide needed in-home services that would otherwise be unaffordable or unobtainable.

Danigelis and Fengler (1991) have argued that aging-in-place is an important element of emotional well-being. Homes typically harbor memories of times past and loved ones now gone. Most single elderly homeowners are women who have spent most of their adult lives living in a particular home and the thought of dismantling the household may be devastating.

Neighborhood supports are also lost when the elderly are displaced. They may no longer be able to attend their area church or visit with long-time neighbors and friends. At a time in their lives when spouse and friends are frequently lost through illness and death, the continuity provided by familiar surroundings may become increasingly important.

The continuity of care, which can be provided through successive homesharing arrangements, can indefinitely postpone the necessity of moving elderly homesharers to institutional arrangements. Those who begin with an arrangement designed to ease financial burdens may progress to service arrangements as their health declines. Although securing new housemates may be stressful, it may be less emotionally trying than leaving one's home and neighborhood.

Security and Safety

A second benefit shared by most homesharers is the proximity of help should a medical emergency arise (Schreter, 1986). Many single elderly people and their families fear that a heart attack, stroke, or fall may leave the elderly person unable to summon help. The presence of a housemate may alleviate some of the worry associated with these possibilities.

A third general benefit to homesharers is a greater feeling of personal security (Schreter, 1986). Many elderly people live in deteriorating neighborhoods where criminal activity is increasing. Having a younger person in the house may allay the fears often associated with being alone.

Companionship

The amount of companionship derived by elderly homesharers is very much a function of the type of match. In independent matches, housemates have on-going, separate social lives, and homesharers do not desire or require companionship from homeseekers. They may even consider social interaction an intrusion.

Functionally limited homesharers in transitional matches may be unable to maintain many social relationships outside of the home. They may benefit from the increased social interaction which occurs during the performance of routine household chores and joint recreational activities.

Homeseekers may provide the primary source of companionship for very frail dependent homesharers. Often unable to maintain any outside relationships, these homesharers may come to view their housemates as not only personal caregivers, but confidantes as well.

Disadvantages to Homesharers: Lack of Privacy

Older adults who share their homes experience at least one common disadvantage; all must relinquish some degree of privacy. This is the most common deterrent to homesharing. Most people are reluctant to have a stranger come to live in what has previously been their refuge against the rest of the world. Often only extreme hardship or very poor health will force people to turn to this option. The degree of hardship that the invasion of privacy represents depends greatly on the type of arrangement, but it is felt by many. Overcoming the initial reluctance to share that arises from the fear of loss of privacy is perhaps the greatest challenge to assisting agencies.

Lack of privacy is not as much an issue in independent matches. While homesharers may not like the idea that a stranger has access to their private possessions, private areas for each resident are often well separated. Because few services of any kind are expected from homeseekers, they may spend little or no time in the common areas of the home resulting in increased privacy for homesharers.

Privacy is more precarious in transitional matches in which homeseekers are required to spend more time in the common areas of the home to accomplish the tasks they have contracted to perform. Homesharers may feel that their privacy has been invaded because homeseekers must handle their possessions in the performance of their duties. But private areas of the home may remain off-limits to housemates and some degree of privacy may be maintained. Visits by friends and relatives may be arranged at times when homeseekers are out of the home, or homeseekers may be asked to refrain from using common areas during visits.

The frail dependent elderly suffer the most complete invasion of privacy. The services provided by homeseekers require their frequent presence in all areas of the home. The provision of personal services exposes the homesharer's physical person as well. The inability to maintain privacy may be a factor in producing the emotional attachments often expressed by dependent housemates.

Incompatibility

Problems of incompatibility also differ between types of arrangements. In an independent match, the paths of home-sharers and homeseekers rarely cross and the relationship is very business-like. Incompatibility is generally not an issue because a great deal of social distance is maintained. There may be problems if there are misunderstandings about house rules, but the wishes of the more powerful homesharer usually prevail (Jaffe & Howe, 1988).

Incompatibility does become an issue in transitional matches in which interaction is more frequent. Problems may arise when homesharers have unrealistic expectations for services or homeseekers do not live up to their contractual obligations. If the physical health of the elderly person declines, the homeseeker may be unwilling or unable to provide increased services. This, in turn, may lead to conflict and possible dissolution of the match (Jaffe & Howe, 1988).

In a dependent match, power is often concentrated in the hands of the homeseeker. Jaffe and Howe (1988) found that dependent housemates were the most compatible and argued that because homeseekers felt some guilt about the amount of power they had over another's home and person, they worked harder to make the match compatible.

Short Duration of Matches

The typically short duration of matches can be a source of stress for homesharers and may be related to the degree of privacy they maintain. Independent homesharers may be inconvenienced by seeking new matches, but the social distance inherent in these matches prevents them from having to make major adjustments when and if they are rematched.

Due to the reduced social distance between housemates in transitional matches, it may be more difficult for transitional homesharers to find suitable and compatible housemates. When services become involved in the arrangement, contracts must be carefully negotiated to assure an equitable arrangement, and changing housemates may require the homesharer to adapt to new schedules or changing services.

Dependent homesharers suffer the most from matches of short duration. The personal nature of services provided by homeseekers requires the sharer to place a great deal of trust in his or her housemate. Emotional attachments are often formed causing distress when a match dissolves. Frail elderly homesharers may find it very stressful to negotiate a series of personal care contracts with strangers.

Benefits and Disadvantages to Homeseekers

The primary advantage to all homeseekers is financial and few homeseekers would choose this option if they did not require inexpensive housing. Financial advantages range from affordable rent for independent homeseekers to free room and board (and in some cases income) for dependent homeseekers. The short duration of matches which is sometimes disadvantageous for homesharers often works to the advantage of homeseekers who rarely view homesharing as more than a temporary housing solution.

For the independent homeseeker an additional benefit may be the ability to live in a more desirable neighborhood than could otherwise be afforded. An increased sense of security may also be derived from the presence of another person in the dwelling, especially at night. Disadvantages may include restrictions on visitors, noise levels, and use of common areas.

Additional benefits to transitional homeseekers may include companionship, advice from an experienced older person, and greater freedom of use of common areas in the home. Disadvantages include the possibility of incompatibility leading to early termination of the match, the requirement that homeseekers be available at specified times to provide household services, and increasing service demands by elders experiencing declining health.

Dependent homeseekers may experience all of the advantages listed above and more. Young homeseekers, especially those who have recently left their family homes, may find that homesharing also provides them with a sense of emotional security which might be lacking in other available living arrangements. For dependent homeseekers, homesharing may create a smoother transition to independent living. Dependent homeseekers may also experience the greatest disadvantages. Personal care services place high demands on both their time and emotional resources, potentially keeping them from developing relationships with peers. Homesharers' family members may come to depend on homeseekers to make decisions regarding the homesharers' future which homeseekers may not be prepared to do. Some of these problems can be alleviated through agency-delivered respite care and counselling.

Benefits to Society

Homesharing has the potential to provide substantial financial benefits to society as well as to individuals. Many frail elderly persons living in nursing homes are the recipients of Medicaid assistance, the largest item in most state budgets. Although service-oriented agencies find dependent matches difficult to arrange, most do serve at least some dependent homesharers. Keeping only one frail elderly nursing home candidate in his or her own home for a single year could pay much of the annual cost of operating a typical homesharing program.

Transitional homesharers may be entitled to government assistance for home-care services. Jaffe and Howe (1989) noted that in 1983 the state of Wisconsin allowed payment of as much as $8,400 per person per year for home care. In transitional homesharing matches many of the services for which the taxpayer would otherwise pay are provided as part of the exchange between homesharers and homeseekers. Further, the use of available, low-cost space in the homes of the elderly could also reduce the demand for student dormitories, low-income housing, and homeless shelters, all of which are subsidized, in one form or another, by tax revenues.

A final potential benefit is the intergenerational quality of most homesharing matches. In a society that has become increasingly age-segregated, homesharing offers individuals the opportunity to create the sort of intergenerational relationships which they may have experienced as natural in their families, but which are often discouraged by the highly segregated nature of our housing and job markets. Homesharing specifically, and intergenerational programming generally, offer some hope of decreasing the social distance between generations along with the stereotypes and ill will that often accompany such distance.

The many benefits of shared housing for elderly home-sharers, younger homeseekers, and society suggest that communities and funding agencies should view homesharing as a cost-effective, socially progressive, and viable alternative living arrangement. Efforts should be made to increase public awareness of this alternative which allows elderly people the opportunity to remain in their homes and active in their communities.

REFERENCES

Danigelis, Nicholas L. and Alfred P. Fengler. 1991. *No Place Like Home: Intergenerational Home Sharing Through Social Exchange*. New York: Columbia University Press.

Hareven, Tamara K. 1989. "American Families in Transition: Historical Perspectives on Change." 39–57 in Arlene S. Skolnick and Jerome H. Skolnick, eds., *Families in Transition*. Glenview, Ill.: Scott, Foresman and Company.

Howe, Elizabeth and Dale J. Jaffe. 1989. "Homesharing for Homecare." 101–117 in Dale J. Jaffe, ed., *Shared Housing for the Elderly*. Westport, Conn.: Greenwood Press.

Howe, Elizabeth, Barbara Robins, and Dale J. Jaffe. 1984. "Evaluation of Independent Living's Homeshare Program." Unpublished report for Independent Living of Madison, WI.

Jaffe, Dale J. 1989. *Caring Strangers: The Sociology of Intergenerational Homesharing*. Greenwich, Conn.: JAI Press.

Jaffe, Dale J. and Christopher Wellin. 1989. "The Nature of Problematic Homesharing Matches: The Case of Share-a-Home of Milwaukee." 181–193 in Dale J. Jaffe, ed., *Shared Housing for the Elderly*. Westport, Conn.: Greenwood Press.

Jaffe, Dale J. and Elizabeth Howe. 1988. "Agency-assisted Shared Housing: The Nature of Programs and Matches." *The Gerontologist*. 28:318–324.

————. 1989. "Case Management for Homesharing." *Journal of Gerontological Social Work*. 14(3/4): 91–110.

Maatta, Norma, Karen Hornung, Mary Hart, and Karen Primm. 1989. "Homesharing in a Rural Context." 37–46 in Dale J. Jaffe, ed., *Shared Housing for the Elderly*. Westport, Conn.: Greenwood Press.

Mantell, Joyce and Mary Gildea. 1989. "Elderly Shared Housing in the United States." 13–23 in Dale J. Jaffe, ed., *Shared Housing for the Elderly*. Westport, Conn.: Greenwood Press.

Pynoos, Jon and Arlyne June. 1989. "The Matchmakers of Santa Clara County." 141–158 in Dale J. Jaffe, ed., *Shared Housing for the Elderly*. Westport, Conn.: Greenwood Press.

Robins, Barbara and Elizabeth Howe. 1989. "Patterns of Homesharing in the United States." 25–36 in Dale J. Jaffe, ed., *Shared Housing for the Elderly*. Westport, Conn.: Greenwood Press.

Schreter, Carol A. 1986. "Advantages and Disadvantages of Shared Housing." *Journal of Housing for the Elderly*. 3:121–138.

Stack, Carol B. 1975. *All Our Kin: Strategies for Survival in a Black Community*. New York: Harper & Row.

Thuras, Paul D. 1989. "Habits of Living and Match Success: Shared Housing in Southern California." 159–172 in Dale J. Jaffe, ed., *Shared Housing for the Elderly*. Westport, Conn.: Greenwood Press.

CHAPTER 11

Assisted Living: Improving the Quality of Housing for Older Adults

Patricia K. Suggs
Katherine M. Logan

As individuals age, accommodation and relocation become important issues. At the extreme, accommodation can involve relocation to a less challenging but more restrictive environment. So important is this topic that some (Netting & Wilson, 1991) believe accommodation decisions are an inevitable part of aging. At any age, however, a change in living arrangements represents a major life event, and the impact of such an event should never be underestimated. Of course, sometimes an older person actively wishes to move and has made an informed decision. For many others, however, a less stressful solution is to investigate ways of improving the existing environment to meet changing needs (Garret, 1992).

Even when assistance is needed, relocation may be unnecessary for those with family members or friends who are willing and able to either locate services or provide the needed assistance. For those who lack these support resources, relocation, and its attendant stressful adaptations, may be the only available option. Because of this, there has been increasing interest in incorporating supportive services into existing housing programs in an attempt to maintain older adults in familiar housing and delay or eliminate the need for relocation.

Housing Models

A variety of housing models, all of which attempt to meet the changing needs of older adults, have been developed over the past few decades. In 1980, for example, Lawton, Greenbaum, and Liebowik presented two conceptual models for dealing with increasing resident frailty within a retirement community. In the first of these, labeled the Constant Model, an elderly person is likely to be relocated to a more supportive environment once the individual becomes frail and is no longer able to maintain an independent lifestyle. In the other model, labeled the Accommodation Model, increasingly intense services are provided as residents age-in-place.

Similarly, Hofland (1990) has suggested four distinct models of housing that form a continuum. Hofland's Model I compares with Lawton's Constant Model (Lawton, Greenbaum, & Liebowik, 1980) described above. In this model, as long as the older resident remains functionally independent, the resident resides in independent housing. Once frailty or disability become a problem, however, relocation is necessary.

Hofland's Model II represents a social service model which provides for a "least restrictive environment." This compares with Lawton's Accommodation Model (Lawton, Greenbaum, & Liebowik, 1980) which, according to Hofland, fosters dependence in that services are often provided whether the resident actually needs them or not.

Model III focuses on the structure and delivery of supportive services. This model describes housing that attempts to meet the needs of a heterogeneous older population in which the best "fit" between functional ability and the environment is sought.

Model IV represents a direct challenge to societal perceptions of older people by focusing on their unique contributions and needs. This model calls attention to the need for social reform in housing policies and is in sharp contrast to existing residential arrangements.

Both of these efforts at categorization, as well as the many others that have appeared in recent years, can be seen as attempts to make conceptual sense of a very complex set of concerns consisting of functional needs, personal preferences, societal resources, and social willingness to provide alternative housing arrangements.

Housing Options

In general, current conceptual models of specialized housing attempt to categorize housing types by the needs they are designed to meet. The purpose of any such model is to simplify an otherwise complex set of elements that are constantly changing in order to meet the special needs of a resident population which itself is changing. The list of nontraditional responses to the housing needs of older people is a large one, yet nontraditional housing options remain only a very small portion of the overall response to these housing needs. As discussed in earlier chapters, substantial demographic changes in the composition of the elderly have been projected. Therefore, it has been suggested that the ability of nontraditional housing to meet the needs of the elderly will become an important issue.

The Concept of Assisted Living

The concept of "assisted living" refers to a coordinated combination of housing and support services for the elderly. Assisted living is viewed as a means of providing a non-institutional living arrangement for those who are neither functionally independent nor totally dependent. Supportive housing options range from shared sleeping space in a single family home to totally self-contained apartments in a building with shared common and support service space. Some offer limited access to staff and selected hotel-type services, while others provide ongoing personal and nursing care. These forms of housing are generally not regulated uniformly, although most forms of assisted living are licensed by state agencies (Leak, 1991).

According to Kane, Illsont, Kane, and Nyman (1990), assisted living, as a specialized type of housing, offers great promise in meshing housing with services for the most vulnerable and frail older individuals. The basic model for assisted living includes activities designed to "normalize" the living environment, proactive strategies to enhance client functioning, a carefully planned response to prevailing cultural values, and a conscious effort to refine service management and practices.

A critical element in housing arrangements, and one that assisted living is intended to address, is meeting the needs of older adults while at the same time allowing those individuals to maintain personal control over their lives (Berkowitz, Waxman, & Yaffe, 1988). Much recent research has been concerned with decreased control among the elderly and the resultant impact on their physical and psychological well-being. The concept of personal control has been found to be a powerful variable in human behavior. Increased choice and control in community and sheltered care settings for the elderly lead to more positive social environments, better resident functioning, lower resident turnover, and more positive perceptions of the environment by both residents and outside observers (Moos and Igra, 1980).

Despite its inherent attractiveness, assisted living has not been vigorously pursued by policymakers or developers in the United States. This has been at least partially due to restrictive federal policies regarding the inclusion of supportive services in housing programs (Wilson, 1988). Historically, housing and supportive services have been viewed as separate issues falling within the separate and exclusive domains of various federal and state agencies. For example, the original statutory mandate of the Older Americans Act is to serve older adults in their "own" homes. As a consequence, those living in age-segregated housing, such as public housing for the elderly, were often excluded from services with the assumption that their service needs were already being met.

Medicare and Medicaid also serve to strengthen the separation of housing and supportive services. The Social Security Administration's medical model of long-term care, which requires that most services be authorized and performed

Assisted Living 249

by specially trained individuals (e.g., physicians, nurses, and certified personnel) in designated institutions (e.g., hospitals and nursing homes), has had the consequence of formalizing the separation of housing and service components as official federal policy. Because of this, the number of age-segregated independent living units for the elderly that are without services has continued to increase. As a further consequence, the number of nursing home beds has also increased (Wilson, 1992).

The legislation that served as the basis for Medicaid programs for older people identified only two types of living arrangements: (1) totally independent living; and (2) confinement to a skilled nursing facility or intermediate care facility. The role of supportive housing falling between these two extremes was neither recognized nor legitimized. However, additional service options were created such as boarding homes (Newcomer and Stone, 1985). As a consequence, board and care has become the housing of last resort for the very poor who can not qualify for nursing home placement under Medicaid regulations. At the same time, the private market saw an increase in the demand for supportive housing (Newman, 1985; 1988; Regnier et al., 1991; Zedlewski, 1989).

By the late 1970s, the "continuum of care" consisted of independent living options, with limited support services routinely available, and the various types of boarding homes and nursing homes. Efforts to expand this continuum of care focused mainly upon community-based care options for individuals residing in their own homes. Such options usually included home repair, nutrition site meals, chore services, and property tax relief programs.

By the early 1980s, increases in the cost of nursing home care resulted in more emphasis being placed on "targeted" services aimed at meeting the needs of the vulnerable older population. Homecare and adult daycare were implemented to reduce the risk of institutionalization. Also during this time, changes began to occur in populations of older persons living in all types of age-segregated housing. In general, they were getting older and more frail. By the mid 1980s, "aging-in-place" and "delayed entry" began to appear in the gerontological literature to describe this phenomenon and its attendant problems. At the same time older adults were "aging-in-place" they were becoming less willing to accept a groundless belief in the inevitability of nursing home placement (Wilson, 1992).

This resistance led to expanded efforts to enhance the availability of traditional "scattered site" services such as in-home health, meals-on-wheels and remote emergency-care monitoring. In addition, some efforts were made to create programs aimed at keeping older adults in single family homes. These efforts included homesharing, accessory apartments, reverse annuity programs, Elder Cottage Housing Opportunity (ECHO) housing, and managed care programs such as ON-LOK in California (1979). These few examples have had little impact in states with increasing numbers of frail older adults needing ongoing services. Obviously, as Newman (1990) has suggested, new options are needed which will serve the more impaired older individuals, that will cost less than traditional nursing home placement, and that will be more acceptable to older consumers and their families.

Assisted Living

The growth of the frail elderly population and rapid increases in the cost of long-term care have resulted in several efforts to keep older persons in their communities and, consequently, out of nursing homes, for as long as is possible. One particularly promising effort has been assisted living.

In spite of the absence of a cohesive federal policy, states have begun to explore the development and regulation of new forms of supportive housing (Leak, 1991). Also under consideration are ways to define and regulate that broad category of services and housing that has become known as assisted living. Most assisted living programs utilize the principle of environmental and client normalization which reduces the effect of individual impairment through manipulation of the physical setting and involves systematic intervention which focuses upon increasing individual competence (Manfredini & Smith, 1988). The residential environment creates a recognizable private household, while at the same time utilizing materials in common or public spaces that are intended to replicate, as closely as possible, those used in private individual residences (Wilson, 1992). Emphasis on these structural elements overlaps with strong beliefs surrounding the emotional and social context of "home." Tully (1986) defined elements of home to include security, small familial groups, control over the course of daily life, unity of purpose and group identity. Taken together these reflect the general goals of assisted living in the United States.

Assisted living has the potential to incorporate even the most complex and intense need for systematic intervention. In contrast, current programmatic interventions have tended to focus on bundles of service assumed to be generally appropriate in select settings. One consequence of this is a bi-modal system consisting of in-home services delivered in single units by multiple providers and institutional services delivered in fixed packages by a single provider. Both of these often result in a poor fit between available services and actual individual service need. Improving this fit involves re-evaluating how services could be delivered to more closely match individual preferences and actual need. Conceptually, this means coordinating unbundled services that would be more cost effective and would focus on client normalization. One obvious approach is to expand the scope, range and mix of services in settings where multiple clients live in close proximity.

One such approach that has been used successfully in Winnipeg, Manitoba, Canada is a 400-unit housing complex for older adults (Blandford, Chappell, Marshall, 1989). In 1984 the Provincial Department of Health funded a Tenant Resource Coordinator (TRC) position for the entire housing facility. The primary function of this full-time employee was to develop and serve as a facilitator for supportive services needed by the residents. In addition, the TRC was to serve as a liaison with existing formal and informal sources of support that were already involved in the housing environment. The success of this approach should serve as a model for existing housing facilities.

Examples of Assisted-Living Programs
in the United States

Oregon

An assisted-living program in Oregon originated in 1983 as a private pay option. By merging consumer preference (home care) with need (core care capability), a new type of supportive housing emerged. Three events which heavily influenced the program were: (1) a new mode of financing (bond financing through the State Housing Agency); (2) the decision to license the project under existing state rules for residential care; and (3) those involved in developing the prototype were new to the field of supportive housing. Assisted living in Oregon adheres to five principles that are believed to be essential to quality long-term care. These include: individual choice, personal dignity, independence, privacy, and a homelike environment.

In 1987 Oregon developed a pilot project for Medicaid clients in one of two existing assisted-living projects. As an outgrowth of this, the assisted-living program involved construction of a building designed for the care of more than 100 frail elderly persons. Residents of this building are encouraged to furnish their dwelling units with their own belongings and a professional staff is available at all times to provide an array of services. The resulting model calls for meeting individual needs in areas such as assessment, meals, laundry, social activities, transportation, personal care, nursing and medical care, support for behavior difficulties, and household management. Funding is on a flexible cost basis with the rate of payment determined by levels of client impairment (Wilson, 1992).

Since the project's opening, its goal has been to provide incentives for state agencies to expand the model as a means of illustrating the beneficial role supportive housing could play in long-term care. Thus, in Oregon at least, assisted living could become an important long-term care option in the future. In fact, some agencies in the state have suggested that the assisted-living model will become the predominate mode of custodial care.

North Carolina

The North Carolina Division of Aging was awarded a grant to develop the Housing Independence for Older North Carolinians project. The resulting program was strongly influenced by the Oregon model described above. Through this grant, older adults will be assisted in securing and maintaining maximum independence and dignity in a home environment with appropriate supportive services. The philosophy is to recognize the varying and changing needs of older persons and to support a social model which emphasizes assistance. The primary goal of the program, jointly administered by the North Carolina Division of Aging and the North Carolina Housing Finance Agency, is to develop a set of policy recommendations that encourage linkages between housing and community-based in-home care for frail older adults. Under this model, service intensity is determined by the functional limitations of each resident. Services will be provided based on a written individualized assistance plan, developed through a team approach with resident and family participation.

Two principal activities of the program include program and policy development and the establishment of at least four replicable demonstration program sites. Various forms of multi-unit housing built expressly for older adults were included by utilizing the following programs: (1) an incentive grant whereby existing local housing units and service agencies can establish a link to housing with services; and (2) a pre-development loan program which will aid in financing "up-front" expenses associated with obtaining permanent capital financing for housing with services projects. Loans are to be offered on a competitive basis and a preference will be given to nonprofit agencies. Currently there are seven sites which include three under the incentive grants program and four under the pre-development loan program.

A follow-up grant has been awarded by the Robert Wood Johnson Foundation. In this project, the North Carolina Housing Finance Agency will work with eighteen housing units in North Carolina to coordinate supportive services for seniors in subsidized housing. These projects will rely heavily on consumer choice to determine the services to be offered.

Implications for Managers and Staff

Increased interest in the incorporation of services into existing housing facilities has serious implications for managers and staff who may lack training in service delivery to frail older adults. Studies in public housing units demonstrate the tremendous need both for education of housing managers and staff and for the linkage between housing units and community services. One study, dealing with subsidized housing for the elderly, involved a survey mailed to 248 housing managers in the State of New York. The results indicated that 62 percent of managers were not familiar with how to gain access to the key health and human services in their communities, hampering their ability to accommodate the environment to the changing needs of their residents (NCOA, 1989).

In a North Carolina study of housing managers in the early 1980s, public housing authorities reported that they had written eligibility and continued residence policies, but few reported having services offered within their projects. Of those with 50 percent or more elderly residents, over half reported no resident staff persons for their projects and 42 percent did not require special training of managers in meeting the needs of older adults (Suggs, Stephens, & Kivett, 1987).

Heumann (1988) conducted a study of site managers of subsidized housing in three Illinois state agencies concerned with housing and support needs of elderly persons. The primary goal of this study was to obtain the managers' estimates of problems related to aging in place by determining how many of their residents were at a level of frailty where additional support was necessary. A mail survey was conducted to determine the ability of staff to monitor, support, transfer, or retain frail residents. Managers were asked to estimate the number of hours per month spent by on-site staff on each of twenty-three activities grouped into three dimensions: basic physical management and administrative activities; basic tenant interaction activities; and tenant support activities. Most site managers appeared to be hired for their fiscal and property management skills, yet approximately 26 percent of management problems involved support services, or the lack of them, for frail elderly tenants. It was believed to be detrimental to relocate older adults when untrained site managers were the ones making the decisions. The quality of support issue is a major factor to be considered. Typically, when there is no family and no affordable assisted living option, the only remaining alternative is to relocate to a long-term care institution—usually a nursing home. It is certain that policies are needed which address both the aging-in-place phenomenon as well as the need for services in subsidized housing for independent elderly people.

Conclusion

Dramatic changes in the size and needs of the older population are likely to further stretch the already inadequate boundaries of existing housing policies. Much recent housing research has been concerned with the impact of decreased control on the well-being of older adults. The findings generally support the notion that control of one's living environment is an important element in psychological and physical well-being. Specifically, studies by Langer and Rodin (1976), Rodin and Langer (1980), and Schulz and Brenner (1977) have confirmed the beneficial psychological impact of increasing an individual's control over her or his environment.

Research has also confirmed that increased choice and control in community and sheltered care settings for the elderly lead to more positive social environments, better individual functioning, lower resident turnover, and more positive perceptions of the environment by both residents and outside observers (Moos, 1981; Moos & Igra, 1980). Further, a clear positive relationship has been established between internal locus of control and life satisfaction (Kuypers, 1972). Butler (1975) has also pointed out that loss of choice is one of the most significant changes in later life and that such a loss promotes helplessness.

In terms of self-esteem, Chown (1977) has argued that both retirement and relocation may produce decreases in self-esteem and she related this process to an increase in helplessness.

As the elderly confront increasing frailty and the need for assistance, environmental adjustment, including renovation and relocation, become major coping mechanisms (Jackson, Longino, Zimmerman, & Bradsher, 1991). Assisted living is particularly relevant in situations where supportive needs are increasing at the same time functional abilities are declining. Specifically, assisted living can enhance the feeling of control by older adults by allowing them a choice of where they live. We can no longer ignore the importance of supportive services to maintaining the preferred lifestyles of frail older adults. Because of this, as the older population grows and as the need for coordinated and integrated supportive services becomes more critical, some form of assisted living is likely to emerge as a viable, efficient, and above all else a preferable living arrangement for frail elderly people.

REFERENCES

American Association of Housing for the Aging Provider News, 7(4), 1992 "Housing the elderly" p. 10.

Baker, P.M. (1987). A survey of the need for sheltered housing for the elderly in greater Victoria. Paper presented at the meeting of the Canadian Association on Gerontology, Calgary, Alberta.

Berkowitz, M.W., Waxman, R., and Yaffe, L. (1988). The effects of a resident self-help model on control, social involvement and self-esteem among the elderly. *The Gerontologist, 28*(5), 620–624.

Blandford, B.A, Chappell, N., and Marshall, S. (1989). Tenant resource coordinators: An experiment in supportive housing. *The Gerontologist, 29* (6), 826–829.

Bolda, E. (1991). Initial Report on North Carolina Domiciliary Care Policy. Prepared for inclusion in the North Carolina Long Term Care Bibliographic Database, The Long Term Care Resources,

Duke University Center for the Study of Aging and Human Development.

Butler, A. (1983). Housing and the elderly—a sheltered response. In Butler, A. and Tinker, N. Housing *Alternatives for the Elderly.* Centre for Applied Social Studies, University of Leeds, England, Occasional Paper no. 10.

Butler, R.N. (1975). *Why Survive? Being Old in America.* New York: Harper & Row.

Chown, S.M. (1977). Morale, Careers, and Personal Potentials. In J.E. Birren & K.W. Schaie (Eds.), *Handbook of the Psychology of Aging* (pp. 672–691). New York: Van Nostrand Reinhold.

Garret, G. (1992). But does it feel like home?: Accommodation needs in later life. *Professional Nurse, 7*(4), 254–257.

Goldberg, S.L. (1972). Nonprofits will flourish in 90s. *AAHA Provider News, 7*(1).

Heumann, L.F. (1988). Assisting the frail elderly living in subsidized housing for the independent elderly: A profile of the management and its support priorities. *The Gerontologist, 28* (5), 625–631.

Hofland, B.F. (1990). Value and ethical issues in residential environments for the elderly. In D. Tilson (Ed.), *Aging in place* (pp. 241–271). Glenview, IL: Scott, Foresman.

Jackson, D.J., Longino, C.F., Zimmerman, R.S., Bradsher, J.E. (1991). Environmental adjustments to declining functional ability, *Research on Aging, 13*(3), 289–309.

Jaffe, D.J., and Howe, E. (1988). Agency-assisted shared housing: The nature of programs and matches. *The Gerontologist, 28*(3), 318–324.

Kane, R., Illsont, L., Kane, R., and Nyman, J. (1990). "Meshing Services with Housing: Lessons from Adult Foster Care and Assisted Living in Oregon." Minneapolis: University of Minnesota Care Decisions Resource Center.

Kuypers, J.A. (1972). Internal-External Locus of Control, Ego Functioning, and Personality Characteristics in Old Age. *The Gerontologist, 12*(2): 168–173.

Langer E.J., & J. Rodin. (1976). The Effects of Choice and Enhanced Responsibility for the Aged: A Field Experiment in an Institutional Setting. *Journal of Personality and Social Psychology, 34:* 191–198.

Lawton, M.P. (1990). Knowledge resources and gaps in housing the aged. In D. Tilson (Ed.), *Aging in place* (pp. 287–309). Glenview, IL: Scott, Foresman.

Lawton, M.P., and Weeden, J. (1985). Introduction, *Generations, 9:* 4–8.

Lawton, M.P., Greenbaum, M., & Liebowik, R. (1980). The lifespan of housing environments for the aging. *The Gerontologist, 20*(1), 56–64.

Leak, S. (1991). State Housing with Services Programs: New initiatives, striking diversity. *Long Term Care Advances, 3:* 2–7.

Manfredini, D., and Smith, W. (1988). The concept and implementation of active treatment. In M. Janicki, M. Krauss, M. Seltzer (Eds.), *Community Residence for Persons with Developmental Disabilities: Here to Stay.* Baltimore: Paul Brooks Publishing Company.

Moos, R.H. (1981). Environmental choice and control in community care settings for older people, *Journal of Applied Social Psychology, 2:* 23–43.

Moos, R.H., and Igra, A. (1980). Determinants of the social environments of sheltered care settings. *Journal of Health and Social Behavior, 13:* 88–98.

National Council on Aging (1989). Knowledge gaps among housing managers. *Networking, 1*(2), 4.

——— (1992). Annual Report, *Perspectives on Aging* (March–June), p. 6.

——— (1992). Annual Report, *Perspectives on Aging* (March–June), p. 10–11.

Netting, F.E., and Wilson, C.C. (1991). Accommodation and relocation decision making in continuing care retirement communities. *Health and Social Work, 16*(4), 266–73.

Newcomer, R., and Stone, R. (1985). *Board and Care Housing. Generations, 9:* 39–41.

Newman, S. (1985). The shape of things to come. *Generations, 9:* 24–27.

——— (1990). The frail elderly in the community: An overview of characteristics. In D. Tilson (Ed.), *Aging in Place.* Glenview, IL: Scott, Foresman.

Regnier, V., Hamilton, J., and Yatabe, S. (1991). *Best Practices in Assisted Living.* Los Angeles: Long Term Care National Resource Center at UCLA/USC.

Rodin, J., & Langer, E.J. (1980). Aging Labels: The Decline of Control and the Fall of Self Esteem. *Journal of Social Issues, 36:* 12–29.

Schulz, R., & G. Brenner. (1977). Relocation and the Aged: A Review and Theoretical Analysis. *Journal of Gerontology, 32:* 323–333.

Suggs, P.K., Stephens, V., Kivett, V.R. (1987). Coming, going, remaining in public housing: How do the elderly fare? *Journal of Housing for the Elderly,* 4(1), 87–104.

Tilson, D. (Ed.). (1990). *Aging in Place.* Glenview IL: Scott, Foresman.

Tully, K. (1986). *Improving Residential Life for Disabled People.* New York: Churchill Livingstone.

Wilson, K. (1988). Beyond loving care. Paper prepared for the Oregon Gerontological Society, Portland.

Wilson, K.B. (1992). Assisted living: A model of supportive housing. To be published in *Advances in Long Term Care.* New York: Springer.

Zedlewski, S., Barnes, R., Burt, M., McBride, T., and Meyer, J. (1989). *The Needs of the Elderly in the 21st Century.* Washington, D.C.: The Urban Institute.

CHAPTER 12

Medical Care in Residential Settings: The Nursing Home in Transition

Richard A. Lusky
Stanley R. Ingman

Introduction: The Rise of the Modern Nursing Home

For nearly three decades, the nursing home has been synonymous with long-term care in America. While there is overwhelming evidence that the majority of older adults would prefer to cope with illness and infirmity in their own homes, growing numbers end up doing so in residential settings. This is true in spite of the introduction of in-home services, adult daycare, respite care and other intended deterrents to institutionalization. This chapter examines the nursing home as a residential and health-care setting for the elderly. Apart from its medical trappings, the nursing home can also be seen as a form of organized housing for the elderly where many tenants try to create a home-like environment within a social context that is primarily controlled by others.

Origins of the Nursing Home

The roots of the contemporary nursing home may be traced to the English Poor Laws and their emulation in colonial America. The first such law, the Elizabethan Poor Law of 1601, set a precedent for public responsibility for care of the poor, the aged, the disabled, and the chronically ill. Significantly, it fostered in-home rather than institutional care, requiring that each local community provide the resources required to enable such individuals to remain in their own homes. By 1722, however, concern with the costs of this program led to a new Poor Law which created almshouses, or workhouses, where economies of scale might reduce the costs of care. Over time, the development of new programs for the blind and other specialized groups left these establishments with the responsibility of providing the aged and the indigent with acute and long-term medical care as well as a place to live. As medicine became more effective in treating infectious diseases, further specialization took place and the management of short-term illnesses shifted to the newly emerging hospitals. This left the public facilities and their dispensaries with the responsibility for providing long-term care to the chronically ill poor, including many aged (Allen, 1987, pp. 107–111).

Development of the Nursing Home Industry

Economic development, public health measures, and the introduction of sulfonamide and antibiotics brought dramatic declines in death rates during the late 1800s and early 1900s. As longevity increased, cities, counties and states sought federal relief from the responsibility of providing long-term care to growing numbers of indigent elders. Concerned with both the potential cost of such care and the unsavory reputation of the county homes and state mental hospitals, which had replaced the earlier public workhouses, the federal government resisted funding any residential care of the elderly. As a result, it limited its principal vehicle for assisting the elderly, the Social Security Act of 1935, to cash payments to noninstitutionalized persons.

Eventually, however, state and local officials sought and won court approval of payment for services rendered to Social Security recipients in privately owned boarding homes. This set the stage for full federal participation in the financing of residential long-term care through the Medicare and Medicaid amendments of the mid-1960s, and for the development of a publicly supported nursing home industry in the private sector (Allen, 1987, pp. 112–114).

The Growing Need for Nursing Home Care

According to Allen (1987, p. 176), "The nursing home industry, on the scale we know it, would not be possible without Social Security checks and reimbursement of Medicare and Medicaid bills for patients." While it is true that these programs facilitate access to the nursing home, few elders would opt for nursing home placement if they or their families did not need (or perceive a need for) the services which nursing homes provide. Three major factors tend to fuel the demand for residential care:

(1) *Continued Population Aging.* Continued improvement in the mortality rates of Americans and the concomitant improvements in life expectancy have brought steady increases in the number and percent of citizens aged sixty-five and older. These increases will become even more dramatic early in the next century when individuals of the post-war baby-boom generation, born between 1950 and 1970, begin to turn sixty-five. In 1900, the nation's 3 million citizens aged sixty-five and older represented only about 4 percent of its total population of 76 million. By 1990, the nation's population had tripled to nearly 250 million. In contrast, the older population had increased tenfold to 31 million or 12.5 percent of the total population. During this same period, those aged eighty-five and older represented the fastest growing segment of the older population, their numbers increasing nearly twenty-five fold compared to thirteen fold among those aged seventy-five to eighty-four and eight fold among those aged sixty-five to seventy-four. Bureau of the Census "middle series" population projections suggest that these trends will continue between 1990 and 2050, with the

number of all elders doubling from 31 million to 68.5 million, and the number of those aged eighty-five and older more than tripling, from 4.6 million to 15.2 million. By 2050, when the surviving baby-boomers will have reached advanced ages, those aged sixty-five and older are likely to represent approximately 23 percent of the total population, and those aged eighty-five and older, 5 percent (United States Bureau of the Census, 1992, Table 2–1).

(2) *Higher Rates of Morbidity and Infirmity at Advanced Ages.* Remarkably, these increases in longevity have not been accompanied by comparable improvements in health and functional status. Rather, increased longevity has been associated with increases in the prevalence of disabling chronic conditions requiring continuous medical and/or personal care in their advanced stages. While there are gender and racial differences, the rates of arthritis, hypertension, hearing impairment and heart disease, the most common chronic conditions experienced by the elderly, all increase with advancing age (U.S. Senate Special Committee on Aging, 1991, pp. 112–113). Moreover, the elderly are more likely to be subject to co-morbidity, with the number of chronic conditions increasing with advancing age. By age eighty, 53 percent of males and 70 percent of females report two or more such conditions (National Center for Health Statistics, 1989a, pp. 3–4).

Not surprisingly, the rates of functional impairment also increase with advancing age. A recent analysis of 1984–1985 data on community dwelling and institutionalized older adults found that the rate of functional dependency in basic self-care activities, such as bathing or dressing, and/or more complex tasks, such as meal preparation or shopping, grew from 20.2 percent among those aged sixty-five to seventy-four to 35.1 percent among those aged seventy-five to eighty-four to 66.2 percent among those aged eighty-five and older. (National Center for Health Statistics, 1990, p. 23). One frequent explanation for the anomaly of increasing longevity in the face of continued illness and infirmity among the "old old" is that improvements in general health status and medical technology are enabling elders to survive otherwise fatal conditions, leaving them to cope with residual disabilities.

(3) *Changing Social and Financial Resources.* As more and more Americans have reached the age where the risk of chronic illness and impairment are great, there have been important changes in the resources which elders can muster to preserve their independence. Traditionally, care of the chronically ill and the functionally dependent has been a family matter. While it is still true that most long-term care is provided by informal caregivers, the availability of such care is threatened by gender differences in life expectancy (which favor elderly women only to leave them living alone in the latter years of life); steady reductions in family size, the advent of dual wage-earner families and increased geographic mobility (which can reduce the number of siblings and children available for assistance in times of need); and the increasing prevalence of very old individuals who must depend on adult children who are aged themselves (and less likely, therefore, to be capable of providing such assistance).

In part, the declining availability of informal supports has been offset by improvements in the financial resources of older persons during the 1970s and 1980s. After adjustment for inflation, the average income for elderly families increased by 18 percent between 1969 and 1984, while the average income of elderly individuals grew by 34 percent. These improvements, associated with a shift away from reliance on earnings, families, and charities for retirement income to savings, pension plans, and public programs, reduced the poverty rate among the elderly from 25.3 percent to 12.4 percent during this period (U.S. General Accounting Office, 1986, pp. 18–19). While a great many older persons were still left below or marginally above the poverty level, substantial numbers achieved the reserves required to purchase at least part of their formal care if informal support mechanisms failed.

In sum, this century has seen a dramatic growth in the number and proportion of older Americans. This growth has been most rapid among the "old old," who are at greatest risk for chronic health problems which are often accompanied by physical impairments and functional limitation. This trend has occurred at a time when other social changes in our society have begun to limit the availability of the informal care upon which elders traditionally relied in times of disability. At the same time, the advent of public programs to assist the elderly and the general improvement in their economic conditions have put elders in a better position to secure formal care in times of need. Together, these developments have fueled the growth of a "long-term care industry" with the nursing home as the principal provider.

The Organization and Functioning of Nursing Homes

Essential Features of the Nursing Home

Kane and Kane have defined long-term care as, "a set of health, personal care, and social services delivered over a sustained period of time to persons who have lost or never acquired some degree of functional capacity." They note that, ideally, these services are provided in the least restrictive environment possible. They also note that, while the aged typically constitute the majority of long-term care patients, younger persons may require long-term care as a result of impairments present at birth, the early onset of disabling chronic diseases such as multiple sclerosis or AIDS, or physical trauma (1987, pp. 3–4).

The functional limitations which may lead to long-term care are often grouped into limitations in the Activities of Daily Living (ADLs), involving such basic self-care activities as dressing, bathing and feeding (Katz, et al., 1963, pp. 914–919) and limitations in Instrumental Activities of Daily Living (IADLs) involving more complex activities required for independent living such as meal preparation, housework, and shopping (Lawton & Brody, 1969, pp. 179–186).

The nursing home was the first health-care provider to secure public financing for the provision of long-term care, first under the Old Age Assistance provisions of the Social Security Act and subsequently under Medicare and Medicaid. As a result, the modern nursing home has been, for better or for worse, the cornerstone of formal long-term care services in the U.S. for more than fifty years. Despite this fact, there is no single universally accepted definition of a nursing home. When we hear the term "nursing home," we tend to think of free-standing facilities in which dozens or even hundreds of patients live out their days under the care of a trained nursing staff.

To the lay public, any facility for the residential care of older people, even "board-and-care homes," which provide no formal nursing supervision, may constitute a "nursing home." Moreover, even health-care professionals may have some difficulty distinguishing new forms of housing for the elderly, especially those which mix independent living arrangements with supportive services, from the traditional nursing home.

For the purposes of this chapter, the term "nursing home" will be defined using the definition developed by the National Center for Health Statistics in its National Nursing Home Surveys. The most recent NNHS survey, defines a nursing home as:

> ... nursing and related-care homes in the conterminous United States that had three beds or more set up and staffed for use by residents and that routinely provided nursing and personal care services. A facility could be free standing or could be a nursing care unit of a hospital, retirement center, or similar institution as long as the unit maintained financial and employee records separate from the parent institution. (p. 1)

Places providing only room and board, those limited to the treatment of specific health problems such as alcoholism, and facilities identified as providing "residential care" were excluded (National Center for Health Statistics, 1989b, p. 1). This definition captures most facilities qualifying for Medicaid and Medicare reimbursement for "nursing home care."

Kane and Kane (1987, pp. 225–228) have further enumerated the varied goals which may underlie nursing home care, including: (1) the prolongation of life through the treatment of disease; (2) maintenance or improvement of physical function; (3) discharge to home or a lesser level of community care; (4) reduced use of acute hospitals and emergency rooms; (5) social well-being and involvement; (6) improved cognitive functioning and a reduction in behavioral problems; and (7) patient satisfaction.

In all but the smallest of facilities, these goals are pursued through the efforts of a range of professional, paraprofessional, and support personnel functioning in a complex of formally organized units. The depiction of nursing home structure presented here draws heavily on Allen's classic text on nursing home administration.

While organizational configurations may vary according to size or individual history, the nursing department is the heart of every nursing home. Most members of the nursing staff are nursing aides; paraprofessionals who perform the majority of personal care and basic nursing activities under the supervision of Licensed Practical Nurses (LPNs), Registered Nurses (RNs), and/or university-trained nurses.

Medical services departments typically include pharmacists, physical and occupational therapists, speech pathologists, and other health professionals who may care for a nursing home's patients on either a full or part-time basis. Also included may be dentists, podiatrists, optometrists, and, in some larger homes, laboratory and X-ray technicians.

In principle, all medical decisions, including use of all of the nursing and medical services described here, as well as issues of diet, exercise, and recreational activities, are made by the physician responsible for a patient's care. This may be the patient's "attending physician" from the community, a full or part-time physician medical director, or in larger facilities, a physician serving as a salaried staff member.

The remaining services provided within the nursing home are often organized around an administration department. They include services related to administratively processing patients (admissions, medical records, and bookkeeping departments), providing social services including placement upon discharge (recreation departments and social work departments), and furnishing room and board (dietary, housekeeping and maintenance departments).

Allen notes that, while organizational arrangements and staffing may vary, the state and federal regulations require that facilities make provision for carrying out all of these nursing, medical, and administrative functions (Allen, 1987, pp. 65–72).

The Nursing Home Industry

The demographic, social and political developments outlined above have resulted in dramatic growth of the nursing home industry in the United States. This growth is evident in the marked increases in the number and size of facilities, in growing utilization rates, and in expanding nursing home employment.

Allen (1987, p. 142), assembling statistics from several sources including the National Center for Health Statistics' biannual National Master Facility Inventory, has shown that growth of the nursing home industry was most spectacular in the decades immediately following the introduction of Social Security in 1935. He estimates the number of nursing homes in 1939 at approximately 1,200. By 1960, the number had grown by more than 500 percent to 9,582 facilities, containing more than 330,000 beds. Since 1960, the rate of growth in the industry has moderated, with fewer but larger new facilities being built. Since the mid-1970s, the number of nursing home beds has essentially kept pace with the growth of the older population, fluctuating around fifty-seven beds per thousand persons age sixty-five and older.

Despite a leveling off in the number of new beds, data from the 1985 National Nursing Home Survey show that the number of nursing homes has doubled since 1960, reaching 19,100 facilities in 1985. Growth in nursing home capacity during the same period has been even more pronounced, with the number of beds quadrupling to 1.6 million (National Center for Health Statistics, 1987, pp. 2–4).

Contemporary patterns of ownership and certification in the nursing home industry reflect continuing trends towards public financing and away from public operation of long-term care facilities. Three out of every four (74.9 percent) of the 19,000 nursing homes identified by the National Nursing Home Survey in 1985 were proprietary facilities. Another 19.9 percent of the homes, 3,800 voluntary nonprofit facilities, also were classified as operating in the private sector. Only one in twenty (5.2

percent) was government-owned. The average size of a nursing home in 1985 was eighty-five beds. Of the three types of ownership, proprietary facilities tended to be the smallest facilities, averaging about seventy-eight beds per home. Voluntary nonprofit facilities were, on average, about twenty beds larger. Government-operated homes were by far the largest, averaging about 132 beds. As a result of these differences, the voluntary nonprofit and governmental facilities tended to control a somewhat larger share of the nation's nursing home beds than might be expected from their numbers; about 23 percent and 8 percent respectively. With more than 1.1 million beds, which is 69 percent of all beds in the country, however, proprietary facilities continue to represent the mainstream of the nursing home industry.

Over three-fourths (75.8 percent) of all nursing homes in 1985, and 73.4 percent of proprietary facilities, were approved for the care of patients eligible for Medicare or Medicaid benefits. Of those approved for these public insurance programs, about one-fourth (24.3 percent) specialized in skilled nursing care exclusively. Just over one-third (36.8 percent) were limited to an intermediate level of nursing care recognized by the government through the late 1980s. The remaining 39.6 percent offered both levels of care (National Center for Health Statistics, 1987, p. 3). Since the survey, these two levels of care have been merged into a single "skilled" level of care.

Findings from the 1985 National Nursing Home Survey also provide evidence of the increasing importance of larger facilities and multiple facility ownership in the industry. Smaller facilities continued to dominate the industry, with two-thirds (65.5 percent) of all facilities containing fewer than one hundred beds and one-third (33.0 percent) containing fewer than fifty beds. As a group, however, these smaller homes accounted for only 36.7 percent of the nation's nursing home beds. In contrast, homes with 100–199 beds, representing only 28.3 percent of all facilities, accounted for 43.2 percent of existing beds. Still larger homes, representing only 6.3 percent of all facilities, controlled one out of every five beds (20.1 percent). In all, fully 44 percent of the private sector homes were owned by a proprietary or nonprofit "chain" (National Center for Health Statistics, 1987, p. 3).

Growth in the number of nursing homes and nursing home beds has been coupled with more intensive use of these resources as measured by admission and discharge rates, length of stay, occupancy rates, and staffing levels. This has been due, in large part, to cost containment measures in both the long-term care and acute care arenas. From the mid-1970s on, many states, in an effort to control their shares of Medicaid reimbursable long-term care costs, attempted to restrain growth of the nursing home industry by requiring developers to demonstrate a need for proposed expansions. At the same time, the federal government, attempting to check the elderly's rising Medicare reimbursable hospital costs, introduced a new payment model (i.e., the Prospective Payment System) which generally led to earlier hospital discharge. The elderly, leaving the hospital at an earlier stage of convalescence, were, in turn, both more likely to require the services of a nursing home, to be more (medically) demanding nursing home patients, and to spend a longer period in such facilities once there (Morrissey, Sloan, & Valvona, 1988, pp. 685–698; Swan, de la Torre, & Steinhart, 1990, pp. 323–324; National Center for Health Statistics, 1989b, p. 5). Between 1973 and 1985, admissions to U.S. nursing homes grew by 17 percent while discharges grew by only 13.5 percent. Together with longer lengths of stay, these patterns brought occupancy rates up from 86.5 percent to 91.6 percent. (National Center for Health Statistics, 1987, p. 2). By 1989, the national occupancy rate for nursing homes had reached 95.1 percent (American Association of Retired Persons, 1992, p. 2).

At the same time, the growing number of facilities and, presumably, the more intensive care needs of the nursing home and personal-care home patients, brought about a dramatic explosion in residential long-term care employment. This expansion outstripped even the extraordinary growth in overall health care employment. Between 1970 and 1990, the number of civilians employed in health care grew from 4.2 million, or about 5.5 percent of all employed civilians, to 9.7 million, or about 8.0 percent of all employed civilians. In all, this represented a 102 percent increase in the number of American civilians employed in health care. During the same period, the number of civilians employed in nursing and personal care facilities grew from 509,000 to 1.5 million, a 203 percent increase which brought the proportion of health care employees working in long-term care up from 12.0 percent to 16.3 percent (National Center for Health Statistics, 1992, p. 242).

Statistics on the size of the long-term care work force in relation to the number of available beds suggests that these increases were not due simply to the growing number of nursing home beds in the country. Between 1973 and 1985, the number of full-time equivalent employees (FTE) in nursing homes per one hundred beds grew steadily from about forty-one FTE to about forty-nine FTE (National Center for Health Statistics, 1987, p. 2).

The Nursing Home Population

Younger people often believe that a substantial proportion, even a majority, of older persons live in nursing homes. While gerontologists have been quick to correct this misconception, it now appears that the professional community has, in the past, been guilty of substantially underestimating the likelihood of older persons entering such facilities. According to the Bureau of the Census, there were 1,772,032 Americans residing in nursing homes in 1990. This represented a 24.2 percent increase over the comparable number in 1980, and about 0.7 percent of persons of all ages (United States Bureau of the Census, 1992, Table 6–6). Since the elderly constitute only 12.5 percent of the population and about 88 percent of nursing home residents, the proportion of older persons residing in nursing homes is considerably greater; about 5 percent.

Data from 1973, 1977, and 1985 National Nursing Home Surveys show that, while persons aged sixty-five and older have, on average, gotten significantly older, the 5 percent nursing home residency rate has remained stable. This has had the effect of increasing the age of older nursing home residents. Between 1975 and 1985, for example, the proportion of residents under age sixty-five shrank from 14 percent to 12 percent while the proportion aged eighty-five and older grew from 35 percent to 40 percent (National Center for Health Statistics, 1989b, p. 3).

As life expectancy increases, even with some success at preventing institutionalization, a substantial proportion of older citizens can expect to reside in a nursing home for some period of time before they die. This proportion has been estimated at somewhere around a 43 percent of those sixty-five and older (Murtagh, Kemper, & Spillman, 1990). Of course, the dominant image is that admission to a nursing home is a final step before death. However, many older adults experience a temporary admission, typically a post-hospital stay for convalescence or for rehabilitation. Also, there has been questionable decisionmaking regarding quick transfers to and from the local hospital and nursing home just prior to death. In response, both facilities have erected barriers to prevent what they see as "patient dumping." At the same time, there are financial incentives for hospitals to accept transfers from nursing homes even when the value of hospitalization to the individual patient might be questionable.

Historically, the ease by which nursing home admission has been accomplished has been *the* major problem for policymakers trying to control facility growth in the country. It has been estimated that 30 to 60 percent of the residents being admitted are being inappropriately placed in these facilities. Developing alternatives to institutionalization, along with case management and pre-admission screening programs, represent mechanisms aimed at solving this problem. In the United States, where residential long-term care is still provided in the context of a private marketplace, these programs have had limited acceptance and success. In Canada, where all long-term care options, including nursing home care, community-based care, and home care, are becoming controlled by provincial care coordinators, decreases in nursing home utilization can be more clearly tied to growth in the volume of community care.

In most societies, however, developing a system whereby the social and health status of the resident matches the level of service needed, whether it be institutional or noninstitutional, remains problematic. Sometimes it is best handled at the time of admission, using care coordinators or primary care practitioners of various types. Otherwise, programs or facilities must adjust their service capabilities to meet the increasing frailty of their residents. Often, this means crossing traditional service barriers. For example, inviting community-based providers into the nursing home, nursing home personnel into the community, or coordinating the efforts of providers in these two arenas. Public housing authorities, as well as healthcare providers and family members, can play key roles in avoiding needless transfers to nursing homes.

Regulating Long-Term Care

While the nursing home industry emerged principally in the private sector, nursing homes have been continuously subject to governmental influence and control. This control has been exercised directly through explicit governmental regulation of the facilities and indirectly through governmental reimbursement policies.

Both mechanisms have been employed by federal and state government on behalf of two concerns. First, they have kept a watchful eye on profit-oriented nursing homes serving patients who, because of their infirmities, have been deemed particularly vulnerable to inadequate care or to physical, mental, social, or financial mistreatment. Second, they have attempted to influence the availability, utilization, and cost of long-term care. Historically, these concerns and their regulatory and financing counterparts have taken somewhat different forms.

Initially, standards of quality and quality-assurance mechanisms in nursing homes tended to parallel those developed in acute-care hospitals. In these facilities quality of care has traditionally been ensured by state licensure for operation, accreditation of the facilities by professional bodies, and certification of the facilities for reimbursement by federal insurance programs. The overlapping licensing, accreditation, and certification requirements have tended to focus on the resources available for care in the facility rather than the actual care provided or the outcomes of such care. In the nursing home setting, this has meant that regulatory concerns primarily have addressed such issues as space, cleanliness, staff-to-patient ratios, provisions for the safety of residents, and similar issues.

Despite regulatory mechanisms such as these, the quality of care in the nursing home industry has been subject to more or less continuous criticism in the professional and public press (Butler, 1975; Vladeck, 1980). In particular, critics have argued that residential long-term care facilities often approximate other "total institutions" (Goffman, 1961), such as mental hospitals and prisons, where organizational interests dominate patient or inmate needs (Gubrium, 1975). Inadequate medical supervision, limited nursing care, the excessive and unnecessary use of physical or chemical restraints, and physical or mental abuse have been documented at many institutions, most recently by the Institute of Medicine in its ground-breaking study on means of improving the quality of care in nursing homes (Institute of Medicine, 1986). This study has led to a new federal program of quality assurance in which the process of delivering care and the outcomes of care are evaluated through a new survey process (Coleman, 1991).

Persistent Problems and Lessons for Housing

Access to Care: The Problem of Distributive Justice

Full access to nursing homes, especially in terms of access to similar quality facilities, is not a reality in any society in our modern world. Various nations have made attempts to narrow the gap between high and low income elders, or at least low and moderate income elders, as they enter retirement. For example, some societies provide a flat rate of payment upon retirement regardless of the amount paid into the governmental retirement system.

In terms of nursing home care, individuals and their family members currently select a facility on the basis of what is available. If this decision is made when a crisis occurs there are far fewer options. If the person has no resources, placement in nursing homes that accept Medicaid is the only available option. And, increasingly fewer nursing homes are accepting Medicaid payments (U.S. General Accounting Office, 1990).

Individuals with some resources may begin as private-pay patients. However, with the high costs of nursing home care, from $30,000 to $50,000 a year, private resources can be quickly depleted, moving the resident from private pay to Medicaid eligibility and public support. As public-pay patients they may be allowed to keep only $3,000 of their own funds for future burial needs. Given the economic vulnerability of this population, Medicaid has become the dominant funding source for nursing home care. The disturbing scenario of the "spend-down process," as it currently exists in the United States, faces most Americans as a very real possibility (U.S. General Accounting Office, 1979).

Medicaid status often means that nursing home patients are restricted to as little $25 per month in discretionary funds. Some of these unfortunate patients can be seen, near the end of each month, rummaging through garbage cans in search for food or something of value that they can sell (Diamond, 1992). The emergence of two separate classes of residents, the "have-nots" (those on Medicaid or welfare) and "haves" (those still on private pay), represents a crude but important distinction. Sometimes various floors within facilities maintain this distinction in reimbursement.

The development of a private-public partnership between insurance companies and government represents one of many attempts to protect all citizens against the spend-down problem (Rivlin & Wiener, 1988). In Manitoba, Canada, the government uses general tax revenues and gatekeepers (called "care coordinators") to provide universal access to both nursing home care and in-home care. In Connecticut the insurance industry and state government have joined together to encourage citizens to purchase private long-term care insurance to cover the front-end costs of care, with government programs picking up the long-term costs. In Switzerland, some cantons (the Swiss equivalent of states) require that all facilities accept 25 percent of their admissions from economically deprived individuals to prevent the creation of "low income facilities" and to ensure that a two-class system of care does not develop. Elderly private and public housing, facing the issue of "ghettoization" in our society, may be able to learn from the nursing home arena as housing officials struggle with differential economic well-being of the elderly who live in the units.

Quality of Care: The Challenge of Aging in Place

As discussed above, the quality of nursing home care continues to be an important issue in the 1990s. The much discussed Omnibus Budget Reconciliation Act of 1987 (OBRA) attempts to address this issue in a variety of ways. The Nursing Home Ombudsman Program of the Administration on Aging is another federal attempt. Calls to introduce stronger physician involvement, together with attempts to strengthen medical direction in nursing homes, represent another thrust which has been encouraged for more than twenty years. With the dominance of low-paid aides on the nursing home staff, many have called for salary increases, improved training, and related methods of nurturing this giant but largely invisible work force with its massive turnover rates (Tellis-Nayak and Tellis-Nayak, 1989).

One major dilemma relates to the definition of quality. For historical reasons, the nursing home industry has been largely defined by regulators and governmental officials as a medical facility, despite the use of the terms "nursing" and "home" within its title. Nurses have only recently discovered the health model, but perhaps too late for this arena. As Diamond (1992) graphically shows, however well-meaning, the monitoring of body functions tends to dominate the daily lives of residents. And, too often, the business of living becomes lost. This is not, of course, to argue that it is easy to prevent or reverse "the general medicalization of many societal problems" (Binney, Estes, and Ingman, 1990).

As medical and nursing home care moves outside the nursing home and the hospital into the homes of elderly citizens, public housing will have to face some major challenges (Hanes-Spohn, Bergthold, & Estes, 1987, pp. 25–55). As more outsiders (for example, nurses and home-health aides) enter the home to provide care ranging from social to nursing to medical care, quality of life and care will both become, in part, a responsibility of housing officials and supervisors. Various housing units will attempt, rightly or wrongly, to exclude the ill resident on the grounds that they "are unable to handle such cases." However, as the population ages and their own residents become more frail and ill, such exclusionary policies will become less viable. Housing officials will be forced to become more creative in their policies and approaches to programming.

Ensuring Responsible Care: The Problem of Public Accountability

Public accountability can be appropriately defined in terms of the ability of the public, in our case relatives and residents and the general society, to affect the operation of nursing home facilities; that is, primarily, the quality of service offered. Of course, the administration, the staff, and the owners have the most direct control. State regulation, typically disdained by nursing home owners, administrators, and staff, is one means that the state, and thus the public, has to affect the quality of nursing home care. The new OBRA regulations, as they relate to nursing home operation, attempt to improve the overall quality of care for both elderly and nonelderly residents of nursing homes. The Institute of Medicine, with its extensive review of "the problem of quality control," set the stage for these new regulations (Institute of Medicine, 1986). While many of the new OBRA regulations specifically address the issue of quality of care, it is clear that regulation is not the total answer to the quality-of-care gap.

Cross-national comparisons have led many to argue that the issue of ownership is at the core of the recurring crisis in nursing home care. As outlined above there are three basic forms: private for-profit, which dominates the industry, voluntary nonprofit, and governmental ownership. European societies have a nursing home sector dominated by the latter two forms of ownership. Many Europeans argue that the care of frail and helpless residents whose relatives are ill equipped to advocate for them, requires that the profit motive be eliminated from this sector (Kayser-Jones, 1981; Lemke and Moos, 1989). While government or voluntary nonprofit facilities can, of course, be insulated from public influence, the development of more effective ombudsman programs, together with the encourage-ment of community ownership and visibility, should lead to greater accountability and reduce the chances that abuses can occur.

REFERENCES

Allen, J.E. (1987). *Nursing Home Administration*. New York: Springer.

American Association of Retired Persons (1992). *Reforming the Health Care System: State Profiles 1991*. Washington, DC.: AARP Public Policy Institute.

Binney, L., Estes, C. and Ingman, S. (1990). "Medicalization, Public Policy and the Elderly: Social Services in Jeopardy?" *Social Science and Medicine*, 761–771.

Butler, R.N. (1975). *Why Survive?* New York: Harper & Row.

Coleman, B. (1991). *The Nursing Home Reform Act of 1987: Provisions, Policy, Prospects*. Boston: University of Massachusetts Gerontology Institute.

Diamond, T. (1992). *Making Gray Gold: Narratives of Nursing Home Care*. Chicago: University of Chicago Press.

Goffman, E. (1961). *Asylums*. Garden City, NY: Doubleday & Company.

Gubrium, J.F. (1975). *Living and Dying at Murray Manor*. New York: St. Martin's Press.

Hanes-Spohn, P., Bergthold, L., and Estes, C. (1987). "Cottages to Condos: The Expansion of the Home Health Industry Under Medicare." *Home Health Quarterly, 8*, 25–55.

Institute of Medicine (1986). *Improving the Quality of Care in Nursing Homes*. Washington, D.C.: National Academy Press.

Kane, R.A., and Kane, R.L. (1987). *Long-term Care: Principles, Programs, and Policies*. New York: Springer.

Katz, S. (1963). "Studies of Illness in the Aged: The Index of ADL." *Journal of the American Medical Society, 185*, 114–919.

Kayser-Jones, J. (1981). *Old, Alone and Neglected: Care of the Aged in the United States and Scotland*. Berkeley: University of California Press.

Lawton, M.P. and Brody, E. (1969). "Assessment of Older People: Self-Maintaining and Instrumental Activities of Daily Living." *The Gerontologist, 9*, 179–186.

Lemke, S. and Moos, R. (1989). "Ownership and Quality of Care in Residential Facilities for the Elderly." *The Gerontologist 29*,(2), 209–215.

Morrissey, M., Sloan, F., and Valvona, J. (1988). "Medicare Prospective Payment and Posthospital Transfers to Subacute Care." *Medical Care, 26*, 685–698.

Murtagh, C.M., Kemper, P., and Spillman, B.C. (1990). "The Risk of Nursing Home Use in Later Life," *Medical Care, 28*, 952–962.

National Center for Health Statistics (1987). *Nursing Home Characteristics: Preliminary Data From the 1985 National Nursing Home Survey*. Advance Data from Vital and Health Statistics No. 131. Hyattsville, MD: Public Health Service.

———— (1989a). *Aging in the Eighties: The Prevalence of Comorbidity and its Association with Disability*. Advance Data from Vital and Health Statistics No. 170. Hyattsville, MD: Public Health Service.

———— (1989b). *Nursing Home Utilization by Current Residents: United States, 1985*. Vital and Health Statistics Series 13, No. 102. Hyattsville, MD: Public Health Service.

———— (1990). *Long-term Care for the Functionally Dependent Elderly*. Hyattsville, MD: Public Health Service.

———— (1992). *Health, United States, 1991*. Hyattsville, MD: Public Health Service.

Rivlin, A.M., and Wiener, J. (1988) *Caring for the Disabled Elderly: Who Will Pay?* Washington, D.C.: The Brookings Institution.

Swan, J., de la Torre, A., and Steinhart, R. (1990). "Ripple Effects of PPS on Nursing Homes: Swimming or Drowning in the Funding Stream?" *The Gerontologist, 30* (3), 323–331.

Tellis-Nayak, V., and Tellis-Nayak (1989). "Quality of Care and the Burden of Two Cultures: When the World of the Nurse's Aide Enters the World of the Nursing Home." *The Gerontologist, 29*(3), 307–313.

U.S Bureau of the Census (1992). Current Population Reports, Special Studies, pp. 23–178, *Sixty-Five Plus in America*. Washington, D.C.: U.S. Government Printing Office.

U.S. General Accounting Office (1979). *Entering A Nursing Home: Costly Implications For Medicaid and the Elderly.* Washington, D.C.: U.S. Government Printing Office.

—— (1986). *An Aging Society: Meeting the Needs of the Elderly While Responding to Rising Federal Costs.* Washington, D.C.: U.S. Government Printing Office.

—— (1990). *Nursing Homes: Admission Problems for Medicaid Recipients and Attempts to Solve Them.* Washington, D.C.: U.S. Government Printing Office.

U.S. Senate Special Committee on Aging et al. (1991). *Aging America, 1991.* Washington, D.C.: U.S. Department of Health and Human Services.

Vladeck, B. (1980). *Unloving Care: The Nursing Home Tragedy.* New York: Basic Books.

Part IV: Housing Issues for the Twenty-first Century

Concepts and Measurement of the Housing Quality of Older Adults: Developing a Public-Health Approach

Roger T. Anderson
Charles F. Longino

Introduction

This is an unusual chapter. Housing-quality issues as they relate to older adults are usually handled in the context of environmental psychology, not public health. Environmental psychology (Parmelee & Lawton, 1990) has a long tradition of exploring the connections between environmental influences and health and well-being. Some of the early empirical work in this tradition focused on designing intermediate and advanced care facilities for functionally impaired older adults, and the stresses associated with rehousing (Carp, 1976; Lipman & Slater, 1977; Boles, 1983).

Another research emphasis has focused on the role of the community (Schooler, 1967; Lawton & Cohen, 1974; Lawton & Yaffe, 1980) and housing conditions on emotional well-being and quality of life for adults living in the community (Lawton & Yaffe, 1980; Barresi, Ferraro & Hobey, 1983–84; Pastalan & Pawlson, 1985; Husaini, Moore & Castor, 1991). This chapter develops a public health approach to the housing quality of older adults, combining the traditional public-health focus on general housing conditions, with the rich contributions of environmental psychology and the gerontologic rehabilitative sciences regarding the special environmental needs of older adults. In doing so, we will concentrate on epidemiological, conceptual, and methodological issues of housing-quality research in community samples of older adults.

Housing quality is worthy of consideration in public health, in part, because our homes present potential environmental hazards to our health in that they are constructed of physical, chemical, and structural properties (Spengler, 1990). It is this issue that has received the most attention as public policy is translated into minimal housing codes. Gerontological interest comes to bear particularly because older persons are frequently long-term occupants of homes of antiquated construction (Chevan, 1987; Struyk & Soldo, 1980). In many instances substantial renovation and repair would be needed to meet current housing codes, a task made difficult by the reduced income and earning potential of the older occupant.

Regardless of the gross environmental hazards that they may embody, however, homes are also the primary living spaces where self-care and routine daily living activities occur for the elderly. The extent to which the physical features of a home support the safe and efficient conduct of these activities may have important long-term effects on health and morale.

At some point, for most of us at least, age becomes an index not only of survival, but of increasing physiological deficits. And these deficits represent potential problems in the way we negotiate our living environments. Aging is empirically associated with an increased prevalence of a variety of physical, mental, and social impairments which result in disability and, in an objective sense, a diminished quality of life. Regardless of whether such changes are the product of biological aging, disease processes, lifestyle, or a combination of these factors, the variability in functioning at older ages (Dawson, Hendershot & Fulton, 1987) has caused medical gerontologists to search for the best ways to magnify and expand health and quality of life in advanced old age. From a practical standpoint, successful aging should include bringing the environment into balance with an individual's needs and capabilities for secure and productive living.

The correspondence of the housing unit to the primary needs of the occupant, of course, changes over time. As they age, people adapt to their living environments by behavioral changes and housing modifications. In this regard, housing quality follows a life course of its own and should be considered in terms of its successful adaptation rather than solely in terms of its abstract properties. For example, the level of physical or mental challenge from environmental features becomes a more salient issue as the occupants reach advanced ages. Homes designed for families, or that require substantial upkeep, may become burdensome in later years. Similarly, with advancing age, the neighborhood characteristics may challenge previous perceptions of safety and pose barriers to access in the community. This dynamic quality has not received adequate consideration in operationalization and measurement of housing quality.

The Public Health Framework

The founding interest of public health as a separate discipline was to reduce the toll of disease in the population. Originally, the emphasis was on environmental engineering and sanitization. In the last half-century, however, the framework of public health has expanded to include enhanced immunity, positive health behaviors, better health education, and a more focused health-care practice and policy (Faden, 1987). While the field of public health may be seen as the overlapping of several domains or disciplines, it is the environmental, institutional, and population-based emphases in public health that make it distinct from other sciences (Winett, King & Altman, 1989). Public health, in part, uses knowledge gained about basic disease mechanisms, and causal processes within individuals to study the distribution of risk for disease and illness in society; to quantify the toll of exposure on the health of a population; to identify high-risk groups; and to develop strategies for preventing disease and promoting health. Other applications involve uncovering clues about causal processes from associations between exposures and disease in the population.

An important contribution to environmental epidemiology, within public health, is risk assessment. Risk assessment seeks to determine how risk increases if a group of people are exposed to a certain amount and type of hazard for a certain period (Gothfeld, 1992). Careful attention is given to assessing risk exposure and the form of association with a health-related outcome. This information is used to establish an acceptable level of exposure, and an appropriate policy approach to protect the public from greater exposure. Within this area, a vast amount of research has been conducted on chemicals in the soil, water, air, and food (Frank, 1992).

In the following discussion, we develop a broad-based model of housing quality, and discuss measurement issues salient to research. The approach is distinctively a public-health approach to the issue of housing quality. This chapter is focused on two major considerations, the first is definitional and the second is methodological. The primary questions to be answered are: what is housing quality and how can it be measured?

Toward a Public Health Approach to Housing Quality

Several issues have converged to bring a public health emphasis to the housing environments of older adults. These developments include: a broadening of public-health goals to include health-promotive living environments; demographic trends that point to a rising proportion of housing units that are owned and occupied by older adults; clinical goals in geriatric medicine that increasingly aim to slow or halt functional declines associated with advancing age; and, health policy trends toward a gradual shift in rehabilitative care from the hospital setting to the home.

From a public-health perspective, there are two fundamental goals when housing-quality research is considered. The first is the role of housing in enhancing health and well-being of older adults. The second is the place of housing in health interventions for older adults. For example, what is the impact of the housing environment on functional decline for older residents, what kinds of housing-related risk factors predict acute injury among these residents, and what gains can be achieved by modifying or controlling these factors?

While these goals are legitimately within the scope of public health in general, there are some major impediments to addressing them. First, a unified conceptual framework for housing quality has not been developed. For example, while there is some research to suggest little overall impact of housing quality on physical health (e.g., Kasl, 1990), the indicators of housing quality are typically gross conditions such as the presence or absence of plumbing, built-in heating, and running water, and the extent of crowding. Such models are apt to underestimate both the magnitude of the role of housing on a given health-related outcome and overall health and well-being.

Table 1

Typology of Conceptual and Measurement
Issues of Housing Quality

Phenomenological	Evaluative	Quantitative
Form	**Form**	**Form**
comprehensiveness	objective	gradient
single outcome	subjective	present/absent
Dimensional	**Method**	**Characteristics**
general public	trained observer	frequency
person specific	occupant	severity/intensity
social/community	archival	duration

Second, there is a critical need to develop valid, sensitive, and reliable measures of housing quality. The goal of instrument development goes far beyond the scope of this chapter, nevertheless, a discussion of critical measurement issues is the necessary starting point, and it will be a major consideration in this chapter.

In Table 1, we have outlined several critical definitional and measurement considerations for housing quality research from a public health perspective.

Defining Housing Quality

The phenomonological issues concern the way in which housing quality is defined. Models of housing quality in public health should be comprehensive in their relevance to the range of health outcomes, and multidimensional in covering all relevant aspects of the construct. For the former, Table 2 shows our typological model of the comprehensive range of adverse outcomes of housing environments of the elderly salient from a public health perspective. Examples are given of corresponding exposures for each class of outcomes listed. For any given study, the actual range of exposures will depend upon the scope and aims of the investigation. Our approach is that a comprehensive assessment of housing quality of older adults should be relevant to risks for disease and illness, disability, and injury.

Disease and Illness

The first class of adverse outcomes in Table 2 concerns disease and illness. The potential sources include either causal agents within the home environment (e.g., toxins or chemical agents) or conditions, equipment, or facilities that influence their concentration, contact, or dispersion (e.g., home structure, ventilation, plumbing) (Lowry, 1989; Spengler, 1990). Physical hazards may include outmoded facilities such as lead pipes, toxic chemicals, gases or fumes from cooking, fuel combustion, or building materials using, for example, asbestos, formaldehyde, or carbon monoxide. Other sources may arise from neglect or improper maintenance of the home.

The home environment may also support growth or transmission of bacteriological agents. Structural deficits can produce damp conditions and standing water that become reservoirs for pathogens or portals of entry and habitat for vermin and insects. Plumbing and facilities for waste removal are another important potential source for the spread of infection. Health outcomes may include processes within the internal organs or tissue, external or anatomical sites, or a combination of these. Finally, depression and psychological distress are listed under both illness and disability. Potential pathways for an effect of housing on emotional distress are indirect—through housing satisfaction, and direct—through neighborhood characteristics (e.g., social contacts, security), and resources to meet housing needs (e.g., financial burden, upkeep, and maintenance).

Table 2
Typology of Outcomes and Exposures
in the Home Environment

Class	Exposure	Disruption	Outcomes
Disease/ Illness	Chemical	Internal/ Organ	Hypothermia
	Heat		Poisoning
	Pollutant	External/ Bodily	Food or Water- Borne Disease
	Sanitation		
	Ventilation		Depression and
	Other reservoir/		Anxiety
	Vectors		Mortality
	Neighborhood		
Disability	Stairs	Upper/Lower	Mobility
	Doorways	Extremities	Self-Care
	Layout of Home		Physical Fitness
	Facilities		Depression and
	Locks/Safety	Psychological/	Anxiety
	Neighborhood	Emotional	
	Community		Satisfaction
Injury	Design	Internal/ Organ	Hypothermia
	Structure		
	Stairs		Burns
	Lighting		
	Layout of		
	Home	External/Bodily	Falls
	Furnishings		
	Facilities/	Cognitive	Fractures
	Devices		Mortality

Disability

A second type of hazard in the home environment has to do with features that promote disability. Disability refers to performance deficits within the physical and social environments resulting from anatomical, physiological, or psychological impairment (Granger & Gregham, 1984). Although the direct cause of disability is impairment, features in the home environment may be important modifiers of disability through their potential to support or enhance behaviors and performance levels (Verbrugge, 1990). Housing conditions can indirectly influence physiological heartiness by promoting a higher level of physical activity and vigor, and they can also promote better emotional health by fostering activities of personal meaning and social importance. The fields of occupational and physical therapy and geriatric rehabilitation are a rich source of information about interior features of the home that enhance physical and social functioning and reduce the risk of injury to older adults.

It is within the context of disability that public-health concerns for elderly housing draw the most heavily from traditions in environmental and behavioral psychology (Lewin, 1935; Murray, 1938). Discussions of housing for the elderly usually begin with Lawton (1970, 1976, 1982), who developed a theoretical framework for understanding how person-environment relations change with the aging process. According to this framework, an individual's behavior and functioning is the product of a combination of environmental parameters (environmental press) and the individual's competence for performance. Competence includes the individual's biological health, sensory and perceptual capacities, motor skills, and cognitive capacity. Lawton's model suggests that optimal functioning, or adaptation, occurs when a state of balance is reached between environmental demands and individual competence. Negative or maladaptive behavior results when a balance is not achieved or cannot be maintained (Lawton, 1982). Low competence heightens vulnerability to environmental press in marginally adequate environments and thus reduces adaptation. In contrast, high competence promotes greater independence from environmental press and more dependence on personal factors.

With advancing age, gradual changes in competence, due either to normal aging processes or chronic disease, increases vulnerability to environmental press. Some of the major sources of disability are listed in Table 2. They include: (1) design of stairs and staircases; (2) lighting adequate for visual acuity; (3) functioning of doors, windows, and locks; (4) size of doorways; (5) presence of handrails in stairs and bathrooms; (6) ease of use of furnishings; and (7) presence of a telephone in the home. These environmental exposures may disrupt physical performance, due to functional impairment in the upper and lower extremities caused by joint pain, balance, or grip strength, or cognitive functioning; due to perception and sensory functions, or emotional health; or due to isolation, insecurity, or dissatisfaction.

Emotional health is included under disability to emphasize its toll in terms of quality of life. One of the most common ways of attempting to measure disability in public health research is to pay special attention to functional performance, especially the existing measures of activities of daily living (ADLs). Physical limitations and capacity measures are also important, such as muscle strength and range of motion of limbs.

Injury

A third class of health-risk factors in a public-health approach to housing quality is the home injury of older adults. In recent years, development in public health of the epidemiology of injury has transformed the concept of "injury" from a random or unpredictable event to a predictable event based on probabilities. Injury is a risk that systematically arises within the physical environment (Haddon, 1968). In the environmental context, injuries are a consequence of design features, behavioral guides, and systematic person-environment relations. This public-health emphasis, together with Lawton's competence-press theoretical framework, is useful in identifying susceptibility factors for injury in older adults. Thus, the role of gait, balance, visual acuity, use of medications, and activity should be viewed in combination with environmental features in hazard identification.

Some of the most obvious home environment factors important to injury include: (1) architecture of stairs, staircases, and thresholds; (2) lighting appropriate for visual acuity in all living areas; (3) placement of loose rugs, or torn carpets; (4) secure and appropriately placed grab bars and handrails; (5) properly working and safe appliances, smoke alarms; and (6) unstable or inappropriate furniture. Areas of disruption include internal function and structure due to trauma to joints or bones, regulatory processes, external function and structure, such as trauma to skin and tissue, and cognitive function and structure, particularly sensory feedback.

Injuries may also involve burns from cooking appliances or water temperature, hypothermia from inadequate heating facilities or insulating structures, and falls and fractures. It is obvious that people can, and do, die from injuries and that some injuries may have an indirect impact on health issues as well. In public-health terms, mortality and declines in general health status are also included as possible injury outcomes.

A second phenomenological aspect of housing quality of older adults shown in Table 1 is its multidimensional nature. Regardless of the public-health outcome of interest or the measure used, the indicators should represent key dimensions of housing quality. Historically, a major distinction between public health and psychological research on environments has been that the former places unusual emphasis upon specifying the important dimensions in terms of objective conditions of the housing unit that are relevant to hygiene and health promotion. The latter, while not ignoring objective considerations, places a considerable emphasis on subjective or meaningful consider-ations of the individual. This difference is most evident in the view of housing satisfaction. As a subjective state, housing satisfaction serves as a valid indicator of housing quality. However, in causal models in environmental epidemiology, housing satisfaction is viewed as an outcome or mediating variable rather than an environmental "exposure." Exposure is on one side of the equation, and satisfaction, along with health factors, is on the other side of the equation. Determinants of housing satisfaction include adaptations, sentiments, and expectations regarding housing, and these are forged over many years. As a result, they may respond to objectively defined housing conditions, or they may bear little systematic relationship to them.

In our view, housing quality for older adults should be conceptually based upon both public health standards that are important to the health and safety of all occupants and on the specific circumstances and needs of older adults. Specifically, housing quality should encompass:

1. General public health standards. These include physical conditions of the housing unit relevant to public health standards for safety and well-being of the general public.
2. Person-environment adaptations. These include the physical conditions of the housing unit that are relevant to safe access and the use of the living environment to meet the needs of the older occupants.
3. Social accessibility. This includes access to community resources and the outdoor environment.

The general dimension refers to objectively defined conditions for safe habitation which should be provided in the general population by each housing unit. This reflects the traditional public health emphasis on environmental exposure. In most communities this aspect of housing quality is defined by minimum housing codes. Housing quality measured in this way includes structural strength, sanitation, adequate light and ventilation, being rodent-free, and being safe from the threat of fire or other hazards to life and property. However, the potential list of items is quite long and unwieldy including properly working appliances, presence of safety devices like smoke detectors, properly working doors, locks, and windows, and many others.

At a minimum, this dimension should include general housing conditions: (1) base equipment; (2) facilities; (3) light and ventilation; (4) the electrical system; (5) exterior and interior structure; (6) space and use; and (7) sanitation. These dimensions are proposed as generic dimensions of housing quality. In a particular study, the need for additional and more specific dimensions would largely depend upon the aims of the study and the characteristics of the sample.

The objective physical properties of housing relevant to public health and well being are not referenced specifically to older occupants. We have added a person-specific phenomeno-logical dimension of housing quality using the emphasis on adaptation in environmental psychology (Lawton, 1970, 1976, 1982), and the gerontologic rehabilitative sciences (Kemp, Brummel-Smith, & Ramsdell, 1990). In this dimension, objective conditions of the home are assessed by taking individual behaviors and functional needs of older occupants into account. For example, in the home environment the criterion "properly working" or "adequate" need to be references to the occupant's ability to use or interact with the system in question. Additional-ly, as a result of the variety of age-associated changes in functional capability, such as gait, strength, balance, and perception, older adults have important needs in housing quality that are not the same as those of other groups (Reddick, 1984–85; Tobis et al., 1990). Thus, exposures relevant to this dimension include environmental barriers and supports which impact daily functioning, and risk for injury in the functionally impaired older occupant.

Our focus has been on objective conditions of housing as the primary determinant of environmental adaptation. However, individual perceptions and social resources play an important role as mediators or moderators of housing quality. As Wister (1984) has noted:

> ... perceptions of housing or support inadequacies, knowledge of alternatives and individual housing, and living arrangement preferences will interact with social and economic resources [and] constraints to affect environmental adaptation. (p. 272)

Social supports and living arrangements also play an important role (Kahana, 1975; Golant, 1986; Wister, 1984). Thus, it is important to carefully consider intervening variables in developing applied models of housing quality.

The third and final dimension of housing quality involves accessibility to the neighborhood and the larger community, to shopping, medical facilities, hobbies and leisure activities, and to social contacts (Reddick, 1984–85). Older adults are more dependent than others on their neighborhood environment for goods and services and social activity (Lawton, Nahemow, & Yeh, 1980). Two salient demands which affect access are the location of the home in terms of distance and the perceived safety and ease of negotiating structures and traffic flow within the neighborhood. This dimension is also not represented in previous public health research on housing quality.

Measuring Housing Quality

In this section we will review some of the salient issues and approaches to measuring housing quality. In Table 1, these are the evaluative and qualitative choices in measurement. Unfortunately, there are no existing well-validated measurement systems appropriate to the comprehensive nature and major dimensions of housing quality we have proposed.

The Evaluative Dimension of Exposure Assessment

The phenomenological and evaluative dimensions of exposure assessment are closely tied, such that the nature of the dimension constrains both the feasibility and the applicability of the evaluation. Characteristics of the form of evaluation of an exposure are also referred to as the "mode" of measurement. The criteria for determining the adequacy or sufficiency of any form of data collection are its reliability, validity, sensitivity, and the quality of the data collected. Key operational assumptions are that: (1) the evaluator or respondent must have reasonable access to the housing environment; (2) the assessment should not pose an unreasonable burden to complete (e.g, time); (3) the complexity of information collected should be matched to the respondent's skill and capability to generate appropriate responses; and (4) respondent bias is limited or unimportant. In addition to the nature of the dimension, the strengths and weakness also depend on the amount of study resources (e.g., time, personnel, financial) allocated for the planned assessment.

We begin with the general dimension of housing quality in our public-health model. Data of this nature may be obtained with a checklist using either the occupant's ratings or those of a trained examiner. Occasionally, these data may also be obtained from archival sources. Each of these modes carries a unique set of advantages and disadvantages which must be carefully weighed in the context of the study design, resources, and aims. The use of trained raters produces higher levels of detection and data quality with regard to substandard housing conditions. A further advantage of using trained raters is the wide range of technical conditions that they can assess.

The cost of this accuracy and precision, however, can be considerable and may include large travel and personnel costs, which for large-scale community samples may make this mode of data collection prohibitively expensive. A further limitation is that the assessor must gain permission from the occupant to inspect the home. Often such requests are viewed with suspicion and wariness, producing large refusal rates, and thereby raising questions about sample bias.

Because of their lower cost, most of the data on housing conditions in the United States are collected from the housing-unit occupant (Chen & Newman, 1987). This mode of measurement allows broad coverage, particularly by adapting the instrument to phone or mail surveys. The shortcomings may be substantial depending on the depth of detail required in an investigation. Some of the more important shortcomings include response bias through purposeful under or over-reporting of housing conditions, response sets, and errors in recognition or discrimination of housing states.

Unfortunately, there are few published comparisons of housing assessments made by trained evaluators and those made by the occupants. However, it is likely that errors in occupants' reports are smallest for responses on objective housing conditions or states. Examples of such queries include presence or absence of a built-in heating systems, the number of years since the roof was reshingled, and the working condition of exterior doors. However, this assumes that occupants are not purposefully misleading the investigator.

Yet another measurement mode involves the occupant's subjective appraisal or judgment of the quality of the housing unit. This approach may ask for a subjective assessment of whether or not the house is "in need of repair" or "adequate" which are partly based on occupant's knowledge, manner of use, capabilities, and expectations. Chen and Newman (1987) reported significant discrepancies between trained housing inspectors and occupant's assessment of need for repair in a checklist of housing attributes.

Perhaps the most important limitation of this subjective approach is that occupant reports will be most imprecise where aspects of housing quality require trained evaluation. Such aspects include, for example, the adequacy of steps, handrails, porches, and other structures to bear normal loads. This limits the range of housing conditions that can be fruitfully measured by subjective appraisal.

A salient issue to the occupant interview method concerns the use of proxy sources. The possibility exists of encountering an older occupant who is unable to appropriately respond to a questionnaire. This issue may be important enough to warrant concern about nonresponse or missing data (Rodgers & Herzog, 1992). In this circumstance, the use of a proxy reporter must be weighed against excluding the housing unit from study. In the 1984 supplement on aging (SOA) to the National Health Interview Survey, proxies were used in 8.5 percent of the interviews of people fifty-five years and older, and 26.6 percent in those aged eighty-five years and over (Fitti & Kovar, 1987). If these numbers are typical of the general population of older people, surveys that exclude respondents on the basis of competency to respond will be biased toward younger samples. This bias, in turn, will be compounded by other socio-demographic factors associated with chronic disease. Ideally, the choice of a proxy should be someone who lives with the occupant and thus has knowledge of the housing conditions of interest.

One other approach to assessing the physical condition of housing is the use of archival data from local government agencies, such as departments of housing, and the tax assessor's office. To limit costs associated with survey research, data are sometimes sought from less expensive sources such as existing records stored in a central location. With regard to potential sources of housing information, data on plumbing, heating, and water supply are often compiled for each residence in a county area through the issuance of building permits by the local government. These data are continuously updated over time through tax assessment and renovation permits. The advantages of this approach, reduced costs, reduced collection time, and broad coverage must be weighed against its drawbacks. They are considerable.

First, only minimal data on housing quality can be obtained with this mode of assessment. Further, this mode is prone to serious misclassification error. The latter can occur when the homeowner fails to report home improvements that he has made in order to avoid higher taxation or when he is not familiar with local regulations for permits and the reporting of housing improvements. Record-keeping errors by local government agencies also reduce the quality of these data. From a research standpoint, the nonreporting of improvements or changes represents a potential for detection bias and may be most serious in rural areas, in homes of long tenancy, and in older homes constructed when the local data collection policies differed. Often there are also intra-county and regional differences in rates of home assessments or record keeping that confuse the issue. Unfortunately, archival data may also contain deliberate deceptions generated by unscrupulous or incompetent inspectors.

As with the other measurement approaches, there are few published studies comparing archival data and objective home inspection data. Anderson, Shiferaw, & Mittelmark (1992), however, examined the correspondence between county tax assessment records and occupant's reports on presence of heating equipment, plumbing apparatus, and the availability of running water. Approximately 23 percent (487) of owner-occupied homes listed by the county as substandard were occupied by a householder aged sixty-five years or over. In a random sample of 222 of these housing units, 195 householders were located, and in-home interviews were completed in 154 of the homes (79 percent).

The results are disturbing. While approximately 92 percent of the sample was identified by the county records as lacking built-in heating and the remainder (twelve homes) were listed as lacking either plumbing, or both plumbing and built-in heating only four of the occupants (3 percent of the sample) reported lacking heating, while none of the occupants reported lacking plumbing and running water. While objectively assessed housing conditions were not available in this study and, therefore, the true prevalence of inadequacies was not known, these results underscore the potential for low reliability in measurement between approaches.

In the person-specific dimension, it is not housing quality in general that concerns us, but the housing quality of older persons. In the context of housing quality, older adults may be more susceptible to certain environmental qualities than younger persons through changes in physiological systems. For example, advanced age does affect immunological responses, bone density, and impairment from disease. It may also affect appraisal of the housing environment. In this sense, objective housing quality is a relative concept with the type and potency of exposures specific to the population and the individual's characteristics. Unfortunately, measures of housing quality currently found in the literature lack content areas sensitive to such adaptational needs.

One area which strongly influences the approach to measurement is the need to conceptually separate the occupant's health status and life circumstances from objective states of housing quality. This is a critical issue in studies of disability. For example, should inability to safely use the stairs in a home be viewed as an indicator of housing quality, impairment of the individual, or both? The person-specific approach to this problem is to define barriers or risks to safe access and use of the home environment as demands which impede routine access or use by similarly impaired individuals. Correspondingly, environmental supports are features, such as modifications or repairs of the environment or its use (Struyk & Katsura, 1987) which reduce environmental demands in daily activity.

Demands and supports can be categorized as associated with at least three major classes of activity in the home:

1. access to living space (indoors and outdoors)
2. household activities
3. self-care

Representative examples of demands include: number and height of steps; height of bathtub; location of washer/dryer; width of doorways and hallways; and access to transition and outside living areas (e.g., garage, patio, backyard). Environmental supports may include handrails, lighting, grab bars, specific home repairs or modifications (e.g., installation of ramps), and adaptive equipment.

The major challenge from a measurement perspective is to accurately estimate the match between individual capability level for an activity with the corresponding environmental demands and supports. Unlike general housing conditions which can be presented in a standard list, methods to account for person-environment fit have not been standardized and depend heavily on study resources. The most extensive and resource-intensive procedure involves collecting objective data on functional capability and home supports via individual assessments made by a skilled assessor, such as by an occupational or physical therapist. A determination would be made whether environmental deficits exist in the home, such as lack of grab bars, hand rails, and raised thresholds, relative to the functional capacity of the occupant. This strategy would yield person-environment fit scores for each major living space use or function. While this method can provide rich data about housing quality relative to the occupant's needs, inter-rater and intra-rater reliability studies are needed to check the accuracy and consistency of these assessments.

In studies where intensive data collection is not feasible, an alternative is to collect survey data on both Activities of Daily Living (ADL) and Instrumental Activities of Daily Living (IADL) functioning with matching physical assessments of barriers and supports in the home environment. One option involves simply asking the occupant what problem they have with their housing environment. Other queries can be made about any modifications that may have been made to the home and which enhance functioning. The problem with this approach is that it rests solely on the person's knowledge of what environmental problems are, and conversely what level of functioning they could achieve in an ideal housing environment. Such a measure is unlikely to have sufficient sensitivity, and it is likely to be biased by social status and perceptions about housing quality.

A more desirable approach is to construct an environmental checklist that contains salient features or aspects of the home which relate to demands and supports. Such physical assessments might include the presence or absence of hand rails, an obstacle-free pathway to living spaces, the number and height of steps, the height of the bathtub, and others. The validity of this approach may be enhanced when the checklist is developed to pertain to documented needs of a specific population of older adults, such as impairment level, or for a specific outcome within the class of disease, disability, or injury, such as falls. A primary example of this has been developed for occupant or observer evaluations to assess risk for falls (e.g., Reinsch, MacRae, Lachenbach, & Tobis, 1992). Generally, information about environmental conditions collected by self-report, without a trained interviewer or physical inspection, has the same strengths and weaknesses as discussed for general conditions, above.

Indicators of access to the neighborhood and community should include objective conditions salient to the general public, the perceived conditions relative to safety, and the person-environment fit specific to individual capabilities. These dimensions closely relate to Lawton's (1976) typology of conceptual bases of neighborhood and community environments. The "physical resource environment" includes objective physical conditions in the neighborhood that may be described or recorded empirically. Indicators of this aspect relevant to public health outcomes include noise, traffic, the incidence of area crime, distance to resources such as medical facilities, and others.

This type of data is typically collected by trained assessors, using formal criteria for coding the environment, such as the number of reported crimes, volume of vehicular traffic per unit of time, and measured physical distance to goods and services. If census tracts are used as the unit of analysis, data on population density, vacant buildings, and crime rates can be obtained from government sources such as the U.S. Bureau of the Census. The use of occupant reports is problematic, as with physical conditions of the housing unit, since individual perceptions may reduce the accuracy of the estimates.

Lawton's "perceived resource environment" includes appraisals, knowledge, and judgments made about an environment. Perceived safety of the neighborhood is an important community access issue, and depends on the occupant's perceptions. Accordingly, these data should be collected by self-report. The validity of proxy responses will depend on the type of proxy and study population. In cases where the target person cannot answer or complete a questionnaire due to physical or cognitive limitations, the caregiver would be a more logical choice of respondent since it is the caregiver who is the gatekeeper to the community. In other circumstances, where the participant is unavailable for contact but otherwise independent, proxy responses from family members are generally preferable to those from friends (Rodgers & Herzog, 1992).

A final aspect of community environment listed by Lawton is the "functional resource environment." It refers to the aspects of the environment that are actually used by the respondent in the context of the person-environment fit perspective discussed earlier. Similarly, measuring adaptation needs in the home environment raises the issue of how to disentangle person-based risk such as physical disability from environmental exposures. If a person does not report full or adequate access to their environment, what role has the environment played in this situation? It is important in studying the housing quality of the older adults to obtain data on barriers relative to health and disability status of the individual.

The Quantitative Dimension
of Exposure Assessment

The form of the quantitative dimension of exposure assessment is statistical. It concerns the relationship between the exposure and the outcome. In epidemiology, this is referred to as the underlying etiologic or causal model of disease. For analytical purposes, assessing the goodness of fit of statistical models of risk is aided by knowledge of what kind of relationship is hypothesized. This issue is important at the measurement stage because the response format of the instrument employed should correspond to the "dose-response" or model of association of interest. In Table 1, two forms of association listed were gradient, and the dichotomy present or absent. An hypothesized gradient form of relationship between an exposure and outcome may rely on ordinal, interval, and ratio levels of measurement, depending on the nature of the exposure. Because of the recency and sparseness of public health data on housing quality and health and well-being for the elderly, little information is available about the form of association between exposure and outcome.

A related consideration in assessing exposures in the housing environment is the characteristic of exposure. There are three principal characteristics of exposure that should be considered. These include: (1) the frequency, or number of times a discrete exposure has occurred in a given time period; (2) the intensity of exposure; and (3) the duration of exposure. These epidemiological concepts have typically not been applied to housing quality research but are useful to guard against error in most forms of assessment.

These characteristics of exposure benefit us by increasing our power to detect hypothesized effects. If exposures are hypothesized to have a cumulative effect on health or well-being over time, then to be appropriate the measures must be capable of estimating the duration of exposure. For example, barriers to physical activity in the home may lead to gradual decrements in functional status through deconditioning. In such a study, it would be important to assess whether baseline levels of physical activity are chronic, accounting for potential modifications to the home or the reliance on social support. Similarly, when an effect is constant, as opposed to cumulative, such as with falls, the probability for the outcome, the fall, will increase as a function of the frequency of exposure (Mantonoski, 1988), such as exposure to loose carpet. Both duration and frequency may be assessed through a questionnaire format by explicitly referring to a time frame of exposure and by designs with repeated measures. Finally, the probability for the outcome may depend on the level, or intensity of the exposure. In this case physical measurements will have to be made of the active or "toxic" property of the housing condition.

Conclusion

We have argued in this chapter that there is a need for the systematic study of the complex effect that housing environments have on health outcomes of older adults. In doing so, we have synthesized a public-health perspective from three sources: (1) a focus on the objective and physical environment; (2) environmental psychology's emphasis on the person-environment fit when examining the relationship between older persons and their housing; and (3) environmental issues related to access to community resources and to functioning. We would further argue that a public-health model of housing quality should include not only these dimensions in risk assessment, but must also be comprehensive with regard to the scope of health and well-being outcomes.

In this chapter, we have begun a discussion of methodological issues that we feel must be addressed if progress is to be made in epidemiological research on housing and health of older adults. We have provided only a beginner's guide to the issues but we hope that epidemiologists in the field of public health will turn their attention to the special living environments of older Americans.

REFERENCES

Anderson, R.T., Shiferaw, B., & Mittlemark, M.B. (1992). Older Adult's Perceptions of Housing Quality: The Forsyth County Aging Study. Paper presented at the Southern Gerontological Society, Nashville, TN, March 18–21.

Barresi, C.M., Ferraro, K.F., & Hobey, L.L. (1983–84). Environmental satisfaction, sociability and well-being among urban elderly. *International Journal of Aging and Human Development*, 18(4), 277–293.

Boles, W. (1983). A sociological, psychological, and physiological profile of three groups of older adults as related to housing needs and norms. *Journal of Applied Gerontology*, 2: 44–60.

Carp, F.M. (1976). A senior center in public housing for the elderly. *The Gerontologist*, 16(3) 243–249.

Chen, A., & Newman, S. (1987). Validity of homeowners' housing evaluations. *The Gerontologist*, 27(3) 309–313.

Chevan, A. (1987). Homeownership in the older population. *Research on Aging*, 9(2): 226–255.

Dawson, D., Hendershot, G., & Fulton, S. (1987). Aging in the eighties: Functional limitations of individuals age 65 and over. *Advance Data No. 33*, National Center for Health Statistics.

Faden, R.R. (1987). Health psychology and public health. In G.C. Stone, S.M. Weiss, J.D. Matarazzo, N.E. Miller, J. Rodin, C.D. Beler, M.J. Follick & J. Singer (Eds.), *Health Psychology: A Discipline and a Profession*. Chicago: University of Chicago Press, 1987.

Fitti, J.E., & Kovar, M.G. (1987). The supplement on aging to the 1984 National Health Interview Survey. Vital and Health Statistics, Series 1, No. 21. DHHS pub no. (PHS) 87–1323. Hyattsville, MD: National Center for Health Statistics, 1987.

Frank, A.L. (1992). The status of environmental health. In J.M. Last & R.B. Wallace (Eds), *Public Health and Preventative Medicine*, 13th Edition, Norwalk, CT: Appleton & Lange.

Golant, S.M. (1986). Subjective housing assessments by the elderly: A critical information source for planning and program evaluation. *The Gerontologist*, 122–127.

Gothfeld, M. (1992). Principles of toxicology. In J.M. Last & R.B. Wallace (Eds), *Public Health and Preventative Medicine*, 13th Edition, Norwalk, CT: Appleton & Lange, 1992.

Granger, C.V., & Gregham, G.E. (1984). *Funtional Assessment in Rehabilitative Medicine*. Baltimore: Williams & Wilkins Press.

Haddon, W. (1968). The changing approach to the epidemiology, prevention, and amelioration of trauma: The transition of approaches etiologically rather than descriptively based. *American Journal of Public Health*, 58: 1431–1438.

Husaini, B.A., Moore, S.T., & Castor, R.S. (1991). Social and psychological well-being of black elderly living in high-rises for the elderly. *Journal of Gerontological Social Work*, 16(3/4): 57–78.

Kahana, E. (1975). A congruence model of person-environment interaction. In P. Windly, T.O. Byerts, and F.G. Ernst (Eds.), *Theory and Development in Environmental Aging*. Washington, D.C.: Gerontological Society, 1975.

Kasl, S.V. (1990). Quality of the residential environment, health, and well-being. *Bulletin of the New York Academy of Medicine*, 66(5):479–489, Sept/Oct.

Kemp, B., Brummel-Smith, K., and J. Ramsdell. (1990). *Geriatric Rehabilitation*. Boston: College-Hill Press.

Lawton, M.P. (1970). Assessment, integration and environments for the elderly. *Journal of Gerontology*, 10:38–49.

—— (1982). Competence, environmental press, and adaptation of older people. In M.P. Lawton, P.G. Windley, & T.O. Byerts (Eds.), *Aging and the Environemnt: Theoretical Approaches*. New York: Springer Publishing Co.

—— (1976). The impact of the environment on aging and behavior. In J.E. Birren and F.W. Schaie (Eds.) *Handbook of the Psychology of Aging*, New York: Van Nostrand.

Lawton, M.P., & Cohen, J. (1974). Environment and the well-being of elderly inner-city residents. *Environment and Behavior*, 6(2).

Lawton, M.P., & Nahemow, L. (1973). Ecology and the aging process. In C. Eisdorfer and M.P. Lawton (Eds), *The Psychology of Adult Development and Aging*. Washington, DC: American Psychological Association.

Lawton, M.P., & Yaffe, S. (1980). Victimization and fear of crime in elderly public housing tenants. *Journal of Gerontology*, 35:768– 779.

Lawton, M.P., Namehow, L., & Yeh, Tsong-Min (1980). Neighborhood environment and the well-being of older tenants in planned housing. *International Journal of Aging and Human Development*, 11(3), 211–227.

Lewin, K. (1935). *A Dynamic Theory of Personality*, translated by D.K. Adams & K.E. Zener. New York: McGraw-Hill, 1935.

Lipman, A., & Slater, R. (1977). Homes for old people: Toward a positive environment. *The Gerontologist*, 17(2).

Lowry, S. (1989). Housing and health. *British Medical Journal*, 299:1439–1442.

Mantonoski, G.M. (1988). Issues in the measurement of exposure. In L. Gordis (Ed.) *Epidemiology of Health Risk Assessment*. New York: Oxford University Press.

Murray, H.A. (1938). *Explorations of Personality*. New York: Oxford University Press. 1938.

Parmelee, P.A., and Lawton, M.P. (1990). The design of special environments for the aged. In J.E. Birren and K.W. Schaie, (Eds.), *The Handbook of the Psychology of Aging*, 3rd Edition. New York: Academic Press.

Pastalan, L.A., and Pawlson, G. (1985). Importance of the physical environment for older people. *Journal of the American Geriatrics Society*, 33(12):874.

Reddick, J. (1984–85). The interdependence of health and housing for the elderly. *Journal of Housing for the Elderly*, 2(4):77–83 Winter.

Reinsch, S., MacRae, P., Lachenbach, P.A., & Tobis, J.S. (1992). Attempts to prevent falls and injury: A prospective community study. *The Gerontologist*, 32:450–456.

Rodgers, W.L., & Herzog, A.R. (1992). Collecting data about the oldest old: Problems and procedure. In R.M. Suzman, D.P. Willis, and K.G. Manton (Eds), *The Oldest Old*. New York: Oxford University Press.

Schooler, K.S. (1967). The relationship between social interactions and morale of the elderly as a function of environmental characteristics. *The Gerontologist*, 9:25–27.

Spengler, J.D. (1990). Shelter for the twenty-first century. *Environmental Health Perspectives*, 86:281–284.

Struyk, R., & Katsura, H. (1987). Aging at Home: How the Elderly Adjust Their Housing without Moving. *Journal of Housing for the Elderly*, 4(2), 1–192

Struyk, R.J., & Soldo, B.J. (1980). *Improving the Elderly's Housing*. Cambridge, MA: Ballinger Publishing Co.

Tobis, J.S., Block, M., Steinhaus-Donhan, C., Reinsch, S., Tamura, K., & Weil, D. (1990). Falling among sensorially impaired elderly. *Arch. Phys. Med. Rehibil.*, 71:144–147, 1990.

Verbrugge, L. (1990). Disability. *Epidemiology of Rheumatic Disease*, 16(3): 741–761, August.

Winett, R.A., King, A.C., & Altman, D.G. (1989). *Health, Psychology and Public Health: An Integrative Approach*. New York: Pergamon Press.

Wister, A.V. (1984). Environmental adaptation by persons in their later life. *Research on Aging*, 11(3), 267–291, September.

CHAPTER 14

Home Equity as an Income Source for Older Adults

David P. Higgins

There was a time, not too long ago, when most elderly people were poor by today's income standards. Many had lived through the harsh years of the 1930s and had been unable to save. Most had no pension income because pension plans were not common then. Also, many were self-employed as farmers, tradesmen, or small business owners. Those who survived middle age were often forced to seek the assistance of family members or neighbors. Because of this assistance, these individuals were not completely without resources but, in terms of income, many were certainly poor.

Fortunately, this characterization of old age as a time of extreme need and dependence no longer describes the reality faced by most older adults. For example, in 1980, the per capita annual after-tax income of an elderly person (65 years or older) was $6,300, compared to $5,964 for the population as a whole (Schulz, 1992, p. 15). This change in the economic status of elderly people is attributable to the expansion of employer pension plans, the ability to save created by economic prosperity in the years following World War II, and the old-age benefits provisions of the social security program. In 1988, for people over age sixty-five, 38 percent of income was from social security, 17 percent from private pension plans, 17 percent from work earnings, 25 percent from savings and investments, and 3 percent from other sources (Grad, 1990, table 47). Thus, the weight of evidence suggests that today's older population is, as a whole, reasonably well-off financially. In fact, the living standard of older adults tends to be similar to that of the entire population (Schulz, 1992, p. 16).

The problem with this conclusion is that it is based on a comparison of averages. If we look at the distribution of income, we discover wide differences. According to Crystal and Shea (1990, p. 441), when income from all sources is aggregated for people over age sixty-five, the lowest 20 percent received only 5.5 percent of the total income of the entire group, and the lowest 40 percent received 16 percent of the total income. This disparity is exacerbated by differences of race, gender, and marital status. In 1987, median income was $8,975 for white persons over age sixty-five, $5,081 for African Americans, and $5,292 for Hispanics (U.S. Senate Special Committee on Aging, 1988, table 2–5). In 1986, older unmarried men had a median annual income of $8,510 compared to $6,870 for women (Grad, 1990, table 12). In 1988, older married couples had a median income of $20,305 compared with $7,928 for unmarried persons (Grad, 1990, table 12). Clearly, there is income disparity. According to the U.S. Department of Health and Human Services, 28 percent of all people over age sixty-five had incomes below 150 percent of the poverty level in 1986 (U.S. Senate, 1988). This measure includes people classified as poor, near poor, and economically vulnerable. For people in the lower range of the income continuum, a modest increase in income has the potential to substantially enhance their economic independence and quality of life.

It is reasonable to ask whether home equity has a role to play in economic welfare. Specifically, is the amount of wealth stored in the nation's stock of elderly-owned housing sufficient to substantially enhance the economic well-being of older adults? The simple answer is yes, because the store of equity value in homes is immense, and because most elderly people own their homes outright or carry only a small mortgage balance. For example, in 1984, 52 percent of all elderly households had at least $40,000 of home equity, and 44 percent of all households possessed equity in the $20,000 to $100,000 range (Schulz, 1992, table 1–2). During 1983–1984, the 20 percent of elderly households with the lowest incomes had an average home equity of $35,948 (Crystal and Shea, 1990, p. 441). Much of this equity resulted from price inflation during the 1970s and early 1980s. In 1985, there were 18.2 million elderly households in the United States. About three-fourths of these householders owned and occupied their homes, and 83 percent of these had no mortgage balance. The median value of the homes was $52,300, with a median of $30,700 for African-American elderly households, and $49,900 for Hispanic elderly households (American Association of Retired Persons and Administration on Aging, 1989). By 1989, the median value of homes owned by people over sixty-five had risen to $65,944 (American Seniors Housing Association, 1992).

The store of wealth in the form of home equity is significant, even for many low income people. In effect, this group of elderly people is "asset rich" and "income poor." The need is to convert the value stored in home equity into an income stream. There are a number of ways this can be done. For example, the home could be sold, the proceeds invested in marketable securities such as bonds, stocks, or mutual funds, and income derived from the investments. Alternatively, the owner could lease the home to others to derive rental income. The problem, of course, is that such approaches require elderly homeowners to meet their need for housing in some other way. The real need is to convert the store of equity wealth into an income stream without having to sacrifice ownership or occupancy, and this is the intended purpose of a reverse mortgage. If the equity value of the home is sufficient and certain other criteria are met, a reverse mortgage can be a satisfactory solution to income inadequacy. As might be expected, older persons with lower incomes tend to own homes with lower market values. Studies demonstrate that homes with modest market values do not generate a very large monthly cash flow, both absolutely (Crown, 1989, p. 118; Higgins & Folts, 1992, pp. 190,198), and relative to income (Venti & Wise, 1991, p. 393).

Nevertheless, even a modest increase in income can be very important. To the extent that it preserves an older person's economic independence, it also reduces dependence upon government assistance programs and preserves the power for self-direction while, at the same time, allowing older people to live in their own homes and in familiar surroundings. Even a small amount of additional monthly income may also permit the purchase of a few nonessential extras that add pleasure to living, make leisure travel possible, or make it easier to obtain assistance at home for chronic ailments or with daily living activities. Taken together, these are the kinds of things that are described by the general phrase "quality of life."

Principles Governing Reverse Mortgages

Most people borrow a large amount of money in a lump-sum to finance the purchase of a home, then pay off the loan in installments over many years. If the loan is paid off on schedule these people enter their retirement years with a debt-free home. Due to increases in the general level of prices over the years, the home may have a market value considerably in excess of the original purchase price. This value represents a store of wealth that may be accessed through a reverse mortgage. The relationship between a reverse mortgage and a regular mortgage is implied in its name. In a regular mortgage, a large debt is acquired and then slowly reduced over a period of years through a series of payments, which represent a "cash expense" stream. In contrast, the reverse mortgage builds up a large debt over time through the systematic borrowing of small amounts against the equity value of the home, which represents a "cash income" stream. For both types of mortgages, borrowing is made possible by using the market value of the home as collateral or security for the lender. Of course, at some point the debt built up by borrowing against the equity value will have to be repaid. Typically, this will be done by selling the home and using all or part of the cash proceeds to extinguish the debt. So, reverse mortgage is the term used to describe a process which converts home equity into debt through an orderly system of payments to a home owner by a lender. The home owner does not make any payments to the lender while this process is under way; although, at some point the loan will have to be repaid.

There are several types of reverse mortgages, which will be discussed shortly. However, in order to develop an understanding of the general principles involved we will look first at a particular type in more detail, the reverse annuity mortgage. It is the type associated with a fixed monthly payment received without interruption over a period of time.

Suppose that you place $100 in a bank savings account that pays you 6 percent interest once each year. At the end of the first year your account value would be $106, obtained by adding the principal (P) of $100 and the interest (I) of $6. In fact, you derived the interest amount by multiplying the principal amount by the interest rate (r), or $(P)(r) = (\$100)(.06) = \$6$. If you left the $106 in the savings account for another year, the interest you would receive in the second year would be $(P)(r) = (\$106)(.06) = \$6.36$, and the value of your account would be $\$100.00 + \$6.00 + \$6.36$, or $112.36. This is a simple demonstration of the principle of compounding. We can see how it works more clearly by developing a general approach for computing a future value (FV). We know that the future value at the end of one period is

$$FV_1 = P + I \tag{1}$$

We also know that $I = (P)(r)$, so we can substitute $(P)(r)$ for I in equation (1) and write

$$FV_1 = P + (P)(r) \tag{2}$$

Now, we can factor out P and write

$$FV_1 = P(1 + r) \tag{3}$$

In our example, letting $P = \$100$ and $r = 6$ percent, for one year we have $FV_1 = \$100(1 + .06)$ or $106. For the second year, we would compute the end-of-year value as

$$FV_2 = FV_1 (1 + r) \tag{4}$$

which produces $FV_2 = \$106(1 + .06)$ or $112.36. Suppose, however, that we want to place $100 in the savings account for two years, so that we wish to compute directly how much we will have at the end of the second year. Since equation (3) is the expression for FV_1, we can substitute it into equation (4), giving us

$$FV_2 = P(1 + r)(1 + r), \text{ or}$$

$$FV_2 = P(1 + r)^2 \tag{5}$$

Our computation of the ending value would then be $100 (1 + .06)^2$, yielding $100 (1.1236) or $112.36. Now, we can generalize the equation for any specific number of years we choose by letting the number of years be represented by n, and writing the equation as

$$FV_n = P(1 + r)^n \tag{6}$$

Equation (6) is termed the general formula for the value of a sum to be received n years in the future. If we left our $100 on deposit for 8 years, n would be 8, and we would have

$$FV_8 = P(1 + r)^8$$

$$FV_8 = \$100(1 + .06)^8$$

$$FV_8 = \$100(1.5938)$$

$$FV_8 = \$159.38$$

Of course, how much the $100 would grow to become depends upon the interest rate and how long our original deposit earns interest. An example of the relationship between time and rate of interest is shown in Table 1.

The ending amount is always larger, the higher the interest rate and the longer the time period. Especially important to observe, however, is that the ending amount increases at an increasing rate over time due to the compounding effect. Note that for a given interest rate, the value of the savings account increases by more in any five-year period than in the preceding five-year period, which results from beginning each five-year period with an amount that is larger than the amount at the beginning of the preceding five-year period.

This characteristic of compounding has an important implication for how useful a reverse mortgage can be as a producer of an income stream. It means that a reverse mortgage constructed to generate a monthly cash stream over more than just a few years may not generate a very large monthly amount for the home owner. To see this idea more clearly, we have to shift our thinking from moving from the present to a future point in time, to moving from a future point in time back to the present.

Table 1

Relationship Between Time and Interest Rate. Future Values of $100 Deposited for n Years at Rate r

Year	6%	8%	10%	12%
0	$ 100.00	$100.00	$100.00	$100.00
1	106.00	108.00	110.00	112.00
2	112.36	116.64	121.00	125.44
3	119.10	125.97	133.10	140.49
4	126.25	136.05	146.41	157.35
5	133.82	146.93	161.05	176.23
10	179.08	215.89	259.37	310.58
15	239.66	317.22	417.72	547.36
20	320.71	466.10	672.75	964.63
25	429.18	684.85	1083.47	1700.01

Recall that $100 deposited in the savings account produced a value of $112.36 in two years, when the yield on the savings account was 6 percent. If you were an investor, and I asked you how much you would lend me now in exchange for my promise to pay you $112.36 at the end of two years, you would agree to lend me $100 now if you required an annual rate of return of 6 percent on your investment. Table 2 illustrates how much a lender would be willing to advance in the form of a single sum now based on a promise to pay at various later dates. Clearly, the amount becomes smaller as the length of time to repayment increases.

This means that a reverse mortgage is most viable as a source of supplemental income if the length of time to actual or expected repayment is relatively short. For people who expect to occupy their home for many years, a reverse mortgage may not produce enough additional income to substantially improve their quality of life. On the other hand, for very elderly people who have reason to expect that they will vacate their home after only a few years, perhaps to enter an assisted-living or a nursing facility, a reverse mortgage may generate sufficient cash income to enable them to fully enjoy their remaining years of physical independence. In this regard, it is interesting to note that the average reverse mortgage borrower is a single woman, age 76 (Brackey, 1992, p. 1B).

Table 2

Single Sum Loan Amounts Based on Repayment of $100,000 at Different Times under Three Interest Rates

Repayment at End of Year	6%	8%	10%
3	$83,962	$79,383	$75,131
6	70,496	63,017	56,447
9	59,190	50,025	42,410
12	49,697	39,711	31,863
15	41,727	31,524	23,939
18	35,034	25,025	17,986

The size of the monthly receipt is also influenced by the interest rate on the loan. The higher the rate, the smaller will be the monthly cash receipt. This is because the lender, expecting a fixed amount at the end of some specified period of time, can only experience an increase in rate of return if the amount loaned is reduced. Stated formally, the size of the cash stream a homeowner may receive through a reverse mortgage is inversely related to the interest rate on the loan. This idea is also expressed in Table 2.

To this point we have seen that the size of the monthly receipt generated by a reverse mortgage is inversely related to the length of the loan and the interest rate. To make these points we have used examples involving a single sum. In fact, a reverse annuity mortgage is a stream of payments equal in amount and evenly separated in time, usually monthly. The principles presented apply to annuity payments in the same way they apply to single sum payments. The only difference is that the size of a single payment in a stream of payments will be much smaller than a one-time lump sum payment, simply because there are many more payments. The contrast may be observed by assuming that the $100,000 lump sum repayment assumed in Table 2 is used to pay off $100,000 of indebtedness built up through monthly receipts over the various time periods. Table 3 illustrates the size of monthly receipts that will result in $100,000 of debt after the number of years indicated at three interest rates. Again, note that the size of a single receipt is inversely related to the length of the cash stream and the interest rate on the loan.

Table 3
Monthly Loan Amounts Based on Repayment of $100,000 at Different Times under Three Interest Rates

Repayment at End of Year	Number of Receipts	6%	8%	10%
3	36	$2,542	$2,467	$2,393
6	72	1,157	1,087	1,019
9	108	701	635	575
12	144	476	416	362
15	180	344	289	241
18	216	258	208	167

The size of the monthly receipt also depends upon the appraised value of the home and percentage of this amount a lender is willing to advance. Lenders call this the loan-to-value ratio. If an elderly borrower owns a home with an appraised value of $50,000, and the lender will advance 80 percent of this amount, the lender's computation of the monthly payment to the home owner will be based on a maximum allowable indebtedness of $40,000. An 80 percent loan-to-value ratio is assumed in Table 4, which shows the interactions among the home's appraised value, the interest rate on the loan, and the number of monthly receipts.

Table 4

Term Reverse Annuity Mortgage: Monthly Cash Receipts
at Three Interest Rates and Five Maturities,
with an 80 percent Loan-to-Value Ratio

Monthly Cash Receipt at:

Appraised Value	Loan Value	For Number of Years (Months)	For Loan Interest Rate: 7%	9%	11%
$20,000	$16,000	4 (48)	$290	$278	$267
		8 (96)	125	114	105
		12 (144)	71	62	54
		16 (196)	44	38	31
		20 (240)	31	24	18
$30,000	$24,000	4 (48)	$435	$417	$400
		8 (96)	187	172	157
		12 (144)	107	93	81
		16 (196)	66	56	46
		20 (240)	46	36	28
$40,000	$32,000	4 (48)	$580	$556	$534
		8 (96)	250	229	209
		12 (144)	142	124	108
		16 (196)	88	75	62
		20 (240)	61	48	37
$50,000	$40,000	4 (48)	$725	$695	$667
		8 (96)	312	286	262
		12 (144)	178	155	135
		16 (196)	110	94	77
		20 (240)	77	60	46
$60,000	$48,000	4 (48)	$869	$834	$801
		8 (96)	374	343	314
		12 (144)	214	186	162
		16 (196)	132	113	92
		20 (240)	92	72	55

Types of Loans Secured by Home Equity

An elderly person may require cash on a regular basis, or to satisfy a one-time need, or on an irregular basis to meet an occasional need for extra funds. The types of equity-based loans available are categorized according to these three motives in Table 5, which is the basis for the following discussion.

Table 5
Types of Home Equity Loans

Need	Loan Type
Regular Periodic Income	Reverse Mortgage Term Annuity Split-Term Annuity Tenure Annuity Shared Appreciation Annuity
A Large Amount Once	Deferred Payment Loan
Lumps of Cash Occasionally	Property Tax Deferral Loan Line-of-Credit Loan

Reverse mortgages normally imply an annuity payment, although any loan secured by the home requires execution of a mortgage instrument to provide the lender with security. Thus, all of the loans listed in Table 5 are reverse mortgages. A *term mortgage* is the most straight forward type of reverse annuity mortgage. It is the type depicted in Table 4, and requires that the full loan balance be paid at the end of the designated term. Since this normally requires the sale of the home, it is not well suited for most elderly people because it is not possible to foresee precisely when the home will have to be vacated due to death or the need to move to a more supportive environment. An older adult could hedge their guess about when they expect to vacate the home by selecting an annuity horizon that exceeds their expected period of residency; but this would reduce their monthly cash income.

The *split-term* reverse annuity mortgage is one solution to this problem. Like the term mortgage, the cash receipt stream is received for a fixed period; but, the lender may not require repayment of the debt until the owner dies, vacates, or sells the home, even if the owner occupies the home for many years after the annuity payments have ended. This arrangement solves the potential problem of forcing the elderly person from the home, but it does not address the income problem that would arise if the owner chose to continue residing in the home after the annuity stopped. There is an additional problem. If the lender cannot be sure when the loan will be repaid, the lender must reduce the risk by lowering the size of the monthly payment. In other words, to ensure that the projected rate of return will be experienced, the lender bases the size of the annuity payment on a period of time which exceeds the length of time the home owner is expected to reside in the home. Even though the resident may occupy the home for an even longer period, the lender ensures the required investment return by diversifying this risk across many loans of this type. This is simply an application of the type of risk spreading practiced by insurance companies.

A somewhat better solution is a *tenure* reverse annuity mortgage whereby the older home owner receives a fixed monthly cash income for as long as the home is occupied. In this arrangement, it is not possible to outlive the payment stream. However, tenure reverse annuity mortgages produce an even lower monthly cash inflow to the home owner because the lender cannot know when the home will be vacated, yet must continue payments until it is vacated. Monthly cash incomes from these three annuity forms can be contrasted with an example.

Assume that a lender agrees to make a ten-year, 8 percent interest rate loan based on 80 percent of an appraised value of $50,000. Assume further that the elderly occupant is expected to reside in the home for ten years. In the case of the *term* reverse annuity, the lender's monthly payment to the home owner would be $219. In the *split-term* arrangement, assume that the lender reduces risk by assuming the home will be occupied for fifteen years. In this situation, the occupant would receive $179 per month for ten years. For the *tenure* reverse annuity mortgage, suppose that the lender bases the monthly payment amount on the actuarial assumption that payments will be made for fifteen years, even though they are expected to be made for ten years. The monthly payment would then be $116.

In addition, a variation of these financing schemes is called a *shared appreciation* mortgage. This type grants all or part of any potential appreciation in the value of the home to the lender. The advantage to the borrower is higher monthly receipts during the period of occupancy because the lender shares in any increase that may occur in the home's market value from the time the loan agreement is initiated until the loan is paid off. While this is an interesting idea, lenders have not been willing to base a larger monthly payment on the possibility that real estate values will increase.

Suppose a couple in their early to mid-sixties has recently retired. If they are in good health and have adequate income for normal living expenses, they may expect to reside in their home for many years. If the home was purchased long ago, they may want to renovate existing space or make additions to the house. Either of these is a significant cost. A *deferred payment* loan is intended to meet this need. The retired couple borrows a large sum, all at once, to cover the cost of repairs, refurbishment, or an addition. The loan is secured with the equity value of the home. As an example, if $15,000 were borrowed at 8 percent and expected to be repaid twenty-five years hence, the home's current equity value would have to be at least $110,103 to support the loan. The amount is large because the $15,000 will accrue interest for twenty-five years. If, on the other hand, the needed refurbishment cost only $5,000, the appraised value needed to support the loan would be one-third of $110,103, or $36,701.

A *property tax deferral* loan is intended to preserve the economic independence of elderly people with limited incomes by removing the burden of annual property taxes. These loans are available for this specific purpose, and a cash draw against the equity value of the home can be made periodically to pay the tax. If a home owner borrowed $1,500 per year for fifteen years at an 8 percent interest rate to pay taxes, the equity value of the home would have to be $40,728 to support the periodic borrowing. A line-of-credit loan is similar, but the purpose for borrowing is not restricted. The elderly person may borrow at irregular intervals according to his or her need or desire for funds. Property tax payments could be one need, but borrowing might also take place to pay for medical costs, travel to visit children, home repairs, or a number of other reasons. Of course, the equity value of the home will set an upper limit on how much could be borrowed over time.

Two additional ways of increasing monthly income involve selling the home. In a *sale-and-leaseback*, the home owner sells the home and leases it back. This option is most often used when an elderly person sells his or her home to an adult child. The child makes a down payment, and the parent carries the mortgage, collecting monthly payments of principal and interest from the child. Selling the home can be advantageous if the parent has not used the allowable one time exclusion of up to $125,000 in capital gains on a home. In fact, most people would bear no liability for capital gains tax since the median increase in market value over purchase price was $47,905 for persons over sixty-five in 1989 (American Seniors Housing Association, 1992).

The parent should use the child's down payment to purchase a deferred annuity (i.e., an annuity that will be paid for the duration of the parent's life). Such annuity contracts are available from insurance companies. The parent also collects mortgage payments from the child. Since the child is able to depreciate the home as rental property and experience the tax benefits of depreciation expense, it is possible to arrange a monthly lease payment that is less than the monthly sum of cash income from the child's mortgage payment and the deferred annuity income. This approach to increasing income is best used if there is a desire to keep the home in the family, but even then, it is a complicated arrangement, and since title to the home transfers from the elderly occupant to their child, the parent becomes a tenant rather than an owner (Thompson, 1987, p. 70).

A final option is to establish a *life estate agreement* wherein the elderly person exchanges ownership, upon their death, for the right to live in the home for the remainder of their lives. The elderly person normally receives no income, and remains responsible for property taxes, insurance, and normal maintenance expenses. The only real advantage is a gift tax deduction based on the value of the home. Since a life estate generates no income, it has little appeal except for persons who are wealthy enough to take advantage of the gift deduction and those who may have a philanthropic motive.

Life estate agreements are most often used when an elderly person wishes to leave the value of their home to a charitable organization, a university, or a religious group. The only enduring life estate program that is specifically aimed at assisting elderly people by providing them with an income stream and other assistance is operated by the city of Buffalo, New York. In exchange for the value of the home upon death, the city will make major repairs and perform maintenance on the home without cost to the homeowner. The city also forgives property taxes as long as the older person resides in the home. In addition, the city offers the homeowner the choice of a lump sum payment or a monthly payment for life (Scholen, 1990, pp. 38–39). This type of program has not met with much success in other localities because of its legal and administrative complexity.

Cautions When Considering a Reverse Mortgage

Many elderly people are reluctant to mortgage a home they have spent years paying for and now own debt free (Crown, 1989, p. 101; DeZube, 1990, p. 34; Springer, 1985, pp. 11–12). The first consideration should be whether it is necessary to become a debtor again. Reverse mortgages are not government assistance programs, they are self-supporting financing programs. Retired persons who are short of income should first test their eligibility for government assistance programs. Low-income elderly people may be eligible for Supplemental Security Income under provisions of the Social Security Act in addition to their normal social security old-age benefit. Eligibility is based on income and asset tests, and should be investigated by low income homeowners, especially since qualifying for Supplemental Security Income benefits may determine eligibility for other government benefit programs (Scholen, 1992, pp. 279–280). Low income people should also investigate this option first, because income from a reverse mortgage may give them sufficient combined income to disqualify them for Supplemental Security Income benefits.

Even when there is good reason for concern about medical (or other) costs, it may be more judicious to preserve the equity value of the home specifically for this purpose rather than deplete it for day-to-day expenses. Reverse mortgages can be expensive. Recall that the amount owed increases rapidly because interest accrues on an ever increasing level of indebtedness. To this interest cost must be added normal loan origination costs such as application fees, real estate appraisal fees, loan interest points, and closing costs. If the time from origination to repayment is short, so that origination costs are spread over only a few years, the effective rate of interest on the mortgage may be considerably higher than the stated interest rate. Since reverse mortgages are not assistance programs, they are economically self-supporting. Thus, while the costs may be fair, reverse mortgages are not necessarily a bargain.

One cost advantage is that the cash receipts are not taxed as income because the homeowner is actually borrowing money, and borrowed funds are not taxed (Dunn, 1990, p. 82). Offsetting this advantage, however, is the tax treatment of the interest on the mortgage. Interest is deductible only in the year in which it is paid, so while interest accrues over time, it is not actually paid until the loan is paid off. Thus, there is no tax benefit arising from interest expense during the life of the loan (Scholen, 1990, p. 44).

Lastly, many elderly people want to bequeath an estate to their children, or some other beneficiary. This is an important consideration for many people, so serious introspection should precede a decision to deplete the equity value of a home. In general, a reverse mortgage should not be used unless the income supplement it will yield is needed to maintain economic independence or to materially improve an older person's quality of life. It is best suited for people who are quite old and who expect to need supplementary income for a rather short time, who are reasonably certain they will not need this equity value for some other purpose, and who have no strong desire to bequeath wealth upon their death.

Recent Advances in Funding Mechanisms

Economists, gerontologists, government policymakers, and private lenders have studied and experimented with equity conversion ideas for at least two decades. The programs that were developed tended to be initiated by state or local governments, and focused upon elderly clienteles with specific characteristics in particular geographic areas. Only recently have programs been developed that are available to elderly people as a general clientele. A look at why these programs have been slow in arriving permits an understanding of the institutional mechanisms and loan features needed to make equity conversion plans operationally feasible and attractive to larger numbers of elderly people.

Many of the early programs provided term or split-term reverse mortgages. Elderly people were understandably reluctant to commit themselves to these mortgages for reasons already discussed. The introduction of contracts which guaranteed income throughout the period of occupancy was a major step in reducing this source of consumer reluctance. Difficulties also arose in attempting to create awareness of equity conversion plans among elderly people. Newer programs are accompanied by better information and more widespread promotional efforts.

Several major obstacles have thus far inhibited lenders. First, there is a general and simple lack of experience with these mortgages. Most lenders are hesitant to accept a large amount of risk until repayment expectations are confirmed by experience (Crown, 1989, p. 101). Although that experience has been lacking, new efforts to promote reverse mortgages by advocacy groups as well as the federal government have increased lender interest in these financial transactions.

Second, the costs of originating and servicing loans were high because few loans were made. A large number of mortgages must be put in place in order to obtain the needed operational economies (Sichelman, 1991, p. 23). Creation of standardized mortgages that possess attractive characteristics, and installation of an application process that is understandable and rather easy to pursue were prerequisites to more wide-spread acceptance by elderly people.

Third, mortgage lenders prefer to shift the risk that they may not be repaid to a third party. This preference is particularly strong where reverse mortgages are concerned because the lender experiences a continual outflow of cash for what may be many years, and generally does not know precisely when repayment will occur. Mortgage insurance provided by a third party has been the solution to this problem (Scholen, 1992, pp. 240–241). Third-party mortgage insurance simply means that in the event of repayment default, due to any cause, the insurer will pay the lender on behalf of the borrower.

Fourth, a lender may be neither willing nor have the financial ability to sustain the continuous cash outflow associated with a large number of reverse mortgages. The solution here is to provide a simple way for the lender to sell the mortgage to a third party who has the resources to make cash payments to large numbers of home owners, and who obtains the right to pay-off when the homes are vacated. This alternative leaves the lender with the tasks of loan origination and, perhaps, loan servicing. The lender is then, in fact, not the ultimate lender to the homeowner; rather, it processes loan applications for a fee, and may service the loan, also for a fee. Servicing the loan entails making the cash payments to the homeowner, collecting and transferring the insurance premium to the insurer of the loan, paying property taxes that have been escrowed or are paid with loans against the equity value of the home, keeping track of the loan balance and sending the homeowner periodic statements, and making sure that the borrower remains in compliance with the contractual requirements of the loan (Scholen, 1992, p. 222). If the organization that originates the loan does not wish to service it, this task may be contracted to a third-party organization that specializes in servicing loans.

The fifth difficulty is also related to a lender's ability to sustain large cash outflows over time. In the end, some organization must own the loan contract, and thus obligates itself to make payments to homeowners. How can the organization amass the amount of funds necessary to make reverse mortgage loans? The answer is to *securitize* the mortgages. The lender sells debt instruments termed *Collateralized Mortgage Obligations* to investors in public securities markets as a means of raising large amounts of money. It collateralizes this debt with the mortgages themselves which, in turn, are secured by the homes on which the loans are being made. In the case of reverse mortgages, a form of zero-coupon bond is most appropriate. A zero-coupon instrument pays no interest, but it sells initially for less than its face or maturity value (a U.S. Savings Bond is an example of a zero-coupon debt instrument). Investors receive their return by collecting more at maturity than they paid initially. So, funds are collected over time as mortgages are paid off, with enough funds accumulated to pay off the bonds when they mature. This approach to funding reverse mortgages is still in its infancy. The first collateralized mortgage obligation was issued by HomeFirst, a San Francisco mortgage lender (Schultz & Clow, 1991, pp. 15–16).

Debt instruments that trade in public securities markets fill another important need. They make it possible for any investor to enter and exit mortgage-backed securities markets simply by buying and selling debt instruments. They are not locked into specific pay-off schedules because the debt instruments are liquid, that is, the timing of entry (investment) and exit (disinvestment) is entirely at the discretion of the investor. This flexibility is necessary in order to induce large numbers of investors to supply funds to finance mortgages.

A dramatic step toward creating a large pool of funds to finance mortgages was taken when the Federal National Mortgage Association (Fannie Mae) agreed to purchase Federal Housing Administration (FHA)-insured reverse mortgages issued under the auspices and direction of the U.S. Department of Housing and Urban Development (HUD). Fannie Mae is a quasi-governmental corporation whose purpose is to raise funds for insured mortgages by issuing debt and equity securities in public markets, which permits the amassing of funds because it meets investors' demands for diversification, third-party insurance guarantees, and liquidity.

Reverse Mortgage Programs

The HUD-FHA reverse mortgage program is an extension of a program authorized by Congress in 1987 titled the Home Equity Conversion Insurance Demonstration, in which 2,500 reverse mortgages were issued nationally on a test basis. The current program expands the number which may be issued up to a maximum of 25,000 mortgages through September, 1995. The loans are available from over 8,000 HUD approved lenders on a first-come, first-served basis until the limit of 25,000 is reached (American Association of Retired Persons, 1991, p. 2).

Five types of loans are currently available. *Term, tenure,* and *line-of-credit* mortgages were discussed earlier in this chapter. Two variants combining either term or tenure mortgages with a line-of-credit are also available under the program. A *modified term* loan allows the borrower to reserve a portion of the equity value of the home to be drawn upon to meet unexpected or occasional cash needs, in exchange for a smaller monthly cash income over the payment term. A *modified tenure* loan is the same in concept, the difference being that monthly cash payments are received so long as the home is occupied (Fannie Mae, 1991b, p. 1).

Monthly payments will be smaller with any tenure mortgage compared to a similarly structured term mortgage. These mortgages are funded by Fannie Mae, insured to the lender by the FHA, and serviced by Wendover Funding, Inc., of Greensboro, North Carolina (AARP, 1992, p. 4). The maximum amount that can be borrowed depends upon the borrower's age, the interest rate on the loan, the value of the home, and other factors. Currently, the maximum amount that ultimately may be borrowed, termed the maximum claim amount, ranges from $67,500 to $124,875, depending upon the above factors. There is no minimum amount that must be borrowed (Fannie Mae, 1991a, p. 2).

To be eligible, a borrower (and any co-borrowers) must be at least sixty-two years of age, and either own the home or have a very small mortgage balance. If there is a mortgage balance owed, it will be paid off with Fannie Mae funding and the amount applied as initial indebtedness under the HUD-FHA loan. Borrowers are also required to attend a mortgage counseling session from a counseling agency approved by HUD (Fannie Mae, 1991a, p. 2). The purpose of the counseling is to ensure that the potential borrower has investigated alternative sources of income, understands the costs, obligations, estate and possible tax implications of entering into a reverse mortgage, and to encourage thorough consideration of all factors before committing (Scholen, 1990, p. 25). Borrowers are responsible for upkeep of their property and are required to purchase hazard insurance just as they would be with any type of mortgage (Fannie Mae, 1991b, p. 3).

There are also a number of fees the borrower must pay. These include the loan origination fee, closing costs, and 2 percent of the maximum claim amount as a premium for mortgage insurance. In addition, there is a $1/2$ percent annual mortgage insurance premium. It is possible to finance the origination fee up to 1 percent of the maximum claim amount, the closing costs, and the one-time 2 percent insurance premium, although doing so will create immediate indebtedness against the maximum claim amount and thus reduce the monthly cash receipt (Fannie Mae, 1991a, p. 4).

The borrower is also required to pay loan servicing costs of $25 to $30 monthly, which are deducted when determining the monthly amount to be disbursed to the home owner (Fannie Mae, 1991b, p. 4).

The HUD-FHA program permits the borrower to choose between two methods for determining how much interest accrues on the monthly income receipts. Both are adjustable rate methods. One provides for the loan interest rate to be adjusted annually, with a maximum per year change of 2 percent in the loan interest rate and a 5 percent lifetime cap on change from the initial rate. The second method provides for monthly changes in the interest rate, but the rate charged may never be more than 10 percent above the initial rate, and there is no floor on the minimum rate (Fannie Mae, 1991b, p. 2).

The HUD-FHA program is a good one for the protections it provides. To repeat a point made earlier, reverse mortgages are not assistance programs, they are financing programs, so there is no cost subsidy to the borrower. There are a number of details to be evaluated, and persons interested should contact a HUD approved lender.

Private lenders have begun to enter the reverse mortgage market providing both insured and uninsured loans. Like the HUD-FHA program, they permit occupancy in the home for life or until the home is sold. Insured loans are made by a lender who initiates and holds enough mortgages to create its own "pool" of insured loans. They charge borrowers an insurance fee, and in this way protect themselves and the borrowers against the financial risk that a home owner with a tenure mortgage will accumulate a debt in excess of the market value of the home.

There are variations in the way interest is computed on these loans, so the borrower should exercise care when choosing a method. This type of reverse mortgage involves significant up front costs, and loan interest rates can be high. Consequently, the cost of private insured loans can be quite high if the borrower does not occupy the home for more than a few years. Currently, there are three major lenders that operate in this area. As experience with reverse mortgages increases, as the pool of loans grows, and as competition enters the market for reverse mortgages, it is possible that the costs of these loans may decline (Scholen, 1990, pp. 25–30).

Uninsured mortgages can be less costly because there is no insurance premium added to or imbedded in the monthly interest charge. Lenders, however, limit their risk by making only term loans. As noted earlier, a borrower should have definite reasons for believing that he or she will occupy their home for a fixed period of time before entering into a term loan since the full amount falls due when the term of the cash receipt stream ends. Uninsured reverse mortgages are presently available in only a few states (Scholen, 1990, pp. 30–33).

Deferred payment loans and *property tax deferral loans* share certain characteristics. Borrowing only takes place if the homeowner wishes, interest rates are lower than on annuity mortgages, and up-front costs are lower. The costs are less because these loans are typically made by a state or local government agency. Some of these programs impose rather stringent eligibility requirements based on income and assets. Also, since many of the programs are operated by localities, they are not widely available. They are worth investigating, however, because of their relatively low cost. The best information sources are local councils on aging, city housing authorities, or community development agencies.

Deferred payment loans may be referred to locally as home repair loans or accessibility loans, so it is important that the borrower describe his or her intended purpose for the loan. Property tax deferral loans are available in about a third of the states, and may be made by state or local agencies. To locate information, interested parties should contact their local taxing authority, state housing department or state revenue office, a local council on aging, or an area agency on aging (Scholen, 1990, pp. 10–14).

Sale-and-leaseback arrangements represent contractual agreements between two parties. Consequently, there are no organized programs to promote this approach or to finance the loan. An elderly person who is interested in a sale-and-leaseback arrangement should contact an attorney and an accountant who have experience with such arrangements.

The Future

Equity conversion plans are still quite new. Lenders' requirements in the area of risk bearing, and the institutional need for market instruments that raise large pools of funds have been solved. As a result, we may expect to see a proliferation of private sector lenders, and an increase in the number and types of securitized debt instruments issued to the investing public, all of which bodes well for the availability of reverse mortgages (AARP, 1992, p. 4). It is unlikely that we will see changes in the HUD-FHA loans until the current program ends in 1995 (Scholen, 1992, p. 305), although there may be improvements in delivery. Specifically, there has been some criticism that the counseling requirement is neither readily available nor accessible. There is also concern about the quality of counseling delivered by some counseling agencies. Too, there is concern that the counseling requirement causes elderly people to infer that reverse mortgages are dangerous economic ventures (AARP,

1992, p. 5). These concerns can be dealt with through the exercise of planning and care, and as experience is gained, the approach used may be improved.

One important improvement likely to occur at some time is to allow elderly people to take annuity receipts for life, irrespective of where they live (Scholen, 1992, pp. 306–307). The idea here focuses upon continuing the payments to the older person even if they must vacate their home to move into a care facility (although they may vacate for other reasons, too). Possibly, the home could be leased to provide additional income to the elderly person, which would help with the cost of care. Such an option would reduce the monthly receipt, but it might represent the preferred choice for some people.

An elderly person who chooses a reverse mortgage can ill afford to have the payments stop because both the lender and the insurer of the loan fail financially. This risk is real, if not large, with private market lenders and insurers. Effort should and probably will be made by states to require insurers to commit themselves to a risk pooling arrangement wherein the mortgages of a failed insurer are reinsured by those companies remaining in the pool (Scholen, 1992, p. 311).

All insurers are regulated by states in an attempt to ensure that they maintain economic viability. A risk-pooling scheme would add to pressure to avoid undue risk or suspect management practices because the insurers in the pool would have incentive to police the behavior of one another.

We are likely to see new types of shared appreciation reverse annuity mortgages in the future. Lenders lost interest in them when real estate values ceased to appreciate rapidly; but it is easy to imagine a new form of these mortgages that would permit the monthly cash receipt to increase if the market value of the home increases. The lender could protect itself by increasing the monthly receipt according to some percentage of the increase in the value of the home, even if this percentage is small. Of course, if the home did not appreciate, there would be no increase in the size of receipts. The significant advantage, however, is that there would be some increase in the elderly person's monthly income during periods when the general level of prices is rapidly escalating.

Sources of Information about Home Equity Conversion Programs

Available from:
American Association of Retired Persons (AARP)
Home Equity Information Center
Consumer Affairs Section
1909 K Street, N.W.
Washington, DC 20049

Home-Made Money: Consumer's Guide to Home Equity
Conversion. Publication D12894

Home Equity Conversion in the United States: Programs
and Data. (Write to AARP, Center for Elderly People
Living Alone, 601 E Street, N.W., Washington, DC 20049.)

Summary of Reverse Mortgage Plans. A state-specific
listing of reverse mortgage programs, updated quarterly.
Publication D13253

HEC Hotline. An occasional bulletin providing updates on
developments in home equity conversion. (To be placed on
the mailing list, write to AARP at the above address.)

Available from:
National Center for Home Equity Conversion
1210 East College Drive, Suite 300
Marshall, MN 56258

Retirement Income on the House: Cashing in on Your
Home with a "Reverse" Mortgage. Book. $24.95 plus $4.50
postage and handling.

Fact Sheet on Reverse Mortgages. A listing of public and
private lenders that make reverse mortgages. $1.

REFERENCES

American Association of Retired Persons. (1991). *Fact Sheet: Home Equity Conversion*. Washington, DC: Author.

American Association of Retired Persons and Administration on Aging. (1989). *A Profile of Older Americans: 1989*. Washington, DC: Author.

American Association of Retired Persons, Program Coordination and Development Department, Consumer Affairs Section. (1992, Spring). Progress and Challenge Mark 30 Years of Reverse Mortgage Lending. *AARP Housing Report*, 4–6, Washington, DC: Author.

American Seniors Housing Association. (1992, December). *Seniors Housing Update* (Newsletter). Washington, DC: Author.

Brackey, H.J. (1992, May 11). Homeowners Take Payday. *USA Today*, pp. 1B–2B.

Crystal, S., & Shea, D. (1990). Cumulative Advantage, Cumulative Disadvantage, and Inequality Among Elderly People. *Gerontologist*, 30(4), 437–443.

Crown, W.H. (1989). Trends in the Economic Status of the Aged and the Implications for State Policy. *Journal of Aging and Social Policy*, 1 (3/4), 89–128.

DeZube, D. (1990). A Slow Start for Reverse Mortgages. *Mortgage Banking*, 51, Issue 3, 33–34, 36, 38–39.

Dunn, D. (1990, January 22). House–Rich and Cash–Poor? Then Let the Bank Pay You. *Business Week*, No. 3142, 82–83.

Fannie Mae (1991a). *Home Equity Conversion Mortgage (HECM) Information*. Washington, DC: Author.

——— (1991b). *Our Participation in HUD's Home Equity Conversion Mortgage Program*. Washington, DC: Author.

Grad, S. (1990). *Income of the Population 55 or Older, 1988*. Washington, DC: U.S. Department of Health and Human Services.

Higgins, D.P., & Folts, W.E. (1992). Principles and Cash Flow Expectations of Reverse Mortgages. *Journal of Applied Gerontology*, 11, 187–199.

Scholen, K. (1990). *Home-Made Money: Consumer's Guide to Home Equity Conversion*. Washington, DC: American Association of Retired

Persons, Home Equity Information Center, Consumer Affairs Section.

——— (1992). *Retirement Income on the House*. Marshall, MN: National Center for Home Equity Conversion.

Schultz, A., & Clow, R. (1991, December 9). HomeFirst Set to Securitize Reverse Mortgage Loans. *Investment Dealers Digest*, 57, Issue 49, 15–16.

Schulz, J.H. (1992). *The Economics of Aging, Fifth Edition*. New York: Auburn House.

Sichelman, L. (1991, November). A Tough Sell. *Mortgage Banking*, 52, Issue 2, 22–26.

Springer, P.B. (1985). Home Equity Conversion Plans as a Source of Retirement Income. *Social Security Bulletin*, 48 (9), 10–19.

Thompson, B. (1987). A Mortgage That Pays You. *Changing Times*, 41 (7), 67, 70–71.

U.S. Senate Special Committee on Aging. (1988). *Aging America, Trends and Projections*, 1987–1988 Edition. Washington, DC: U.S. Department of Health and Human Services.

Venti, S.F., & Wise, D.A. (1991). Aging and the Income Value of Housing Wealth. *Journal of Public Economics*, 44, 371–397.

CHAPTER 15

Bofellesskab: The Danish Import[1]

Kay E. Rodabough

Peter and Marie still lived in the family home but their children, except for one son, had grown up and moved away. The house was large and was becoming more difficult to manage. Peter and Marie were approaching retirement and it became obvious, to both of them, that their lives were changing. For one thing, they both realized that it would soon be more complicated to live on their own. Each of them was concerned about that time when one or the other of them would be alone. There was much to remind them that the old neighborhood was changing. Friends and long-term neighbors had begun to move to more supportive environments. Underlying their thoughts was the fact that both Peter and Marie had observed how their own parents had experienced retirement. For their parents, retirement was a period characterized by loss of contact with friends and colleagues and increasing isolation despite living in their own home. Peter and Marie had different plans for their own retirement. It was important for them to continue their involvement in their community and with their neighbors.

Because of their concerns and their determination not to repeat the patterns of their parents, Peter and Marie called together a group made up of friends and others who all shared an interest in creating a new and innovative type of living arrangement. This new type of community would be designed to meet the specific needs of all members of the group and would simultaneously focus on the need for privacy and the desire to promote social interaction. In their own words, Peter and Marie described their feelings about this new approach to community life:

> We realized that social contact would become more limited and, as we aged, we would spend more time in our home. Windows facing the center of the community would function to provide a feeling of involvement. Watching children play and seeing people coming and going would support our continued need for involvement and being a part of the community.

Another of the innovations discussed by this group was the inclusion of a "common house" which would further expand opportunities for community interaction. The group decided to locate the common house at the entrance so that residents could meet each other on their way in and out of the community. Large windows were designed for each of the dwelling units to enhance "casual observation," allowing residents the choice of interacting with their neighbors.

After long and detailed discussions about priorities for space in the community, the group then hired an architect to help them transform their ideas into reality. Together, they developed a community whose physical design reflected each future resident's preferences for closeness and social interaction, while at the same time addressing their desire for privacy.

The Danish Cooperative Housing Model

Peter and Marie had helped to establish a new way of life which provided a range of choices and which reflected an underlying desire to remain in their own home, actively involved in the community, and surrounded by neighbors with similar preferences. The name given to this new type of living arrangement was Bofellesskab which, in Danish, means "people who live or reside jointly."

Pronounced "bo-fell-ess-cob," these communities have been established throughout Denmark as a response to a growing number of people whose need for community interaction has not been met by traditional single-family housing. A Bofellesskab community offers each resident opportunities for privacy in their own dwelling unit while, at the same time, providing common areas that encourage community interaction and involvement. In the United States, a similar concept, based on the Bofellesskab model, is gaining support among those interested in innovative and supportive community based housing. The American version of the Danish Bofellesskab has been labeled CoHousing.[2] CoHousing is a registered trademark of two architects: Kathryn McCamant and Charles Durrett. As a result of their architectural studies in Denmark, McCamant and Durrett (1988) wrote a book entitled: *CoHousing: A Contemporary Approach to Housing Ourselves*. This seminal work has been used as a model by all of the over one hundred groups who have expressed interest in establishing this type of housing in the United States.

The process of establishing a Bofellesskab community in Denmark, or Cohousing community in the United States, differs from one group to another because of the wide variation in interests that are typically found in these groups. However, McCamant and Durrett (1988) have outlined four related features which they believe are common to all such efforts.

One of the most important identifying characteristics of this type of housing community is its inherent participatory process. Future residents are expected to be involved in all aspects of the community from designing what the community will become to the actual day-to-day management. This process alone distinguishes the Danish model from housing options currently available in the United States.

Another characteristic identified by McCamant and Durrett (1988) is specifically related to the design of the community. The design typically involves "clustered" homes situated around pedestrian streets that encourage opportunities for interaction among neighbors. The result is a feeling of closeness, belonging, and security that is absent in many other housing alternatives.

The inclusion of large areas designated as "community space," both indoors and outdoors, is also characteristic of these communities. Typically, a separate "common house" is constructed for meals, community socializing, and other group activities. The emphasis is clearly on group activities and the spatial design of these communities reflects that emphasis.

Finally, the fact that each resident is expected to participate in the day-to-day management of the community allows residents to formulate the best responses to change. This emphasis on involvement is not only characteristic of these communities, but it is a very important element that binds the residents together and permits what can best be described as "management by consensus." An additional common feature is that private spaces, including the dwelling unit itself, are typically smaller than traditional single-family homes. In a sense, each household contributes a small portion of its private space to common areas in the community.

Although all of these characteristics are consistently present, at least to some extent, each community that is developed is distinct and reflects the unique interests, desires, and priorities of those who create it. Each of the communities also reflects the political, social, and financial environments within which they are created and operate.

Cooperative Housing and Older Adults

In the United States, the Danish Bofellesskab housing model is more than merely a concept for an innovative, if somewhat unusual, housing type. Largely due to the work of McCamant and Durrett, there are now over one hundred groups, located all across the United States, in various stages of establishing these communities. Four of these groups are currently living in Bofellesskab-type cooperative communities. The potential of this housing option has far-reaching implications for older adults. Essentially, this type of community is an effort to integrate and accommodate all residents—of all ages—into a single community setting characterized by involvement and dedication to common community goals.

Today, in the United States, there is a growing awareness that continued involvement by older people can be beneficial for all age groups. Cohen (1982) notes, however:

> the paradox is that older adults are often forced into socially nonproductive roles precisely at the time when society most seriously needs their participation. (p. 37)

The participatory process inherent in this type of housing involves residents making meaningful choices about the way they will live. This latter point is important because, historically, older adults have not been active participants in designing their own housing. As reported by Brennan, Moos, and Lemke (1988):

> ... although architects and behavioral scientists have identified several important sets of physical design features of residential settings, older adults themselves have seldom have been asked about their preferences for these features. (p. 85)

Bofellesskab type living arrangements offer older adults the opportunity to make meaningful contributions to the design of the communities and the houses within which they will grow older. The importance of this contribution cannot be overstated because, for many of these people, it will have been their first opportunity to have their needs and preferences seriously considered and actually incorporated into their dwelling units and neighborhoods. In a broader context, the preferences expressed by these older "pioneers" will be a valuable source of information for all segments of the housing industry. In one sense, the older adults who are involved in designing these communities are contributing to the shape of elderly housing for the future.

Bofellesskab Communities in Denmark

To better understand how these cooperative living arrangements fit within the broader context of housing for older adults, I visited Bofellesskab communities located throughout Denmark. The following are summary accounts of my experiences and illustrate the important potential benefits of this lifestyle to some older adults.

Midgard

Winding through busy city streets early one morning, I walked past vacant factories, crossed railroad tracks, and moved along small store fronts and restaurants to enter a large housing development. A green courtyard with benches and flower gardens welcomed me as I approached my destination—a four-story building were nine women had created their own special place.

The community of Midgard got its start when several retired women signed up for a class that required them to reflect on their retirement years. Intrigued by the ideas presented in the class, and motivated by a mutual desire for involvement in their community, the women began looking for ways to make their ideas a reality. When they heard about a proposal for developing a large apartment complex, the women decided to present their ideas to the planning staff. As a result, they were asked to become active participants in the development process and a portion of one of the buildings was designed to incorporate the needs and preferences of these nine women. After five years of planning and anticipation, Midgard had become a reality.

Several years later, I sat in the common room with some of these women discussing what their lives were like now. All agreed that they would not want to live anywhere else. In fact, the title of an educational film about these nine women expressed their commitment to their community: "Gak Hen" (Go and do likewise). Although Midgard was specifically designed to address the needs and preferences of these older women, Bofellesskab communities can be an attractive housing alternative for any age group.

Kolding

I was also invited to spend a week in an intergenerational Bofellesskab community near the Danish town of Kolding. The community consisted of 15 row houses and a common house, all forming a square. A large community play area was located in the center of these buildings. The common house was intentionally located so that people entering or leaving the community would pass this central location. The placement of large windows in the common house purposely enhanced casual observation and gave residents a choice about whether to participate in community gatherings. Kitchen windows were purposely placed at the front of each house, allowing residents to share in the supervision of the community's children who could play in the central square. This arrangement also encouraged social interaction when neighbors passed.

Many of the residents invited me into their homes where they shared their feelings about living in the community. One resident said, "What is really important to me is that people have learned to care for each other by sharing activities." One woman in the community added that the intergenerational relationships that have developed for her have been one of the most important things she values about the way she now lives. She went on to say that since her parents did not live nearby, having older people in the community had proven to be beneficial in many ways. For example, she said:

> when my husband and I moved into the community, there were four families with school-age children. [These] families needed a place for the children to stay before school started. At a community resident's meeting, the families discussed their dilemma. One of the older couples in the community helped solve the problem for all families by offering to care for the children.

On my last night in this community, the residents gathered around candlelit tables in their common house. As they shared coffee and Danish sweet breads one of the residents summed up his feelings about this community when he said: "It is a good form of life."

Bofellesskab Communities in the United States

The Danish cooperative housing movement, coupled with the American tradition for individual choice and privacy, provides the foundation for the development of this type of community in the United States. There are presently over one hundred communities being discussed, in various locations around the United States, that are based on the model described here. Four of those communities have actually begun operation.

The Commons on the Alameda

The Commons on the Alameda in Santa Fe, New Mexico, is one of four Bofellesskab communities currently operating in the U.S. This particular community is made up of individuals who are interested in working at home. Although the community is only partially completed, a total of twenty-eight houses are planned and the community will be intergenerational with older and younger families included.

The Santa Fe community started when a group of about twenty-five people became interested in developing an alternative living arrangement. Weekly meetings were scheduled and agendas were developed to help the group work through the primary issues associated with developing the type of housing they wanted. This group explored a variety of topics, including: the potential for on-site daycare, work-at-home opportunities, the possibility of offering rental units, and renting guest rooms in the common house. The group also discussed developing a community which would include all age groups and family types. And, recognizing that no two situations were the same, the group decided that each house would need to reflect the uniqueness of its owner. A local developer obtained a site where the community could be built which helped focus the group's discussions of how their community could be structured.

To achieve the group's goal of privacy and their preference for work-at-home, a central plaza was designed as an extension of the common house. Residents who were to have business-related visitors chose housing sites on the central plaza. An individual's business was designed to open onto the plaza while residential units faced the private areas of the community.

In interviews with a number of older adult residents in this community, several gave me their perspective on how they felt the Danish community framework would meet their needs. A woman in her seventies shared how she felt about the intergenerational aspect of the community:

> I never had any children. There are a lot of kids at our meetings. The children scratch your knee so you will hold them. This makes me feel intimately involved with children in a way I have never been in my life. . . . I am building a small attached house which I will rent; however, if I ever need to, I will have someone live there who can help me.

She went on to say that when she lived in Connecticut she felt terribly alone. She was in a community where it was not easy to make close contacts. "Here," she said, "I know people would be aware if I did not appear."

In this same community a son and his mother are working on an arrangement where she is purchasing a lot in the community in exchange for his labor to build her house. Separately, neither of them would be able to purchase a home and property in Santa Fe. The design of this community was flexible enough to incorporate both a house for the son and his family and an attached "guest" house for the mother. I asked the mother how she anticipated the community would meet her future needs as she aged. Her response was that she felt it would provide a place she could afford, security where people would know her, work opportunities, her own private house, and opportunities for socializing. And, when she could no longer drive, she felt that family, neighbors or public transportation would be available to help her.

Muir Commons

Muir Commons, located in Davis, California, highlights an additional component of using the constructed environment to support all levels of physical capabilities. The community's houses are universally designed and are clustered along an eight-foot-wide pedestrian street. Muir Commons was the first Danish Bofellesskab type community completed in the United States. The community includes twenty-six houses which are clustered on 2.9 acres.

A total of forty adults, nineteen children and five teenagers live in Muir Commons. Among the adults are five older people. While about half of the adults are married several single mothers live in the community. One resident described how the participatory design process helped her meet some of the needs of her 7-year-old son who had been confined to a wheelchair since the age of 3. She said:

> My husband and I had looked to purchase a house in Davis for three years. One of our hopes was that we could own a home where our son, now seven, could fully participate in his environment. We wanted this house to have features that would help support his independence as he grew up. One strength of this community is that you get to hear and see other people's needs. The process seems so humane. When we started talking about the design of the community, physical features came up, issue by issue; so when we talked about front doors, bathrooms, upstairs and downstairs, doorways and hallways, height of the windows, everyone became aware of the issues as they related to our son's needs. Everyone decided to make their front door accessible because they wanted him to be able to visit.

Doyle Street

A third community that has been developed in the U.S. is located in the San Francisco Bay Area in Emeryville, California. Doyle Street is unique in that it is situated in an urban "infill" site previously reserved for commercial development. There are a total of twelve units in the Emeryville community housing eighteen people. Of these eighteen people, four are middle-aged adults. One of the residents of the Doyle Street Community mentioned she felt that a real benefit of this type of living arrangement was its integration with the surrounding area. A park is under construction nearby, an organic community garden is available, and a cafe and bakery are located across the street. Further, the Emeryville Public Market is within walking distance.

The Winslow Community

The Winslow Community is the fourth community completed in the United States. This community is located on Bainbridge Island, Washington and consists of five acres separated from downtown Seattle, Washington, by a 30-minute ferry ride. Houses on the site are clustered around three neighborhoods and are organized along two pedestrian streets. There are a total of thirty units ranging in size from 518 square feet to 1,500 square feet. Currently, 77 people live in the community including 48 adults and 29 children. Eleven of the adults are age 50 and above.

After reading McCamant and Durrett's book on CoHousing, the developer responsible for this project placed fliers in store windows in Winslow, the Island's small town of 2,500. The developer has said:

> The key to developing the Danish Bofellesskab in the United States is to focus on the norms which are presently acceptable. Another essential area to consider is affordable housing. The way this can be addressed is that house plans can be standardized and residents can customize their house once it is complete.

Aging in Place and the Intergenerational Issue

None of the Bofellesskab type communities currently operating in the U.S. has fully addressed the issue of assistance and care. And, so far at least, there has been little attention paid to the related issue of aging in place. However, the involvement of the residents in all levels of operation of this type of housing would suggest that the Bofellesskab model possesses a unique capacity to adapt to the changing needs of all its residents.

Besides meeting the basic needs for shelter for all age groups, this Danish model is designed to provide needed physical and social support for a broad spectrum of ages, incomes, lifestyles, and family structures. At its very base, this new type of community is an effort to provide an additional option with the capacity to integrate all age groups by addressing a variety of needs.

We must look to creative approaches that address the issue of housing and care and, as a broader goal, the development of a model that creates environments for "successful" aging and integration. For, as Stephen Golant (1984) has reminded us:

> . . . we have learned . . . that as people live increasingly long lives, a society that adapts to that fact may become an "enabling" society for both young and old. An aging society is not a specter that should frighten us. We would do better to think what the spirit of our aging society might become and to what extent it might be a beneficent spirit that could assure a range of options for people of all ages. (p. 165–166)

NOTES

1. Copyright © 1992 Kay E. Rodabough. Used with permission.

2. "CoHousing" is a term coined by Kathryn McCamant and Charles Durrett, authors of *CoHousing: A Contemporary Approach to Housing Ourselves*, Ten Speed (1988), to describe this specific housing model. CoHousing is a service mark of McCamant & Durrett.

REFERENCES

Brennan, Penny L., Rudolf H. Moos, and Sonne Lemke. (1988). "Preferences of older adults and experts for physical and architectural features of group living facilities." *The Gerontologist*, 28(1), 84–90.

Cohen, Marlene C. (1982). "The intergenerational caregiving program." *Aging*, March–April, 37–38.

Golant, Stephen M. (1984). *A place to grow old*. New York: Columbia University Press.

McCamant, Kathryn and Charles Durrett. (1988). *CoHousing: A Contemporary Approach to Housing Ourselves*, Berkeley, California: Ten Speed Press.

———. (1989). "Good Housekeeping: Cohousing can reincorporate community into the American dream." *Utne Reader*, May/June, 68–72.

Moos, Rudolf H., Sonne Lemke, and Thomas G. David. (1987). "Priorities for design and management in residential settings for the elderly," in V. Regnier & J. Pynoos (Eds.), *Housing the aged: Design directives and policy considerations*, New York: Elsevier.

CHAPTER 16

Older Mentally Retarded Persons: A Housing Issue in Need of Clarification

Dale O. Robinson
Dale E. Yeatts
John S. Mahoney

There is a need to address the growing shortage of housing designed especially for mentally retarded older adults. In recent decades, this need has emerged as an issue of national concern (Rose & Ansello, 1987) partly as a result of the deinstitutional-ization movement, partly because of dramatically improved life expectancies among those with mental retardation, and also because of the anticipated loss of extended family support networks that presently provide care to the elderly with various levels of mental retardation.

The elderly, as was discussed in previous chapters, have a population growth rate that is several times that of the general population. Today, nearly 32 million Americans are age sixty-five or older. This number will increase to nearly 65 million by the year 2030 and will comprise over 21 percent of the U.S. population. As a general demographic trend, the population of older persons suffering from mental retardation, as well as other developmental disabilities, has been steadily increasing. However, there is still considerable disagreement about the actual size of the mentally retarded older population.

Most estimates have been based on the prevalence of mental retardation in the general population. DiGiovanni (1978), for example, used a 1 percent prevalence rate and suggested that the maximum number of mentally retarded aging (age fifty-five to sixty-four) and elderly (age sixty-five and over) Americans could be as high as 382,000. Seltzer and Seltzer (1984) on the other hand, suggested that the rate is closer to 3 percent and they estimated that as many as 1.38 million people age fifty-five and over are mentally retarded. Jacobson, Sutton, and Janicki used a more conservative estimate based upon participation in or registration with service systems. They concluded that in 1982, nearly 196,000 individuals age fifty-five and over suffer some form of mental retardation. Applying this conservative estimate to current population projections (U.S. Bureau of the Census, 1989), the anticipated number of aging and elderly Americans who suffer from mental retardation will be approximately 234,000 in the year 2000; and 400,000 by the year 2030.

Thus, while the number of aging and elderly mentally retarded Americans is likely to rise sharply over the next few decades, existing research suggests that there has been no substantial increase in the availability of publicly supported services—including housing—for this group. In fact, Rose and Ansello (1987) have pointed out that the supply of publicly supported housing for older persons suffering mental retardation has actually been declining at a time when the number of persons needing such housing is increasing.

U.S. housing legislation has typically been formulated so that the elderly and the mentally retarded are treated as a single categorical target population. As a result, housing designated as "elderly" housing must also be made available to persons with mental retardation—regardless of age. The consequences of this are discussed in detail in other chapters of this book; however, the general result of this policy is that the special needs of both groups are largely unmet.

The rationale for such inclusion of the elderly and the mentally retarded in a single category has been the stereotypical assumption that older persons and persons who are mentally retarded have similar housing and service needs. It is argued that many elderly persons develop significant health problems, lose at least some degree of physical mobility, retire from their jobs, and lose a significant portion of their income and financial flexibility. As a result, or so this reasoning goes, older persons lose valued social roles, some mental ability, and often become dependent on others (Willer and Intagliata, 1984). Furthermore, those who view these separate groups of individuals as a single categorical population believe that, because of these losses, older persons take on many of the same characteristics as those who are mentally disabled.

One consequence of this line of reasoning has been that little attention is focused on the unique housing and service needs of persons who are both mentally retarded and old. Kauppi and Jones (1985) have pointed out that the mentally retarded elderly are subject to what amounts to "double stereotyping" and they argue that services to mentally retarded people have suffered from the assumption that there is only "one way" to provide services. They further suggest that a contingency approach to the problem would be more efficacious. Such an approach would focus on the needs of the individual clients and would provide flexibility in fitting existing programs to the special needs of elderly mentally retarded persons. Service providers and policymakers have only recently begun to develop or restructure programs so that they can better meet the needs of aging persons with mental retardation. Given the relative infancy of these programs, it is not surprising that contemporary programmatic practices and residential services are underdeveloped and have been largely unable to meet even the present need.

Types of Housing for Older Persons with Mental Retardation

There are currently a variety of types of housing that are appropriate for older persons suffering from mental retardation or other types of developmental disabilities. These include mental institutions, nursing homes, community-based public housing facilities, "foster family care" residential facilities, apartments, and boarding homes. Although the conceptual options are many, the practical alternatives are few. Apart from the traditional response of institutionalizing these individuals, none of the options listed above is currently supported at a level that would make them a viable alternative for even a meaningful proportion of those who need them.

Mental Institutions

During the colonial period in the United States, the care of mentally retarded individuals, as well as older individuals, was considered the absolute responsibility of the family. That few mentally retarded individuals survived to old age in the harsh and unforgiving physical and social environments of the colonies made attention to this group of individuals of little practical concern. However, rapid growth in the general population and the equally rapid development of commerce in the colonial towns produced public concern for increasing numbers of what were labeled "dependent" and "deviant" individuals. At the same time, changing social and economic demands on the family made it increasingly difficult to care for family members at home.

As a result of these developments, and other changes that were taking place, the first publicly supported facilities designed to care for the "dependent" or "deviant" were established. While most persons with mental retardation and most older adults who needed care continued to be cared for by family members, the beginning of the nineteenth century saw a rapid increase in the placement of some of these individuals in almshouses for the poor, asylums for the mentally ill, and penal institutions for criminals (Vitello and Soskin, 1985).

By the mid-nineteenth century, the United States was still primarily an agrarian society but it was rapidly becoming industrialized. The increasing demands for an urban labor force were being met, to a large extent, by the rapid influx of immigrants from Europe. Persons with mental retardation were being called "imbeciles" or "idiots" and were still generally cared for by family members. The most severely retarded persons typically had short life expectancies, whereas those less severely retarded most often were capable of living useful lives as workers on the family farm (Willer and Intagliata, 1984).

World War II triggered a massive change in the housing patterns of most of the industrialized world. The movement from farms and small communities to cities, and from large households to small families, brought with it far-reaching upheavals in the traditional lifestyles of the period (Laurie, 1977). One of the major consequences of these changes was the emergence of the federal and, to a lesser extent, state governments as institutions with ultimate social responsibility for the care of those unable to care for themselves—the disabled, the aged, and others with special needs.

Since World War II, the United States has supported several major housing policies affecting older persons with mental retardation. In the 1950s and early 1960s institutionalization was the solution to the lack of housing and home service arrangements for the growing numbers of older persons with varying degrees of mental retardation and other cognitive impairments. There were several types of institutionalization that emerged at this period in history. These ranged from geriatric hospitals and altruistic segregated residences in Great Britain to the development of the nursing home "industry" in the United States. Denmark alone pioneered an apartment building with a mix of disabled and nondisabled persons, including special provisions for a few disabled by poliomyelitis who required respiratory aids (Landesman and Vietze, 1987). As Chapter 15 suggests, it appears that Denmark continues to develop and provide innovative housing options for its citizens with special needs.

The institutionalized populations of most countries increased until the late 1960s, when corrective measures began to occur under the influence of the "normalization principle." Normalization is generally viewed as an enhancement in the quality of life of individuals with functional or mental impairments. Further, normalization cannot be accomplished, according to most advocates, by forcing persons with mental or physical limitations to live in large, isolated buildings. Nor is it "normal" for most persons to live in groups that are ten to one hundred times the size of the average family (Wolfensberger, 1983). The principle of normalization dictates that the best living environment for adults with mental retardation is a small, family-sized home, blending inconspicuously in a typical residential neighborhood and offering its residents as much opportunity to participate in the community as other community residents (Wolfensberger, 1983).

Since 1967 the size of all institutional populations, with the exception of nursing home populations, has declined dramatically (Landesman and Vietze, 1987). This decrease is largely due to efforts at "deinstitutionalization" at the state level and reflects acceptance of the concept of normalization—at least in principle. As a result, recent years have witnessed a significant increase in the availability of small scale living arrangements and greater emphasis on community, social, and service integration in residential facilities.

Community-based Public Housing Facilities

Traditionally, community-based public residences for persons with mental retardation have been funded through specialized, targeted government programs. The sources of funding have usually included: special categorical or grant programs from a state or local mental retardation/developmental disabilities agency; income supports from Supplemental Security Income (SSI) or Social Security Disability Income (SSDI); and the Medicaid Intermediate Care Facility for the Mentally Retarded (ICF/MR) Program (Janicki, Wyngaarden, and Seltzer, 1988). ICFs/MR are specially designated facilities that provide food and shelter to four or more persons unrelated to the proprietor and, in addition, provide some treatment or services that meet some need beyond the basic provision of food and shelter. In general, these programs are characterized by stringent staffing and treatment requirements exceeding those typically found for other types of residential programs serving mentally retarded adults (Seltzer and Krauss, 1987). In addition to these funding programs, community residences have been financially supported by client fees and private donations.

By the late 1970s, a number of new housing programs became available through the U.S. Department of Housing and Urban Development (HUD), such as rental subsidies (Section 8) and direct loans (Section 202). Further, within the U.S.

Department of Agriculture, the Farmers Home Administration (FmHA) provided a housing program specifically for persons with mental retardation (Janicki, Wyngaarden, and Seltzer, 1988). The ICF/MR waiver program specifically addressed the policy of deinstitutionalization of persons with mental retardation and the development of community-based residential care. Since its passage in 1978, over thirty-five states have used it to finance small, family-sized, community-based group home housing projects. Other long-term community-based group home options for older persons with mental retardation have included adult homes, foster family care, and apartment and group homes. These specialized and generic residential and day-service programs are typically administered locally by a variety of community groups and in most instances are funded through state agencies (Rose and Ansello, 1987).

"Foster Family Care" Residential Facilities

Historically, foster family care programs have ranged from those which are primarily custodial in orientation to those that were meant to be rehabilitative. The concept of foster family care includes the provision of support services, supervision, and/or personal care. It is apparent that one problem in the development and evaluation of foster family care is that of regulatory definitions. Official regulations differ both geographically and across time. Names that have been given to programs that are similar to the concept of foster family care include: alternate homes; home care; family care; alternate families; community living; community residential care; supportive living; and cooperative living (Sherman and Newman, 1988). The dictionary definition of foster family care includes the notions of promoting growth, encouraging development, and providing nurturance.

Early foster family care programs for persons with mental retardation were instituted in New York State in 1931 and in Massachusetts about a decade later. In the early use of foster family care for persons with mental retardation, older persons were not included. Typically, this residential type included only individuals with relatively high levels of functional ability since the foster family care placement was usually located in a rural setting and involved help with farm chores. These placements offered benefits to both the residents and the host family. However, in the 1940s and 1950s foster family care was less often a residential option even for the highly functioning since the changing philosophy was toward institutionalization rather than community placement. Additionally, there was less demand for farm workers because of increasing mechanization (Sherman and Newman, 1988).

In the 1960s, with a shift back to deinstitutionalization, foster family care again came to be used for persons with mental retardation. In recent years, the foster-family-care setting has come to have a more habilitative orientation, either to serve as a transitional placement or as a less restrictive setting. This has made it more suitable for older persons than its earlier orientation toward farm labor. Janicki and Jacobson (1984) found, in a national survey, that all states operated some form of generic foster family care program and most operated some type of specialized program. In an attempt to examine specifically whether the program served older persons with mental retardation, Seltzer and Krauss (1987) conducted a national survey of institutional and community-based day and residential programs. They found only twenty-six programs offering foster family care services for older persons with mental retardation. In the homes surveyed, the average age of the residents was sixty-four years with an average of 3.7 persons per home. They also found that few services were available. However, when services were available, transportation and recreation were the most commonly offered services (Sherman and Newman, 1988).

Today, older mentally retarded individuals are disproportionately found among those in foster family care settings (Sherman and Newman, 1988). Foster family care has often been considered the most appropriate residential setting for older adults with mental retardation, partly because it provides a residential setting for persons for whom habilitation may not be expected. Further, foster family care provides the opportunity to integrate an older person with mental retardation into the life of a family and provide access to the community, while at the same time offering a protective environment (Sherman and Newman, 1988). However, in many instances, there is a need for the environment to be therapeutic rather than merely custodial (Sherman and Newman, 1988).

Foster family care can be viewed as a valuable post-institutional residential placement as well as a means of preventing or delaying institutionalization. Increasingly, there is a recognition that with adequate community support, many older persons with mental retardation may be kept out of institutions. It is generally accepted that persons without family supports have an increased risk of institutionalization (Sherman and Newman, 1988). At the same time, there is some question whether family members are capable of providing a long-term therapeutic environment for older mentally retarded adults. It may well be that artificially created "families" that generally have less emotional involvement are better able to tolerate difficult behavior and thus, care for mentally retarded older adults.

Similarly, limited economic and social resources, both of which may be particularly problematic for the very old, are highly associated with the risk of institutionalization. This higher risk, coupled with an understandable aversion to institutionalization of any type, offers a compelling argument for placing older persons with mental retardation in foster families (Sherman and Newman, 1988).

The issue of how best to care for older mentally retarded individuals is very complex. One of the more important related issues involves the aging of the family caregiver. There is likely to come a time when family caregivers, because of their own aging, are increasingly less able to continue providing care within the home environment. Furthermore, institutionalization of older adults who are mentally retarded frequently leads to a break in the family bond with a retarded relative (Willer and Intagliata, 1984). This, in turn, has led to decidedly negative outcomes for the older individual's quality of life. Foster family care would appear to offer an attractive alternative when primary care by the natural family is inadequate or altogether absent.

Apartments and Boarding Homes

For many older persons suffering from mental retardation, apartment living, both supervised and unsupervised, can provide high levels of normalization and promote self-sufficiency. It appears that this community alternative has been growing in demand as an increasing number of higher-functioning persons with mental retardation have outlived their parents. Apartment clusters are often composed of several apartments, in close physical proximity, functioning to some extent as a single housing unit. The residents typically are supervised by staff members who reside in one of the apartments. Co-residence arrangements consist of one or two adult staff members (often college students) and two or three persons who are mentally retarded living together as roommates. Single maximum independence apartments are occupied by two to four residents with mental retardation, with all supervision and assistance supplied by a citizen advocate or a caseworker employed by a residential service agency. Persons with mental retardation, who are more capable, may live in apartments with minimal supervision, either alone or with roommates (Vitello and Soskin, 1985).

Boarding homes and board-and-care homes are another type of residential care facility used as placement for older deinstitutionalized individuals with mental retardation. These residences differ from an apartment setting in that care providers are responsible for providing food and shelter as well as some supervision of the residents' daily living activities. They differ from health-related facilities because they do not provide nursing services to their adult residents (Willer and Intagliata, 1984).

Nursing Homes and Older
Mentally Retarded Persons

Nursing homes have been used extensively in some states as major sources of placement when, because of advanced age, persons with mental retardation can no longer remain in a community residential setting. Unfortunately, the level of habilitative programming and therapy, if offered at all, has typically been poor, as has the general level of resident activity and integration into the nursing home community (Vitello and Soskin, 1985). Willer and Intagliata (1984) have reported that because persons with mental retardation are typically a minority in nursing facilities, they have usually been given less attention and care by staff and, in some cases, have been ignored or even avoided.

It is interesting to note that some researchers have found older persons with mental retardation to be more likely than nonimpaired aged peers to adjust to institutionalization in a nursing home (Evans, 1983). While most older persons with mental retardation have spent some time in an institution or other kind of group living setting, nonretarded persons usually live in family settings prior to entering residential facilities. As a result, persons with mental retardation probably do not face quite the same adjustment problems as nonimpaired persons.

The Growth of Community-based Services

Since the 1970s, the deinstitutionalization of persons with mental retardation has become federal public policy. It was reasoned that moving people from public institutions to community-based settings would help approximate mainstream society as closely as possible, increase functional independence, and improve quality of life. However, as Seltzer, Finaly, and Howell (1988) have reported, many of the people who left mental institutions were placed in nursing homes where the restrictiveness of their environment was close to that of their former institutions and where fewer specialized services were provided.

On August 13, 1981, the Home and Community-based Medicaid Waiver Program, known as Section 2176, was enacted. Section 2176 granted the Secretary of Health and Human Services authority to waive certain existing Medicaid (Title XIX) statutory requirements to permit states to finance "noninstitutional" (i.e., community-based) long-term care services for individuals who would otherwise be eligible for Medicaid. The 2176 waiver program, as it applies to persons with mental retardation, was designated to provide community services to those who would otherwise be institutionalized (Heal, Haney, and Amado, 1988).

Waiver authority has given states some flexibility to provide community services that respond to individual needs. The designation, "waiver," came about because, under Section 2176, states are authorized to waive certain Medicaid requirements in order to forestall the federal cost of housing persons in institutional settings—primarily nursing homes. Among those directly benefitting from the Section 2176 Medicaid Waiver Program were older mentally retarded adults. In keeping with the financial goal of reducing costs, one requirement for receiving these funds has been that a state must demonstrate that the cost of the home or other community-based services are no greater than what would have to be paid if the "waiver" recipients had in fact been institutionalized (Heal, Haney, and Amado, 1988).

Section 2176 specifies seven basic services that states can offer: (1) habilitation; (2) case management; (3) homemaker services; (4) home-health aid; (5) personal care; (6) adult health services; and (7) respite care. In addition to these basic services, states may request to offer other services (e.g., various therapies or modifications to individuals' homes), provided they show how these services are cost effective and necessary to avoid institutionalization (Heal, Haney, and Amado, 1988).

The Health Care Financing Administration (HCFA) of the Department of Health and Human Services (DHHS) has recently taken steps to provide incentives in current Supplemental Security Income (SSI) and Medicaid eligibility rules so that some individuals whose health problems are less severe can remain in a community setting by having their medical needs met (Willer and Intagliata, 1984). This is done by providing the level of care needed within their home or residence (e.g., home health-care aides and visiting nurses), without resorting to placing them in an institutional setting. This alternative has been viewed as supporting the general intent of deinstitutionalization, while controlling, at least to some extent, the costs involved.

Another helpful program is the Community Support Services Program administered by the Developmental Disabilities Administration. Community Support Services are provided in order to assist individuals to remain in their own homes or with family members. Furthermore, these services are specifically aimed at enhancing the individual's ability to function in the community. The program allows for an array of services to be provided in accordance with the individual's needs (Rose and Ansello, 1987).

Targeting Issues for the New Century

As was discussed earlier, estimates vary widely regarding the number of older persons with mental retardation and their housing and service needs. However, experts agree that this population can be expected to grow rapidly in the future (Schalock, 1983) and may double between the year 2000 and 2030. Government housing programs that do not distinguish between older persons with mental retardation and the general elderly population do a disservice to both groups (Schalock, 1983). Older mentally retarded persons do not receive the types of community support they need in situations where a single housing program serves both populations. At the same time, the general elderly population has been somewhat vocal about being categorized and housed with persons suffering from a variety of mental deficits, including retardation. Only by disassociating the two groups can each receive the specialized attention needed (Schalock, 1983).

Policy decisions in the new century are likely to continue their emphasis on deinstitutionalization. This will require a variety of additional supports including: community-based support services; neglect, abuse, or exploitation prevention services; and services aimed at promoting social acceptance via increased community living skills. At the same time, increased public financial assistance to help persons with mental retardation to obtain and afford a residence in the community is essential.

It is also important to recognize that the aging of individuals with mental retardation will pose increasing challenges to public agencies, both those accustomed to meeting the needs of persons with mental retardation and those serving the elderly population. Historically, public agencies serving the mentally retarded have not dealt with large numbers of clients who have reached old age. Similarly, the aging network has had little experience with elders who suffer from mental retardation. A 1987 report from the University of Maryland National Center on Aging and Disabilities indicated that there is a critical shortage of programs and services for older adults suffering from mental retardation. This shortage is occurring both within the aging network and the state developmental disabilities system and there has been very little meaningful interaction between the two aimed at planning or providing needed services. Rose and Ansello (1987) concluded that there was no comprehensive partnership to address coordinated services for older persons with mental retardation. Without coordination, expensive dual systems of overlapping services have developed. They further argue that, in the long run, integrated services would cost less and be more effective in addressing the needs.

The special housing needs of older persons with mental retardation have been largely overlooked by researchers and policymakers alike. It has been argued by some that, as the financial burdens grow, the traditional lack of attention cannot continue (Rose and Ansello, 1987). Researchers, service providers, and those responsible for planning and administering residential and other services should give this special population a high priority. The current literature suggests that a contingency model based on specific service needs—including housing needs—of older mentally retarded individuals offers a more humane and more efficient approach than currently exists. Such a model does not necessarily imply added expense. However, much research is needed to define placement guidelines and to explore appropriate modifications to existing facilities and programs.

REFERENCES

DiGiovanni, L. (1978). The Elderly Retarded: A Little-known Group. *The Gerontologist*, 18(2), 262–266.

Evans, D.P. (1983). *The Lives of Mentally Retarded People*. Boulder, CO: Westview Press.

Heal, L.W., Haney, J.I., & Novak Amado, A.R. (1988). *Integration of Developmentally Disabled Individuals into the Community*. Baltimore: Paul H. Brooks Publishing Co.

Jacobson, J.W., Sutton, M.S., & Janicki, M.P. (1985). Demography and the Characteristics of Aging and Aged Mentally Retarded Persons. In M.P. Janicki and H.M. Wisniewski (Eds.), *Aging and Developmental Disabilities: Issues and Approaches*. Baltimore: Paul H. Brooks Publishing Co.

Janicki, M.P., & Jacobson, J.W. (1984). *Behavioral abilities of older mentally retarded persons*. Paper presented at the 108th Annual Convention of the American Association on Mental Deficiency, May 1984, Minneapolis, MN.

Janicki, M.P., Wyngaarden, M.K., & Seltzer, M.M. (1988). *Community Residences for Persons with Developmental Disabilities: Here to Stay*. Baltimore: Paul H. Brooks Publishing Co., 1–59.

Kauppi, D.R., & Jones, K.C. (1985). The Role of the Community Agency in Serving Older Mentally Retarded Persons. In M.P. Janicki and H.M. Wisniewski (Eds.), *Aging and Developmental Disabilities: Issues and Approaches*. Baltimore: Paul H. Brooks Publishing Co.

Landesman, S., & Vietze, P. (1987). *Living Environments and Mental Retardation*. Washington, DC: NICHD Mental Retardation Research Center Series, 19.

Laurie, G. (1977). *Housing and Home Services for the Disabled*. Hagerstown, MD: Harper & Row Publishing Co.

Rose, T., & Ansello, E.F. (1987). *Aging and Developmental Disabilities: Research and Planning* (FINAL REPORT). College Park: Maryland State Planning Council on Developmental Disability.

Schalock, R.L. (1983). *Services for Developmentally Disabled Adults: Development, Implementation, and Evaluation*. Baltimore: University Park Press, 219–220.

Seltzer, G.B., Finaly, E., & Howell, M. (1988). Functional Characteristics of Elderly Persons with Mental Retardation in Community Settings and Nursing Homes. *Mental Retardation, 26*(4), 213–218.

Seltzer, M.M., & Krauss, M.W. (1987). *Aging and Mental Retardation: Extending the Continuum*, Washington, D.C.: American Association on Mental Retardation.

Seltzer, M.M., & Seltzer, G.B. (1984). The Elderly Mentally Retarded: A Group in Need of Service. In G. Getzel and J. Mellor, (Eds.), *Gerontological Social Work Practice in the Community*. New York: Haworth Press.

Sherman, S.R., & Newman, E.S. (1988). *Foster Families for Adults: A Community Alternative in Long-Term Care*. New York: Columbia University Press, 13–22.

Summers, J.A., & Reese, R.M. (1986). *The Right to Grow Up: An Introduction to Adults with Developmental Disabilities: Residential Services*. Baltimore: Paul H. Brooks Publishing Co.

U.S. Bureau of the Census. (1989). *Current Population Reports, Series P-25, No. 1018, Projections of the Population of the United States by Age, Sex, and Race: 1988 to 2080* (by Gregory Spencer). Washington, DC: U.S. Government Printing Office.

Vitello, S.J., & Soskin, R.M. (1985). *Mental Retardation: Its Social and Legal Context*. Englewood Cliffs, NJ: Prentice Hall Press.

Willer, B., & Intagliata, J. (1984). *Promises and Realities for Mentally Retarded Citizens*. Baltimore: University Park Press, 111–146.

Wolfensberger, W. (1983). Social Role Valorization: A Proposed New Term for the Principle of Normalization. *Mental Retardation, 21*, 234–239.

CHAPTER 17

Demographic, Economic, and Political Factors Related to Housing for the Elderly

R. Steven Daniels

Introduction

Shelter is a basic human need. The presence or absence of adequate, safe, reasonably priced, and accessible housing directly affects a household's quality of life (Pynoos, 1987). For older adults, the issue of adequate housing is a major one with implications for every aspect of their lives. Older adults are less likely to move, and are, therefore, more likely to develop considerable psychological attachment to their "home" (Lawton, 1985; Longino, 1990; Pynoos, 1987; Rogers & Watkins, 1987). In addition, the elderly are more likely to have difficulty maintaining a house and may find a structure increasingly unsuited to their needs (Huttman, 1977; Longino, 1990; Malozemoff, Anderson, & Rosenbaum, 1978; Struyk & Soldo, 1980). Further, substantial proportions of the older population (especially minorities, the poor, renters, and older people with outstanding mortgages) pay more than 30 percent of their income for housing (Kendig, 1990; Struyk, 1987).

Despite the obvious importance of housing as an issue for the elderly, housing policy has generally not received much attention from the federal government or from advocates for the elderly. Pynoos (1987, p. 210) has identified several factors contributing to this lack of emphasis:

1. proportionally, the elderly have benefitted more than other groups from federal housing assistance programs;
2. most elderly own their homes and are aided by homeowner deductions for mortgage interest and property tax abatement or exemption programs available in most states;[1]
3. the housing agenda is dominated by much stronger and better organized producer groups;
4. the elderly have had difficulty generating enough political support to help create a national housing policy, especially at a time when the federal government is rapidly moving away from housing as a priority; and
5. the parameters of federal support for housing itself are somewhat outside the influence of housing interest groups.

In the face of increasing pressure to make deep budget cuts, most recent efforts in the area of elderly housing policy have focused on maintenance of existing programs and on reaffirming the federal commitment to provide housing for older adults.

Despite retrenchment and the lack of a comprehensive housing policy, demographic changes in the aging population suggest that housing will become an increasingly important political issue. The issue is likely to become even more compelling by the increasing numerical impact of the elderly population combined with a continued gap between the need for and the supply of housing suitable for elderly residents (Kendig, 1990). Unfortunately, the lack of accountability produced by a decentralized political structure and the recent dominance of conservative political policies, especially in the area of housing, provide serious obstacles to expanding future housing options.

The Demographic Context of Elderly Housing Policy

Recent demographic trends in the United States suggest that the demand for elderly housing will increase in the next few decades. In 1985 the elderly represented almost 12 percent of the total U.S. population. By 2050, nearly 23 percent of the U.S. population will be sixty-five or older. In absolute numbers, the population over the age of sixty-five will increase from just under 29 million in 1985 to about 69 million in 2050 (Myers, 1990; Schulz, Borowski, & Crown, 1991).

More important for housing policy is that the characteristics of the elderly population will also change in some significant ways. For example, those eighty-five and over will make up an increasing proportion of the older population. In 1985, those eighty-five and over constituted only about 1 percent of the total population and only 9 percent of the population sixty-five and over. By 2050, the eighty-five and over population will be about 5 percent of the total population and nearly 24 percent of the older population (Myers, 1990). Numerous studies have established that those over eighty-five have a higher incidence of frailty, disability, and chronic conditions and use a greater proportion of health care services (Kane & Kane, 1990).

Another predictable change concerns the sex ratio. The older population is disproportionately female at every age. In 1985, the sex ratio in the United States for those over sixty-five was 67.8—that is, there were only sixty-eight males for every 100 females in that age group. And, these ratios decline dramatically with increasing age such that, for those eighty-five and over, the sex ratio is only 40.1. Because of converging life expectancies for men and women over sixty-five, however, demographers anticipate that sex ratios will increase for most of the first half of the twenty-first century until, by 2050, the ratio for those sixty-five and over is expected to reach 74.7 (Myers, 1990).

The long-range policy implications of a predominantly female older population are based on several patterns that are apparent today. For example, older women are more likely to be single, live alone, and have incomes substantially below the national median (Smeeding, 1990). In addition, women have a greater probability of spending time in a nursing home than men (0.5 versus 0.3) some time before they die (Kane & Kane, 1990).

Not only will the elderly population of the twenty-first century be older, but minorities will represent an increasing proportion of that population. In 1985, nonwhites comprised slightly less than 10 percent of the elderly; by 2050, the proportion is projected to increase to over 21 percent (Myers, 1990). Under current conditions, minorities of all ages are more likely to pay a greater percentage of their income for housing. This problem is magnified for older minorities. Kendig (1990) suggests that certain segments of the population, including minorities, the poor, renters, and older people with outstanding mortgages, pay "excessive costs" for housing.[2] Older minorities generally fall into more than one of these categories.

These changes, along with others, in the characteristics of the elderly population are likely to have a substantial impact on future housing policy. The increasing proportions of historically underrepresented groups (for example those over eighty-five, males, and minorities) is likely to increase demand for specialized and low-cost housing options (Butler, Oldman, & Greve, 1983; Jaffe, 1989; Lawton & Hoover, 1981a; Malozemoff, Anderson, & Rosenbaum, 1978; Morrison, Bennett, Frisch, & Gurland, 1986; American Association of Retired Persons [AARP] Public Policy Institute, n.d.).

The Economic Context of Elderly Housing Policy

The economic condition of the elderly population has engendered considerable debate in recent years. The "old wisdom" suggested that the elderly population was bearing more than its fair share of the poverty burden. This perception resulted in a general expansion of government assistance to the elderly. It also justified the disproportionate expenditure of more general welfare resources on the low-income elderly (Jacobs, 1990; Kendig, 1990). However, this traditional view has begun to be challenged by a different perception. This "new view" envisions the elderly as well-off, in many cases more so than the general population (Binstock, 1983a, 1983b). These new attitudes may have already produced a backlash against government support for programs aimed at older adults.

Today's elderly are generally believed to be better off, economically, than their predecessors (Schulz, 1988). In 1986, for example, with income including realized capital gains, private and public health insurance, food stamps, public housing and imputed rent on owner-occupied housing and excluding federal, state, and local taxes, the mean and median income ratios for all elderly to all nonelderly were 1.05 and .99, respectively (Smeeding, 1990). Moreover, real adjusted family income between 1970 and 1987 grew nearly 50 percent for the elderly while growing only 20 percent for all families and unrelated individuals. Most of this growth can be attributed to expanded Social Security benefits (Smeeding, 1990). The increase in income has been reflected in sizable reductions in the elderly poverty rate. In 1959, 35 percent of the elderly population was below the poverty level compared to slightly over 22 percent for the entire population. By 1987, the elderly rate had fallen to 12 percent, whereas the overall rate was just over 13 percent (Smeeding, 1990; see also, Chen, 1985). Nevertheless, considerable variation exists within the elderly population. Women, the elderly over seventy-five, and minorities are all overrepresented among those living below the poverty level. Further, these groups are more dependent on Social Security as their sole source of income (Struyk & Soldo, 1980).

The reduction in the poverty rate also disguises considerable variation across elderly demographic and age groups. Smeeding (1990) reports that in 1986 poverty rates for the elderly varied from 6.0 percent for households headed by a white male to 49.4 percent for households headed by an African-American female.

It is also true that not all of those with incomes above the poverty level are financially secure. The evidence indicates that near-poverty rates (rates between 100 and 125 percent of the poverty level) have not declined substantially for the elderly since the 1970s (Smeeding, 1990). Smeeding (1990) also notes that many of those elderly with incomes between 125 and 200 percent of the poverty level (the "economically vulnerable") receive from one-third to two-thirds of that income from Social Security. This dependence on a single source of income makes this subgroup susceptible to economic shocks such as sudden increases in housing costs, unexpected medical bills, or the death of a spouse.

The Economic Context of Elderly Housing

Housing policy for the elderly in the United States has been profoundly affected by the traditionally high rates of home ownership among the older population. Approximately 75 percent of the population over sixty-five owned their own homes in 1983. And, among older homeowners, 83 percent had no mortgages (U.S. Bureau of the Census, 1984). This rate is a substantial increase from 1940 when only about 48 percent of those over sixty-five owned homes (Chevan, 1987; Kendig, 1990). Because housing values appreciated faster than inflation during this period, the value of real property has become a significant part of household wealth (Kendig, 1990; Lawton & Hoover, 1981b). The imputed rent from owner-occupied housing substantially reduces the percentage of income taken up by housing costs (Schulz, 1988; Smeeding, 1990). Thus, most owner-occupiers spend less than 25 percent of income on housing.

Nevertheless, elderly homeowners face a number of serious problems. First, the homes owned by the elderly population tend to be older and in less desirable locations. Second, although mortgage-free home ownership does reduce the monthly housing costs for the older population, housing equity is extremely difficult to convert into liquid assets should the need arise. Several options, including reverse annuity mortgages, exist to facilitate that transformation (Hoeflich, 1987; Jacobs and Weissert, 1987; Kendig, 1990; Trichilo, 1987). However, most economic research indicates that the older population rarely spends its accumulated equity, instead, transferring it as part of their estate (Feinstein & McFadden, 1989; Venti & Wise, 1989).

Additional problems become apparent once the unequal distribution of housing wealth is accounted for. In 1980, older adults with annual incomes of over $2,000 (in constant 1967 dollars) had home ownership rates of 71 percent. By contrast, the home ownership rate of older Americans with incomes of less than $1,000 (in constant 1967 dollars) was 27 percent (Chevan, 1987; Kendig, 1990). Widows, minorities, and single older people were disproportionately in this latter group.

The unequal distribution of housing wealth is of serious consequence because renters are more vulnerable to shifts in the housing market and the economy and often live in higher cost urban areas. Nearly 50 percent of elderly renters paid more than 30 percent of their income on housing in 1976. By comparison, only 38 percent of elderly homeowners with mortgages and 14 percent for elderly homeowners without mortgages paid more than 30 percent (Struyk & Soldo, 1980).

Older renters face additional problems. One of the most serious is gentrification—the upgrading of the class composition and housing stock within a neighborhood (Eckert & Murrey, 1987). As the upper-middle class and the wealthy begin to move back into the central city to take advantage of cultural facilities, proximity to work, and relatively low housing costs (compared to the suburbs), significant numbers of low-income and middle-income families are correspondingly displaced. Typically, the new immigrants move into buildings or housing renovated to appeal to more affluent people. Research findings suggest that gentrification is most likely to take place in neighborhoods with high proportions of elderly (Henig, 1981). The older renters generally cannot afford the costs of the newly renovated housing. When combined with the historically low vacancy rates in many central cities, the displacement often results in the shift of older renters into poorer and, frequently, more expensive housing.

The Political Context of Housing for the Elderly

These economic and demographic problems place great pressure on the political system. Although housing has traditionally not been a high priority item on the political agenda, the changing demographic and economic circumstances of the elderly population increase the likelihood that housing will become a significant issue in the near future. The sheer size of the elderly population and the basic demand for housing that these numbers suggest would be enough to alter the agenda, even without the additional needs of the disadvantaged segments of the elderly population.

These shifts in the political agenda are likely to generate increasing demands for policy change. Policy choices do not occur in a vacuum. These choices reflect governmental policy structures, economic resources, political culture, public opinion, and past policy choices. Because the structure of American government is fragmented and decentralized, most policy choices become sensitive to a variety of factors. Thus, policy choices can vary dramatically across U.S. political jurisdictions.

For housing policy, two characteristics of the American political system are relevant. The first is the focus of the political culture on free markets and procedural democracy. The second is the policy incapacity and policy incoherence that arise from political decentralization and fragmentation.

Free Markets and Political Choices

Several sets of values have shaped American political culture. One set includes economic rights such as individualism, personal freedom, sanctity of contracts, and the right to acquire and own property.[3] A second set focuses on more political values like equal treatment under the law, political equality, and equality of opportunity. A third set of cultural values encompasses religion and the centrality of the nuclear family. Conflicts about and among these values have often been the focus of political controversy in the United States.

The intellectual paradigm shaping most of the choices among these competing values has been a belief in the efficiency of free markets in allocating goods and services. Under such a system, government's role is to ensure procedural democracy, to guarantee the maintenance of certain political norms such as competitive markets, private property, representative government and equality of opportunity. The attraction of the free market is powerful because it justifies both laissez-faire capitalism and representative democracy.

The success of the market as an allocation device rests on a number of critical assumptions, particularly the existence of "perfect information" about the goods and services the market has to offer, open entry to the market, and fair competition among producers. If these conditions held, the marketplace would produce the maximum output using the minimum resources. Although this model cannot predict outcomes, it is designed to produce the greatest utility (happiness) for the greatest number of people.

Unfortunately, the American economic system meets few of these conditions. Few consumers have perfect information about the goods and services being offered by the market. As a result, the market outcomes often reward inefficient producers. Second, a few organizations dominate major sectors of the economy. Open entry to the market is not the general rule. Third, because oligopolies dominate so much of the market, the major organizations can restrict competition. The absence of the essential conditions for a free market generally means that resources are not allocated efficiently. An inefficient market, in turn, places enormous pressure on the political system to either justify or rectify the faults of the economy.

Policy Incapacity and Policy Incoherence

In many ways, the political system suffers the opposite dilemma from the economic system. Whereas the economic system is often too concentrated to meet the conditions of a free market, the political system is too decentralized and fragmented to compensate for the weaknesses of the market. Robertson and Judd (1989) have identified the U.S. Government policymaking structure as one of limited policy capacity and policy incoherence. They further suggest that structure has an important independent impact on both policy demands and policy outcomes in most political systems. The structure determines the rules for making demands, the acceptable definitions for public problems, the availability of alternatives, the decision rules, and the implementation of the final choices (Kingdon, 1984; Mazmanian and Sabatier, 1983).

The American political structure is characterized by fragmentation and decentralization. Political authority is distributed between the national government and the state governments (federalism) and is further divided across branches of government within each level (separation of powers). This division of authority has several policy consequences.

First, a fragmented political structure also fragments political and economic demands by various interest groups within the population (Keefe, 1988; Ornstein and Elder, 1978). As Robertson and Judd (1989, p. 7) note, "[G]overnment rules affect the way that groups and citizens interact with one another and with government." Election rules, lobbying laws, and regulatory statutes define the conditions under which political organizing can take place. As a result, political conflict will be directed toward those levels of government and those institutions whose rules allow the expression of political demands (Robertson and Judd, 1989).

Second, the decentralized nature of the American political process constrains the procedures by which policy is made. In general, the system rewards short-term, ad hoc distributive policies over long-term, comprehensive redistributive policies. Elected politicians are rewarded for planning in two-year cycles. Similarly, bureaucracies, and the career bureaucrats who make them function, are rewarded with incremental budget increases and agency survival.

Third, the American policy process severely limits policy making capacity and generates policy incoherence (Robertson and Judd, 1989). Capacity refers to the ability of a government to carry out its policy mandates. One major aspect of capacity can be measured by a political jurisdiction's ability to raise revenue. Although most restrictions on the capacity to tax have been eliminated at the national level, most state constitutions place severe limits on the revenue-raising capacity of state and local governments. For example, many state constitutions require that a state budget be balanced and some even restrict the sources of revenue the state or local governments may utilize.

However, even if capacity could be maximized at all levels of government, the division of authority among levels and across branches of government almost guarantees that policy will be uncoordinated. This policy disorganization becomes increasingly critical when the levels and branches exercise independent authority. Such fragmentation generates policy incoherence "because (1) it increases veto points; (2) it allows formal and informal changes in policy goals; and (3) it produces the need for expedient compromises" (Robertson and Judd, 1989, 11).

These policy weaknesses are particularly severe at the state and local levels. The limitations on governmental capacity and the prohibition against state interference with interstate commerce means that state and local governments have little control over the flow of capital across their borders (Peterson, 1981). Under such circumstances, state governments become sensitive to variations in economic performance and will seek to maximize state property values rather than assure minimum standards of living (Peterson and Rom, 1990).

The Policy Domain of Elderly Housing

Housing policy for the elderly and the nonelderly in the United States reflects both the weaknesses of the marketplace and the fragmentation of the American policy process. Housing policy choices tend to be made at the national level with state and local governments generally responding to federal initiatives (Pynoos, 1987). Nevertheless, many of the most significant constraints on housing selection and location reflect state and local political decisions. Many of the policy choices are also heavily influenced by the housing industry, especially the materials producers, builders, and real estate developers.

Most national housing policies exhibit the characteristics of a relatively closed policy system dominated by the Department of Housing and Urban Development (HUD), the various policy-relevant committees in Congress (including the Housing Subcommittees of the Senate and House Banking committees, and the corresponding subcommittees of the House and Senate Appropriations committees), and several significant housing interest groups (most prominently, the National Association of Home Builders and the National Association of Realtors). For elderly housing, the Subcommittees on Housing and Consumer

Interests of the Select Committee on Aging and the Senate Special Committee on Aging, the Department of Health and Human Services (HHS) and the Office of Management and Budget (OMB) also play significant roles (Pynoos, 1987). By contrast, housing consumers have relatively less influence. This is especially true for the low-income elderly.

Traditionally, there have been three major foci of the relatively closed system just described. These areas of concentrated effort have been: (1) the maintenance of the owner-occupied, single-family residence as the dominant form of housing in the United States; (2) opposition to regulation of the housing industry; and (3) support for construction of specialized housing for the elderly. The overarching goal has been maintaining the production of new housing units and keeping interest rates down (Pynoos, 1987).

In recent years, this system has been affected by a shift in goals. Whereas the improvement of housing stock had once been the dominant issue for both the general population and the elderly population, the gradual amelioration of the worst housing conditions, started in the 1970s, began to change the focus of housing policy to income-based issues. In addition, proposed policy changes also began to explore more creative uses of existing housing stock. Thus, the language of aging policy began to include such new phrases as house sharing, shared housing, accessory apartments, ECHO housing, home equity conversions, and reverse annuity mortgages. The federal government also began to deemphasize housing assistance and shifted remaining assistance from public housing to direct-cash housing assistance programs (Pynoos, 1987).

These shifting goals have begun to expand the scope of conflict in housing policy (Schattschneider, 1960; Van Horn, Baumer, and Gormley, 1992). The expanded issues have increased the number of active interest groups and government organizations with an interest in the outcomes of housing policy. In particular, new coalitions of elderly interest groups such as the National Low-Income Housing Coalition and the Ad Hoc Coalition for Elderly Housing have begun to have an impact on housing policy choices. Academic and professional organizations have also begun to contribute to the housing debate.

Nevertheless, the one group whose influence on housing policy has been minor is the elderly population itself. For the most part, policy choices have been made without substantial input from potential consumers. Much of the difficulty lies in the relative invisibility of housing policy. Housing remains a relatively low priority at the national level (Pynoos, 1987). The policy network has managed to define most housing choices as private choices and has tended to limit the scope of government intervention. These policy definitions fit well with the free market philosophy of both the government and the general public. In addition, at least as it relates to housing, the elderly themselves have yet to become a cohesive political force (Dobson, 1983). The result is conflicting demands by different elderly groups that can be played off against each other and can be used to limit the extent of policy change.

Housing policy in the United States clearly reflects the dominance of private incentives. Most national policy decisions reflect the marketplace (Van Horn, Baumer, and Gormley, 1992). For example, the single most significant national housing policy is not public housing or housing allowances; it is the income tax deduction for mortgage interest (Pynoos, 1987). The fact that mortgage interest is deductible for tax purposes reinforces the single-family dwelling focus of the housing industry and guarantees that private housing choices will have political consequences. Political choices in the housing bureaucracy and the Congress tend to simply mirror these incentives. The housing bureaucracies at the national and state level, the Congress, and state legislatures are all highly sensitive to organized lobbying by the trade associations of the housing industry. The absence of effective lobbying organizations for housing consumers and the weakness of public opinion among the elderly virtually insure that these private incentives will remain central to housing policy choices (Van Horn, Baumer, and Gormley, 1992).

Elderly Housing Policy Consequences

The social, economic, and political context of elderly housing portends serious policy conflict in the future. The rapid aging of the American population suggests that the demand for housing of all kinds by the elderly will increase in the future. Although much of this demand will be for single-family dwellings, major changes in the demographic composition of the elderly population itself will increase demand for more specialized housing. Demographic projections indicate that, in the future, the older population will contain much larger proportions of minorities, males, and those over eighty-five. These changes will increase demand for low-income housing and for specialized housing that provides for a continuum of long-term care (Kendig, 1990).

Much of this demand will continue to be met with owner-occupied single-family housing. The nature of the tax incentives and the interest group system are unlikely to change in the near future. Thus, most of the construction occurring in the United States will continue to be single-family homes. The design of these homes will undoubtedly continue to reflect the needs and preferences of households with heads in the twenty-five to fifty-four-year-old age range. To date, despite extensive academic interest, the housing industry has paid little attention to issues of design and retrofitting for the elderly population (Baumhover, Clark-Daniels, Daniels, Beall, & Gillum, 1991; Streib, Folts, & Hilker, 1984; Woodward, 1987).

Traditionally, national housing policies under HUD have reflected the influence of the mortgage interest tax credit, construction of new public and private housing, and rental assistance (Hancock, 1987). The primary difficulty with current federal programs is their limited scope. The programs tend to aid only a small segment of the older population. Only about 4 percent of the population over sixty-five lives in subsidized housing (Kendig, 1990; Turner, 1986). Most elderly Americans live by themselves in houses they own. The greatest demand, therefore, will be for programs that provide services and supports for elderly homeowners. Unfortunately, under both the Reagan and Bush administrations, funding for public housing has been curtailed, public housing money has been transferred into rent subsidies, and severe cutbacks have occurred in the various block grant programs that provide services (Pynoos, 1987). As a result, very little of the necessary infrastructure to meet the increasing demand will be in place in the near future.

Housing decisions at the state and local level are bound, at least to some degree, by national choices. State and local budgeting flexibility is also limited by balanced budget provisions in state constitutions and city charters. As a result, most innovation at the state and local level comes from the resources of not-for-profit agencies and volunteer organizations (Eckert & Murrey, 1987). For example, shared housing projects, congregate housing, and community housing are usually funded and administered by nonprofit organizations (Eckert & Murrey, 1987; Jaffe, 1989; Malozemoff, Anderson, & Rosenbaum, 1978). State and local governments are also faced with competing objectives. A significant source of housing for many single, elderly males is the "single-room occupancy (SRO)" hotel (Daily, 1987). However, the presence in the central city of many of these facilities generally fosters demands either for redevelopment or historical preservation. Because the populations who occupy these facilities lack vocal and visible defenders, there are few who would argue for expansion or improvement in this type of living arrangement. Thus, state and local policies aimed at development or preservation often displace these segments of the elderly population.

At the local level, the most consistent obstacle to innovative housing solutions has been local zoning ordinances (Daily, 1987). Typically, zoning ordinances restrict the number of unrelated people who can live together. These restrictions are reinforced by eligibility requirements for Supplemental Security Income and federal rent subsidies. In addition, restrictive single-family zoning ordinances often prohibit the expansion of a residence with such innovative alternatives as accessory apartments or ECHO housing.

On the other hand, zoning ordinances can be used to provide opportunities for increasing elderly housing (Shifman, 1987). In *Village of Belle Terre* v. *Boraas*, 416 U.S. 1 (1974), the U.S. Supreme Court ruled that restricting the occupancy of a zoned area to a particular group was permissible if it accomplished a valid legislative purpose and was done reasonably. Since that decision, several jurisdictions have passed ordinances aimed specifically at providing residential zones for elderly residents and setting residential standards for such zones. However, these ordinances are still comparatively rare and remain controversial.

Overall, current policy options have a limited potential for responding to the changes in housing demand produced by the major demographic and economic changes of the 20th century. The current focus on development and promotion of single-family dwellings and housing assistance reflects an earlier era of housing choices. The new policy frameworks being pursued by academics and activists focus more directly on the innovative use of existing housing stock. Yet, the programs providing these innovative services are usually nonprofit, underfunded, and reach only marginal segments of the older population. The primary difficulty in housing experimentation comes because the political structure does not currently reward innovation. The system clearly rewards short-term solutions at the expense of long-term planning. The decentralized and fragmented political process undermines the development of a coherent policy.

Housing Options: Possibilities for Change

How, then, can the expected demand for elderly housing be met? Earlier chapters of this book have outlined a number of promising options. The various home-sharing programs initiated by nonprofit and voluntary organizations hold promise for providing both a means of freeing the equity in homes owned by older residents and providing a residence and companionship for single, older individuals (Eckert & Murrey, 1987). Home equity conversions and reverse annuity mortgages also hold some promise. However, because of structural and personal factors that are just now beginning to be understood, few older Americans have availed themselves of any of these alternatives (Trichilo, 1987). Some potential also exists in elderly-specific zoning ordinances (Shifman, 1987).

Unfortunately, the available alternatives are characteristically underfunded and aimed at a relatively narrow segment of the population. Too many of the future elderly, especially those over eighty-five and minorities, will not have access to these alternatives. These older citizens will likely face a shrinking pool of public housing and diminishing housing subsidies. And, they are more likely to be the victims than the beneficiaries of the conversion of apartments to condominiums or cooperatives. Too poor to buy their converted apartments, many of them will be displaced to less adequate and more expensive living arrangements.

If current trends continue, prospects for the oldest-old are particularly grim. One serious problem is the absence of anything even remotely resembling a continuum of care. A substantial portion of the current nursing home population (between 20 percent and 40 percent by some estimates) may not require the level of care available in skilled nursing and intermediate care facilities (Daily, 1987). However, because few facilities exist that provide lower levels of care, the oldest-old are in the uncomfortable position of having to choose between too much care or too little care.

For the poor elderly who are dependent on Supplemental Security Income, the only alternative may well be personal care facilities or boarding homes (AARP, n.d.). These facilities have arisen, at least in part, because of the lack of alternatives to nursing home care. The regulation and licensing of such facilities is haphazard at best. Some state and local jurisdictions provide better regulation than others; however, in most states policies are inconsistent. The federal government has attempted to regulate the industry through the Keys Amendment to the Social Security Act, but the penalty mechanism places the burden on the recipient of SSI. Additional regulation has been provided through the Board and Care Act of 1990, but under this legislation, penalties involve the removal of Older Americans Act funds. The irony is that, despite the weaknesses of the industry, board-and-care facilities fill a real need that the various levels of government have been unable to provide.

In short, unless the national government intervenes to make housing policy more coherent, the options produced by the existing policy will continue to be piecemeal and incomplete. Unfortunately, the potential risks of such short-run thinking are enormous.

Under what conditions, then, is this negative assessment likely to change? The primary obstacle to significant policy change is the inertia of the political process. Current policy directions are likely to continue unless acted upon by a sufficiently strong outside force. And, it is the permeability of the American political process that provides a measure of hope (Van Horn, Baumer, & Gormley, 1992). Despite the closed nature of the politics of the federal bureaucracy and the Congress, both arenas are permeable by outside forces. If significant policy direction can come from the other arenas of American politics, specifically the executive branch or public opinion, the scope of conflict can be expanded to include elderly housing policy.

What such a change will require, though, is a recognition by actors in the policy process that housing policy is a significant issue and a top priority agenda item. Unfortunately, at no time in the last twenty years, has housing been considered an important item on the agenda of any level of government.

NOTES

1. The property tax subsidy would be more important than the mortgage subsidy because over 80 percent of all older Americans have no mortgages and therefore would not receive a mortgage deduction.

2. "Excessive" usually means 30 percent of household income for renters and 40 percent for owners based on standards developed by the Department of Housing and Urban Development (Kendig, 1990).

3. Much of the discussion in the following section is drawn from Van Horn, Baumer, & Gormley, Jr. (1992, pp. 30–33).

REFERENCES

American Association of Retired Persons. Public Policy Institute. (n.d.). *Preserving independence, supporting needs: The role of board and care homes* (edited by Marilyn Moon, George Gaberlavage, and Sandra J. Newman). Washington, D.C.: Author.

Baumhover, L. A., Clark-Daniels, C. L., Daniels, R. S., Beall, C., & Gillum, J. L. (1991). *Final report: The housing industry in Alabama, preparing for the 1990s and the 21st century* [Report to the Alabama Commission on Aging and the U.S. Administration on Aging]. Tuscaloosa: University of Alabama. College of Community Health Sciences. Center for the Study of Aging.

Binstock, R. H. (1983a). The aged as scapegoat. *The Gerontologist, 23*(2), 136–143.

———— (1983b). The elderly in America: Their economic resources, income status, and costs. In W. P. Browne, & L. K. Olson (Ed.), *Aging and public policy: The politics of growing old in America* (pp. 19–33). Westport, CT: Greenwood Press, Inc.

Butler, A., Oldman, C., & Greve, J. (1983). *Sheltered Housing for the elderly: Policy, practice, and the consumer*. London: George Allen & Unwin.

Chen, Y. (1985). Economic status of the aging. In R. H. Binstock, & E. Shanas (Ed.), *Handbook of aging and the social sciences* (2nd ed.) (pp. 641–665). New York: Van Nostrand Reinhold Company.

Chevan, A. (1987). Homeownership in the older population, 1940–1980. *Research on Aging, 9*, 226–255.

Daily, L. (1987). Housing options for the elderly. In J. A. Hancock (Ed.), *Housing the elderly* (pp. 227–244). New Brunswick, NJ: Center for Urban Policy Research. Rutgers University.

Dobson, D. (1983). The elderly as a political force. In W. P. Browne, & L. K. Olson (Ed.), *Aging and public policy: The politics of growing old in America* (pp. 123–144). Westport, CT: Greenwood Press.

Eckert, J. K., & Murrey, M. I. (1987). Alternative housing modes. In J. A. Hancock (Ed.), *Housing the elderly* (pp. 57–80). New Brunswick, NJ: Center for Urban Policy Research. Rutgers University.

Feinstein, J., & McFadden, D. (1989). The dynamics of housing demand by the elderly: Wealth, cash flow, and demographic effects. In D. A. Wise (Ed.), *The economics of aging* (pp. 55–86). Chicago: University of Chicago Press.

Hancock, J. A. (1987). Appendix A: Major programs of the Department of Housing and Urban Development (HUD) to assist the elderly and federal outlays benefiting the elderly. In J. A. Hancock (Ed.), *Housing the elderly* (pp. 267–270). New Brunswick, NJ: Center for Urban Policy Research. Rutgers University.

Henig, J. R. (1981). Gentrification and displacement of the elderly: An empirical analysis. *The Gerontologist, 21,* 67–75.

Hoeflich, M. (1987). Home equity conversions. In J. A. Hancock (Ed.), *Housing the elderly* (pp. 121–128). New Brunswick, NJ: Center for Urban Policy Research. Rutgers University.

Huttman, E. D. (1977). *Housing and social services for the elderly: Social policy trends.* New York: Praeger Publishers.

Jacobs, B. (1990). Aging and politics. In R. H. Binstock, & L. K. George (Ed.), *Handbook of aging and the social sciences* (3rd ed.) (pp. 349–361). San Diego: Academic Press, Inc.

Jacobs, B., & Weissert, W. (1987). Home equity financing of long-term care for the elderly. In J. A. Hancock (Ed.), *Housing the elderly* (pp. 151–176). New Brunswick, NJ: Center for Urban Policy Research. Rutgers University.

Jaffe, D. J. (ed.). (1989). *Shared housing for the elderly.* Westport, CT: Greenwood Press.

Kane, R. L., & Kane, R. A. (1990). Health care for older people: Organizational and policy issues. In R. H. Binstock, & L. K. George (Ed.), *Handbook of aging and the social sciences* (3rd ed.) (pp. 415–437). San Diego: Academic Press, Inc.

Keefe, W. J. (1988). *Parties, politics, and public policy in America* (5th ed.). Washington: CQ Press.

Kendig, H. L. (1990). Comparative perspectives on housing, aging, and social structure. In R. H. Binstock, & L. K. George (Ed.), *Handbook of aging and the social sciences* (3rd ed.) (pp. 288–306). San Diego: Academic Press, Inc.

Kingdon, J. W. (1984). *Agendas, alternatives, and public policies.* Boston: Little, Brown.

Lasswell, H. (1958). *Who gets what, when, how.* Cleveland: Meridian Books.

Lawton, M. P. (1985). Housing and living environments for older people. In R. H. Binstock, & E. Shanas (Ed.), *Handbook of aging and the social sciences* (2nd ed.) (pp. 450–478). New York: Van Nostrand Reinhold Company.

Lawton, M. P., & Hoover, S. L. (eds.). (1981a). *Community housing choices for older Americans*. New York: Springer Publishing Co.

———— (1981b). Housing for 22 million older Americans. In M. P. Lawton, & S. L. Hoover (Ed.), *Community housing choices for older Americans*. New York: Springer Publishing Company.

Longino, Charles F. (1990). Geographic distribution and migration. In R. H. Binstock, & L. K. George (Ed.), *Handbook of Aging and the Social Sciences* (3rd ed.) (pp. 45–63). San Diego: Academic Press, Inc.

Malozemoff, I. K., Anderson, J. G., & Rosenbaum, L. V. (1978). *Housing for the elderly: Evaluation of the effectiveness of congregate residences*. Boulder, CO: Westview Press.

Mazmanian, D. A., & Sabatier, P. A. (1983). *Implementation and public policy*. Glenview, IL: Scott, Foresman.

Morrison, I. A., Bennett, R., Frisch, S., & Gurland, B. J. (eds.). (1986). *Continuing care retirement communities: Political, social, and financial issues*. New York: Haworth Press.

Myers, G. C. (1990). Demography of aging. In R. H. Binstock, & L. K. George (Ed.), *Handbook of aging and the social sciences* (3rd ed.) (pp. 19–44). San Diego: Academic Press, Inc.

Ornstein, N. J., & Elder, S. (1978). *Interest groups, lobbying, and policy-making*. Washington: CQ Press, Inc.

Peterson, P. E. (1981). *City limits*. Chicago: University of Chicago Press.

Peterson, P. E., & Rom, M. C. (1990). *Welfare magnets: a new case for a national standard*. Washington, DC: The Brookings Institution.

Pynoos, J. (1987). Setting the elderly agenda. In J. A. Hancock (Ed.), *Housing the elderly* (pp. 209–223). New Brunswick, NJ: Center for Urban Policy Research. Rutgers University.

Robertson, D. B., & Judd, D. R. (1989). *The development of American public policy: The structure of policy restraint*. Glenview, IL: Scott, Foresman.

Rogers, A., & Watkins, J. (1987). General versus elderly interstate migration and population redistribution in the United States. *Research on Aging, 9,* 483–529.

Schattschneider, E. E. (1960). *The semi-sovereign people*. New York: Holt, Rinehart, Winston.

Schulz, J. H. (1988). *The economics of aging* (4th ed.). Dover, MA: Auburn House Publishing Co.

Schulz, J. H., Borowski, A., & Crown, W. H. (1991). *Economics of population aging: The "graying" of Australia, Japan, and the United States*. New York: Auburn House.

Shifman, C. R. (1987). Increasing housing opportunities for the elderly. In J. A. Hancock (Ed.), *Housing the elderly* (pp. 95–117). New Brunswick, NJ: Center for Urban Policy Research. Rutgers University.

Smeeding, T. M. (1990). Economic status of the elderly. In R. H. Binstock, & L. K. George (Ed.), *Handbook of aging and the social sciences* (3rd ed.) (pp. 362–381). San Diego: Academic Press, Inc.

Streib, G.F., Folts, W.E., & Hilker, M.A. (1984). *Old Homes—New Families: Shared Living for the Elderly*. New York: Columbia Press.

Struyk, R. J. (1987). The economic behavior of elderly people in housing markets. *Housing Studies, 2*(4), 221–236.

Struyk, R. J., & Soldo, B. J. (1980). *Improving the elderly's housing: A key to preserving the nation's housing stock and neighborhoods*. Cambridge, MA: Ballinger Publishing Company.

Trichilo, V. J. (1987). Home equity conversions. In J. A. Hancock (Ed.), *Housing the elderly* (pp. 121–128). New Brunswick, NJ: Center for Urban Policy Research. Rutgers University.

Turner, L. (1986). Public policies and individual housing choices. In R. J. Newcomer, M. P. Lawton, & T. Byerts (Ed.), *Housing an aging society: Issues, alternatives, and policy* (pp. 42–52). New York: Van Nostrand Reinhold.

U.S. Bureau of the Census. (December 1984). Financial characteristics of the housing inventory for the United States and regions: 1983. Current Housing Reports Series H-150–83, *Annual Housing Survey: 1983 Part C*. Washington, D.C.: Government Printing Office.

Van Horn, C. E., Baumer, D. C., & Gormley, W. T., Jr. (1992). *Politics and public policy* (2nd ed.). Washington, D.C.: CQ Press.

Venti, S. F., & Wise, D. A. (1989). Aging, moving, and housing wealth. In D. A. Wise (Ed.), *The economics of aging* (pp. 9–48). Chicago: University of Chicago Press.

Woodward, A. (1987). Housing the elderly. In J. A. Hancock (Ed.), *Housing the elderly* (pp. 3–13). New Brunswick, NJ: Center for Urban Policy Research. Rutgers University.

Addendum

The issue of housing, especially as it relates to older adults, is obviously a very complex topic. So too, as is amply demonstrated by the variety of chapters in this volume, there are many perspectives from which one might embark on the study of housing. Given this complexity, it is important that the historical perspective is not lost in the discussions about contemporary alternative housing arrangements. As editors of this volume, we were faced with a quite extraordinary dilemma. The following chapter, written by Dr. Wesley Rogers, clearly addresses the historical underpinnings of housing for the elderly. However, at the same time, it is unique and doesn't seem to "fit" with the other chapters. Rather than lose this important information, we decided to exercise our editorial prerogative and include it, albeit unconventionally, as an addendum to the main body of the volume.

W.E.F.
D.E.Y.

The Ancient Foundations of Institutional Health Care

Wesley W. Rogers

Introduction

There is evidence that caves were the original habitats of humanity. First individuals and then, much later, bands of individuals probably sought the relative safety of caves to escape from the environmental, animal, and possibly human, dangers that constantly threatened them. In modern times, numerous caves have been found that indicate the prehistoric cave-dwelling population was extensive. Although caves were, in all likelihood, the residence of choice for much of human history, they have some serious limitations that provided the impetus for humans to seek shelter elsewhere.

An obvious drawback to cave dwelling is that a cave is immobile so that the inhabitants are at the mercy of the environmental conditions in and around the cave. If the environment is more or less benign and food is plentiful, the immobility of a cave is not a serious problem. However, even seasonal changes were likely to be enough to cause shortages of food and, thus, force cave dwellers to leave their relatively safe caves behind.

Another obvious problem associated with cave dwelling is that, lacking modern tools and machinery, cave dwellers were severely limited in the modifications they could make. This limitation on the stone-age equivalent of "decorating" also meant that caves were difficult to modify to meet any special needs their inhabitants might have.

Even if these rather serious limitations were not sufficient to cause stone-age humans to seek other means of sheltering themselves, there remains the fact that caves are limited both in number and in availability. In fact, one can imagine a time in the distant and prehistoric past when competition for cave space with large animals and other human creatures created the first "housing shortage." One can also imagine that somewhat significant day when other means of shelter were devised and humans were at last freed to move out of the caves and into more useful, even if less protective, shelter.

The first housing units, outside the caves, were probably temporary structures that could be moved or abandoned with little effort or cost in resources. Eventually, housing began to be more permanent, at first built from sticks and branches covered with hides, later from logs, and still later from stone and mortar. Along with what we would now call "purpose built" structures came the level of social organization necessary for groups to begin to plan for and anticipate their collective futures.

The caves remained, however, as sanctuaries for individuals who were either unable or unwilling to build the new types of structures. In fact, there is evidence of this even in historical times for it was into the caves that lepers fled when pronounced unclean by the Hebrew priests almost three thousand years ago. Lepers, however, were not the only ones seeking sanctuary in caves. The biblical personalities Elijah and David found safety in them and many early prisons were located in convenient caves. Ultimately, there is evidence to suggest that caves became the favored burial grounds for many societies.

There is a great gap, of unknown length, in the time between cave dwelling, dwelling in human-built structures, and the accommodation of weaker members of society in housing designed to meet their particular needs. However, at some point, bands of humans began to care for those who could not provide for themselves. Again, at some unknown point in our historical development, we also began to notice an advantage to concentrating those with similar needs in a central location. Although it would be comforting to suggest humanitarian motives for this development, lacking information to the contrary, it is just as likely that this concentration was due to selfish expediency rather than concern for others. Still, it is a somewhat comforting notion that, for whatever motives, those who were not full participants in early human social bands began to be accommodated rather than eliminated.

Although there is no reliable and comprehensive historical record of the development of what we now call institutions, many ancient societies left references to a variety of institutional living arrangements. In fact, based on the evidence that does exist, it is not unreasonable to suggest that most ancient human societies made some provision for groups of people who were thought of as having some form of deficit keeping them from full participation in the social life of the community.

The Ancient Poorhouse: *Ptoxion*

The earliest reference to a poorhouse was in the Code of Zeno (1.2.5; Tierney, 1959), the first of which dates to the fifth century B.C. It uses the Latinized word, ptochotrophium. By the sixth century, the Justinian Code uses both a shorter word, *ptoxion*, and the longer *ptochotrophium*. The latter term was also that employed by the historian Procopius Caesriensis in the sixth century.

A ptoxion was the residence of a beggar. There is evidence that paupers and beggars frequently sought the company of others with similar characteristics. Further, they congregated in out-of-the-way places where they were not likely to be hindered from gathering. At first, they gathered in the much-used caves and, much later they began to seek out tombs and abandoned buildings from which to practice their "trade." At another unknown point in time, newly organized cities began to provide shelter for these beggars and cave-dwelling, as a "normal" housing choice at least, passed silently into history.

The Egyptian Sanitoria

The Egyptian sanitoria may be the oldest of all true care institutions. Most of what we know about these institutions has been gleaned from the reports of Egyptian priest-physicians (Garrison, 1929). These reports suggest that an invalid would be carried to the sanitorium, which was usually a portico, a balcony, a nearby room, or even a grassy spot near a temple. The individual took an offering and sought out the specialist who, perhaps, worked from his quarters in the city where he kept his potions, amulets, and powders. The pilgrim took up residence in the sanitoria for as long as was necessary for a cure to be attempted. The family, if any, was responsible for the care and feeding of the sick person. They brought food, took care of the sick person's personal needs, provided transportation, arranged for hygiene, and, in general, took care of the housekeeping duties.

Celtic *Oppidium*: Shelter for the Aged

Practically every Celtic clan had a congregate facility for the aged and infirm. These were not hospitals as were other early facilities. Instead, they were living facilities with personal care much like domiciliary units of today. Frank (1959) has located a regulation requiring that the heads of aged persons who lived in the shelter of Celtic *oppidiums* (townships) be washed at least every twelfth day. The original report was attributed to Julius Caesar.

Because everyone was related within a Celtic clan and the size of the clan seldom reached more than 500 members, the older adults simply moved to the shelter reserved for them within the oppidium. There was adequate help from the family units to provide the needed personal care. Usually the more able older persons cared for those unable to care for themselves. There was not a large population of older Celts to care for due to the simple fact that not many Celts survived young adulthood. The fierceness of the Celtic lifestyle was somewhat inconsistent with long life. With their riotous festivities, dangerous sports, and constant war with other clans, life to old age was rare indeed. Still, it is interesting that even the Celts developed some means to care for groups of clan members with what were defined as functional deficits.

The Jewish Guest Room: *Katalumati*

An early facility specifically designed to provide care was the Jewish guest room. It may have originated as early as 1000 B.C. It was first a room attached to the home of a Hebrew family. Its purpose was to give quarters and sanctuary to the traveler, the stranger, the visiting relative, or simply to the weary neighbor. Levitical law required that "strangers" be cared for. Because of that, a guest room was usually built in a small area on the roof of the family dwelling. The roof of the average Hebrew family home was used for a number of purposes such as drying foods, an evening retreat, or a place of storage. And, it often doubled as the site for secluded quarters for a visitor. It is not difficult to imagine how what was a room for guests was an attractive alternative as a room for family members who needed special care in times of illness or old age.

The *Pandochium* or Ancient Jewish Sickhouse

The *pandochium* was a natural outgrowth of the Jewish guest house. In later years, it became a sickhouse. Gradually, it was split away from the residential structure and stood alone as a permanent health-care facility. The location of the sickhouse within a settlement compound served to meet the health-care needs of the sick, the aged, and the infirm. The earliest reference to a pandoxeion is in the biblical story of the good Samaritan. It is to a pandochium that the good Samaritan took the man who had been beaten by robbers. The descriptions in this story imply that emergency care as well as long-term care were dealt with in an organized fashion not unlike the modern care institution.

The Greek Infirmary: *Hygiastirion*

While the Egyptians may have had the first true "physicians," the later Greek physicians perfected the art of healing. With their great medical schools, their Aesculapian Temples, and their knowledge of pharmacy, the Greeks made greater progress than did the Egyptians in dealing with the various conditions afflicting humans. In fact, the care institutions that developed through Hellenistic influences were to overshadow those of all other cultures for many centuries.

The hygiastirion is thought to be an infirmary type of structure that was attached to the home of a physician. There is some evidence that physicians provided several beds for patients who were unable to live on their own. Because homecare was the primary method of that day, the physicians of Greece expected to make house calls and treat the sick in their own beds. Family instruction in bedside care was an expected part of the Greek physician's treatment.

However, there were likely to have been many occasions in which homecare was either not possible or was not expedient. The traveler, the homeless, the warrior, the mariner, and many older persons were all likely to lack both a family and a suitable home for this type of care. Thus, the early Greek physician was also expected to care for people who appeared at his door but who had no place to reside. The hygiastirion is likely to have become that place.

The *Xenodochium* or Roman Inn

There is considerable evidence that one of the first institutions for ambulatory care was the *xenodochium* of Rome. The Romans adopted the same guest room concept as did the Hebrews. However, unlike early Hebrew houses, the ancient Roman homes became huge compounds with many rooms. In the ruins of Pompeii, there is what is believed to be the remains of a Roman xenodochium. If the Pompeii example is, in fact, a xenodochium, then it was much more elaborate than the typical

Hebrew or Greek guesthouse. The Pompeii example is a building of several rooms attached to the home of a physician. That a physician lived in this particular house is evidenced by the numerous medical and surgical instruments that were unearthed. Although Frank (1953) called it a nursing home, the excavation was more likely a hospitality house or inn used for convalescence similar to the Greek hygiastirion or infirmary. There is nothing to suggest that it had a long-term care function.

Valetudinaria: Roman Sickhouse

Valetudinaria were built by the Romans wherever they took their military forces which was in most parts of Europe and Asia Minor. These facilities, however, were not exclusively used by the garrisoned forces but were also available for gladiators and slaves. One was patterned after the Aesculapian temple hospital on the Insula Tiberine built about 300 B.C. Because home care was the typical mode of health care for patrician society, the valetudinaria was probably a charitable institution for those without homes or families. At first valetudinaria also served as sickhouses for slaves. Later, as the military forces began to spread themselves across the known world, the military administration provided valetudinaria for the soldiers. Finally, when Christianity became a state religion under Constantine the Great (325 A.D.), the valetudinaria became a charity hospital for the indigent.

Despite these multiple uses, the Roman facility was to set the pattern for health-care facilities for a thousand years. It was typically built around a courtyard square. The buildings opened onto the courtyard, and only one gate led to the outside. The administration building was kept separate as were the kitchen and the sanitary buildings. Rooms were small, with only a bed for furnishing. The courtyard style with surrounding wards was found to be very functional. As a result, most Arabian hospitals adopted this system.

The Ancient Home for the Aged: *Gerontochium*

By the close of the pre-Christian era, the time was ripe for a specialized institution for older people. This development was a natural outgrowth of several influences. Our information concerning homes for the aged before the Christian era is mostly biblical. That they existed, however, is attested to by the Justinian Code. Although the Code dates from 533 A.D., it is a compilation of earlier Roman laws, some of which pre-date the Christian era. The idea of a gerontochium did not originate with Justinian, but much earlier since there was a gerontochium in the huge hospital complex of St. Basil in 367 A.D.

The word gerontochium is interesting because it is the Latinized version of a combination of Greek words meaning house for poor old people (*geras* meaning old or aging; *ptochus* a name for a class of poor people; and *oixious* a name for a type of house). Thus the Greek *gerontoxeion*, Latinized to gerontochium, meant, quite literally, a home for poor old people. Even in much later times the same word appears to describe hospitals for old people.

Health Resorts

During the first ten centuries of the Christian era, a number of health resorts grew up around mineral springs or oceanside scenic areas. The idea of retreat from the pressures of life for a period of vacation is an ancient one. However, the influence of religion gave it a more permanent character. The Anchorites of the third century through the seventh century (A.D.) renounced all worldly life and retreated into isolation. This form of asceticism which was found in many forms from India to Egypt was borrowed by the early Christians. Thus, some Monasteries were essentially retreats.

At Gheel, Belgium, there is the tomb of St. Dymphna where the belief arose that a visit to the tomb could cure disease. In the sixth century, many pilgrims came to the site seeking relief from their afflictions. So many, in fact, that the surrounding town's people took those who were ill into their homes and cared for them. Eventually, a hospital was built, but the people continued to take into their homes those who could not get into the hospital. The home health movement, so important in Europe even to this day, can probably be traced to such early practices.

The most significant health resort of the period was perhaps Salubrious Salerno. The history of this resort dates from the time of Horace in the first century B.C. Only thirty miles from Naples near the sunny Tyrrhenian Sea, it was perhaps the choice resort for a thousand years. Its significance is that for several centuries it was also the medical center of Europe. And, the centralization of medical care made it necessary to establish facilities to temporarily house those who sought that care. It is not difficult to imagine that at least some of those housing facilities became segregated based on the type of affliction from which a majority of its patrons suffered. The result would be facilities identified as appropriate for certain classes of care.

Monasteries and Long-Term Care Facilities

During the first millennium, the major contribution to the development of long-term health-care facilities was an unexpected consequence of the new religious movement that was related to the development of monasteries. Many nations and beliefs had those who sought refuge or withdrawal from the world, but it was the Christian monasteries of the middle ages that became a place of refuge for the sick and a residence for the frail aged as well.

The lifestyles of the monks who inhabited these monasteries were of two distinct types: cenobite (communal) or anchorite (alone). The monasteries were operated directly by the individual order without interference of the local bishop or secular noble, and were under the direct protection of the Pope. The original concept was related to withdrawal from society, but the originators found they built small societies wherever they went. The first monastic monks began to build their quarters in isolated places but some others chose sites that were near existing towns and villages.

It appears that most of the early monasteries had at least one thing in common—they were the chief care centers in their locale. The pattern was usually the same. At first a bishop would establish his residence or a missionary would establish a monastic house. As the need arose, a guest house would be erected. It was also usually necessary for the facility to have an infirmary. Sometimes this was the same as the pandochium and in others it was a separate facility detached from the chapel or cathedral. Usually, the monastery was a large complex surrounded by a courtyard and protected by a rock wall.

Those who were ill were usually classified in one of three categories: (1) the superannuated who slept in the infirmary; (2) the sick who were infectious and were likely to be isolated; and (3) the convalescent. Some monasteries had specialized health care such as the blood-letting house at the monastery of St. Gaul or the leprosarium of Saint Radegunde. Others had pesthouses, almshouses, and hospitals. Further, sick monks were usually segregated from lay persons. Thus, a monastery could have as many as six separate health facilities.

The basis of this special treatment in separate facilities is usually traced to the pronouncement of Saint Benedict who said:

> Before all things and above all things care of the sick must be taken so that they be served in every deed as Christ himself... therefore, let the abbot take the greatest care that they suffer no neglect. For these sick brethren let there be assigned a special room and an attendant.... (Henderson, 1892, p. 274)

Ancient Almshouses

The Cathedral of Notre Dame (founded in 375 A.D.) originally stood directly opposite the Ile de la Cité on the banks of the Seine River in Paris. In the eighth century, the basilica was abandoned in favor of another site, also abandoned in the eleventh century, in favor of the present site. The first basilica that was abandoned was used as an almshouse in 651 A.D. A large hall was subdivided into wooden cubicles with canvas awnings. These were built in rows with each cubicle no larger than a bed. However, the first beds accommodated five persons. It was not uncommon during the great plague for a resident to awaken and find that a bed-mate had died during the night.

Other than rearranging things to accommodate additional residents, the almshouses remained unchanged for almost 400 years. It was during this period of expansion that they began to be called hospitals. Tierney (1959) suggests that the term hospital, as it was used during the medieval period, is misleading since these institutions cared for the sick, were homes for the aged, took in orphans, and generally were the health-care centers of their communities.

Hôtel Dieu of Lyon was established for use as an almshouse, and like the Hôtel Dieu of Paris, it was later to be called a hospital. However, this was after it had been in operation as a general almshouse for several centuries. It dates even earlier than its Paris counterpart, having been established in 542 A.D. by King Childebert and his spouse, Ultrogatha.

The almshouse was a general service facility. It usually housed the aged, the chronically ill, the physically limited, or, during times of plague, the acutely ill. In later times, it served as a facility for the poor and was comparable to the poorhouses of a later period. Those who were mentally ill were also housed in the almshouses as long as they could safely be cared for. Further, in the Middle Ages, a traveler could find sanctuary and rest from his journey at the local almshouse.

The earliest record of an almshouse in England was that erected by the Bishop of Winchester in 1130 A.D. It originally housed thirteen "impotent men," a medieval designation for the aged. The original builders did not consider the frailty of the aged inhabitants, however, constructing the almshouse much like the thatched-roofed peasant homes of that era. The ground floor was for daily living and dining. There were tables and chairs, a fireplace over which the meals were cooked, and little else. Sleeping was on mats spread over an upstairs loft with access by means of a steep ladder. The Winchester almshouse was enlarged in 1444 to house forty-nine aged residents, but the ladder was retained as were the upstairs sleeping quarters.

Other almshouses followed essentially the same pattern, a living room downstairs and sleeping ward upstairs. In Ewelme, England, in the year 1436, an almshouse for thirteen paupers was constructed on the same plan. The sleeping quarters consisted of a single large ward accessible only by a steep ladder. This almshouse, called God's House, was attached to the abbey of the diocese.

Ancient Hospitals

There is no counterpart of the modern hospital in ancient times. However, there were ancient health care institutions that we may call hospitals. These early facilities served a variety of purposes one of which was to house older infirm people. The first of these institutions were attached to temples and date back five thousand years in Egypt. Further, recent excavations in Crete have discovered health-care facilities in the Minoan culture dating back four thousand years.

Imhotep of Egypt may have been the first to institutionalize health care. Dating from 2700 B.C., this physician-priest of King Zosar performed healing rites on the invalids who were carried to the temple. Sanitoria attached to the temples were set aside for the sick and infirm.

Amenophis IV (also known as Ikhnaton) built an authentic care institution in 1400 B.C. in Egypt, although he still referred to it as a temple. In his temple, worship of the sun and other healing rites were performed. Porticos of the temple, called sanitoria, were dedicated to the sun god, Aton. The ill, the aged, and the infirm went to these for treatment which was little more than exposure to the sun. Unfortunately, the priests of Re, a rival sun god, undertook efforts to stamp out worship of Aton and, in the process, they obliterated most of the evidence of what actually went on in this very early type of care facility.

Early Christian Hospitals

With the conversion of Constantine the Great to Christianity, health care began to be institutionalized. Prior to this time, the primary health-care facilities were the Aesculapian temples. Constantine, by edict, closed the temple incubation halls and forbade priests to practice health care. Almost immediately, the Council of Nicea (325 A.D.), sanctioned by Constantine, called upon each bishop to build a hospital in his diocese. At first, the bishops attached a pandochium, patterned after the Hebrew system, to their homes or built a separate structure within the cathedral complex. Often, it was attached to a monastery which used health care and long-term care as a vehicle for Christian service. Saint Basil started his great hospital enterprise in this fashion in 369 A.D. in Caesarea.

Ephrem in Edessa began a huge hospital system in 375 A.D. It grew in reputation until, by the fifth century, it was known as the second Athens. Others thought it was the successor of Alexandria because of the influence it had on medical and religious thought. Out of it developed the Nestorians. Nestorius and his followers were expelled from Ephrem by the Emperor at the urging of Bishop Cyrus of Alexandria. They fled into Arabia and took up health care as a vehicle of Christian service.

The bishop of Constantinople, St. John Chrysostom, erected a hospital in 398 A.D. Further, he began what may have been the first social work program as a part of the hospital. However, St. Basil's hospital also had some social work and an employment agency at approximately the same time. The social work of St. John was to benefit the patient in returning to a normal home life after a long period of confinement.

Pulcheria, the sister of Theodosius II, later took over operation of the hospital of St. John and founded others. Pulcheria had served as regent to her brother who, at seven, was made emperor. Given the title Augusta, she administered the kingdom admirably, yielding her position when the boy was old enough to assume leadership. She then devoted her remaining years to the administration of the hospital system she had created. There is no doubt the administrative experience she gained while serving as Augusta Regent was beneficial. She was known as the "tender sister," and for her works of charity, she was elevated by the Greek Orthodox Church to sainthood.

Other hospitals of the first millennium included the Cherbourg Hospital founded in 945 A.D. by William the Conqueror and York Hospital, England, founded 936 A.D. by King Athelstane. York Hospital was first a poorhouse for the aged.

Saint Basil's Hospital

The most extensive hospital complex of the early Christians was that of Saint Basil of Caesarea. Because of its magnitude, it became a city within itself. Located in Eastern Turkey, it was a multi-service facility with many different wards or buildings including:

> Orphantrophium, for orphans and foundlings
> Brephotrophium, for infants, a pediatric hospital
> Gerontochium, for the elderly, a home for the aged
> Nosocomium, a hospital for sick and infirm
> Xenodochium, a hospice for travelers
> Leprosarium, for long-term care of lepers
> Pesthouse, for isolation of contagious disease
> Ophthalmontropheum, home for the blind

In addition, there was a workhouse for occupational and vocational training, an employment bureau for placement of patients being discharged, an industrial school, a medical school, and an educational facility for nursing attendants. The complex was so large that it was called "new town." However, it began as a single house attached to the home of the bishop.

Early Arabian Hospitals

The term Dark Ages is descriptive of the general state of early medical knowledge in all but the Arab world. Arabs built a great hospital system stretching from Cairo to Damascus, from Baghdad to Mecca, from Aleppo to Jundipur, and from Cordova to Jerusalem.

The Mansurian Hospital, al-Mansur, founded 874 A.D., had a long-term convalescent section divided for men and women. Garrison (1929, p. 136) describes the al-Mansur hospital as:

> a huge triangular structure with fountains playing in the four courtyards, separate wards for important diseases, wards for women and convalescents, lecture rooms, extensive library, out-patient clinic, dieting kitchens, an orphan asylum, and a chapel. It employed male and female nurses, the patients were nourished upon a rich and attractive diet, [and] the patients [were] lulled to sleep with soft music.

In addition, there were hospitals in Rai, Isphalan, Shiraz, Fez, Algericas, and Alexandria. What was perhaps the first Arabian hospital was built in 597 A.D. in Egypt. Hospitals were also founded in 707 A.D. at Damascus and in Baghdad in 918 A.D.

The Beginning of the Great Hospitals

In the twelfth century, Harun al-Rashid decreed that a hospital, complete with medical college, would be a part of every mosque. He also opened an asylum to treat and house mentally ill patients and generally provided for the care of the aged. When Benjamin of Tudela visited a Baghdad hospital, he found that the Calif provided for the total care of the patients, even giving them a stipend when they were discharged. The Arabian hospital system was to grow to encompass the known world of the Moslems. It stretched from Africa in the South, to Asia Minor in the North and Spain in the West.

At roughly the same time (the tenth century A.D.) in Paris, the Salle St. Denis was built and the existing almshouse moved so the present cathedral of Notre Dame could be constructed. St. Thomas' Convalescent Hospital was added to the growing health care enterprise in 1210 A.D. This facility, along with the Salle de L'Infirmierie which was built in 1225 A.D., was all that remained of the old almshouse at the beginning of the Middle Ages. With the addition of Salle Neuve in 1260 A.D., the facility became a sprawling hospital complex. It was heavily involved in the long-term care of older people throughout its history.

In Rome, Pope Innocent III (1161–1216 A.D.) founded Santo Spirito, Holy Ghost Hospital, on the banks of the Tiber River. Santo Spirito was the first of the great city hospitals which offered twenty-four hour service by nurses called infirmarians. There were wards for the mentally ill, the aged, and the sick. Isolation was practiced for those having communicable diseases. The Pope also ordered hospitals built in every diocese. Thus began the hospital system of Italy.

In London, a court jester to Henry I named Rahare is responsible for the founding of St. Bartholomew's Hospital. Rahare made a pilgrimage to Rome and became ill. He was hospitalized in the newly founded Holy Ghost Hospital and during his illness vowed to return to England and build a hospital. Upon returning, he appealed to Henry I and was granted land. An almshouse was built in 1123 under church control and Rahare served as its first administrator. By 1330, this facility was designated as a hospital and in 1405 it became an asylum for the mentally ill. In 1534, it was closed by order of Henry VIII and remained closed for six years after which it was opened as a publicly supported institution for the infirm.

At Tonnerre, France, the Notre Dame des Fontenilles was founded in 1293 A.D. by the widow Queen Marguerite de Bourgogne. Its wards were even more extensive than that of the Santo Spirito of Rome. Like other hospitals of the time, the ward was divided by cubicles made of wood, row upon row, side by side, all standing independently of the main structure.

By the thirteenth century, there was a growing interest in privacy by the monks of the monasteries (Thompson and Goldin, 1975). This trend is also noted in the construction of hospital wards. The partitioning of the huge wards into private cubicles was complete with a canopy and a curtain. The first partitioning was only the enclosure of the bed. Later enclosures gave the patient a tiny sitting area within and, later still, the size of the enclosure began to increase. Thompson and Goldin (1975) believe the monks, who were seeking privacy in the living quarters of their monasteries, may have transferred that philosophy to the infirmary. It was only a matter of time before the construction of their hospitals, almshouses, and leprosariums would reflect the same desire for patient privacy.

Around Europe, hospitals sprang up in every town that could afford one. In Glasgow, St. John of Polmadie Hospital was organized in the thirteenth century, a leprosarium was founded in the fourteenth century, St. Nicholas Hospital which began 1455 has survived as home for the aged, and Stablegreen Hospital began receiving patients in 1503. At about the same time in Marburg, St. Elizabeth of Hungary began a hospital. In Seina, in the fourteenth century, St. Catherine started her work in a hospital. In Germany, at Rauenburg, in 1448, a hospital began accepting payment for services and thus may have been the first fee-for-service hospital.

Conclusion

Several conclusions stand out in regard to the historical development of long-term care institutions. It seems obvious that care institutions were, in a sense, "reinvented" from time to time. The almshouse development began as a cottage movement inspired by dedicated religious workers. Initially, it included any person in need; the lame, the sick, and the poor. Gradually, however, the almshouses began to "specialize" by admitting only those with specific needs including leprosy, frailty born of old age, or other conditions.

Prior to the Judeo-Christian era, pagan religions overshadowed the existing care systems and were in control until they were outlawed by Constantine in A.D. 325. Thereafter, specialized care facilities, especially homes for the aged, leprosariums, and asylums for the mentally infirm, became common. Sometimes, specialization was forced upon an institution because of a particular and pressing need. Such was the case during the great plague of 1348–1352. Because the plague killed almost the entire population of those afflicted with leprosy, the leprosariums became "pest houses" for those suffering from various pestilent diseases.

There is also a long history of government involvement in institutional care. Regardless of whether government involvement is viewed as interference or as serving a needed regulatory function, there is good evidence to suggest that it was formalized by the actions of Henry VIII and Martin Luther. Further, it is believed by many that the nursing home movement in the United States got its start with passage of the Social Security Act in 1935. Actually, it was the development of the almshouses in New Amsterdam, Jamestown, and Boston almost two-and-a-half centuries earlier that laid the foundation for the development of the modern-day nursing home.

REFERENCES

Bible. King James version.

Frank, Sister Charles Marie. (1959). *Foundations of Nursing*. 2nd ed. Philadelphia: W.B. Saunders Co.

Garrison, F.H. (1929). *An Introduction to History of Medicine*. 4th ed. Philadelphia: W.B. Saunders Co.

Henderson, G.F. (1892). *Historical Documents of Middle Ages*. "Saint Benedict." pp. 274–314. London: W.B. Saunders Co.

Thompson, John D., and Goldin, Grace. (1975). *The Hospital: A Social and Architectural History*. New Haven: Yale University Press.

Tierney, Brian. (1959). *Medieval Poor Law: A Sketch of Canonical Theory and its Application in England*. Berkeley: University of California Press.

SUGGESTED READING

Hunter, Robert. (1904). *Poverty, Social Conscience in the Progressive Era*. New York: MacMillan Company.

Jamieson, Elizabeth M., and Sewall, Mary F. (1949). *Trends in Nursing History*. 3rd ed. Philadelphia: W.D. Saunders.

Lorand, Arnold. (1914). *Old Age Deferred*. Philadelphia: F.A. Davis.

Maceachern, Malcolm T. (1962). *Hospital Organization and Management*. Berwyn, Ill.: Physicians Record Co.

Metchnikoff, Elie. (1908). *Prolongation of Life*. New York: Putnam & Sons.

Newton, Kathleen. (1954). *Geriatric Nursing*. St. Louis: Mosby.

Nostrums and Quackery: Articles on the Nostrum Evil and Quackery Reprinted. Chicago: American Medical Association Press. 1912.

Ray, Dr. I. (1853). *Treatise on the Medical Jurisprudence of Insanity*. 3rd ed. Boston: Little, Brown and Company.

Robbins, H.W., and Coleman, W.H. (1938). *Western World Literature*. New York: Macmillan.

Robinson, Victor. (1929). 2nd ed. *Pathfinders in Medicine*.

———. (1931). *The Story of Medicine*. New York: Tudor.

Contributors

Roger T. Anderson, Ph.D. received his doctorate in behavioral epidemiology and public health from the Johns Hopkins University, and is currently a post-doctoral Fellow in Gerontology at the Bowman Gray School of Medicine of Wake Forest University. Anderson's primary research interests are the pathways by which social class and the social environment affect morbidity, mortality, and health quality of life. His current research activities are focused on investigating health-service needs of functionally impaired elderly residents of substandard housing; developing comprehensive measures of health quality of life in older adults; and investigating the longitudinal effects of housing quality on disability and physical fitness in the elderly.

Lorin A. Baumhover, Ph.D. is director of the Center for the Study of Aging and Professor of Behavioral and Community Medicine in the College of Community Health Sciences at the University of Alabama in Tuscaloosa. He holds a Ph.D. in sociology from Colorado State University. Baumhover's master's degree is from Colorado State University and his bachelor's degree is from the University of Nebraska. Baumhover has been an active researcher and educator in gerontology for over twenty-five years.

David Boyd, M.S. is currently a doctoral candidate in the Department of Sociology at the University of North Texas. His areas of specialization include Gerontology and Rehabilitation Studies. He is also employed by the university to coordinate a program offering job placement to disabled older workers. His

Contributors

current research interests include housing for older adults and the barriers, both social and physical, faced by older persons with functional impairments.

Susan B. Brecht is president of Brecht Associates, Inc. in Philadelphia. She has over a decade of experience in providing consulting services to the retirement housing industry. Brecht has been responsible for conducting studies and assisting clients in the planning and development of retirement communities throughout the United States. Her particular expertise is in the area of market analysis, establishment of design and program characteristics, market positioning, and feasibility studies for the full continuum of housing and services for the elderly. Brecht is the author of the book, *Retirement Housing Markets: Project Planning and Feasibility Analysis,* published by John Wiley & Sons (1991). She has also published several articles in the field and is frequently asked to make presentations at professional conferences and seminars. Brecht has lectured at the Wharton School, Columbia University and the Massachusetts Institute of Technology. She received her bachelor's degree from the University of Pennsylvania.

Carolyn L. Clark-Daniels, Ph.D. received her doctorate in political science from the University of Alabama. Currently Daniels is assistant professor of political science at Iowa State University. Her work in gerontology has appeared in several journals including the *Gerontologist, The Journal of the American Medical Association,* and the *Annals of Emergency Medicine.*

R. Steven Daniels, Ph.D. received his doctorate in political science from the University of Oregon. He is currently associate professor of political science at the University of Alabama at Birmingham. Daniels work has appeared in such journals as the *Gerontologist, The Journal of Elder Abuse and Neglect,* and the *Annals of Emergency Medicine.*

W. Edward Folts, Ph.D. is associate professor of sociology and director of the gerontology program at Appalachian State University. He received his bachelor's and master's degrees from the University of Alabama and his Ph.D. from the University of Florida. Folts is involved in research related to nontraditional housing for the elderly and co-authored, with Gordon F. Streib and Mary Anne Hilker, *Old Homes—New Families: Shared Living for the Elderly* (1984). Folts has co-authored articles appearing in *The Journal of Gerontology, The Gerontologist, Research on Aging, Educational Gerontology, The Journal of Housing for the Elderly, The Journal of Applied Gerontology,* and others.

Carolyn M. Gilker, M.S. is a program analyst for the National Center for Cost Containment of the Veterans Administration located in Milwaukee. She holds a master's degree in interior environments from the University of Wisconsin–Madison.

John Gillum, M.S. is a research associate in the Center for the Study of Aging at the University of Alabama in Tuscaloosa. Gillum holds bachelor's degrees in both speech communication and human environmental sciences from the University of Southern Mississippi and a master's degree in human environmental sciences from the University of Alabama. Recently, Gillum served as project manager for a study of housing needs and preferences of older people funded by the Administration on Aging.

David P. Higgins, Ph.D. is associate professor of finance and director of the Master of Business Administration Program in Corporate Finance in the Graduate School of Management at the University of Dallas. Higgins earned his doctorate in financial management and investment theory at the University of Texas at Austin. He taught at Arizona State University and the University of Wisconsin–LaCrosse before joining the faculty of the University of Dallas. Higgins' research interests have centered on funding care in retirement communities and nursing homes, and home equity conversion. He has presented the results of his research efforts at meetings of the Gerontological Society of America and the Association for Gerontology in Higher Education. His aging-related publications have appeared in the *Journal of Applied Gerontology* and the *Journal of Housing for the Elderly.*

Elizabeth Howe, Ph.D. is professor of urban and regional planning at the University of Wisconsin–Madison, where she heads that program's social planning concentration. She received her master's degree in political science from the University of Chicago and her Ph.D. in city and regional planning from the University of California–Berkeley. Howe has conducted research on social supports for elderly women and on housing code enforcement.

Michael E. Hunt, Arch.D. is associate director of the Institute on Aging and Adult Life and professor and extension housing specialist in the Interior Environments Program of the Environment, Textiles, and Design Department at the University of Wisconsin–Madison. He earned a doctorate in architecture and Specialist in Aging Certificate from the University of Michigan. In addition, Hunt holds a master's degree in community and regional planning from Kansas State University and a B.A. in architecture and urban studies from the University of Arkansas. His duties at the University of Wisconsin include developing and administering educational programs in the Institute on Aging and teaching and conducting research in the areas of housing for older adults, environment and behavior studies, and environmental design research. Hunt is co-author of a book on retirement communities and has published professional journal articles and book chapters on housing for older people and on environmental learning.

Stanley R. Ingman, Ph.D. received his Ph.D. from the University of Pittsburgh. He is currently serving as the director of the Texas Institute for Research and Education in Aging, a joint program of the University of North Texas and the Texas College of Osteopathic Medicine. Ingman also serves as professor of sociology at the University of North Texas. His latest book, an edited volume with Derek Gil, is entitled *Eldercare, Distributive Justice and the Welfare State: Retrenchment or Expansion* and will be available in 1993. His research focuses upon redesigning the long-term care system in various countries, including the United States.

Dale J. Jaffe, Ph.D. is associate professor of sociology at the University of Wisconsin–Milwaukee where he chairs the graduate program in sociology and the Certificate in Aging program. He received both his master's degree and his Ph.D. in sociology at the University of Chicago. His research interests include the living arrangements of the elderly and the impact of living arrangements on identity and the self.

Katherine M. Logan, Ph.D. is assistant professor of sociology and social work at Appalachian State University. She received her master's degree from the University of Kentucky and her Ph.D. from the State University of New York at Buffalo. Logan serves in an advisory capacity for a number of service programs for older adults. Her current gerontological research interest is focused on ways to improve the care and quality of life in long-term care institutions. Logan recently co-authored an article that appeared in the *Journal of Elder Abuse and Neglect.*

Charles F. Longino, Ph.D. is the Wake Forest professor of sociology and public health sciences at the Bowman Gray School of Medicine of Wake Forest University. Longino, who directed the Center for Social Research in Aging at the University of Miami for many years, has had a career-long interest in housing for the elderly. His first grant, funded by the Social Security Administration, was a comparative study of thirteen retirement communities in the Midwest. His articles, with colleagues from this project, have emphasized the selectivity processes that draw retirees to special types of housing, and the support they experience there. Longino also reported findings from this study at the Symposium on the Social and Built Environments sponsored by the Institute of Medicine, National Academy of Sciences, in 1985. A summary of his housing research is found in *Housing an Aging Society: Issues, Alternatives, and Policies* (1986), edited by Robert J. Newcomer, M. Powell Lawton, and Thomas O. Byerts. More recently, Longino and other colleagues have concerned themselves with the issue of retirement migration in the United States.

Richard A. Lusky, Ph.D. is associate professor and director of the Center for Studies in Aging at the University of North Texas. He trained in medical sociology and health services research at the University of Connecticut, where he subsequently founded and directed the school's Gerontology Studies Unit. He has conducted various studies of the health status and needs of older persons, and of the delivery of long-term care services. Lusky has worked as an advisor to numerous state and local governments attempting to address the issues related to health services for older adults.

John S. Mahoney, Ph.D. is currently assistant professor of sociology and administrator of the off-campus educational programs at Virginia Commonwealth University. Mahoney received his Ph.D. from the University of Virginia. His current areas of research include: collective behavior and social movements, minorities, and work organizations.

Wiley P. Mangum, Ph.D. is associate professor of gerontology at the University of South Florida. His Ph.D. in sociology is from the University of Southern California and his B.A. and M.A. are in psychology from the University of Texas, Austin. Mangum's major teaching and research interests are in social gerontology, research methods in gerontology, the demography of aging, social policy in aging, and ethical and legal issues in aging. His major publications include two books on housing for the elderly and a number of articles on retirement housing and other topics in professional journals. Along with Dr. Tom Rich, he was the founding co-editor of the *Journal of Applied Gerontology* from 1982 through 1985. Mangum is a member of the Gerontological Society of America, the American Society on Aging, and the Southern Gerontological Society. He is also a member of the board of directors of Neighborly Senior Services in Pinellas County, Florida.

John L. Merrill, Arch.D. earned his doctorate in architecture from the University of Michigan and has worked as a research associate at the University of Michigan Institute of Gerontology. Currently, Merrill is associate professor and extension housing specialist at the University of Wisconsin–Madison. For over ten years, Merrill has been involved in research and program development in the area of community-based housing for older persons.

Jerold S. Nachison, AICP is the Chief, Services Branch, under the Section 202 program of the United States Department of Housing and Urban Development. This branch administers the Congregate Housing Services Program (CHSP) and services initiatives related to the frail elderly and the nonelderly living in projects for the elderly. Nachison also serves as a HUD consultant to developers and state and local agencies which build and manage congregate housing. Nachison has served as the Chief of Planning, Programs, and Evaluation for the Maryland Commission on Aging. He has also served on the faculty of West Virginia University and with the Peace Corps. Nachison has written over fifty-five articles on housing. He is a graduate of Pennsylvania State University and holds master's degrees from both the University of Missouri and the University of Delaware.

Mary K. Nenno, M.A. received her B.A. from Elmira College, where she was selected as a member of Phi Beta Kappa. She began graduate studies at the Institute of Local and State Government of the University of Pennsylvania and completed her M.A. in government at the University of Buffalo. Nenno was a staff member of the National Association of Housing Redevelopment Officials (NAHRO) from 1960 to 1991. In 1991 she retired from NAHRO as the associate director for policy development. Currently, Nenno is a visiting fellow at the Urban Institute in Washington, D.C. Her areas of specialization are government housing policy and housing for special needs.

Patricia Pawasarat is a research assistant in the department of sociology at the University of Wisconsin–Milwaukee where she is currently pursuing her master's degree. Her interests are in the area of family, gender, and aging.

Dale O. Robinson, M.S. is currently serving as Community Support Program Supervisor with the El Paso State Center, Community Services Division in Alpine, Texas. Robinson has also served as vocational services coordinator for the Denton County (Texas) Mental Health and Mental Retardation Division and as counselor for the Dallas (Texas) Mental Health and Mental Retardation Center. Robinson received his B.S. in sociology from Southwest Missouri State University and his M.S. in aging studies from the University of North Texas.

Kay E. Rodabough, M.S. is a well-known advocate for older adults in the Dallas area. She is currently working with a group of Dallas residents who are interested in establishing an intergenerational cooperative housing community in the Southwestern United States. Rodabough received her master's degree in gerontology from the University of North Texas. Her gerontological interests are focused on innovative inter-generational housing options that prolong functional independence and encourage participation for all age groups.

Wesley W. Rogers, Ph.D. first became interested in the historical foundations of long-term care while serving as program director for nursing home administration during the sixteen years he taught at McLennan Community College. For ten years Rogers and his wife, Janie, owned and served as administrators of a nursing home in Texas. Rogers' professional experiences include serving as an Air Force navigator, service as an educational program director, and service as the executive director of a retirement center in Amarillo, Texas. Rogers is the author of a popular text on nursing home administration. He is now retired and living in Carrollton, Texas.

Gordon F. Streib, Ph.D. is graduate research professor emeritus at the University of Florida in Gainesville. Streib received his master's degree from the New School for Social Research and his Ph.D. from Columbia University. He is the co-author of *Retirement in American Society, Old Home—New Families: Shared Living for the Elderly,* and he has contributed chapters to numerous other books including the *Handbook of Aging and the*

Social Sciences. In addition, Streib's work has appeared in *Research on Aging, The Gerontologist, The Journal of Gerontology, American Sociological Review,* and many other professional journals.

Patricia K. Suggs, Ph.D. is director of the Appalachian Geriatric Education Center and assistant professor, section on internal medicine and gerontology at Bowman Gray School of Medicine of Wake Forest University. She also holds the position of Aging Initiatives Director for the Northwest Area Health Education Center. Suggs holds master's degrees from both the University of North Carolina at Greensboro and Duke University. Her bachelor's degree is from Illinois State University and she received her Ph.D. from the University of North Carolina at Greensboro. Suggs' current research interests include an evaluative study of restorative care programs and development of a curriculum for housing managers and staff.

Jan W. Weaver, M.A., R.N. has worked in nursing management and training positions in various long-term care settings during her nineteen years as a registered nurse. Weaver served as executive director of Adult Day Care of San Angelo, Inc. in San Angelo, Texas, prior to joining the staff of the Texas Institute for Research and Education in Aging as a research associate. Weaver received her M.A. in English from Angelo State University in 1991. She is currently a doctoral candidate at the University of North Texas. Weaver is serving a two-year term as delegate to the National Institute of Adult Day Care and is the immediate past president of the Adult Day Care Association of Texas. She is also the facilitator of a task force that is developing an adult day care program in Denton, Texas, and serves on a steering committee that is involved in implementing an intergenerational dependent care program for faculty, students, and staff at the Texas College of Osteopathic Medicine.

Dale E. Yeatts, Ph.D. is currently assistant professor in the Center for Studies in Aging and the department of sociology at the University of North Texas. His areas of interest include elderly housing, management techniques for health care and housing facilities, and minority elderly. Yeatts' work has been published in a variety of professional journals including *The Gerontologist*, the *Journal of Gerontology*, and *Public Health Reports*. Yeatts received his Ph.D. in sociology at the University of Virginia. In addition, Yeatts received his master's degree from the College of William and Mary and his bachelor's degree from Old Dominion University.

Author Index

Subject Index